POPULATION DENSITY (/km²)	ARABLE AND PERMANENT PASTURE (per cent of total area)	URBAN POPULATION (%)	BIRTH RATE (per 1 000)	DEATH RATE (per 1 000)	PER CAPITA GROSS NATIONAL PRODUCT ($US)
68	59	53	16	8	1 970
v.s.	0	n.a.	n.a.	n.a.	n.a.
279	n.a.	8	26	8	300
96	38	9	28	7	1 050
52	19	34	43	15	570
0.5	1	50	n.a.	n.a.	n.a.
18	n.a.	16	47	23	120
14	n.a.	20	40	25	330
4	13	40	36	6	470
63	31	20	36	16	140
26	38	28	49	14	340
66	13	90	19	5	1 540
14	75	49	18	12	2 140
2	22	86	20	7	5 550
89	54	20	35	15	130
86	9	18	38	17	150
20	11	43	45	16	1 060
25	26	61	48	15	970
44	67	52	22	11	2 370
59	54	86	28	7	3 380
84	68	53	16	10	2 770
15	6	28	46	21	420
82	45	37	31	7	1 140
95	19	72	19	6	3 880
27	14	43	48	15	400
22	10	10	49	16	200
28	16	38	36	9	390
40	23	41	29	9	470
52	n.a.	22	45	8	11 640
14	7	15	45	23	n.a.
68	30	61	40	10	1 080
33	94	5	39	20	120
15	37	28	50	21	330
1	10	29	45	15	3 360
51	56	n.a.	18	8	n.a.
37	51	68	11	12	5 690
25	n.a.	97	25	7	270
13	57	14	50	21	170
41	14	4	48	24	130
35	19	27	39	10	660
93	n.a.	11	50	23	90
4	n.a.	12	50	26	70
24	50	94	18	9	1 060
25	47	33	22	7	1 330
1	36	10	39	25	230
26	67	44	28	7	480
29	52	61	46	8	1 000
1	86	46	40	10	620
38	35	37	46	16	430
12	60	10	43	20	420
38	27	4	43	20	110
37	67	77	14	8	4 880
11	51	81	19	8	4 100
17	13	49	48	14	650
4	14	8	52	25	100
66	24	16	49	23	240
12	3	45	15	10	5 280

COUNTRIES	AREA (10³ km²)	POPULATION (millions)	POPULATION DENSITY (/km²)	ARABLE AND PERMANENT PASTURE (per cent of total area)	URBAN POPULATION (%)	BIRTH RATE (per 1 000)	DEATH RATE (per 1 000)	PER CAPITA GROSS NATIONAL PRODUCT ($US)
Oman	212	0.8	4	n.a.	n.a.	50	19	1 250
Pakistan	804	72.5	90	31	26	44	15	130
Panama	74	1.7	22	19	49	31	5	1 010
Papua New Guinea	462	2.8	6	n.a.	11	41	17	440
Paraguay	407	2.6	6	27	38	40	9	480
Peru	1 285	16.0	12	24	60	41	12	710
Philippines	300	44.0	138	37	32	41	11	310
Poland	312	34.4	108	64	55	18	8	2 450
Portugal	92	8.5	95	55	26	19	11	1 540
Puerto Rico	9	3.2	341	66	58	23	6	2 400
Qatar	10	0.1	8	n.a.	n.a.	50	19	5 830
Réunion	3	0.5	195	33	43	28	7	1 210
Rhodesia (Zimbabwe)	389	6.5	17	17	19	48	14	480
Romania	237	21.5	89	62	42	20	9	n.a.
Rwanda	26	4.4	157	71	3	50	24	80
São Tomé e Principe	1	0.1	82	n.a.	23	45	11	470
Saudi Arabia	2 150	6.4	4	38	18	49	20	2 080
Senegal	197	4.5	22	28	30	48	24	320
Seychelles	0.3	0.06	209	43	n.a.	30	9	n.a.
Sierra Leone	72	3.1	38	82	13	45	21	180
Sikkim	7.3	0.2	29	n.a.	5	n.a.	n.a.	90
Singapore	0.6	2.3	3 819	22	100	20	5	2 120
Somali Republic	638	3.2	5	34	26	47	22	80
South Africa	1 222	25.6	20	84	48	43	16	1 200 (brace)
South-West Africa (Namibia)	824	0.9	1	65	23	46	23	1 200 (brace)
Spain	505	36.0	70	69	61	19	8	1 960
Sri Lanka	66	14.0	208	29	22	28	8	130
Sudan	2 506	18.2	7	12	13	48	18	150
Surinam	163	0.4	3	35	49	41	7	870
Swaziland	17	0.5	28	88	8	49	22	400
Sweden	450	8.2	18	8	81	13	11	6 720
Switzerland	41	6.5	156	58	55	13	9	6 650
Syria	185	7.6	38	69	44	45	15	490
Taiwan	36	16.3	433	25	63	23	5	720
Tanzania	942	15.6	16	50	7	50	22	140
Thailand	514	43.3	80	22	13	36	11	300
Togo	57	2.3	39	42	15	51	23	210
Trinidad & Tobago	5	1.1	229	35	12	26	7	1 490
Tunisia	164	5.9	34	80	40	38	13	550
Turkey	781	40.2	49	70	39	39	12	690
Uganda	236	11.9	47	16	8	45	16	160
Union of Soviet Socialist Republics	22 402	257	12	27	60	18	9	2 300
United Arab Emirates	84	0.2	3	n.a.	65	50	19	13 500
United Kingdom	244	56.1	229	80	76	13	12	3 360
United States of America	9 363	215.3	23	47	74	15	9	6 640
Upper Volta	274	6.2	22	18	7	49	26	80
Uruguay	178	2.8	17	86	80	21	10	1 060
Venezuela	912	12.3	13	24	75	36	7	1 710
Vietnam	336	46.4	138	n.a.	16	37	15	150
Western Sahara	226	0.08	v.s.	n.a.	n.a.	n.a.	n.a.	n.a.
Yemen Arab Republic	195	6.9	33	n.a.	7	50	21	120
Yemen, P.D.R.	287	1.7	6	38	26	50	21	120
Yugoslavia	256	21.5	83	58	39	18	8	1 250
Zaïre	2 344	25.6	10	22	25	45	20	150
Zambia	753	5.1	6	46	34	51	20	480

...n Reference Bureau Inc., Washington, and the 1975 *Statistical Yearbook* of the United Nations. Population estimates are for mid-1976. Most of

The Canadian Oxford School Atlas
Fourth Edition

Oxford University Press
70 Wynford Drive
Don Mills, Ont.
M3C 1J9

First Edition 1957
Second Edition 1963
Third Edition 1972
Fourth Edition 1977
partly based on the
previous three editions
edited by E. G. Pleva
and Spencer Inch

3456789 - 5432109

Printed in Canada by
The Bryant Press Limited

ISBN 0-19-540240-5

Metric Commission Canada
has granted use of the
National Symbol
for Metric Conversion

Prepared by
The Cartographic Department
of the Clarendon Press

Advisory Editor
Quentin Stanford

 Canada Canada
metric métrique

Contents

Canada: Statistics on Population, Production, & Trade

List of Tables and Graphs

Canada: Statistics on Population, Production, & Trade

1. Land Area and Density of Population, 1951, 1961, 1971, and 1976

PROVINCE OR TERRITORY	LAND AREA[1] km²	POPULATION 1951 TOTAL	/km²	POPULATION 1961 TOTAL	/km²	POPULATION 1971 TOTAL	/km²	POPULATION 1976 TOTAL	/km²	AVERAGE ANNUAL GROWTH RATE 1966–71 %	1971–76 %
NEWFOUNDLAND (incl. Labrador)	370 487	361 416	0.98	457 853	1.24	522 104	1.41	548 789	1.48	1.1	1.0
PRINCE EDWARD ISLAND	5 657	98 429	17.40	104 629	18.50	111 641	19.74	116 251	20.55	0.6	0.8
NOVA SCOTIA	52 841	642 584	12.16	737 007	13.95	788 960	14.94	812 127	15.37	0.9	0.6
NEW BRUNSWICK	72 093	515 697	7.15	597 936	8.29	634 557	8.80	664 525	9.22	0.6	0.9
QUÉBEC	1 356 797	4 055 681	2.99	5 259 211	3.88	6 027 764	4.44	6 141 491	4.53	0.8	0.4
ONTARIO	891 198	4 597 542	5.16	6 236 092	7.00	7 703 106	8.64	8 131 618	9.12	2.0	1.1
MANITOBA	548 497	776 541	1.42	921 686	1.68	988 247	1.80	1 005 953	1.83	0.5	0.4
SASKATCHEWAN	570 271	831 728	1.46	925 181	1.62	926 242	1.62	907 650	1.59	−0.6	−0.4
ALBERTA	644 392	939 501	1.46	1 331 944	2.07	1 627 874	2.53	1 799 771	2.79	2.2	2.1
BRITISH COLUMBIA	930 533	1 165 210	1.25	1 629 082	1.75	2 184 021	2.35	2 406 212	2.59	3.1	2.0
YUKON TERRITORY	531 846	9 096	0.017	14 628	0.028	18 388	0.034	21 392	0.040	5.6	3.3
NORTHWEST TERRITORIES	3 246 404	16 004	0.005	22 998	0.007	34 807	0.011	42 237	0.013	4.2	4.3
CANADA	9 221 016	14 009 429	1.52	18 238 247	1.98	21 568 310	2.34	22 598 016	2.45	1.5	1.0

[1]Includes only land area excluding fresh water.

Sources: *Canada Year Book 1970–71*; *1976 Census of Canada*, Statistics Canada.

2. Percentage of Population in Urban Areas, 1851 to 1971[1]

PROVINCE	1851	1871	1891	1911	1931	1951	1961	1971
NEWFOUNDLAND	—	—	—	—	—	43.3	50.7	57.2
PRINCE EDWARD ISLAND	—	9.4	13.1	16.0	19.5	25.1	32.4	38.3
NOVA SCOTIA	7.5	8.3	19.4	36.7	46.6	54.5	54.3	56.7
NEW BRUNSWICK	14.0	17.6	19.9	26.7	35.4	42.8	46.5	56.9
QUÉBEC	14.9	19.9	28.6	44.5	59.5	66.8	74.3	80.6
ONTARIO	14.0	20.6	35.0	49.5	63.1	72.5	77.3	82.4
MANITOBA	—	—	23.3	39.3	45.2	56.0	63.9	69.5
SASKATCHEWAN	—	—	—	16.1	20.3	30.4	43.0	53.0
ALBERTA	—	—	—	29.4	31.8	47.6	63.3	73.5
BRITISH COLUMBIA	—	9.0	42.6	50.9	62.3	68.6	72.6	75.7
CANADA	13.1	18.3	29.8	41.8	52.5	62.4	69.7	76.1

[1]The percentage of the population classified as urban, rural farm, and rural non-farm in 1971 is shown on the various provincial maps in the *Atlas*.

Sources: *Urban Development in Canada* by Leroy O. Stone, *1961 Census Monograph*; *1971 Census of Canada*.

3. Growth Components of Canada's Population, 1851 to 1971

PERIOD	TOTAL POPULA-TION GROWTH 000	BIRTHS 000	DEATHS 000	NATURAL INCREASE 000	RATIO OF NATURAL INCREASE TO TOTAL GROWTH %	IMMI-GRATION 000	EMI-GRATION 000	NET MIGRATION 000	RATIO OF NET MIGRATION TO TOTAL GROWTH %
1851–1861	793	1 281	670	611	77.0	352	170	182	23.0
1861–1871	460	1 370	760	610	132.6	260	410	−150	−32.6
1871–1881	636	1 480	790	690	108.5	350	404	−54	−8.5
1881–1891	508	1 524	870	654	128.7	680	826	−146	−28.7
1891–1901	538	1 548	880	668	124.2	250	380	−130	−24.2
1901–1911	1 835	1 925	900	1 025	55.9	1 550	740	810	44.1
1911–1921	1 581	2 340	1 070	1 270	80.3	1 400	1 089	311	19.7
1921–1931	1 589	2 420	1 060	1 360	85.5	1 200	970	230	14.5
1931–1941	1 130	2 294	1 072	1 222	108.1	149	241	−92	−8.1
1941–1951[1]	2 503	3 212	1 220	1 992	92.3	548	382	166	7.7
1951–1961	4 228	4 468	1 320	3 148	74.5	1 543	463	1 080	25.5
1961–1971	3 330	4 105	1 497	2 608	78.3	1 429	707	722	21.7

[1] Includes Newfoundland in 1951 but not in 1941.

Source: *Canada Year Book 1975*.

4. Components of Population Change by Province, 1961 to 1966 and 1966 to 1971

PROVINCE OR TERRITORY	TOTAL POPULATION CHANGE		NATURAL INCREASE		NET MIGRATION	
	1961–66	1966–71	1961–66	1966–71	1961–66	1966–71
NEWFOUNDLAND...............	35 543	28 708	59 577	49 096	−24 034	−20 388
PRINCE EDWARD ISLAND......	3 906	3 106	8 506	5 207	−4 600	−2 101
NOVA SCOTIA.................	19 032	32 921	59 526	37 418	−40 494	−4 497
NEW BRUNSWICK..............	18 852	17 769	53 229	35 233	−34 377	−17 464
QUÉBEC......................	521 634	246 919	457 717	288 727	63 917	−41 808
ONTARIO.....................	724 778	742 236	487 852	373 072	236 926	369 164
MANITOBA....................	41 380	25 181	70 340	49 260	−28 960	−24 079
SASKATCHEWAN...............	30 163	−29 102	75 691	50 867	−45 528	−79 969
ALBERTA.....................	131 259	164 671	134 607	105 293	−3 348	59 378
BRITISH COLUMBIA............	244 592	310 947	104 103	88 494	140 489	222 453
YUKON TERRITORY & NORTHWEST TERRITORIES......	5 494	10 075	6 745	6 720	−1 251	3 355
CANADA	**1 776 633**	**1 553 431**	**1 517 893**	**1 089 387**	**258 740**	**464 044**

Source: *Canada Year Book 1975*.

5. Vital Statistics Rates, 1930 to 1976

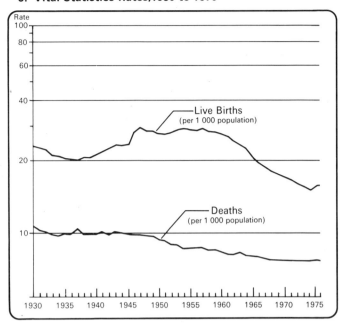

Source: *Quarterly Vital Statistics*, December 1976, Statistics Canada.

6. Immigration to and Emigration from Canada, 1952 to 1976

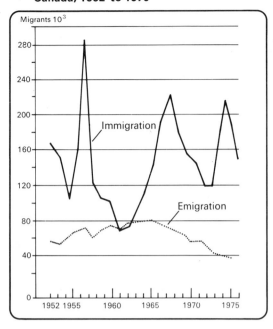

Sources: *Canada Year Book 1974; Canadian Statistical Review*, July 1976, Statistics Canada; *Immigration Statistics Canada*, 1976.

7. Age Groups and Sex Ratio of Canada's Population, Census Years, 1901 to 1971[1]

AGE GROUP	PER CENT OF TOTAL POPULATION							
	1901	1911	1921	1931	1941	1951	1961	1971
0–4	12.0	12.3	12.0	10.4	9.1	12.3	12.4	8.4
5–9	11.5	10.9	12.0	10.9	9.1	10.0	11.4	10.5
10–14	10.8	9.7	10.4	10.4	9.6	8.1	10.2	10.7
15–19	10.4	9.5	9.2	10.0	9.7	7.6	7.9	9.8
20–24	9.6	9.9	8.1	8.8	9.0	7.8	6.5	8.8
25–34	14.9	17.0	15.3	14.4	15.7	15.5	13.6	13.4
35–44	11.7	12.0	13.2	12.9	12.5	13.3	13.1	11.7
45–54	8.3	8.6	9.1	10.4	10.7	10.0	10.3	10.6
55–64	5.7	5.5	5.9	6.4	7.9	7.7	7.1	8.0
65–69	2.0	1.8	2.0	2.2	2.7	3.1	2.7	2.9
70+	3.1	2.8	2.8	3.3	4.0	4.7	5.0	5.2
Total	100.0	100.0	100.0	100.0	100.0	100.0	100.0	100.0
Median age[2]	22.7	23.8	24.0	24.7	27.0	27.7	26.3	26.3
Sex ratio[3]	105.0	112.9	106.4	107.4	105.3	102.4	102.2	100.2

[1] Excluding Newfoundland in censuses prior to 1951.

[2] Fifty per cent of the population lies below the median age, which is given in years and fractions of years.

[3] Males per 100 females.

Source: *Canadian Urban Trends, National Perspective*, Vol. I. Printed with the permission of the Ministry of State for Urban Affairs and Copp Clark Publishing.

8. Ethnic Origin of Canada's Population, Census Years, 1901 to 1971[1]

ETHNIC GROUP	PER CENT OF TOTAL POPULATION							
	1901	1911	1921	1931	1941	1951	1961	1971
BRITISH ISLES........	57.0	55.5	55.4	51.9	49.7	47.9	43.8	44.6
FRENCH...............	30.7	28.6	27.9	28.2	30.3	30.8	30.4	28.7
OTHER EUROPEAN....	8.5	13.1	14.2	17.6	17.8	18.3	22.6	23.0
Austrian...............	0.2	0.6	1.2	0.5	0.3	0.2	0.6	0.2
German...............	5.8	5.6	3.4	4.6	4.0	4.4	5.7	6.1
Greek.................	v.s.	0.1	0.1	0.1	0.1	0.1	0.3	0.6
Hungarian.............	v.s.	0.2	0.1	0.4	0.5	0.4	0.7	0.6
Italian................	0.2	0.6	0.8	0.9	1.0	1.1	2.5	3.4
Jewish................	0.3	1.1	1.4	1.5	1.5	1.5	1.4	1.4
Netherlands...........	0.6	0.8	1.3	1.4	1.8	1.9	2.4	2.0
Polish................	0.1	0.5	0.6	1.4	1.5	1.5	1.6	1.5
Russian...............	0.4	0.6	1.1	0.8	0.7	0.6	0.5	0.3
Scandinavian...........	0.6	1.6	1.9	2.2	2.1	2.0	2.1	1.8
Ukrainian..............	0.1	1.0	1.2	2.2	2.7	2.8	2.6	2.7
Other..................	0.2	0.5	1.0	1.4	1.4	1.5	1.9	2.0
ASIAN................	0.4	0.6	0.8	0.8	0.6	0.5	0.7	1.3
Chinese and Japanese...	0.4	0.5	0.6	0.7	0.5	0.4	0.5	0.7
Other.................	v.s.	0.1	0.1	0.1	0.1	0.1	0.2	0.6
NATIVE INDIAN and ESKIMO.........	2.4	1.5	1.3	1.2	1.4	1.2	1.2	1.4
OTHER and NOT STATED........	0.9	0.7	0.5	0.3	0.3	1.3	1.3	1.0
TOTAL................	100.0	100.0	100.0	100.0	100.0	100.0	100.0	100.0

v.s. Very small.

[1] Excluding Newfoundland in censuses prior to 1951.

Source: *Canadian Urban Trends, National Perspective*, Vol. I. Printed with the permission of the Ministry of State for Urban Affairs and Copp Clark Publishing.

9. Immigration to Canada by Country or Region of Last Permanent Residence, 1946 to 1950, 1963 to 1967, and 1975

COUNTRY	ANNUAL AVERAGE 1946–50	ANNUAL AVERAGE 1963–67	1975
ASIA....................	1 061	11 150	47 382
BRITISH ISLES...........	32 081	42 946	36 076
UNITED STATES........	8 777	15 199	21 055
WEST INDIES...........	446	3 993	17 800
PORTUGAL..............	22	6 495	8 547
ITALY..................	4 010	24 360	5 978
GREECE................	568	6 523	4 062
FRANCE................	956	6 266	3 891
GERMANY (WEST)......	1 996	8 541	3 469
NETHERLANDS..........	5 193	2 905	1 448
OTHERS................	31 537	26 363	29 646
Total...................	86 078	154 027	187 881

Sources: *Immigration and Population Statistics*, Manpower and Immigration; *Canadian Statistical Review*, July 1976, Statistics Canada.

10. Population and Other Characteristics of Census Metropolitan Areas, 1971 and 1976

CENSUS METROPOLITAN AREAS	POPULATION	AVERAGE ANNUAL POPULATION CHANGE		IMMIGRANTS	POPULATION BORN OUT OF PROVINCE	LABOUR FORCE IN MANUFACTURING	COMPONENT MUNICIPALITIES	PREDOMINANT LANGUAGE (MOTHER TONGUE)
	1976	1966–71 %	1971–76 %	1971 %	1971 %	1971 %	1971 No.	1971 %
MONTRÉAL, Qué................	2 758 780	1.3	0.2	14.8	20.5	28.4	103	F66
TORONTO, Ont..................	2 753 112	3.0	1.2	34.0	44.2	27.5	29	E74
VANCOUVER, B.C..............	1 135 774	3.2	1.0	26.5	53.9	18.4	22	E82
OTTAWA-HULL, Ont..........	668 853	2.8	1.6	12.5	34.8	8.7	25	E57
WINNIPEG, Man...............	570 725	1.2	0.8	19.9	34.4	19.7	14	E71
EDMONTON, Alta..............	542 845	3.3	1.9	18.3	39.3	12.6	10	E76
QUÉBEC, Qué..................	534 193	2.0	1.3	2.2	4.3	13.8	36	F95
HAMILTON, Ont...............	525 222	1.8	0.9	26.7	36.0	37.5	12	E80
CALGARY, Alta.................	457 828	4.4	2.7	20.5	49.8	12.1	1	E84
ST. CATHARINES-NIAGARA FALLS, Ont..................	298 129	1.3	0.9	22.9	33.0	36.4	4	E76
KITCHENER, Ont...............	269 828	3.6	2.6	21.8	31.3	42.0	9	E81
LONDON, Ont...................	264 639	2.5	0.9	20.0	28.6	24.4	9	E88
HALIFAX, N.S..................	261 366	1.8	0.9	7.2	26.0	8.9	7	E94
WINDSOR, Ont.................	243 289	1.7	−0.4	21.5	28.8	36.0	12	E74
VICTORIA, B.C.................	212 466	2.3	1.7	24.7	54.4	9.8	8	E91
SUDBURY, Ont.................	155 013	2.7	−0.3	12.4	25.9	14.3	11	E54
REGINA, Sask..................	148 965	1.3	1.2	13.1	26.0	10.3	2	E82
ST. JOHN'S, Nfld..............	140 883	2.4	1.4	3.0	6.8	7.8	14	E99
OSHAWA, Ont..................	133 959	n.a.	2.3	19.9	30.0	42.1	3	E84
SASKATOON, Sask.............	132 291	1.8	0.9	13.9	28.1	10.6	1	E79
CHICOUTIMI-JONQUIÈRE, Qué.....	127 181	0.1	0.1	1.4	3.9	28.4	13	F96
THUNDER BAY, Ont.............	117 988	0.8	0.6	21.1	33.6	17.7	3	E74
SAINT JOHN, N.B...............	109 700	0.5	0.6	4.9	17.2	17.9	15	E92

Source: *Census of Canada, 1971* and *1976.*

11. Unemployment Rates, 1961 to 1976

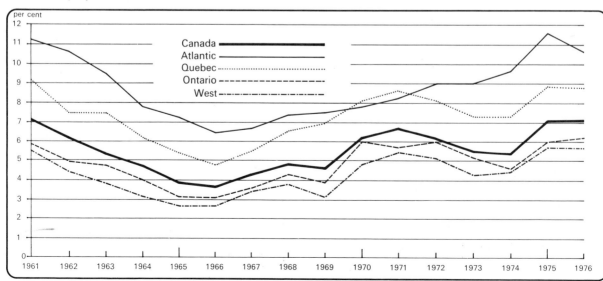

Sources: *Climate for Regional Development*, DREE, 1976; *Labour Force*, December 1976, Statistics Canada.

12. Census-farms[1]—Population, Number, Use of Land, and Capital Value, 1931, 1951, 1961, and 1971

	Unit	1931	1951	1961	1971
POPULATION ON CENSUS-FARMS.....	no.	3 289 140	2 911 996	2 128 400	1 489 565
Percentage of total Canadian population living on census-farms...................	%	31.7	20.8	11.7	6.9
NUMBER OF CENSUS-FARMS.........	no.	728 623	623 091	480 903	366 128
AREA IN CENSUS-FARMS..............	ha	65 245 614	69 618 662	69 020 420	67 867 446
Percentage of total land area of Canada in census-farms..........................	%	7.5	7.7	7.6	7.5
USE OF AGRICULTURAL LAND:					
Improved land...........................	ha	34 292 869	38 741 130	41 361 370	43 259 551
Under crops...........................	ha	23 335 979	24 884 859	24 974 214	27 506 271
Pasture................................	ha	3 204 686	4 002 050	4 099 158	4 090 186
Summer fallow.......................	ha	6 802 911	8 812 824	11 297 354	10 696 291
Other improved land..................	ha	949 292	1 041 396	990 644	996 803
Unimproved land........................	ha	30 952 745	30 877 531	27 659 050	24 607 895
Woodland.............................	ha	10 658 112	9 111 978	6 898 956	4 605 668
Other unimproved land................	ha	20 294 632	21 765 554	20 760 094	20 002 226
Total capital value......................	$	5 247 753 468	9 470 876 372	13 171 221 700	24 067 857 000
Land and buildings......................	$	4 053 282 300	5 527 207 155	8 622 641 300	16 936 043 000
Machinery and equipment................	$	650 664 000	1 933 312 262	2 568 631 500	3 909 184 700
Livestock and poultry....................	$	543 807 168	2 010 356 955	1 979 948 900	3 221 285 970

[1]A census-farm was defined in the 1971 Census as an agricultural holding of one or more acres (0.4 ha) with sales of $50 or more of agricultural products in the year prior to the census.

Sources: *1966 Census of Canada*, Vol. III (3–1), June 1968; *1971 Census of Canada*, Statistics Canada.

13. Average Size of Census-farms, 1931, 1941, 1951, 1961, and 1971

PROVINCE OR TERRITORY	HECTARES (ha)					AVERAGE ANNUAL RATE OF INCREASE	
	1931	1941	1951	1961	1971	1951–61 %	1961–71 %
NEWFOUNDLAND..............	n.a.	n.a.	9.2	12.4	24.0	3.5	9.4
PRINCE EDWARD ISLAND......	37.2	38.4	43.2	52.4	68.4	2.1	3.1
NOVA SCOTIA................	43.6	46.4	54.0	71.2	88.4	3.2	2.4
NEW BRUNSWICK.............	48.8	49.6	52.4	74.8	97.6	4.3	3.1
QUÉBEC......................	50.8	46.8	50.0	59.2	70.4	1.8	1.9
ONTARIO.....................	47.6	50.4	55.6	61.2	67.6	1.0	1.1
MANITOBA....................	111.6	116.4	135.2	168.0	217.2	2.4	2.9
SASKATCHEWAN..............	163.2	172.8	220.0	274.4	338.0	2.5	2.3
ALBERTA.....................	160.0	173.6	210.8	258.0	316.0	2.2	2.3
BRITISH COLUMBIA...........	54.4	61.2	71.2	90.4	126.8	2.7	4.0
CANADA[1]	—	—	111.6	143.6	185.2	2.9	2.9

n.a. Not available.

[1]Includes data for Yukon and Northwest Territories.

Sources: *Agricultural Trends in Canada, 1966 Census of Canada*, Special Bulletin S-403, September 1969; *Selected Statistical Information on Agriculture in Canada*, October 1969, Economics Branch, Canadian Department of Agriculture; and *1971 Census of Canada*, Statistics Canada,

14. Farm Characteristics by Province, 1971

	CANADA	NFLD.	P.E.I.	N.S.	N.B.	QUÉ.	ONT.	MAN.	SASK.	ALTA.	B.C.
Total number of census farms..............	366 128	1 042	4 543	6 008	5 485	61 257	94 722	34 981	76 970	62 702	18 400
AVERAGES FOR CENSUS-FARMS											
Area (hectares per farm)...........	185	24	68	88	98	70	68	217	338	316	127
Improved land (as a % of total farm area)......	64%	30%	64%	29%	37%	60%	68%	67%	71%	58%	30%
Improved pasture (as a % of total farm area)......	6%	13%	15%	8%	7%	16%	15%	4%	3%	6%	7%
Under crops (as a % of total farm area)......	41%	13%	46%	18%	24%	40%	49%	48%	42%	37%	19%
Summer fallow (as a % of total farm area)......	16%	2%	1%	1%	1%	1%	2%	14%	25%	14%	3%
Value of machinery and equipment ($ per farm)..................	10 677	3 934	8 425	6 636	7 402	6 979	9 396	11 762	13 336	13 834	8 868
Total capital value[1] ($ per farm)..................	65 759	30 201	35 636	34 301	31 579	35 919	72 819	58 764	71 353	83 606	87 333
Value of all crops sold ($ per farm)..................	3 760	1 208	3 651	1 967	3 476	1 186	4 207	3 799	5 386	3 953	3 329
Value of all livestock and poultry sold ($ per farm)..................	5 236	2 049	3 477	3 350	2 330	2 986	6 920	4 712	3 452	8 349	4 007
Value of other products sold (dairy, eggs, forest products) ($ per farm)..................	2 332	4 511	1 516	4 214	2 741	4 510	3 404	1 140	356	976	4 053

[1]Includes land, buildings, machinery, equipment, and livestock.

Source: *1971 Census of Canada*, Statistics Canada.

15. Leading World Producers of Wheat, 1974

	PRODUCTION 10^3 t	EXPORTS 10^3 t
USSR............................	83 849	4 700 (1970)
USA.............................	48 806	25 133
CHINA...........................	27 700	n.a.
INDIA...........................	22 072	260
FRANCE..........................	18 905	7 384
CANADA..........................	14 221	10 122
AUSTRALIA.......................	11 700	3 827

n.a. Not available.

Source: *Statistical Yearbook*, United Nations, 1975.

16. Canadian Wheat Statistics, 1965 to 1976

	1965	1966	1967	1968	1969	1970	1971	1972	1973	1974	1975	1976
Hectares seeded (10³)	11 320	11 877	12 049	11 770	9 985	4 993	7 763	8 540	9 464	8 831	9 369	11 012
Yield (kg/ha)	1 539	1 875	1 324	1 486	1 808	1 788	1 835	1 681	1 687	1 486	1 802	2 111
Production (10⁶ t)..........	17.67	22.51	16.13	17.69	18.26	9.02	14.41	14.51	16.15	13.29	17.07	23.52
Exports (10⁶ t)	15.91	14.02	9.14	8.32	9.43	11.84	13.71	15.69	11.41	10.73	12.25	n.a.
Domestic use (10⁶ t)..............	4.28	4.36	4.25	4.48	4.56	4.65	4.79	4.76	4.59	4.60	4.78	n.a.
Carry-over at the beginning of crop year (10⁶ t)	13.96	11.43	15.56	18.30	23.18	27.45	19.98	15.88	9.94	10.08	8.03	8.07

n.a. Not available.

Source: Agriculture Division, Statistics Canada.

17. Census-farms with Sales of $2 500 or More Classified by Type of Product, 1971[1]

PROVINCE	FARMS WITH SALES OF $2 500 OR MORE	TYPE AND NUMBER OF FARMS									
		Dairy	Cattle, hogs, sheep	Poultry	Wheat	Small grains[3]	Other field crops[4]	Fruits and vege- tables	Forestry	Miscel- laneous specialty	Mixed combina- tions
NEWFOUNDLAND..........	282	70	40	54	—	—	30	58	5	5	20
PRINCE EDWARD ISLAND....................	2 780	629	980	21	—	11	616	26	6	8	483
NOVA SCOTIA..............	2 568	1 019	655	169	—	9	76	250	114	109	167
NEW BRUNSWICK..........	2 603	821	535	111	—	4	670	98	119	26	219
QUÉBEC....................	40 932	28 646	5 183	1 561	20	342	1 124	1 472	331	423	1 830
ONTARIO..................	65 667	17 718	28 129	1 912	313	5 189	4 593	3 856	165	1 606	2 186
MANITOBA.................	25 336	1 614	9 829	519	2 738	7 249	376	65	16	209	2 721
SASKATCHEWAN...........	62 930	701	15 913	210	26 516	13 900	112	14	3	128	5 443
ALBERTA..................	46 533	2 490	25 843	413	3 893	9 105	814	40	28	320	3 587
BRITISH COLUMBIA........	8 625	1 633	2 501	644	166	390	387	1 948	162	571	223
CANADA[2]	258 259	55 341	89 610	5 615	33 646	36 199	8 798	7 827	949	3 405	16 869

[1] A criterion of 51% or more total sales was used to determine in which category a farm was placed.
[2] Includes data for Yukon and Northwest Territories.
[3] Includes oats, barley, rye, mixed grains, buckwheat, corn, field peas and beans, flaxseed, soybeans, etc
[4] Includes hay and fodder crops, potatoes, sugar beets, tobacco, etc.

Source: *1971 Census of Canada*, Statistics Canada.

18. Area, Production, and Values of Major Field Crops by Province[1], Various Years

FIELD CROP AND PROVINCE	AREA			TOTAL PRODUCTION			GROSS FARM VALUE		
	Average 1945–49	Average 1963–67	1974	Average 1945–49	Average 1963–67	1974	Average 1945–49	Average 1963–67	1972
	10³ ha	10³ ha	10³ ha	10³ t	10³ t	10³ t	$000	$000	$000
Wheat.................	**9 823.0**	**11 630.0**	**9 391.0**	**9 873.0**	**18 473.2**	**14 220.4**	**587 412**	**1 145 512**	**993 349**
Prince Edward Island........	0.8	1.2	4.0	1.5	2.2	12.8	84	141	530
Nova Scotia...............	0.4	0.4	1.2	0.6	1.0	3.3	34	62	286
New Brunswick............	0.8	1.2	0.8	1.3	2.6	3.9	77	164	253
Québec..................	4.8	9.2	24.0	5.6	16.3	41.8	313	1 024	1 524
Ontario									
Winter..................	248.0	159.0	168.0	492.6	433.3	519.0	28 358	27 547	27 310
Spring..................	16.0	8.0	4.0	22.4	14.4	8.2	1 287	915	738
Manitoba.................	968.0	1 324.0	1 200.0	1 306.3	2 144.6	1 714.6	79 827	132 286	128 340
Saskatchewan.............	5 775.0	7 575.0	6 160.0	5 034.8	11 523.0	8 872.3	301 085	719 844	612 880
Alberta..................	2 766.0	2 509.0	1 800.0	2 939.3	4 261.9	2 993.7	171 983	259 464	217 120
British Columbia...........	42.0	44.0	28.0	71.2	73.9	51.7	4 365	4 064	4 368
Oats....................	**4 605.0**	**3 284.0**	**2 442.0**	**5 034.4**	**5 773.2**	**3 928.7**	**219 370**	**261 224**	**266 733**
Prince Edward Island........	44.0	35.0	20.0	62.8	67.4	43.3	3 113	3 559	2 399
Nova Scotia...............	26.0	11.0	7.6	34.3	19.6	14.2	1 891	1 138	796
New Brunswick............	71.0	32.0	20.0	94.6	53.4	35.4	4 799	2 891	1 775
Québec..................	550.0	430.0	250.0	508.3	654.4	367.2	26 716	36 992	25 029
Ontario..................	601.0	547.0	198.0	875.5	1 117.9	361.1	42 078	56 534	27 134
Manitoba.................	584.0	633.0	480.0	755.7	1 045.6	663.2	31 402	45 526	49 500
Saskatchewan.............	1 634.0	718.0	760.0	1 480.5	1 258.4	1 156.6	60 134	51 872	70 310
Alberta..................	1 058.0	849.0	680.0	1 156.7	1 505.2	1 233.8	46 148	60 542	87 360
British Columbia...........	37.0	28.0	26.0	69.9	51.3	54.0	3 088	2 169	2 430
Barley..................	**2 628.0**	**2 670.0**	**4 600.0**	**3 073.6**	**5 042.0**	**8 584.6**	**133 431**	**226 867**	**646 184**
Prince Edward Island........	2.0	5.0	8.0	3.7	11.8	22.8	172	585	1 606
Nova Scotia...............	2.0	1.2	2.4	3.3	2.6	5.9	172	149	465
New Brunswick............	4.0	2.0	4.0	6.8	4.1	9.7	346	228	432
Québec..................	34.0	6.0	21.0	40.7	12.5	35.9	2 006	688	1 869
Ontario..................	94.0	79.0	136.0	162.8	195.2	336.8	7 148	10 391	22 556
Manitoba.................	706.0	282.0	720.0	914.4	500.8	1 153.9	40 907	23 118	107 100
Saskatchewan.............	942.0	775.0	1 600.0	936.2	1 463.1	2 786.9	39 813	66 146	217 710
Alberta..................	835.0	1 462.0	2 040.0	979.8	2 760.7	4 093.2	42 121	121 832	289 800
British Columbia...........	8.0	57.0	68.0	15.9	91.2	139.3	746	3 730	4 646
Soybeans...............	**29.0**	**103.0**	**178.0**	**40.6**	**202.0**	**300.4**	**3 492**	**20 886**	**53 703**
Ontario..................	29.0	103.0	178.0	40.6	202.0	300.4	3 492	20 886	53 703
Mixed Grains...........	**490.0**	**646.0**	**724.0**	**998.9**	**1 726.2**	**1 831.3**	**36 988**	**68 250**	**103 257**
Prince Edward Island........	19.0	19.0	30.0	42.6	55.9	98.8	1 590	2 269	4 010
Nova Scotia...............	1.6	4.0	3.0	3.1	9.9	8.3	135	473	422
New Brunswick............	1.2	4.0	1.2	2.1	8.7	5.7	79	397	351
Québec..................	76.0	40.0	50.0	111.6	90.2	106.0	4 852	4 590	5 960

Table 18 continued

FIELD CROP AND PROVINCE	AREA			TOTAL PRODUCTION			GROSS FARM VALUE		
	Average 1945–49	Average 1963–67	1974	Average 1945–49	Average 1963–67	1974	Average 1945–49	Average 1963–67	1972
	10³ ha	10³ ha	10³ ha	10³ t	10³ t	10³ t	$000	$000	$000
Ontario..................	366.0	320.0	328.0	803.7	998.0	993.4	29 194	39 415	51 442
Manitoba..................	7.0	61.0	80.0	11.2	128.6	136.1	364	4 943	13 500
Saskatchewan.............	5.0	49.0	80.0	5.8	102.8	145.1	192	3 652	8 460
Alberta..................	13.0	148.0	148.0	16.7	327.5	331.1	512	12 286	18 700
British Columbia...........	0.8	1.6	2.4	1.9	4.5	6.8	70	225	412
Flaxseed	**466.0**	**713.0**	**600.0**	**241.3**	**518.1**	**363.2**	**37 188**	**57 799**	**70 863**
Ontario..................	16.0	7.0	0.0	11.8	7.3	0.0	1 879	787	53
Manitoba..................	180.0	397.0	300.0	108.4	263.1	180.3	16 732	29 182	24 190
Saskatchewan.............	210.0	177.0	220.0	85.3	135.6	119.4	12 872	15 170	35 820
Alberta..................	58.0	122.0	80.0	34.9	102.1	63.5	5 555	11 501	10 800
Rapeseed	**16.0**	**468.0**	**1 304.0**	**672.7**	**429.5**	**1 199.7**	**1 746**	**44 595**	**181 086**
Manitoba..................	—	47.0	200.0	—	40.9	192.8	—	4 262	26 350
Saskatchewan.............	16.0	192.0	600.0	672.7	194.8	544.3	1 746	20 252	79 856
Alberta..................	—	229.0	480.0	—	193.8	442.2	—	20 082	74 880
Shelled Corn	**98.0**	**291.0**	**584.0**	**280.4**	**1 467.8**	**2 588.5**	**14 056**	**77 233**	**164 100**
Québec..................	—	—	66.0	—	—	292.6	—	—	14 359
Ontario..................	92.0	286.0	516.0	272.6	1 449.8	2 291.1	13 726	76 198	148 656
Manitoba..................	5.0	2.0	2.0	7.7	4.4	4.8	330	233	1 085
Potatoes.................	**167.0**	**118.0**	**112.0**	**1 801.0**	**2 182.7**	**2 427.4**	**72 522**	**100 208**	**160 356**
Prince Edward Island........	18.0	18.0	18.4	271.8	402.7	467.4	7 746	16 071	33 212
Nova Scotia..............	6.0	2.0	1.6	80.2	37.4	28.9	3 436	1 787	1 910
New Brunswick.............	24.0	23.0	23.2	396.0	551.2	607.7	13 241	20 944	45 548
Québec..................	47.0	29.0	21.0	406.2	389.4	382.2	17 485	18 153	17 017
Ontario..................	37.0	20.0	17.0	363.1	427.0	368.3	16 877	20 957	32 857
Manitoba..................	8.0	9.0	14.0	63.7	119.4	222.3	2 371	5 571	7 500
Saskatchewan.............	10.0	4.0	1.6	55.8	31.8	24.0	2 570	1 909	1 662
Alberta..................	9.0	9.0	9.2	76.1	136.4	181.4	3 706	8 495	11 275
British Columbia...........	6.0	4.0	5.6	88.0	87.4	145.2	5 089	6 321	9 375
Tame Hay...............	**4 214.0**	**5 121.0**	**5 355.0**	**15 176.0**	**21 368.0**	**23 604.0**	**250 847**	**430 464**	**552 356**
Prince Edward Island........	88.0	72.0	51.0	302.0	296.0	204.0	4 620	4 410	4 019
Nova Scotia..............	161.0	90.0	60.0	634.0	429.0	288.0	11 773	7 668	6 099
New Brunswick.............	214.0	100.0	64.0	678.0	430.0	251.0	11 849	7 305	5 596
Québec..................	1 584.0	1 345.0	1 070.0	5 013.0	5 495.0	4 518.0	87 681	109 928	122 431
Ontario..................	1 348.0	1 354.0	1 080.0	5 559.0	6 701.0	5 733.0	86 292	146 814	147 226
Manitoba..................	130.0	407.0	500.0	504.0	1 571.0	2 177.0	6 021	28 198	40 000
Saskatchewan	192.0	467.0	800.0	617.0	1 579.0	2 903.0	9 029	28 077	52 250
Alberta..................	376.0	1 114.0	1 480.0	1 243.0	3 949.0	6 078.0	19 053	75 507	132 060
British Columbia...........	121.0	174.0	250.0	624.0	917.0	1 451.0	14 530	22 558	42 675

Continued overleaf

Table 18 continued

FIELD CROP AND PROVINCE	AREA			TOTAL PRODUCTION			GROSS FARM VALUE		
	Average 1945–49	Average 1963–67	1974	Average 1945–49	Average 1963–67	1974	Average 1945–49	Average 1963–67	1972
	10³ ha	10³ ha	10³ ha	10³ t	10³ t	10³ t	$000	$000	$000
Fodder Corn	**162.0**	**212.0**	**419.0**	**3 183.0**	**5 594.0**	**10 043.0**	**17 951**	**38 877**	**79 129**
Québec..................	28.0	26.0	64.0	549.0	705.0	1 855.0	4 172	5 506	16 338
Ontario..................	123.0	166.0	336.0	2 531.0	4 579.0	7 697.0	12 910	30 828	58 691
Manitoba................	6.0	15.0	11.0	53.0	213.0	190.0	422	1 599	1 600
British Columbia...........	2.0	2.0	7.0	38.0	77.0	299.0	309	677	2 500

[1] Excluding Newfoundland.

[2] Because of rounding and omissions, columns may not always add up to the totals indicated.

Sources: *Canada Year Book 1961, 1970–71, and 1975; Quarterly Bulletin of Agricultural Statistics 1971.*

19. Value of Mineral Production, 1970 and 1976

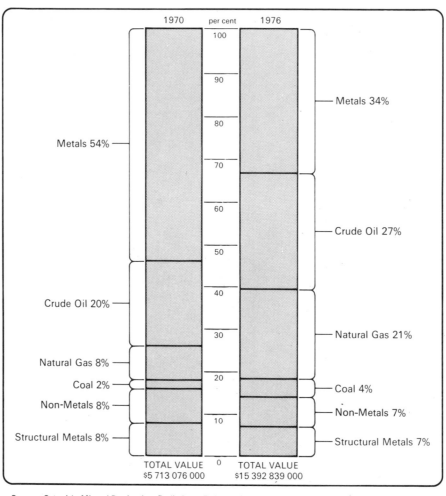

Source: *Canada's Mineral Production, Preliminary Estimate,* Statistics Canada, 1970 and 1976.

20. Value of Production of Principal Minerals, 1976*

Metals	NFLD. $000	N.S. $000	N.B. $000	QUÉ. $000	ONT. $000	MAN. $000	SASK. $000	ALTA. $000	B.C. $000	Y.T. & N.W.T. $000	CANADA $000
COBALT.............	—	—	—	—	9 679	2 090	—	—	—	—	11 769
COPPER.............	10 194	—	14 587	181 500	390 361	85 444	14 463	—	412 308	17 299	1 126 156
GOLD................	1 596	—	460	58 460	90 414	5 674	2 342	—	21 820	27 030	207 796
IRON ORE...........	643 455	—	—	324 607	264 111	—	—	—	9 090	—	1 241 263
IRON, remelt..........	—	—	—	65 086	—	—	—	—	—	—	65 086
LEAD................	4 621	—	30 808	460	3 186	137	—	—	44 264	45 912	129 388
MOLYBDENUM.......	—	—	—	2 946	—	—	—	—	88 927	—	91 873
NICKEL.............	—	—	—	—	993 704	238 439	—	—	—	—	1 232 143
PLATINUM GROUP....	—	—	—	—	48 790	—	—	—	—	—	48 790
SILVER..............	2 194	—	21 497	15 794	67 000	3 817	1 387	—	35 108	28 331	175 128
URANIUM (U_3O_8)†....	—	—	—	—	3 892 kg	—	2 166 kg	—	—	—	6 058 kg
ZINC................	37 833	—	142 432	101 960	265 426	51 367	6 755	—	93 940	162 583	862 296
Total—All Metals....	**699 919**	—	**217 945**	**765 699**	**2 153 488**	**387 330**	**25 116**	—	**710 487**	**281 167**	**5 241 151**
Non-Metallics											
ASBESTOS...........	33 383	—	—	343 164	3 797	—	—	—	30 719	34 460	445 523
GYPSUM.............	2 436	13 804	177	—	2 658	203	—	—	3 628	—	22 906
PEAT................	—	500	5 800	7 800	870	2 470	400	1 100	3 560	—	22 500
POTASH (K_2O)........	—	—	—	—	—	—	361 442	—	—	—	361 442
QUARTZ.............	218	231	—	5 075	5 400	1 517	168	1 125	161	—	13 895
SALT................	—	17 632	—	—	44 272	161	7 833	5 793	—	—	75 691
SODIUM SULPHATE...	—	—	—	—	—	—	22 221	2 657	—	—	24 878
SULPHUR, in smelter gas...........	—	—	781	2 575	7 318	—	—	—	4 780	—	15 454
SULPHUR, elemental...	—	—	—	—	35	15	293	62 280	716	—	63 339
TITANIUM DIOXIDE, &C........	—	—	—	74 410	—	—	—	—	—	—	74 410
Total—All Non-metallics........	**38 699**	**32 927**	**6 758**	**439 174**	**75 742**	**4 366**	**392 357**	**72 955**	**45 078**	**34 460**	**1 142 516**
Fuels											
COAL................	—	54 500	6 300	—	—	—	12 900	223 800	306 500	—	604 000
NATURAL GAS.......	—	—	59	2	5 760	—	8 250	2 302 235	130 137	20 178	2 466 621
NATURAL GAS BY-PRODUCTS.......	—	—	—	—	—	—	5 787	772 414	16 124	—	794 325
PETROLEUM, CRUDE..	—	—	24	—	6 028	32 995	435 675	3 531 100	114 272	8 364	4 128 485
Total—All Fuels.....	—	**54 500**	**6 383**	**2**	**11 788**	**32 995**	**462 612**	**6 829 549**	**567 033**	**28 542**	**7 993 404**
Structural Materials											
CLAY PRODUCTS.....	475	3 915	2 464	14 243	50 926	1 318	3 098	8 727	6 944	—	92 110
CEMENT.............	5 014	7 059	8 967	88 733	116 162	22 606	15 171	36 948	38 499	—	339 159
LIME................	—	—	1 440	20 570	24 236	2 805	—	4 093	955	—	54 099
SAND AND GRAVEL..	9 200	14 400	4 100	75 900	95 200	25 200	10 200	42 100	42 800	—	320 800
STONE...............	2 700	4 400	7 000	117 000	66 500	1 500	—	1 200	9 300	—	209 600
Total—All Structural Materials...........	**17 389**	**29 774**	**23 971**	**316 446**	**353 024**	**53 429**	**28 469**	**93 068**	**98 498**	—	**1 015 768**
Grand Totals 1976....	**756 007**	**117 201**	**255 057**	**1 521 321**	**2 594 042**	**478 120**	**908 554**	**6 995 572**	**1 421 096**	**344 169**	**15 392 839**
Grand Totals 1968...	**309 712**	**56 928**	**88 451**	**728 784**	**1 355 629**	**209 626**	**357 174**	**1 091 749**	**389 311**	**137 002**	**4 725 341**

*Based on rounded figures shown.
†Value of uranium production not available.

Source: *Canada's Mineral Production, Preliminary Estimate*, Statistics Canada, 1976.

21. Petroleum Supply and Demand, 1960, 1965, 1970, 1973, and 1975

	1960	1965	1970	1973	1975
			10^3 t		
SUPPLY					
Production					
Crude and equivalent[1].....................	32 605	55 356	88 571	126 969	106 814
Imports					
Crude...................................	20 586	23 703	34 135	53 024	50 673
Refined Products.......................	5 771	9 749	11 600	7 417	2 778
Total Supply...........................	**58 962**	**88 808**	**134 306**	**187 410**	**160 265**
DEMAND					
Domestic Demand........................	51 604	68 678	87 983	102 678	104 908
Exports..................................	7 377	19 517	45 782	83 808	55 079
Total Demand...........................	**58 981**	**88 195**	**133 765**	**186 486**	**159 987**

[1]Includes plant liquefied petroleum gases.

Source: *An Energy Strategy for Canada*, Energy, Mines and Resources, 1976.

22. Marketable Gas Supply and Demand, 1960, 1965, 1970, 1973, and 1975

	1960	1965	1970	1973	1975
			10^9 m^3		
SUPPLY					
Production...............................	12.53	29.74	52.88	71.34	71.32
Imports..................................	0.15	0.50	0.31	0.42	0.31
Total	**12.68**	**30.24**	**53.19**	**71.76**	**71.63**
DEMAND					
Net Sales................................	9.08	16.29	26.15	35.05	38.17
Pipeline uses[1]..........................	0.32	1.56	3.36	3.68	2.88
Exports[2]................................	3.11	11.45	22.08	29.09	26.80
Reprocessing............................	—	0.61	0.83	2.29	2.41
Stock change............................	0.19	0.34	0.77	1.65	1.38
Total	**12.70**	**30.25**	**53.19**	**71.76**	**71.64**

[1]Includes pipeline fuel consumed in Canada to move gas for export.

[2]Includes pipeline fuel consumed in USA to move gas to central Canada.

Source: *An Energy Strategy for Canada*, Energy, Mines and Resources, 1976.

23. Installed Generating Capacity by Type and Region, 1960, 1970, and 1975

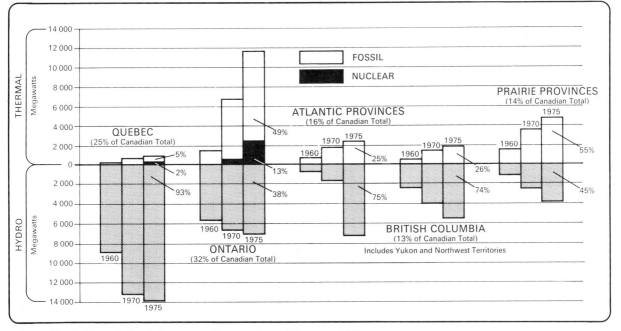

Source: *Electrical Power in Canada*, Department of Energy, Mines and Resources, 1975.

24. Electricity Supply and Demand, 1960, 1965, and 1970 to 1975

	1960	1965	1970	1971	1972	1973	1974	1975
					10^9 kW·h			
Canadian production.....	114	144	205	216	240	263	279	273
Imports...............	1	4	3	3	2	2	2	4
Domestic demand.......	109	144	202	213	232	248	266	266
Exports...............	6	4	6	7	11	17	15	11

Source: *An Energy Strategy for Canada*, Energy, Mines and Resources, 1976.

25. Coal Supply and Demand, 1960, 1965, and 1970 to 1975

	1960	1965	1970	1971	1972	1973	1974	1975
					10^6 t			
Canadian production.....	10.0	10.4	15.1	16.7	18.8	20.5	21.1	25.1
Imports[1]...............	11.5	15.1	18.0	16.7	17.6	15.7	13.0	16.4
Domestic demand.......	20.4	23.4	25.7	25.3	24.2	25.0	24.9	25.4
Exports[1]...............	0.9	1.2	4.3	7.3	8.8	10.6	10.8	12.2

[1]Includes coke.
Source: *An Energy Strategy for Canada*, Energy, Mines and Resources, 1976.

26. Lumber Production and Shipments and Value of All Shipments of the Sawmill and Planing Industry, 1968 and 1973

PROVINCE OR TERRITORY	PRODUCTION		QUANTITY SHIPPED		VALUE OF SHIPMENTS	
	1968	1973	1968	1973	1968	1973
	m³	m³	m³	m³	$000	$000
NEWFOUNDLAND.........	17 310	45 859	25 213	44 583	931	3 203
PRINCE EDWARD ISLAND...................	6 563	2 279	2 305	2 279	73	120
NOVA SCOTIA............	511 294	375 911	439 751	376 107	15 572	24 059
NEW BRUNSWICK........	627 963	658 859	663 549	689 052	24 886	48 117
QUÉBEC..................	3 801 653	5 497 449	3 631 322	5 590 304	135 075	323 735
ONTARIO................	1 985 433	2 445 160	1 736 936	2 361 517	76 824	163 533
MANITOBA...............	79 890	184 861	68 055	176 451	1 849	9 742
SASKATCHEWAN.........	199 185	394 238	251 602	455 443	8 767	23 599
ALBERTA.................	805 896	1 363 278	909 442	1 454 906	29 950	83 808
BRITISH COLUMBIA.......	17 317 436	23 823 777	18 171 589	23 522 533	707 896	1 546 889
YUKON & NORTHWEST TERRITORIES.............	17 296	7 266	18 646	7 266	584	351
CANADA	25 369 913	34 798 930	25 918 404	34 680 461	1 002 407	2 227 156

Sources: *Canada Year Book 1970–71*; *Canadian Forestry Statistics*, Statistics Canada, 1973.

27. Estimated World Newsprint Production and Exports by Leading Countries, 1966, 1969, and 1974

COUNTRY	1966		1969		1974	
	Production	Exports	Production	Exports	Production	Exports
	10³ t	10³ t	10³ t	10³ t	10³ t	10³ t
CANADA.................	8 419	7 764	8 758	8 033	8 661	7 892
UNITED STATES.........	2 408	99	3 232	117	2 924	v.s.
JAPAN.................	1 301	26	1 779	4	2 233	v.s.
USSR..................	972	197	1 358	273	1 334	v.s.
FINLAND...............	1 330	1 210	1 212	1 108	1 219	1 137
SWEDEN...............	760	474	964	659	1 210	944
BRITAIN...............	825	3	876	2	383	v.s.
WORLD.................	18 275		20 850		22 655	

v.s.   Very small.
Sources: *Statistical Yearbook*, United Nations, 1975; *Yearbook of International Trade Statistics*, United Nations, 1974.

28. Pulp Production, 1964, 1969, and 1973

	1964	1969	1973
	10³ t	10³ t	10³ t
QUÉBEC	4 720	5 938	5 590
BRITISH COLUMBIA......	2 564	4 425	5 336
ONTARIO	3 009	3 593	3 668
OTHER PROVINCES........	2 170	2 905	3 965
Total Production.........	12 464	16 861	18 559

Sources: *Canada Year Book 1972*; *Canadian Forestry Statistics*, Statistics Canada, 1973.

29. Pulp Production and Imports and Exports by Leading Countries, 1973

COUNTRY	PRODUCTION	EXPORTS	IMPORTS
	10^3 t	$US millions	$US millions
UNITED STATES.......	43 388	1 007	1 112
CANADA..............	18 559	1 919	44
JAPAN...............	10 086	12	266
SWEDEN.............	9 462	1 318	11
USSR...............	7 767	80	48
FINLAND.............	6 678	349	1

Sources: *Statistical Yearbook*, United Nations, 1975; *Yearbook of International Trade Statistics*, United Nations, 1974.

30. Quantity and Value of Sea and Inland Fish Landed, 1962, 1968, and 1972 and Persons Employed, 1968 and 1972

PROVINCE OR TERRITORY	QUANTITY			VALUE			PERSONS EMPLOYED	
	1962	1968	1972	1962	1968	1972	1968	1972
	t	t	t	$000	$000	$000		
NEWFOUNDLAND.................	249 127	435 972	295 135	17 222	28 007	35 723	19 355	14 452
PRINCE EDWARD ISLAND........	17 065	21 312	25 780	4 361	7 399	9 540	3 301	3 210
NOVA SCOTIA....................	197 682	360 719	286 856	30 928	52 250	66 375	13 108	11 735
NEW BRUNSWICK................	92 746	247 205	162 144	9 182	15 581	19 923	5 942	5 161
QUÉBEC........................	60 512	92 751	83 210	5 534	8 544	11 138	4 945	5 843
ONTARIO.......................	28 924	25 263	19 589	5 341	5 968	8 119	2 044	2 097
MANITOBA......................	16 374	11 670	11 101	4 229	3 276	4 523	4 018	1 827
SASKATCHEWAN.................	6 822	4 976	4 864	1 478	1 382	1 634	2 348	1 800
ALBERTA.......................	4 093	5 389	2 202	714	917	727	4 758	1 547
BRITISH COLUMBIA..............	311 517	121 193	153 060	49 067	57 274	75 128	12 133	9 902
YUKON & NORTHWEST TERRITORIES....................	2 968	1 948	1 625	859	781	866	401	201
Totals..........................	**987 813**	**1 328 403**	**1 045 566**	**128 915**	**181 379**	**233 696**	**72 353**	**57 775**

Sources: *Canada Year Book 1969, 1970–71, and 1975; Fishery Statistics of Canada*, 1971.

31. St. Lawrence Seaway: Type of Traffic, 1975[1]

DOMESTIC	UPBOUND		DOWNBOUND		FOREIGN		UPBOUND		DOWNBOUND	
	No. of Transits	Cargo tonnes	No. of Transits	Cargo tonnes			No. of Transits	Cargo tonnes	No. of Transits	Cargo tonnes
Canada to Canada......	1 275	5 851 957	1 531	15 327 411	Canada	Import	180	508 413	—	—
Canada to United States...............	1 301	12 050 055	33	239 130		Export	—	—	196	1 204 205
United States to Canada..............	51	98 173	1 022	15 234 567	United States	Import	655	3 381 100	—	—
United States to United States.........	97	140 933	100	245 773		Export	—	—	658	6 392 947

[1] Combines Montreal-Lake Ontario and Welland Canal Sections.

Source: *Traffic Report of the St. Lawrence Seaway*, St. Lawrence Seaway Authority, 1975.

32. Water-Borne Cargo Loaded and Unloaded for Six Largest Ports, 1973

PORT & COMMODITY	INTERNATIONAL		COASTWISE		TOTAL	PORT & COMMODITY	INTERNATIONAL		COASTWISE		TOTAL
	Loaded	Un-loaded	Loaded	Un-loaded			Loaded	Un-loaded	Loaded	Un-loaded	
	t	t	t	t	t		t	t	t	t	t
Vancouver (205-115)[2]	24 671 201	3 549 504	2 749 659	4 516 125	35 486 490	Thunder Bay (41-105)	3 658 080	238 276	13 584 692	765 157	18 246 205
Wheat	5 146 171	—	—	—	5 146 171	Wheat	69 886	—	7 897 143	—	7 967 029
Coal	9 084 196	—	—	—	9 084 196	Iron ore and concentrates	2 282 065	—	2 891 255	—	5 173 319
Sept Îles-Pointe Noire (12-92)	21 840 735	568 236	859 564	505 059	23 773 594	Port Cartier (10-21)	11 942 246	2 017 260	22 101	1 646 307	15 627 913
Iron ore and concentrates	21 816 884	—	840 635	—	22 657 519	Iron ore and concentrates	8 764 774	—	9 077	—	8 773 851
Montréal (211-155)	5 579 172	4 716 805	4 069 285	4 844 381	19 209 644	Wheat	1 984 063	900 862	10 563	1 252 613	4 148 101
Wheat	1 750 700	148 822	—	—	1 899 522	Québec (117-55)	4 865 635	5 718 461	1 013 272	2 844 690	14 442 058
Fuel oil	916 237	1 479 529	2 443 058	299 203	5 138 027	Fuel oil	1 298 197	522 930	747 963	655 405	3 224 495
Containerized freight	915 080	654 994	—	—	1 570 073	Crude petroleum	—	3 941 017	—	85 326	4 026 343

[1] Bold figures represent total tonnage and include commodities not listed.

[2] The two figures in parenthesis indicate approximately the total number of international (left-hand figure) and coastwise (right-hand figure) commodities handled by the port in 1971.

Source: *Shipping Report*, Parts II and III, Statistics Canada, 1973.

33. St. Lawrence Seaway Traffic by Classification and Direction— Montreal-Lake Ontario Section—1975

Principal Commodities	Upbound 10³ t	Upbound %	Downbound 10³ t	Downbound %	Principal sources and destinations of commodities
Wheat............................	—		11 260	47.6	Can → Can [66%] USA → Foreign [16%] USA → Can [14%]
Corn.............................	—	—	2 907	12.3	USA → Foreign [48%] USA → Canada [45%]
Oats.............................	—	—	427	1.8	Can → Can [47%] USA → Foreign [28%]
Barley...........................	—	—	2 231	9.4	Can → Can [89%]
Soybeans........................	—	—	1 157	4.9	USA → Foreign [62%] USA → Can [38%]
Total Agricultural Products.........	29	0.1	19 408	82.1	
Bituminous Coal....................	173	0.9	225	1.0	USA → Can [50%] Can → Can [43%]
Coke.............................	311	1.6	522	2.2	USA → Can [45%] USA → Foreign [13%] Foreign → USA [33%]
Iron Ore.........................	13 143	66.1	14	0.1	Can → USA [82%] Can → Can [18%]
Salt.............................	20	0.1	760	3.2	Can → Can [59%] USA → Can [38%]
Total Mine Products...............	14 499	72.9	2 029	8.6	

Continued

Table 33 continued

Principal Commodities	Upbound 10³ t	Upbound %	Downbound 10³ t	Downbound %	Principal sources and destinations of commodities
Fuel Oil........................	1 545	7.7	224	1.0	Can → Can [47%] Can → USA [35%]
Iron and Steel Products.............	2 171	10.9	188	0.6	Foreign → USA [80%] Foreign → Can [8%]
Total Manufactures and Miscellaneous...................	5 292	26.6	2 015	8.5	
Grand Total	19 896	100.0	23 650	100.0	

Source: *Traffic Report of the St. Lawrence Seaway*, St. Lawrence Seaway Authority, 1975.

34. St. Lawrence Seaway Traffic by Classification and Direction— Welland Canal Section—1975

Principal Commodities	Upbound 10³ t	Upbound %	Downbound 10³ t	Downbound %	Principal sources and destinations of commodities
Wheat...........................	—	—	11 870	31.9	Can → Can [69%] USA → Foreign [16%] USA → Can [14%]
Corn...........................	—	—	3 124	8.4	USA → Foreign [44%] USA → Can [46%] Can → Can [10%]
Oats...........................	—	—	450	1.2	Can → Can [49%] USA → Foreign [26%]
Barley...........................	—	—	2 345	6.3	Can → Can [88%] USA → Can [5%]
Soybeans........................	—	—	1 558	4.2	USA → Foreign [46%] USA → Can [52%]
Total Agricultural Products.....	11	—	20 767	55.9	
Bituminous Coal.................	—	—	7 699	20.7	USA → Can [94%]
Coke...........................	304	1.8	499	1.3	USA → Can [49%] Foreign → USA [35%]
Iron Ore........................	11 121	64.8	3 817	10.3	Can → USA [74%] Can → Can [9%] USA → Can [16%]
Stone, Ground or Crushed.........	972	5.7	106	0.3	Can → USA [91%]
Salt...........................	20	0.1	1 336	3.6	Can → Can [51%] USA → Can [45%]
Total Mine Products............	12 899	75.3	13 999	37.7	
Fuel Oil.........................	547	3.2	485	1.3	Can → Can [70%]
Iron and Steel, Manufactured.......	2 012	11.8	112	0.3	Foreign → USA [91%]
Scrap Iron and Steel..............	—	—	559	1.6	USA → Foreign [99%]
Package Freight—Domestic........	241	1.4	39	0.1	Can → Can [100%]
Total Manufactures and Miscellaneous	3 953	23.1	2 182	5.9	
Grand Total	17 134	100.0	37 149	100.0	

Source: *Traffic Report of the St. Lawrence Seaway*, St. Lawrence Seaway Authority, 1975.

35. Regional Shares of Selected National Manufacturing Statistics, Selected Years, 1926 to 1973

	1926 %	1933 %	1942 %	1951 %	1961 %	1971 %	1973 %
Total Employees							
ATLANTIC PROVINCES........	6.4	5.2	4.8	5.3	4.8	4.6	4.9
QUÉBEC.....................	31.3	33.6	34.6	33.2	33.5	31.2	30.0
ONTARIO....................	48.5	48.0	47.1	47.6	46.8	49.1	49.2
PRAIRIE PROVINCES..........	5.9	7.1	5.7	6.5	7.2	7.1	7.1
BRITISH COLUMBIA..........	8.0	6.1	7.8	7.4	7.7	7.9	8.7
CANADA[1]....................	100.0	100.0	100.0	100.0	100.0	100.0	100.0
	558 861	468 366	1 150 616	1 258 375	1 264 946	1 628 404	1 772 109
Salaries and Wages[2]							
ATLANTIC PROVINCES........	4.3	4.4	4.1	4.3	3.9	3.7	3.9
QUÉBEC.....................	29.2	30.9	31.9	30.7	31.1	28.5	27.4
ONTARIO....................	51.5	50.6	50.0	51.0	49.7	52.2	52.2
PRAIRIE PROVINCES..........	6.7	7.6	5.2	6.0	7.0	6.6	6.8
BRITISH COLUMBIA..........	8.3	6.5	8.8	8.0	8.4	9.1	9.7
CANADA[1]....................	100.0	100.0	100.0	100.0	100.0	100.0	100.0
	$625 416	$435 908	$1 681 150	$3 276 281	$5 231 447	$12 129 897	$15 217 314
Census Value Added[2]							
ATLANTIC PROVINCES........	4.3	4.3	3.6	4.3	3.7	3.3	3.8
QUÉBEC.....................	29.5	31.3	32.0	30.0	30.0	27.6	26.2
ONTARIO....................	51.9	50.6	50.5	51.4	50.8	54.1	53.3
PRAIRIE PROVINCES	7.0	7.4	5.6	5.7	7.3	6.7	6.9
BRITISH COLUMBIA..........	7.2	6.4	8.3	8.6	8.1	8.2	9.8
CANADA[1]....................	100.0	100.0	100.0	100.0	100.0	100.0	100.0
	$1 281 021	$918 923	$3 305 495	$6 940 947	$10 682 138	$23 187 881	$30 890 503

[1]Canada shown total.
[2]Total Salaries and Wages and total Census Value Added × $000.

Source: *Canadian Urban Trends, National Perspective*, Vol. I. Printed with the permission of the Ministry of State for Urban Affairs and Copp Clark Publishing.

36. Percentage of Domestic and Foreign Control of Principal Canadian Manufacturing Industries, 1970

INDUSTRY	NUMBER OF ESTABLISHMENTS %			PRODUCTION & RELATED WORKERS %			VALUE ADDED[1] %		
	U.S.A.	Other Foreign	Canada	U.S.A.	Other Foreign	Canada	U.S.A.	Other Foreign	Canada
Food and beverages.....................	6.4	2.4	91.2	21.8	10.7	67.5	28.1	11.8	60.1
Textiles...............................	8.7	3.9	87.4	28.9	9.0	62.1	40.3	10.0	49.7
Paper and related products...............	22.8	9.4	67.7	32.6	15.0	52.4	35.1	14.1	50.8
Primary metals.........................	19.2	8.4	72.5	35.4	7.3	57.3	40.1	6.6	53.3
Transportation equipment................	18.7	2.8	78.6	66.8	6.6	26.6	77.6	5.4	17.0
Printing and publishing..................	1.4	0.8	97.9	5.2	3.3	91.5	8.2	3.0	88.8
Metal fabricating.......................	9.3	2.1	88.7	26.5	5.1	68.4	33.5	5.3	61.2
Electrical products......................	36.5	6.3	57.2	51.7	9.4	38.9	55.0	10.8	34.2
Chemicals and chemical products..........	34.6	12.1	53.3	50.1	22.5	27.4	62.8	21.2	16.0
Total..................................	9.1	2.8	88.1	32.4	8.1	59.5	40.8	10.1	49.1

[1]Value added refers to the value of manufactured goods shipped less cost of materials and supplies used including fuel and electricity.

Source: *Domestic and Foreign Control of Manufacturing Establishments in Canada*, 1969 and 1970, Statistics Canada, March 1976.

37. Principal Manufacturing Industries: National and Provincial Areas Ranked by Value Added, 1973[1]

CANADA

Motor vehicles and parts.............	7.2[2]
Pulp and paper......................	6.3
Sawmills and planing mills...........	4.4
Iron and steel mills..................	4.0
Misc. machinery and equipment.......	2.8
Smelting and refining................	2.2
Commercial printing.................	2.1
Publishing and printing..............	2.1
Communications equipment..........	2.0
Petroleum refining..................	1.9
Total value added ($000)....	**28 825 008**

ATLANTIC PROVINCES

Pulp and paper......................	20.5[2]
Fish products.......................	11.9
Sawmills and planing mills...........	4.6
Dairy products......................	2.6
Breweries...........................	2.4
Fabricated structural metals..........	1.8
Industrial chemicals.................	1.5
Meat processing....................	1.2
Read-mix concrete..................	0.8
Machine shops......................	0.8
Total value added ($000)....	**1 110 712**

QUÉBEC

Pulp and paper......................	7.4[2]
Smelting and refining................	4.5
Sawmills and planing mills...........	2.8
Women's clothing...................	2.5
Misc. machinery and equipment.......	2.3
Petroleum refining..................	2.2
Men's clothing.....................	2.2
Commercial printing.................	2.2
Pharmaceuticals and medicines........	1.9
Dairy products......................	1.8
Total value added ($000)....	**7 672 770**

ONTARIO

Motor vehicles and parts.............	12.9[2]
Iron and steel mills..................	6.4
Misc. machinery and equipment.......	3.4
Pulp and paper......................	3.0
Communications equipment..........	2.6
Commercial printing.................	2.2
Rubber products....................	2.2
Publishing and printing..............	1.9
Metal stamping and pressing..........	1.9
Electrical industrial equipment........	1.8
Total value added ($000)....	**15 055 448**

PRAIRIE PROVINCES

Meat processing....................	7.6[2]
Publishing and printing..............	4.3
Pulp and paper......................	3.7
Sawmills and planing mills...........	3.4
Dairy products......................	3.1
Fabricated structural metals..........	2.5
Commercial printing.................	2.3
Agricultural implements..............	2.3
Breweries...........................	2.3
Bakeries...........................	1.9
Total value added ($000)....	**2 048 771**

BRITISH COLUMBIA

Sawmills and planing mills...........	28.1[2]
Pulp and paper......................	16.4
Veneer and plywood.................	5.1
Fish products.......................	3.2
Misc. machinery and equipment.......	2.7
Publishing and printing..............	2.2
Shipbuilding and repair..............	1.9
Fabricated structural metals..........	1.4
Dairy products......................	1.4
Commercial printing.................	1.2
Total value added ($000)....	**2 934 260**

[1]Value added refers to the value of manufactured goods shipped less cost of materials and supplies used including fuel and electricity.

[2]All figures refer to per cent of total value added by manufacturing for national or provincial areas.

Source: *Manufacturing Industries of Canada: National and Provincial Areas*, 1973, Statistics Canada, April 1976.

38. Major Import Commodities, 1976

		$000
1	Motor vehicle parts, except engines	4 302 964
2	Crude petroleum	3 272 033
3	Passenger automobiles and chassis	2 804 140
4	Trucks, truck tractors, chassis and other motor vehicles	1 177 694
5	Telecommunication and related equipment	1 089 795
6	Motor vehicle engines and parts	979 123
7	Electronic computers and other office machines	738 722
8	Outerwear	603 974
9	Coal	544 285
10	Miscellaneous equipment and tools	539 559
11	Plastic film, sheet and other materials	478 073
12	Wheel tractors, new	443 214
13	Organic chemicals	411 706
14	Photographic goods	391 255
15	Paper and paperboard	333 259
16	Meat, fresh, chilled or frozen	329 206
17	Tractor engines and tractor parts	264 453
18	Raw sugar	253 758
19	Coffee	249 546
	Total—All Imports	**37 390 942**

Source: *Summary of External Trade*, December 1976, Statistics Canada.

39. Major Export Commodities, 1976

		$000
1	Passenger automobiles and chassis	3 629 229
2	Crude petroleum	2 287 976
3	Motor vehicle parts, except engines	2 181 868
4	Wood pulp and similar pulp	2 172 057
5	Newsprint paper	1 993 026
6	Wheat	1 705 489
7	Natural gas	1 616 490
8	Lumber, softwood	1 605 418
9	Trucks, truck tractors and chassis	1 395 248
10	Iron ores and concentrates	916 544
11	Motor vehicle engines and parts	774 785
12	Coal and other crude bitumin substances	560 980
13	Petroleum and coal products	557 168
14	Fertilizers and fertilizer materials	547 224
15	Barley	542 362
16	Agricultural machinery and tractors	538 269
17	Nickel in ores, concentrates and scrap	523 577
18	Copper and alloys	515 864
19	Asbestos, unmanufactured	471 419
20	Aluminum, including alloys	464 551
21	Nickel and alloys	443 609
	Total—All Exports	**37 212 853**

Source: *Summary of External Trade*, December 1976, Statistics Canada.

40. Imports: Principal Nations, 1976

		$000
1	United States	25 661 677
2	Japan	1 523 727
3	Venezuela	1 295 110
4	United Kingdom	1 153 318
5	West Germany	817 855
6	Iran	695 426
7	Saudi Arabia	481 614
8	France	437 721
9	Italy	365 369
10	Australia	340 836
11	South Korea	303 251
12	Taiwan	292 061
	All Countries	**37 390 942**

Source: *Summary of External Trade*, December 1976, Statistics Canada.

41. Exports: Principal Nations, 1976

		$000
1	United States	25 122 901
2	Japan	2 386 190
3	United Kingdom	1 826 797
4	West Germany	694 778
5	Italy	547 917
6	USSR	535 224
7	Belgium & Luxembourg	472 154
8	Netherlands	442 327
9	France	393 464
10	Australia	359 067
11	Venezuela	355 317
12	Brazil	327 588
	All Countries	**37 212 853**

Source: *Summary of External Trade*, December 1976, Statistics Canada.

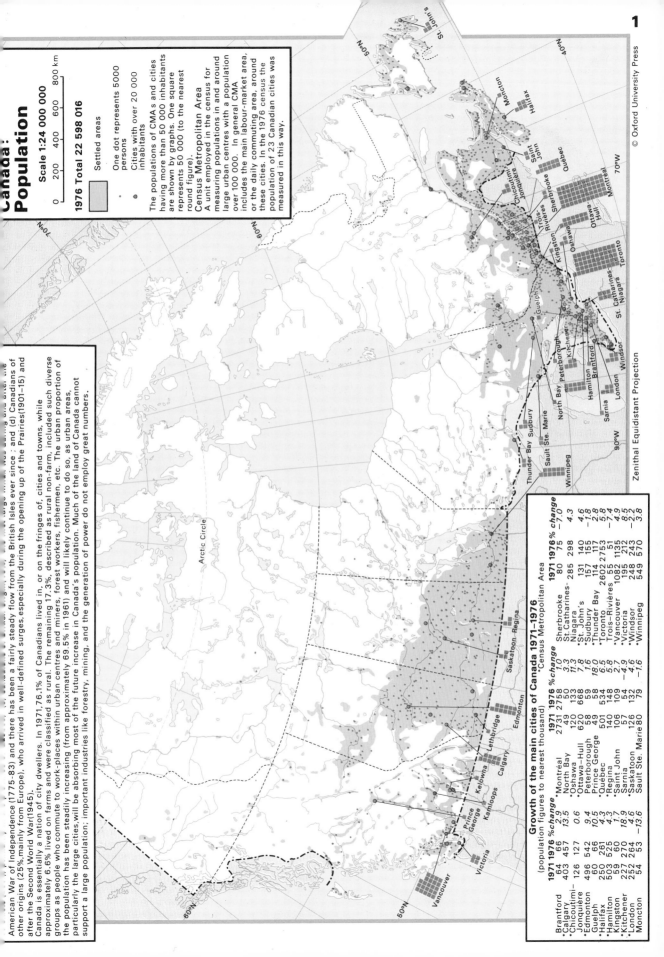

Canada: Population

Scale 1:24 000 000

0 200 400 600 800 km

1976 Total 22 598 016

Settled areas

One dot represents 5000 persons

Cities with over 20 000 inhabitants

The populations of CMAs and cities having more than 50 000 inhabitants are shown by graphs. One square represents 50 000 (to the nearest round figure).

Census Metropolitan Area

A unit employed in the census for measuring populations in and around large urban centres with a population over 100 000. In general CMA includes the main labour-market area, or the daily commuting area, around these cities. In the 1976 census the population of 23 Canadian cities was measured in this way.

© Oxford University Press

American War of Independence (1775-83) and there has been a fairly steady flow from the British Isles ever since ; and (d) Canadians of other origins (25%, mainly from Europe), who arrived in well-defined surges, especially during the opening up of the Prairies(1901–15) and after the Second World War(1945).

Canada is essentially a nation of city dwellers. In 1971, 76.1% of Canadians lived in, or on the fringes of, cities and towns, while approximately 6.6% lived on farms and were classified as rural. The remaining 17.3%, described as rural non-farm, included such diverse groups as people who commute to work-places within urban centres and miners, forest workers, fishermen, etc. The urban proportion of the population has been steadily increasing (from approximately 69.5% in 1961) and will likely continue to do so, as urban areas, particularly the large cities, will be absorbing most of the future increase in Canada's population. Much of the land of Canada cannot support a large population; important industries like forestry, mining, and the generation of power do not employ great numbers.

Zenithal Equidistant Projection

Growth of the main cities of Canada 1971-1976
(population figures to nearest thousand)

	1971	1976	%change		1971	1976	%change
Brantford	64	66	2.9	*Montréal	2731	2758	1.0
*Calgary	403	457	13.5	North Bay	49	50	3.3
*Chicoutimi–	126	127	0.6	*Oshawa	120	133	11.3
Jonquière				*Ottawa–Hull	620	668	7.8
*Edmonton	496	542	9.4	Peterborough	58	59	1.6
*Guelph	60	66	10.5	Prince George	49	58	18.0
*Halifax	261		4.3	*Québec	501	534	6.5
*Hamilton	503	525	4.3	*Regina	140	148	5.8
*Kingston	59	60	1.7	Saint John	106	109	2.7
*Kitchener	227	270	18.9	*Sarnia	57	54	-4.9
*London	252	264	4.6	*Saskatoon	126	132	4.6
Moncton	54	53	-13.6	Sault Ste. Marie	80	79	-1.6

*Census Metropolitan Area

	1971	1976	%change
Sherbrooke	80	75	-7.0
St. Catharines–	285	298	4.3
Niagara			
*St. John's	131	140	4.6
*Sudbury	157	155	-1.8
Thunder Bay	114	117	-2.8
*Toronto	2602	2753	5.8
*Trois-Rivières	55	51	-7.4
*Vancouver	1082	1135	-4.9
*Victoria	195	212	8.5
*Windsor	248	243	-2.2
*Winnipeg	549	570	3.8

Canada: Physiographic Regions

Scale 1:24 000 000

0 200 400 600 km

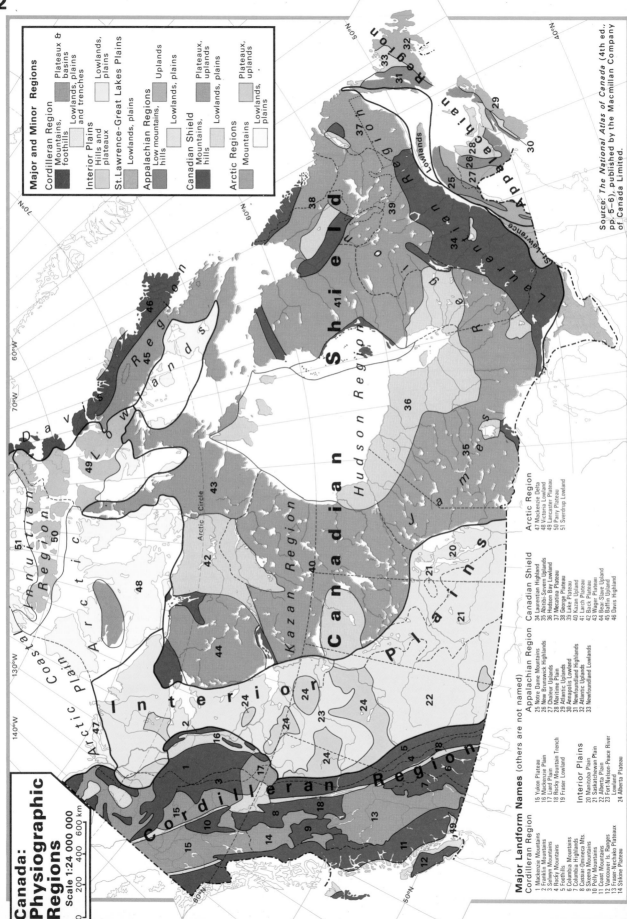

Major and Minor Regions

Cordilleran Region
- Mountains, foothills
- Plateaux & basins
- Lowlands, plains and trenches

Interior Plains
- Hills and plateaux
- Lowlands, plains

St. Lawrence–Great Lakes Plains
- Lowlands, plains

Appalachian Regions
- Low mountains, hills
- Uplands
- Lowlands, plains
- Plateaux, uplands

Canadian Shield
- Mountains, hills
- Lowlands, plains
- Plateaux, uplands

Arctic Regions
- Mountains
- Lowlands, plains

Source: *The National Atlas of Canada* (4th ed., pp. 5–6), published by the Macmillan Company of Canada Limited.

Major Landform Names (others are not named)

Cordilleran Region
1 Mackenzie Mountains
2 Franklin Mountains
3 Selwyn Mountains
4 Rocky Mountains
5 Foothills
6 Columbia Mountains
7 Columbia Highlands
8 Cassiar-Omineca Mts.
9 Skeena Mountains
10 Pelly Mountains
11 Coast Mountains
12 Vancouver Is. Ranges
13 Fraser-Nechako Plateaux
14 Stikine Plateau
15 Yukon Plateau
16 Mackenzie Plain
17 Liard Plain
18 Rocky Mountain Trench
19 Fraser Lowland

Interior Plains
20 Manitoba Plain
21 Saskatchewan Plain
22 Alberta Plain
23 Fort-Nelson-Peace River Lowland
24 Alberta Plateau

Appalachian Region
25 Notre Dame Mountains
26 New Brunswick Highlands
27 Chaleur Uplands
28 Maritime Plain
29 Atlantic Uplands
30 Annapolis Lowland
31 Newfoundland Highlands
32 Atlantic Uplands
33 Newfoundland Lowlands

Canadian Shield
34 Laurentian Highland
35 Abitibi-Severn Uplands
36 Hudson Bay Lowland
37 Mecatina Plateau
38 George Plateau
39 Lake Plateau
40 Kazan Upland
41 Larch Plateau
42 Back Plateau
43 Wager Plateau
44 Bear-Slave Upland
45 Baffin Upland
46 Davis Highland

Arctic Region
47 Mackenzie Delta
48 Victoria Lowland
49 Lancaster Plateau
50 Parry Plateau
51 Sverdrup Lowland

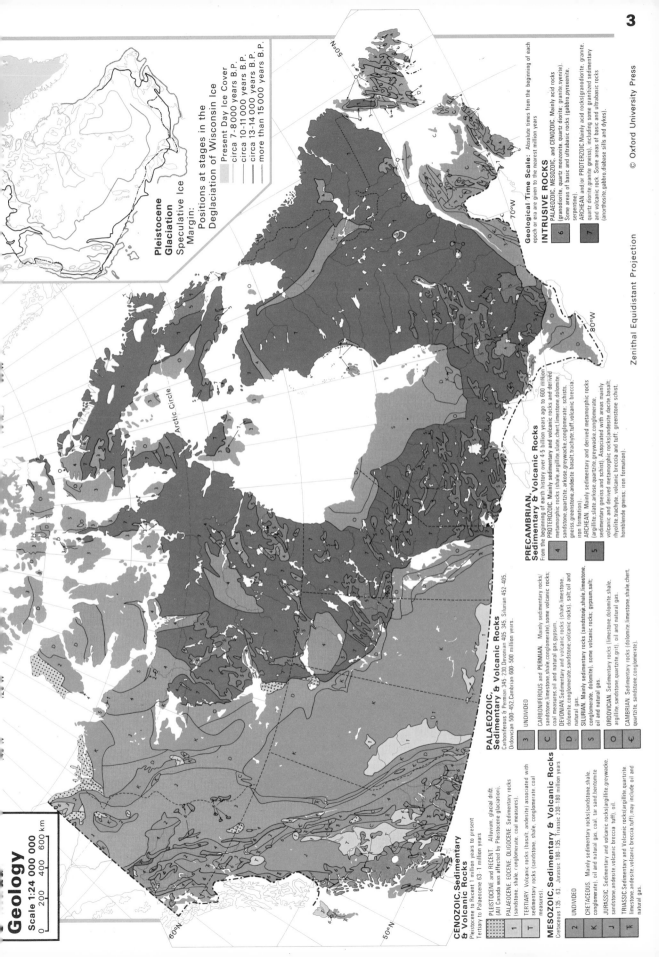

3

Geology

Scale 1:24 000 000

0 200 400 600 km

Pleistocene Glaciation

Speculative Ice Margin:

Positions at stages in the Deglaciation of Wisconsin Ice

Present Day Ice Cover
circa 7-8000 years B.P.
circa 10-11 000 years B.P.
circa 13-14 000 years B.P.
more than 15 000 years B.P.

Geological Time Scale: Absolute times from the beginning of each epoch or era are given to the nearest million years

CENOZOIC, Sedimentary & Volcanic Rocks

Pleistocene to Recent 1 million years to present
Tertiary to Palaeocene 63·1 million years

1 PLEISTOCENE and RECENT Alluvium, glacial drift, sedimentary rocks (sandstone, shale, conglomerate, coal measures). (All Canada was affected by Pleistocene glaciation).

T TERTIARY Volcanic rocks (basalt, andesite) associated with sedimentary rocks (sandstone, shale, conglomerate, coal measures).
PALAEOCENE, EOCENE, OLIGOCENE Sedimentary rocks (sandstone, shale, conglomerate, coal measures).

MESOZOIC, Sedimentary & Volcanic Rocks

Cretaceous 135·63. Jurassic 180·135. Triassic 230·180 million years

2 UNDIVIDED

K CRETACEOUS Mainly sedimentary rocks (sandstone, shale, conglomerate), oil and natural gas. Coal, tar sand, bentonite.

J JURASSIC Sedimentary and volcanic rocks (argillite, greywacke, sandstone, andesite volcanic breccia tuff), oil.

Ŧ TRIASSIC Sedimentary and Volcanic rocks (argillite, quartzite, limestone, andesite, volcanic breccia tuff), may include oil and natural gas.

PALAEOZOIC, Sedimentary & Volcanic Rocks

Carboniferous & Permian 345·230 Devonian 405·345. Silurian 452·405.
Ordovician 500·452.Cambrian 600·500 million years.

3 UNDIVIDED

C CARBONIFEROUS and PERMIAN. Mainly sedimentary rocks (sandstone, limestone, shale, conglomerate), some volcanic rocks; coal measures.oil and natural gas.gypsum.

D DEVONIAN Sedimentary and volcanic rocks (shale, limestone, dolomite,conglomerate,sandstone volcanic rocks), salt, oil and natural gas.

S SILURIAN. Mainly sedimentary rocks (sandstone,shale,limestone, conglomerate, dolomite), some volcanic rocks; gypsum,salt; oil and natural gas.

O ORDOVICIAN Sedimentary rocks (limestone,dolomite,shale, argillite,slate,arkose,quartzite,greywacke,conglomerate.

Ę CAMBRIAN Sedimentary rocks (dolomite,limestone,shale,chert, quartzite, sandstone,conglomerate).

PRECAMBRIAN, Sedimentary & Volcanic Rocks

From the beginning of earth history over 4·5 billion years ago to 600 million years

4 PROTEROZOIC Mainly sedimentary and volcanic rocks and derived metamorphic rocks (shale,argillite,slate,chert,limestone,dolomite, sandstone,quartzite, arkose,greywacke,conglomerate, schists, gneiss,greenstone,andesite basalt,trachyte,tuff,volcanic breccia; iron formation).

5 ARCHEAN. Mainly sedimentary and derived metamorphic rocks (argillite, slate arkose, quartzite,greywacke conglomerate. sedimentary gneiss and schist). Associated with areas mainly volcanic and derived metamorphic rocks(andesite,dacite,basalt, rhyolite,trachyte, volcanic breccia and tuff. greenstone schist. hornblende gneiss, iron formation).

INTRUSIVE ROCKS

6 PALAEOZOIC, MESOZOIC, and CENOZOIC. Mainly acid rocks (granodiorite, quartz diorite. quartz monzonite, quartz diorite. granite,syenite). Some areas of basic and ultrabasic rocks (gabbro,pyroxenite. serpentine).

7 ARCHEAN and/or PROTEROZOIC.Mainly acid rocks(granodiorite, granite. quartz diorite.granite gneiss). including some granitized sedimentary and volcanic rock. Some areas of basic and ultrabasic rocks (anorthosite,gabbro,diabase sills and dykes).

© Oxford University Press

Zenithal Equidistant Projection

4

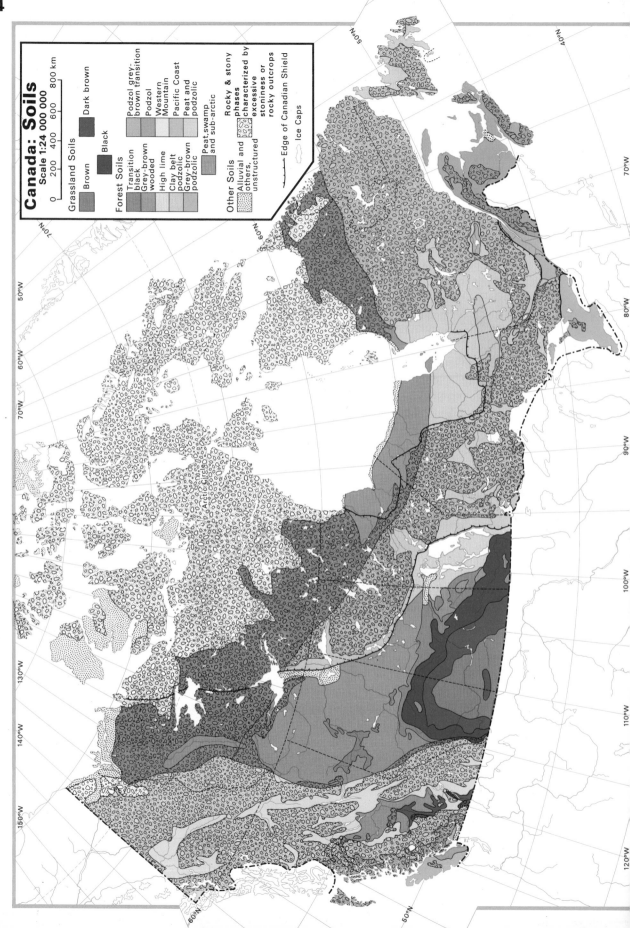

Canada: Soils
Scale 1:24 000 000

0 200 400 600 800 km

Grassland Soils
- Brown
- Dark brown
- Black

Forest Soils
- Transition black
- Grey-brown wooded
- High lime
- Clay belt podzolic
- Grey-brown podzolic
- Podzol grey-brown transition
- Podzol
- Western Mountain
- Pacific Coast
- Peat and podzolic

Other Soils
- Peat, swamp and sub-arctic
- Alluvial and others, unstructured
- Rocky & stony phases characterized by excessive stoniness or rocky outcrops

— Edge of Canadian Shield

Ice Caps

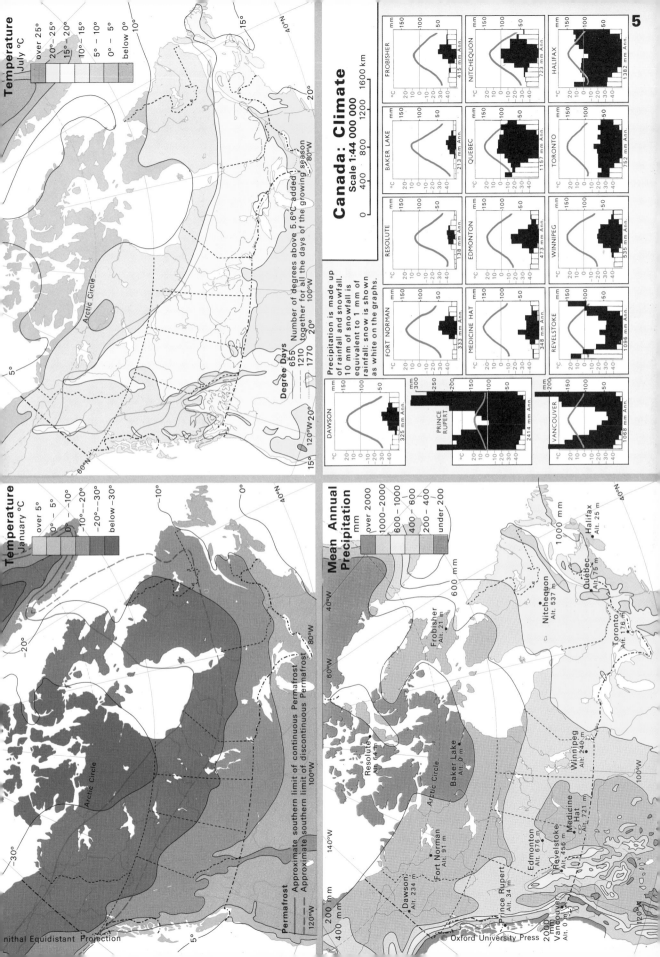

Canada: Climate
Scale 1:44 000 000

0 400 800 1200 1600 km

Temperature
July °C
- over 25°
- 20°–25°
- 15°–20°
- 10°–15°
- 5°–10°
- 0°–5°
- below 0°

Temperature
January °C
- over 5°
- 0°–5°
- 0°–-10°
- -10°–-20°
- -20°–-30°
- below -30°

Mean Annual Precipitation
mm
- over 2000
- 1000–2000
- 600–1000
- 400–600
- 200–400
- under 200

Degree Days
655   Number of degrees above 5.6°C added
1210 together for all the days of the growing season
1770
—— 100°W

Precipitation is made up of rainfall and snowfall. 10 mm of snowfall is equivalent to 1 mm of rainfall; snow is shown as white on the graphs.

Permafrost
—— Approximate southern limit of continuous Permafrost
—— Approximate southern limit of discontinuous Permafrost

Azimuthal Equidistant Projection

© Oxford University Press

5

Climate station graphs: FROBISHER 415 mm Ann., NITCHEQUON 723 mm Ann., HALIFAX 1382 mm Ann., BAKER LAKE 213 mm Ann., QUÉBEC 1157 mm Ann., TORONTO 752 mm Ann., RESOLUTE 138 mm Ann., EDMONTON 473 mm Ann., WINNIPEG 535 mm Ann., FORT NORMAN 333 mm Ann., MEDICINE HAT 348 mm Ann., REVELSTOKE 1096 mm Ann., DAWSON 325 mm Ann., PRINCE RUPERT 2414 mm Ann., VANCOUVER 1068 mm Ann.

Location labels: Resolute Alt. 64 m, Baker Lake Alt. 0 m, Frobisher Alt. 21 m, Nitchequon Alt. 537 m, Halifax Alt. 25 m, Québec Alt. 75 m, Toronto Alt. 175 m, Winnipeg Alt. 240 m, Dawson Alt. 234 m, Fort Norman Alt. 91 m, Prince Rupert Alt. 34 m, Edmonton Alt. 676 m, Revelstoke Alt. 456 m, Medicine Hat Alt. 721 m, Vancouver Alt. 0 m

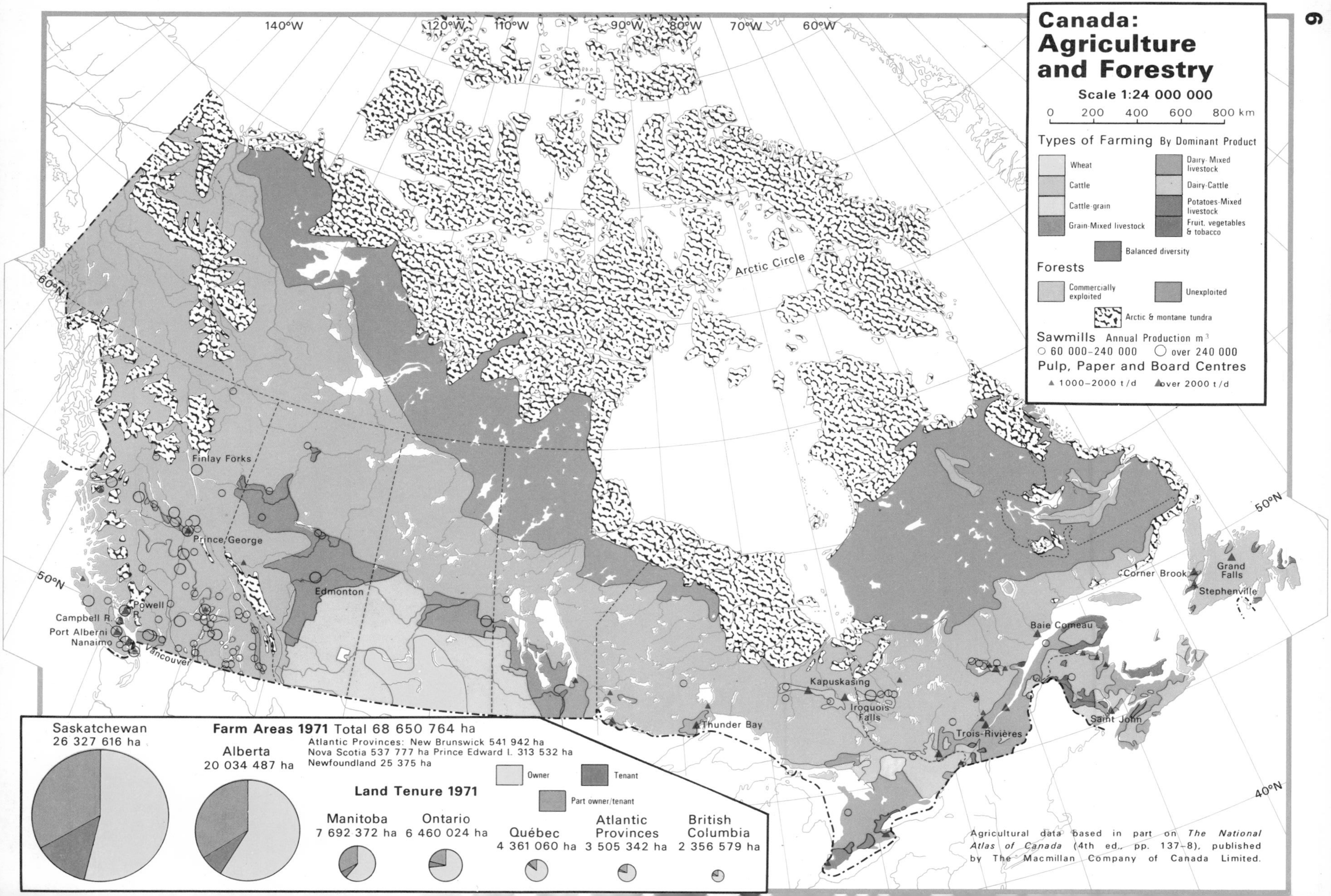

Canada: Agriculture and Forestry
Scale 1:24 000 000
0 200 400 600 800 km
Types of Farming By Dominant Product
Wheat
Cattle
Cattle-grain
Grain-Mixed livestock
Dairy-Mixed livestock
Dairy-Cattle
Potatoes-Mixed livestock
Fruit, vegetables & tobacco
Balanced diversity
Forests
Commercially exploited
Unexploited
Arctic & montane tundra
Sawmills Annual Production m3
60 000–240 000
over 240 000
Pulp, Paper and Board Centres
1000–2000 t/d
over 2000 t/d
140°W
120°W
110°W
90°W
80°W
70°W
60°W
60°N
50°N
40°N
Arctic Circle
Finlay Forks
Prince George
Powell R.
Campbell R.
Port Alberni
Nanaimo
Vancouver
Edmonton
Thunder Bay
Kapuskasing
Iroquois Falls
Trois-Rivières
Baie Comeau
Saint John
Corner Brook
Grand Falls
Stephenville
Farm Areas 1971 Total 68 650 764 ha
Atlantic Provinces: New Brunswick 541 942 ha
Nova Scotia 537 777 ha Prince Edward I. 313 532 ha
Newfoundland 25 375 ha
Land Tenure 1971
Owner
Part owner/tenant
Tenant
Saskatchewan 26 327 616 ha
Alberta 20 034 487 ha
Manitoba 7 692 372 ha
Ontario 6 460 024 ha
Québec 4 361 060 ha
Atlantic Provinces 3 505 342 ha
British Columbia 2 356 579 ha
Agricultural data based in part on The National Atlas of Canada (4th ed., pp. 137–8), published by The Macmillan Company of Canada Limited.

Canada: Water Resources and Electrical Power

Scale 1:24 000 000

0 200 400 600 800 km

River Flow

Average discharge in cubic metres per second (m³/s)

Gauging – average annual flow (10⁶ m³)
△ Gauging station

Electrical Power 1977

Installed capacity (MW)

○ Over 2000
○ 1000–2000
○ 500–999
○ 75–499
○ –75

Proposed

Colour denotes principal fuel used

Hydro Coal Gas Oil Nuclear

1000 MW provides electrical generation to meet the needs of about 500 000 people

Transmission Lines Over 400 kW

Multiple Single Proposed

©Oxford University Press

ARCTIC
Water Flow to the Sea
15 491 m³/s

HUDSON BAY
Water Flow to the Sea
29 453 m³/s

ATLANTIC
Water Flow to the Sea
33 700 m³/s

PACIFIC
Water Flow to the Sea
21 225 m³/s

La Grande
Total capacity 10 190 MW
Completion 1980-1985

Arctic Circle

Churchill Falls 50 539

Manic 2 Manic 3 Manic 5

Manicouagan

Peribonca

St. Maurice

Beauharnois 653 234

Lennox

Saint John

Ottawa

Sir Adam Beck

Lakeview R.L. Hearn Pickering Nanticoke

Bruce

Lambton

Grande Baleine

Eastmain

Rupert

Nottaway

Abitibi

Moose

Mattagami

Albany

Attawapiskat

Winisk

Severn

Nelson Kettle

Reindeer Lake

Cedar Lake

Churchill 68 141

L. Winnipeg

L. Winnipegosis

L. Manitoba

Qu'Appelle

Saskatchewan

North Saskatchewan

South Saskatchewan

Bow

Kootenay

Columbia

Mica

Sundance

Gordon M.Shrum

L. Williston

Peace 66 850

Athabasca

Lake Athabasca

Slave

Great Slave Lake

Great Bear Lake

Mackenzie

Liard

Pelly

Stewart

Yukon

Skeena

Fraser

Thompson

Coppermine

Dubawnt

Thelon

Kazan

Back

George

Kaniapiskau

Feuilles

Churchill

Nelson

Discharge at Selected Stations

Totals in million cubic metres (10⁶ m³)
Graphs show average monthly run-off as a percentage of the total

Churchill

St.Lawrence

Nelson

Columbia

Fraser

Peace

Mackenzie

Zenithal Equidistant Projection

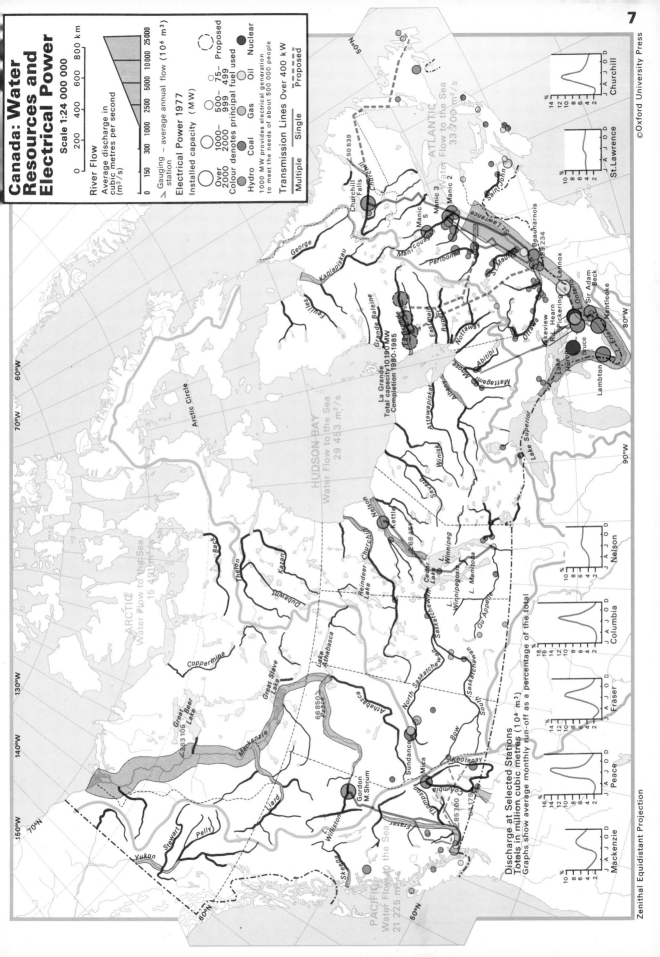

8

Vegetation and Ice

Rocky desert	Boreal forest	Ice-fields
Alpine tundra	West Coast forest	Mean extent of sea ice
Stony sedge	S.E.Mixed forest	Fast ice –winter
Dwarf scrub	S.Broadleaf forest	First year ice
Bog organic	Parkland	Ice clusters
Sub-Arctic forest	Grassland	Old ice

Fuels 1974

Coal Fields

Coking coal   Sub-bituminous coal   Lignite

Coal Mining Centres

● Major   ● Minor

Oil and Natural Gas

▲ Productive fields

Oil and natural gas are found in areas of sedimentary rocks *see* page 3

——— Major pipeline – – – Proposed pipeline

Fishing Resources

Fishing grounds   – – – Coastal lobster fisheries

Cod spawning grounds   Region of salmon spawning rivers

Aquatic mammals frequenting Arctic and coastal waters.
Whales, principal species : beluga (white), pilot, finback, narwhal, minke. Sea lions. Seals, principal species : fur, harbour, hair, ringed, bearded, saddleback, hooded. Walrus. Dolphin.

National and Provincial Parks, Wildlife Reserves

Major areas only

Principal Mammals
Icefields polar bear.
Tundra red and arctic fox, caribou, polar bear, grizzly bear, musk ox.
West Coast Forest Mountain goat, mountain sheep, moose, mule deer, black and grizzly bear, cougar.
Sub-Arctic and Boreal Forest Caribou, moose.
Ubiquitous beaver, muskrat, mink, red-fox, black bear, white-tailed deer, rabbit, porcupine, wolf, raccoon, ermine, marten, wolverine, skunk, otter, lynx. Some species are seldom seen in populated areas and most are not found in the tundra and areas north.

Trapping 1974-75 Season
Approximately 40 000 trappers, operating mainly in the Territories and the northern part of the provinces, produced $25 million worth of wildlife pelts. The leading pelts,in order, were: beaver, muskrat,lynx, hair seal,mink and fox.

Fur Farming 1974-75 Season
Fur farms are found in all parts of Canada and produced pelts valued at $17 million. Mink accounted for 99% of fur farm production.

Conical Orthomorphic Projection

9

Canada: Natural Resources and Native Peoples

Scale 1:19 000 000

0   150   300   450   600   750 km

Native Peoples

Estimated Population 1971 Eskimo 12 000   Indian 20 000

⌂ Settlement   ○ Major settlement
△ Major reserve

Minerals Resources 1974

Mining centres ◆ Major   ◆ Minor

1 Petroleum 2 Natural Gas 3 Aluminum 4 Nickel 5 Copper 6 Iron 7 Zinc 8 Coal 9 Potash 10 Gold
11 Asbestos 12 Silver 13 Lead 14 Molybdenum 15 Platinum 16 Cobalt 17 Uranium 18 Tungsten 19 Mercury
The minerals are listed in order of value.

Most minerals are extracted from composite ores which is why most centres
have several numbers.

Production   12 Exceptionally large   9 Major   5 Minor
Italic numbers mean that the mineral is obtained as a by-product.

See pp. 10–11 Canada: Manufacturing for smelters, refineries and iron
pelletizing plants.

BYLOT IS.
BIRD SANCTUARY

AUYUITTUQ
NATIONAL PARK

Arctic Circle

DEWEY SOPER
BIRD SANCTUARY

Putuniq

Schefferville
Carol Lake
Wabush
Gagnon

Baie Verte
Buchans

Thompson
Wabowden

Murdochville
Ste.Anne des Monts
Bathurst
Newcastle
Glace Bay
CAPE BRETON
HIGHLANDS N.P.

CHICOUTIMI
PROVINCIAL
PARK
LAURENTIDES
PROVINCIAL
PARK

Chibougamau
Chapais
Minto

Red Lake
Uchi Lake
Sturgeon Lake
Manitouwadge
Virginiatown
Kirkland Lake
South Porcupine
Joutel
Noranda
Matagami

Timmins
Pamour
Temagami
Schumacher
Cobalt
Val d'Or
Malartic
MONT
TREMBLANT
P.P.

East Broughton
Thetford Mines
Black Lake
Asbestos

Atikokan
Shabandowan
Wawa
Elliot Lake
Sudbury
Falconbridge
ALGONQUIN
P.P.
Shawville

© Oxford University Press

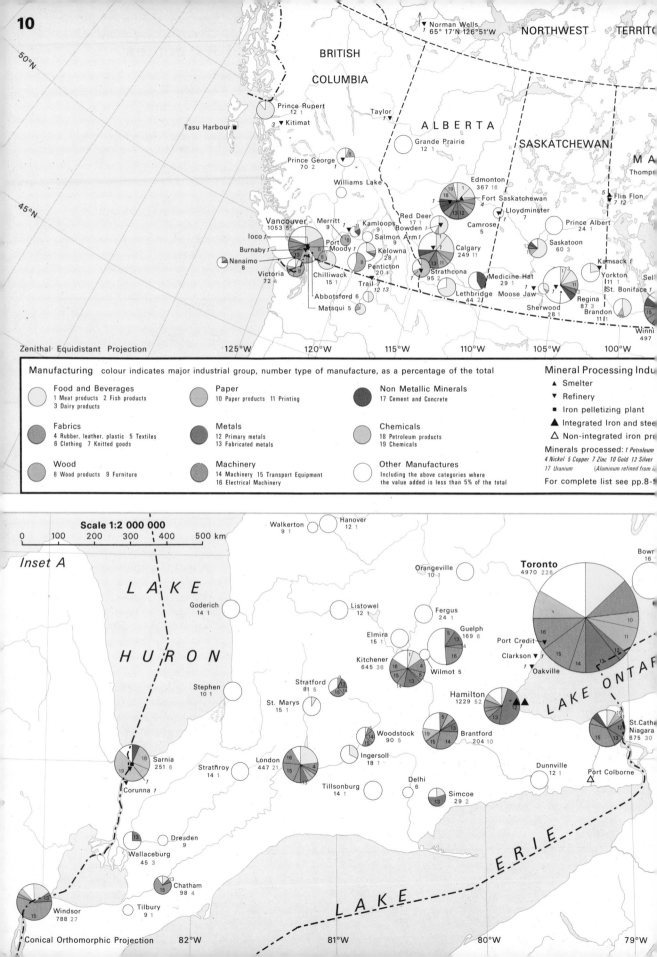

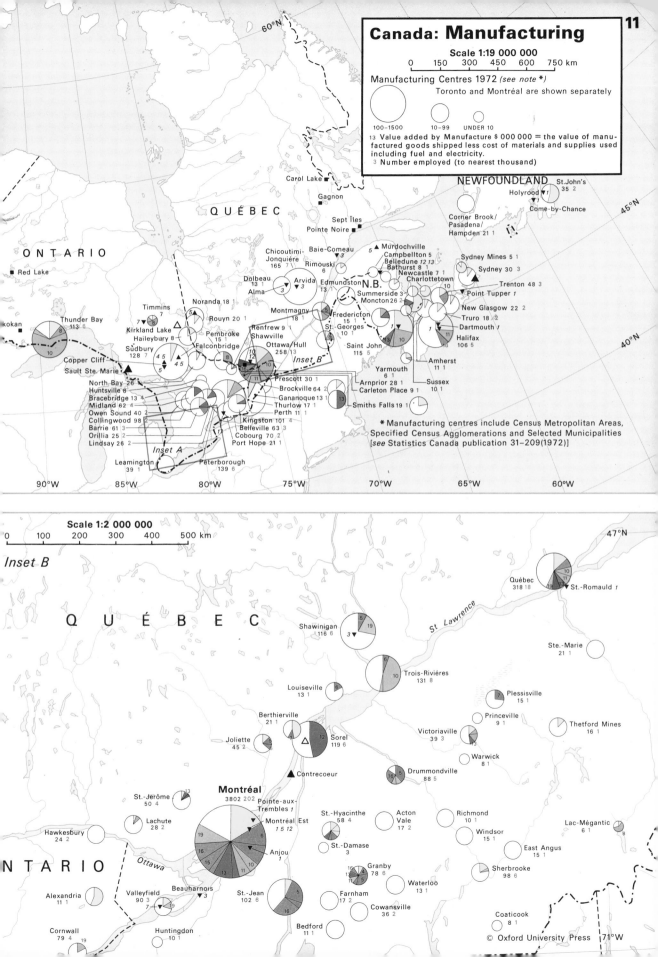

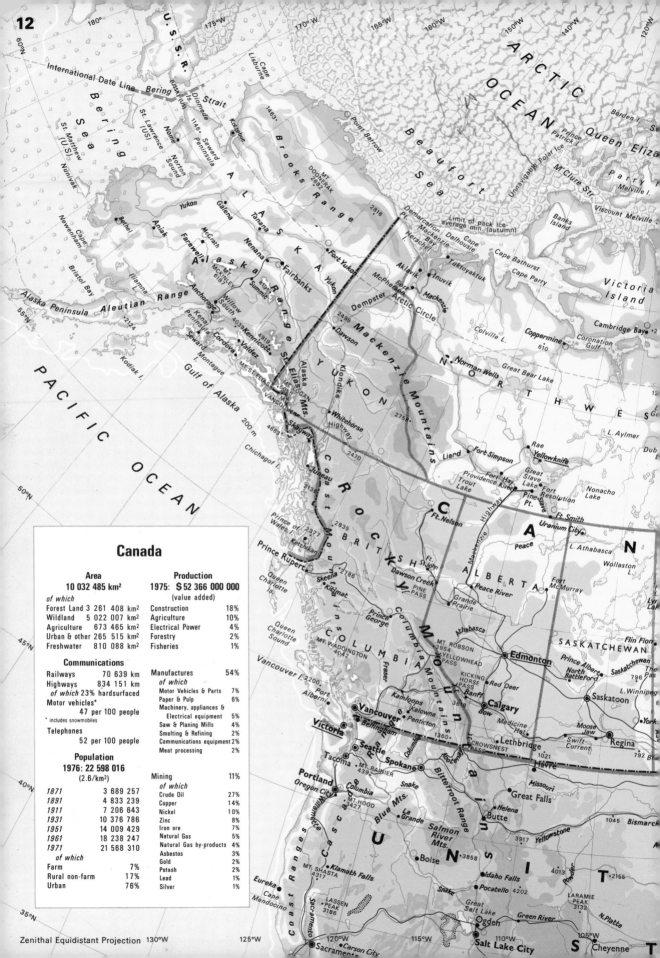

Canada

Area
10 032 485 km²
of which

Forest Land	3 261 408 km²
Wildland	5 022 007 km²
Agriculture	673 465 km²
Urban & other	265 515 km²
Freshwater	810 088 km²

Communications

Railways	70 639 km
Highways	834 151 km

of which 23% hardsurfaced
Motor vehicles*
47 per 100 people
* includes snowmobiles
Telephones
52 per 100 people

Population
1976: 22 598 016
(2.6/km²)

1871	3 689 257
1891	4 833 239
1911	7 206 643
1931	10 376 786
1951	14 009 429
1961	18 238 247
1971	21 568 310

of which

Farm	7%
Rural non-farm	17%
Urban	76%

Production
1975: $52 366 000 000
(value added)

Construction	18%
Agriculture	10%
Electrical Power	4%
Forestry	2%
Fisheries	1%
Manufactures	54%

of which

Motor Vehicles & Parts	7%
Paper & Pulp	6%
Machinery, appliances & Electrical equipment	5%
Saw & Planing Mills	4%
Smelting & Refining	2%
Communications equipment	2%
Meat processing	2%
Mining	11%

of which

Crude Oil	27%
Copper	14%
Nickel	10%
Zinc	8%
Iron ore	7%
Natural Gas	5%
Natural Gas by-products	4%
Asbestos	3%
Gold	2%
Potash	2%
Lead	1%
Silver	1%

Zenithal Equidistant Projection

14

Québec

Production
1973: $11 639 000 000
(Value added)

Construction	18%
Electrical Power	6%
Agriculture	5%
Forestry	2%
Manufactures	65%
of which	
Textiles & Knitting	8%
Paper & Pulp	7%
Clothing	5%
Publishing & Printing	5%
Smelting & Refining	4%
Saw & Planing Mills	3%
Pharmaceuticals	2%
Dairy products	2%
Mining	4%
of which	
Copper	22%
Asbestos	19%
Iron Ore	14%
Zinc	8%
Gold	5%

Population
1976: 6 141 491
(3.98 / km²)

1871	1 191 516
1891	1 488 535
1911	2 005 776
1931	2 874 662
1951	4 055 681
1961	5 259 211
1971	6 027 765
of which	
Farm	5%
Rural non-farm	14%
Urban	81%

1976 * Census Metropolitan Area

*Montréal	2 758 780
*Ottawa-Hull	668 853
*Québec	534 193
*Chicoutimi-Jonquière	127 181
Sherbrooke	75 137
Trois-Rivières	51 772
St.-Hyacinthe	36 832

Area
1 540 733 km²
(15.3% of Canada)

Forestland	696 075 km²
Wildland	566 641 km²
Agriculture	36 864 km²
Urban & other	8 236 km²
Freshwater	232 917 km²

Communications

Railways	8 705 km
Highways	106 400 km

of which 40% hardsurfaced

Motor Vehicles *
45 per 100 people
* includes snowmobiles

Telephones 50 per 100 people

Newfoundland

Production
1973: $763 000 000
(Value added)

Construction	31%
Electrical Power	12%
Fisheries	6%
Forestry	5%
Manufacture	22%
of which	
Paper & Pulp	30%
Fish products	27%
Publishing & Printing	3%
Concrete manufacture	2%
Mining	24%
of which	
Iron ore	84%
Asbestos	5%
Copper	3%

Population
1976: 548 789
(1.35 / km²)

1871	152 500
1891	202 040
1911	242 619
1931	281 500
1951	361 416
1961	457 853
1971	522 105
of which	
Farm	1%
Rural Non-farm	42%
Urban	57%

1976 *Census Metropolitan Area

*St. John's	140 883
Corner Brook	24 789
Labrador City	11 877
Happy Valley-Goose Bay	8 114

Area
403 661 km²
(4.0% of Canada)

Labrador	292 219 km²
Island	111 442 km²
Forest Land	127 492 km²
Wildland	235 672 km²
Agriculture*	65 km²
Urban & other*	828 km²
Freshwater	39 696 km²

*Island only

Communications

Railways	409 km
Highways	11 177 km

of which 32% hardsurfaced

Motor Vehicles 28 per 100 people
Telephones 32 per 100 people

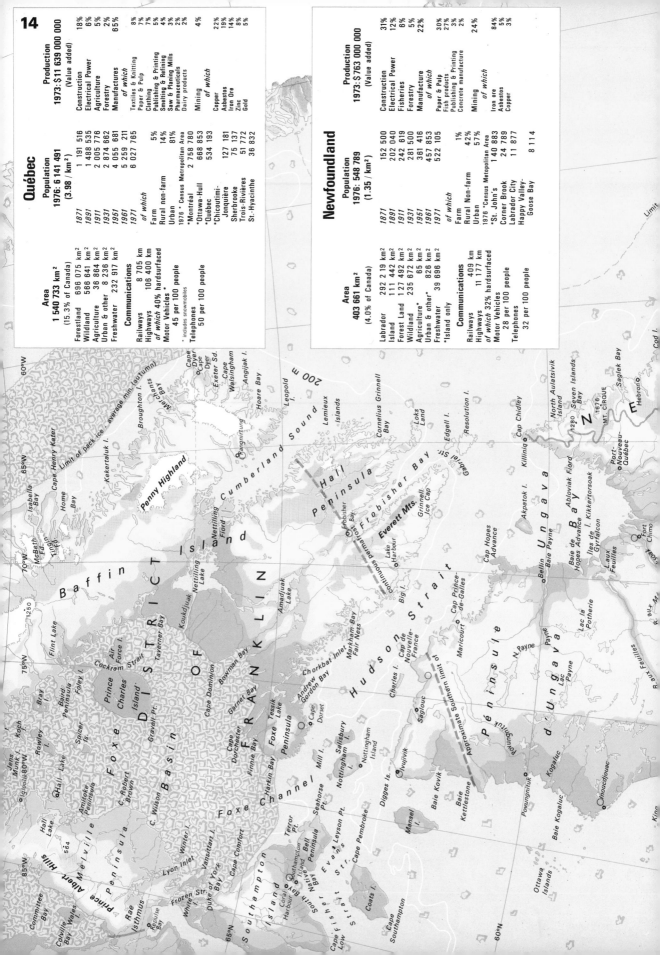

© Oxford University Press

Québec and Newfoundland

Scale 1:8 000 000

Conical Orthomorphic Projection

For legend and layer boxes see pages 16–17

0   100   200 km
0   100   200 m

200 m

QUÉBEC

NEWFOUNDLAND

LABRADOR

NOVA SCOTIA

NEW BRUNSWICK

PRINCE EDWARD ISLAND

MAINE

NEW HAMPSHIRE

VERMONT

NEW YORK

Gulf of St. Lawrence

St. Lawrence

James Bay

L. Ontario

St. John's

Halifax

Sydney

Charlottetown

Fredericton

Saint John

Bangor

Montréal

Ottawa

Québec

Trois-Rivières

Chicoutimi

Sherbrooke

Rochester

Buffalo

Kingston

Watertown

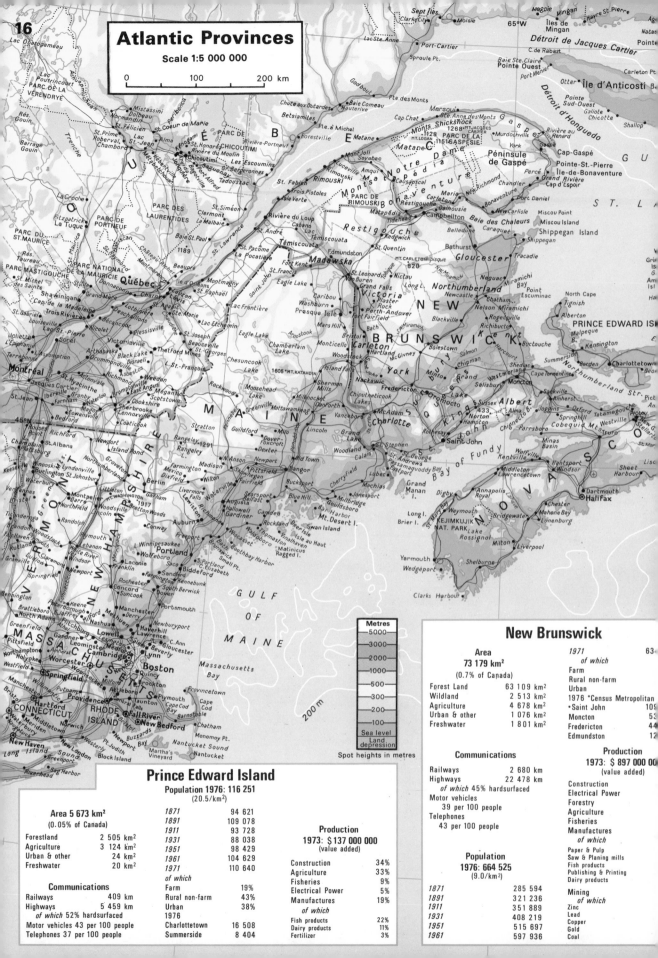

Atlantic Provinces

Scale 1:5 000 000

0   100   200 km

New Brunswick

Area
73 179 km²
(0.7% of Canada)

Forest Land	63 109 km²
Wildland	2 513 km²
Agriculture	4 678 km²
Urban & other	1 076 km²
Freshwater	1 801 km²

Communications

Railways	2 680 km
Highways	22 478 km

of which 45% hardsurfaced

Motor vehicles
39 per 100 people
Telephones
43 per 100 people

Population
1976: 664 525
(9.0/km²)

1871	285 594
1891	321 236
1911	351 889
1931	408 219
1951	515 697
1961	597 936

1971	63‑
of which	
Farm	
Rural non‑farm	
Urban	
1976 *Census Metropolitan	
•Saint John	109
Moncton	53
Fredericton	44
Edmundston	12

Production
1973: $ 897 000 00
(value added)

Construction
Electrical Power
Forestry
Agriculture
Fisheries
Manufactures
of which

Paper & Pulp
Saw & Planing mills
Fish products
Publishing & Printing
Dairy products

Mining
of which
Zinc
Lead
Copper
Gold
Coal

Prince Edward Island

Population 1976: 116 251
(20.5/km²)

Area 5 673 km²
(0.05% of Canada)

Forestland	2 505 km²
Agriculture	3 124 km²
Urban & other	24 km²
Freshwater	20 km²

Communications

Railways	409 km
Highways	5 459 km

of which 52% hardsurfaced
Motor vehicles 43 per 100 people
Telephones 37 per 100 people

1871	94 621
1891	109 078
1911	93 728
1931	88 038
1951	98 429
1961	104 629
1971	110 640

of which
Farm	19%
Rural non‑farm	43%
Urban	38%
1976	
Charlottetown	16 508
Summerside	8 404

Production
1973: $137 000 000
(value added)

Construction	34%
Agriculture	33%
Fisheries	9%
Electrical Power	5%
Manufactures	19%

of which
Fish products	22%
Dairy products	11%
Fertilizer	3%

Metres

5000
3000
2000
1000
500
300
200
100
Sea level
Land depression

Spot heights in metres

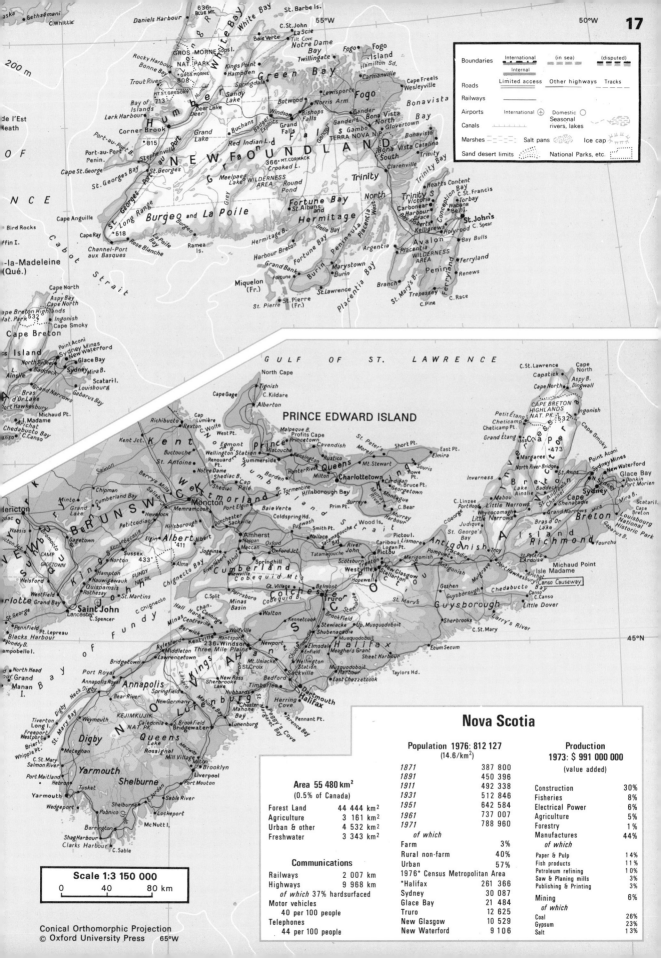

17

Nova Scotia

Population 1976: 812 127
(14.6/km²)

Year	Population
1871	387 800
1891	450 396
1911	492 338
1931	512 846
1951	642 584
1961	737 007
1971	788 960

of which

Farm	3%
Rural non-farm	40%
Urban	57%

1976* Census Metropolitan Area

*Halifax	261 366
Sydney	30 087
Glace Bay	21 484
Truro	12 625
New Glasgow	10 529
New Waterford	9 106

Area 55 480 km²
(0.5% of Canada)

Forest Land	44 444 km²
Agriculture	3 161 km²
Urban & other	4 532 km²
Freshwater	3 343 km²

Communications

Railways	2 007 km
Highways	9 968 km

of which 37% hardsurfaced

Motor vehicles 40 per 100 people
Telephones 44 per 100 people

Production
1973: $ 991 000 000
(value added)

Construction	30%
Fisheries	8%
Electrical Power	6%
Agriculture	5%
Forestry	1%
Manufactures	44%

of which

Paper & Pulp	14%
Fish products	11%
Petroleum refining	10%
Saw & Planing mills	3%
Publishing & Printing	3%
Mining	6%

of which

Coal	26%
Gypsum	23%
Salt	13%

Scale 1:3 150 000
0 40 80 km

Conical Orthomorphic Projection
© Oxford University Press

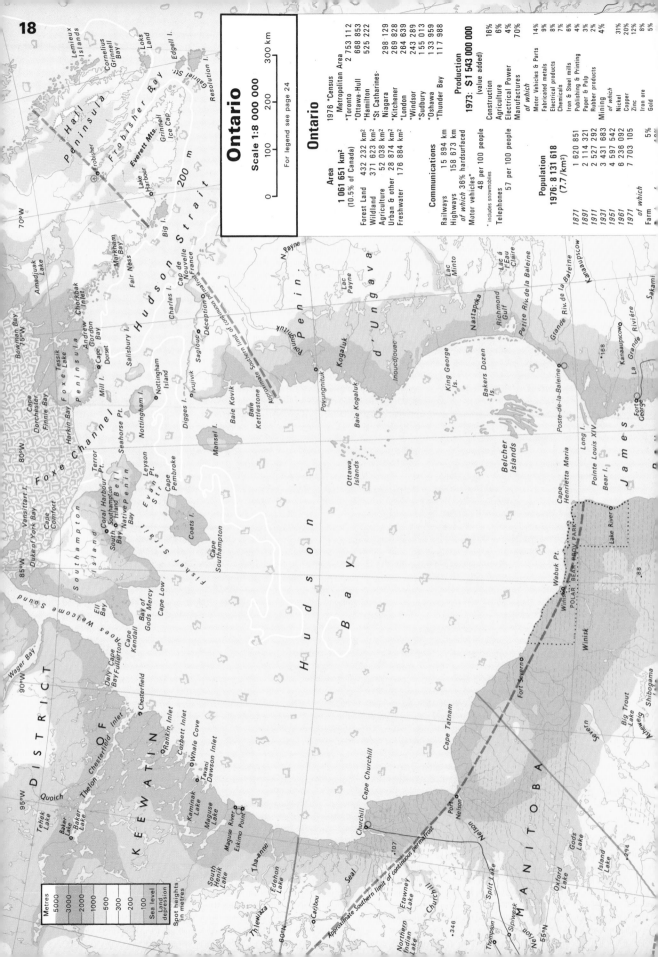

Ontario

Scale 1:8 000 000

| 0 | 100 | 200 | 300 km |

For legend see page 24

Ontario

Area
1 061 651 km²
(10.5% of Canada)

Forest Land	432 232 km²
Wildland	371 623 km²
Agriculture	52 038 km²
Urban & other	28 874 km²
Freshwater	176 884 km²

Communications

Railways	15 894 km
Highways	158 873 km
of which 36% hardsurfaced	
Motor vehicles*	48 per 100 people
* includes snowmobiles	
Telephones	57 per 100 people

Population
1976: 8 131 618
(7.7/km²)

1871	1 620 851
1891	2 114 321
1911	2 527 292
1931	3 431 683
1951	4 597 542
1961	6 236 092
1971	7 703 105
of which	
Farm	5%

1976 *Census
Metropolitan Area

*Toronto	2 753 112
*Ottawa-Hull	668 853
*Hamilton	525 222
*St. Catharines-Niagara	298 129
*Kitchener	269 828
*London	264 639
*Windsor	243 289
*Sudbury	155 013
*Oshawa	133 959
*Thunder Bay	117 988

Production
1973: $1 543 000 000
(value added)

Construction	16%
Agriculture	6%
Electrical Power	4%
Manufactures	70%
of which	
Motor Vehicles & Parts	14%
Fabricated metals	9%
Electrical products	8%
Chemicals	7%
Iron & Steel mills	6%
Publishing & Printing	4%
Paper & Pulp	3%
Rubber products	2%
Mining	4%
of which	
Nickel	31%
Copper	20%
Zinc	12%
Iron ore	5%
Gold	5%

Metres
5000
3000
2000
1000
500
300
200
100
Sea level
Land depression

Spot heights in metres

GREAT LAKES DRAINAGE AREA

The Great Lakes and their connecting waterways are the most important unit of inland water transportation in the world. The St. Lawrence Seaway project (completed 1959) provides 8.23 m navigation from Montréal to the head of the Great Lakes, a distance of over 3200 km. Navigation facilities throughout the Great Lakes have provided 7.62 m navigation from the Lakehead to Prescott, Ontario, since the completion of the Welland Canal by Canada in 1932. The great fleet operating on these inland waters, whose largest vessels are of 27 000 t capacity, is understood to provide the cheapest transportation in the world. Below Montréal the St. Lawrence Ship Channel accommodates all but the largest ocean vessels and has made the city a major world port. But between Montréal and Prescott, Ont. the 4.27 m canals (completed by Canada in 1904) with their small locks let through only small vessels carrying less than 2 500 t. The breaking of this bottleneck was the essential purpose of the Seaway project. Ice closes the Great Lakes to navigation from Dec. to April approx., but a few ports and connecting channels are kept open by ice-breakers.

© Oxford University Press

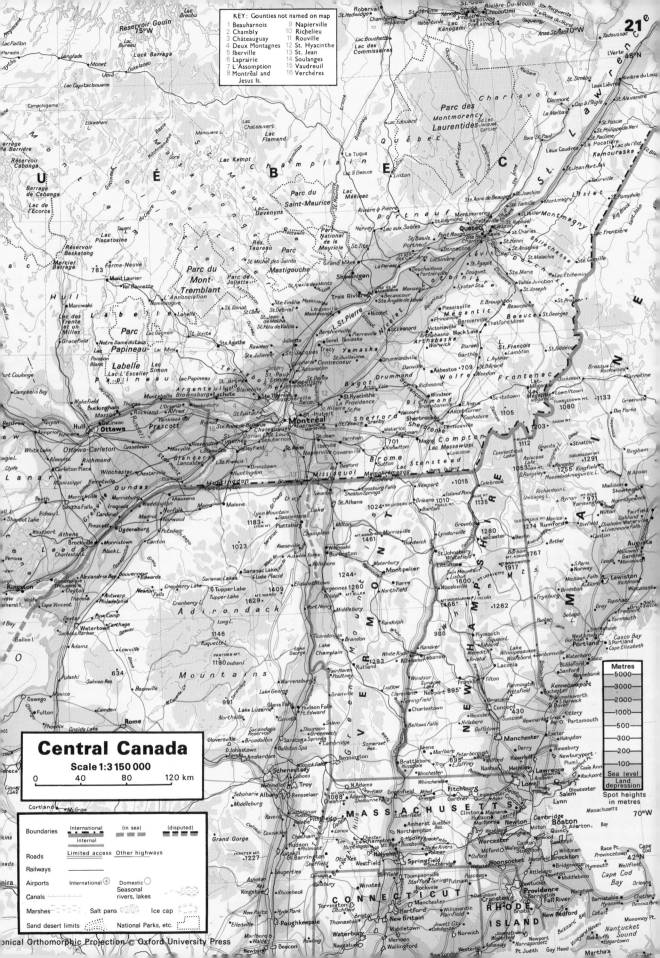

22

80°W · 46°N · 79°W · 78°W · 77°W

Powassan · Fossmill · Kiosk · Brent · Rapides des Joachims · Moor Lake · Deep River · Walt

Port Loring · Trout Creek · Waskigomog Lake · A L G O N Q U I N · Chalk River · Petawawa · Chapeau · Île aux Allumettes · Beach

South River · Bernard Lake · Burntroot Lake · Lac Lavieille · P R O V I N C I A L · Pembroke · Deep River

Wawashkesh L. · Sundridge · Magnetawan · Burks Falls · Big Trout L. · Dickson L. · P A R K · Round Lake · Petawawa · Cobden

Doe L. · Kearney · Ravensworth · Brûlé Lake · Opeongo Lake · Shirley L. · Aylen · Killaloe Sta. · Golden Lake · Eganville

Nobel · Sprucedale · Novar · Algonquin Park · Lake of Two Rivers · Victoria Lake · Bank Lake · Kamaniskeg Lake · L. Clear

Parry Sound · Vernon L. · Huntsville · Ragged L. · Rock Lake · Whitney · Madawaska · Wallace (Princes Lake) · Barrys Bay

Depot Harbour · Otter Lake · Skeleton L. · Kawagama L. · Hay L. · Bird Creek · Childs Mines · Weslemkoon Lake · Lava

Rosseau · Lake of Bays · Dorset · Kennisis L. · Bancroft · Denbigh

Christian Is. · MacTier · Port Carling · Redstone L. · Haliburton · Maynooth · Wilberforce · Turriff · Mazinaw L. · Snow Roa

Georgian Bay · Bala · Bracebridge · 45°N · Minden · Gooderham · Irondale · Baptiste Lake · Skootamatta L. · Big Gull L.

HURON · Torrance · Gravenhurst · Gull L. · Chandos L. · Coe Hill · Bannockburn · Sharbot

Penetanguishene · Severn · Severn Bridge · Head L. · Kinmount · Apsley · Jack L. · Arden

Midland · Port McNicoll · Victoria Hbr. · Washago · Catchacoma L. · Anstruther L. · Kasshabog L. · Kaladar · Tamworth · Enterp

Waubaushene · Coldwater · Coboconk · Kawartha Lakes · Marmora · Deloro · Madoc · Actinolite · Tweed

Elmvale · L. Couchiching · Rathburn · Balsam L. · Bobcaygeon · Buckhorn · Stony Lake · Lakefield · Havelock · Stirling · Newt

Wasaga Beach · Orillia · Atherley · Victoria Rd. · Fenelon Falls · Sturgeon L. · Chemung L. · Norwood · Campbellford · Napane

Steyner · Brechin · Kirkfield · Lindsay · Peterborough · Hastings · Warkworth · Frankford · Belleville · Deseronto

Creemore · Beaverton · Woodville · Omemee · Keene · Rice Lake · Trenton · Bay of Quinte · Adolphus Reach

Angus · Barrie · Big Bay Pt. · Cannington · Bethany · Millbrook · Harwood · Castleton · Stirling · Picton

Lefroy · Georgina I. · Sunderland · Pontypool · Bewdley · Brighton · Consecon · Bloomfield · Prince Edward B.

Alliston · Sutton · Keswick · Myrtle · Hampton · Orono · Colborne · Presqu'ile Point · Wellington

Beeton · Bradford · Mount Albert · Uxbridge · Brooklin · Port Hope · Cobourg · Pt. Petre

Tottenham · Holland Landing · Newmarket · Port Perry · Oshawa · Newcastle · Bowmanville

Schomberg · Aurora · Claremont · Whitby · Ajax · Pickering

Orangeville · Nobleton · King City · Stouffville · Markham · Richmond Hill

Erin · Bolton · Maple · Woodbridge

Inglewood · Bramalea · Brampton · Toronto · Toronto Is.

Acton · Georgetown · Streetsville · Mississauga · Port Credit

Milton · Oakville · Bronte

Waterdown · Burlington · Burlington Beach · Olcott · Wilson · Newfane · Hilton

Dundas · Hamilton · Niagara-on-the-Lake · Youngstown · Sodus

Ancaster · Stoney Creek · Grimsby · Beamsville · Lewiston · Lockport · New · Williamson · Newark

Mount Hope · St. Catharines · Thorold · Niagara Falls · Tonawanda · Lyons

Caledonia · Smithville · Fonthill · Niagara Falls · Chippawa · Phelps · Seneca Falls

Hagersville · Cayuga · Dunnville · Welland · Fort Erie · Port Colborne · Buffalo · Canandaigua

LAKE ERIE · 79°W · 77°W · Geneva

Lake Ontario and Upper St. Lawrence

Scale 1:1 500 000

0 · 20 · 40 · 60 km

L A K E   O N T A R I O

Surface level 75 m above m.s.l.

Conical Orthomorphic Projection

LAKE ERIE (surface level 174 m above m.s.l.)

Metres	
5000	
3000	
2000	
1000	
500	
300	
200	
100	
Sea level	
Land depression	

Boundaries — International (in sea) (disputed) — Internal

Roads — Limited access — Other highways

Railways

Airports — International ⊕ Domestic ○

Canals

Marshes · Salt pans · Ice cap

Sand desert limits · National Parks, etc.

Seasonal rivers, lakes

Spot heights in metres

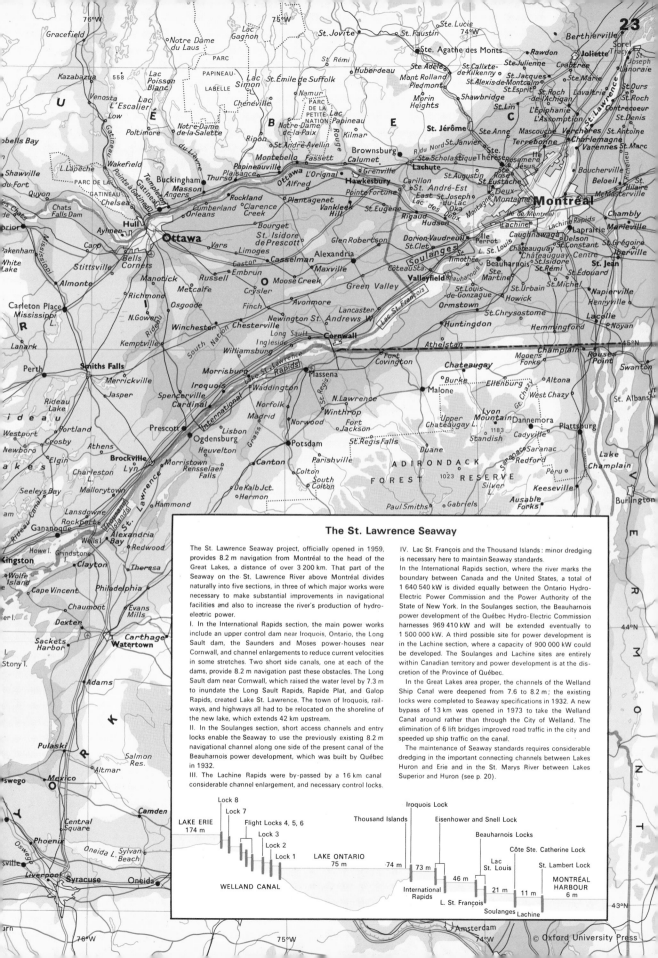

The St. Lawrence Seaway

The St. Lawrence Seaway project, officially opened in 1959, provides 8.2 m navigation from Montréal to the head of the Great Lakes, a distance of over 3 200 km. That part of the Seaway on the St. Lawrence River above Montréal divides naturally into five sections, in three of which major works were necessary to make substantial improvements in navigational facilities and also to increase the river's production of hydro-electric power.

I. In the International Rapids section, the main power works include an upper control dam near Iroquois, Ontario, the Long Sault dam, the Saunders and Moses power-houses near Cornwall, and channel enlargements to reduce current velocities in some stretches. Two short side canals, one at each of the dams, provide 8.2 m navigation past these obstacles. The Long Sault dam near Cornwall, which raised the water level by 7.3 m to inundate the Long Sault Rapids, Rapide Plat, and Galop Rapids, created Lake St. Lawrence. The town of Iroquois, railways, and highways all had to be relocated on the shoreline of the new lake, which extends 42 km upstream.

II. In the Soulanges section, short access channels and entry locks enable the Seaway to use the previously existing 8.2 m navigational channel along one side of the present canal of the Beauharnois power development, which was built by Québec in 1932.

III. The Lachine Rapids were by-passed by a 16 km canal considerable channel enlargement, and necessary control locks.

IV. Lac St. François and the Thousand Islands: minor dredging is necessary here to maintain Seaway standards.

In the International Rapids section, where the river marks the boundary between Canada and the United States, a total of 1 640 540 kW is divided equally between the Ontario Hydro-Electric Power Commission and the Power Authority of the State of New York. In the Soulanges section, the Beauharnois power development of the Québec Hydro-Electric Commission harnesses 969 410 kW and will be extended eventually to 1 500 000 kW. A third possible site for power development is in the Lachine section, where a capacity of 900 000 kW could be developed. The Soulanges and Lachine sites are entirely within Canadian territory and power development is at the discretion of the Province of Québec.

In the Great Lakes area proper, the channels of the Welland Ship Canal were deepened from 7.6 to 8.2 m; the existing locks were completed to Seaway specifications in 1932. A new bypass of 13 km was opened in 1973 to take the Welland Canal around rather than through the City of Welland. The elimination of 6 lift bridges improved road traffic in the city and speeded up ship traffic on the canal.

The maintenance of Seaway standards requires considerable dredging in the important connecting channels between Lakes Huron and Erie and in the St. Marys River between Lakes Superior and Huron (see p. 20).

Alberta

Area	Population	Production
661 207 km²	**1976: 1 799 771**	**1973: $ 5 794 000 000**
(6.5% of Canada)	(2.7/km²)	(value added)

Area		Population		Production	
Forest Land	307 422 km²	*1871*	included in N.W.T.	Construction	19
Wildland	140 670 km²	*1891*	–	Agriculture	18
Agriculture	190 715 km²	*1911*	374 295	Electrical Power	3
Urban & other	5 605 km²	*1931*	731 605		
Freshwater	16 795 km²	*1951*	939 501	Manufactures	18
		1961	1 331 944	*of which*	
		1971	1 627 875	Fabricated metals	9
		of which		Meat processing	9
Communications		Farm	15%	Chemicals	8
Railways	10 021 km	Rural non-farm	12%	Publishing & Printing	6
Highways	152 819 km	Urban	73%	Petroleum refining	6
of which 10% hardsurfaced		1976 *Census		Saw & Planing mills	5
Motor vehicles		Metropolitan Area		Dairy products	3
	57 per 100 people	*Edmonton	542 845		
Telephones		*Calgary	457 828	Mining	42
	55 per 100 people	Lethbridge	46 048	*of which*	
		Medicine Hat	32 263	Oil	69
		Red Deer	31 723	Natural Gas	14
				Natural Gas by-products	12
				Coal	2

Western Provinces

Scale 1:8 000 000

0 50 100 150 km

For layer box see page 30

Boundaries	International	(in sea)	(disputed)
	Internal		
Roads	Limited access	Other highways	
Railways			
Airports	International	Domestic	
Canals			
Marshes		Salt pan	Ice cap
		Seasonal rivers, lakes	
Sand desert limits		National Parks, etc.	

Conical Orthomorphic Projection © Oxford University Press

Saskatchewan

Area	Population	Production
651 923 km²	1976: 907 650	1973: $ 2 474 000 000
(6.4% of Canada)	(1.4/km²)	(value added)

st Land	128 201 km²	1871	included in N.W.T.	Agriculture	54%
land	179 043 km²	1891		Construction	13%
culture	264 269 km²	1911	492 432	Electrical Power	3%
n & other	8 774 km²	1931	921 785	Forestry)	
water	71 636 km²	1951	831 728	Fisheries)	1%
		1961	925 181	Trapping)	
		1971	926 240	Manufactures	12%
		of which		*of which*	
		Farm	25%	Meat processing	8%

Communications

Agricultural implements	5%
Rural non-farm	22%	Petroleum refining	7%
Urban	53%	Agricultural implements	5%
	Publishing & Printing	5%
	Dairy products	4%
ways	13 784 km	Mining	17%
ways	207 033 km	*of which*	
of which 8% hardsurfaced	Oil	51%
r vehicles*	Potash	38%
60 per 100 people	Zinc	5%
les snowmobiles	Copper	3%
phones	
46 per 100 people	

1976 *Census
Metropolitan Area
* Regina 148 965
* Saskatoon 132 291
Moose Jaw 31 884
Prince Albert 28 240
Swift Current 14 523

Manitoba

Area	Population	Production
650 090 km²	1976: 1 005 953	1973: $ 2 021 000 000
(6.4% of Canada)	(1.5/km²)	(value added)

Forest Land	135 472 km²	1871	25 228	Agriculture	27%
Wildland	121 191 km²	1891	152 506	Construction	20%
Agriculture	85 283 km²	1911	461 394	Electrical Power	5%
Urban & other	204 577 km²	1931	700 139	Forestry)	
Freshwater	103 566 km²	1951	776 541	Fisheries)	1%
		1961	921 686	Trapping)	
		1971	988 245	Manufactures	36%
		of which		*of which*	
		Farm	13%	Clothing	9%

Communications

		Rural non-farm	17%	Publishing & Printing	7%
Railways	7 633 km	Urban	70%	Meat processing	6%
Highways	75 920 km			Aircraft & Parts	4%
of which 14% hardsurfaced		Agricultural implements	4%
Motor vehicles	Mining	11%
47 per 100 people	*of which*	
Telephones	Nickel	54%
51 per 100 people	Zinc	32%
	Copper	4%
	Oil	4%

1976 *Census
Metropolitan Area
*Winnipeg 570 725
Brandon 34 481
Portage la Prairie 11 719
Flin Flon 8 431

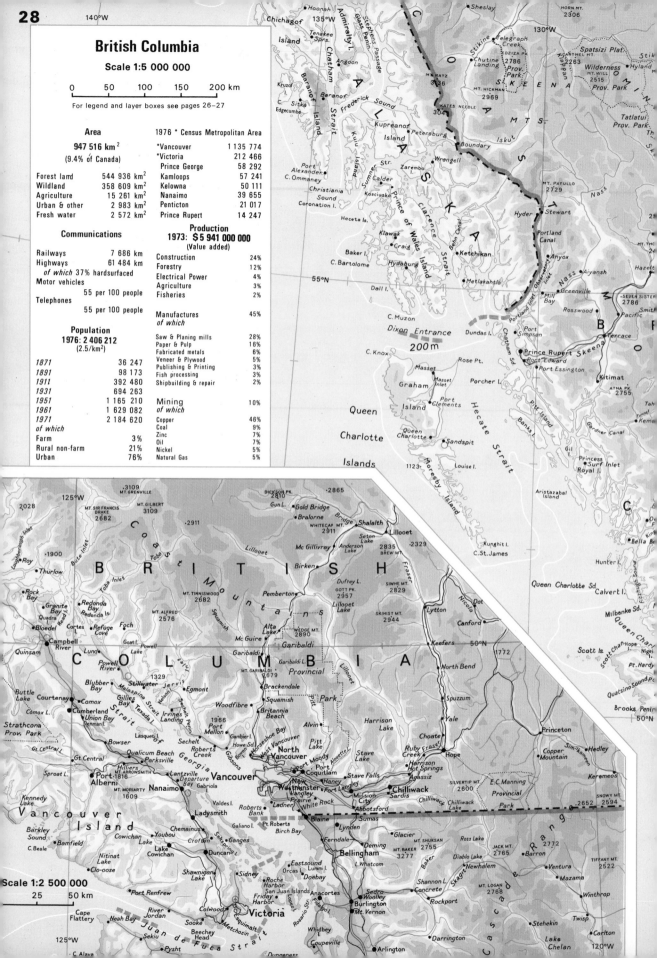

British Columbia

Scale 1:5 000 000

0   50   100   150   200 km

For legend and layer boxes see pages 26–27

Area

947 516 km²
(9.4% of Canada)

Forest land	544 936 km²
Wildland	358 609 km²
Agriculture	15 261 km²
Urban & other	2 983 km²
Fresh water	2 572 km²

Communications

Railways	7 686 km
Highways	61 484 km

of which 37% hardsurfaced

Motor vehicles	55 per 100 people
Telephones	55 per 100 people

Population

1976: 2 406 212
(2.5/km²)

1871	36 247
1891	98 173
1911	392 480
1931	694 263
1951	1 165 210
1961	1 629 082
1971	2 184 620

of which

Farm	3%
Rural non-farm	21%
Urban	76%

1976 * Census Metropolitan Area

*Vancouver	1 135 774
*Victoria	212 466
Prince George	58 292
Kamloops	57 241
Kelowna	50 111
Nanaimo	39 655
Penticton	21 017
Prince Rupert	14 247

Production

1973: $5 941 000 000
(Value added)

Construction	24%
Forestry	12%
Electrical Power	4%
Agriculture	3%
Fisheries	2%
Manufactures	45%

of which

Saw & Planing mills	28%
Paper & Pulp	16%
Fabricated metals	6%
Veneer & Plywood	5%
Publishing & Printing	3%
Fish processing	3%
Shipbuilding & repair	2%
Mining	10%

of which

Copper	46%
Coal	9%
Zinc	7%
Oil	7%
Nickel	5%
Natural Gas	5%

Scale 1:2 500 000

25   50 km

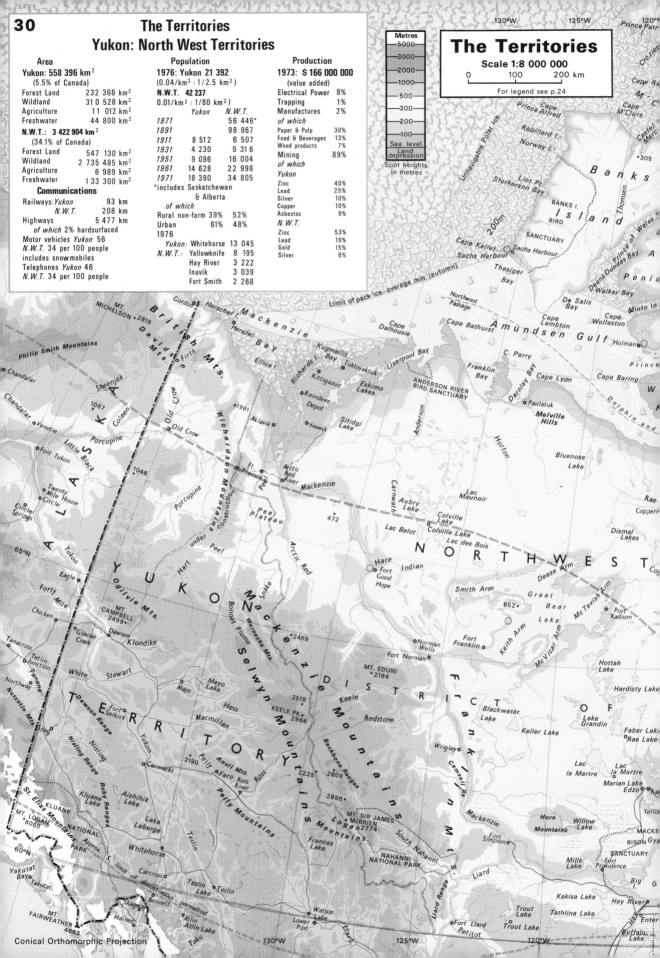

The Territories
Yukon: North West Territories

Area
Yukon: 558 396 km²
(5.5% of Canada)

Forest Land	232 366 km²
Wildland	310 528 km²
Agriculture	11 012 km²
Freshwater	44 800 km²

N.W.T.: 3 422 904 km²
(34.1% of Canada)

Forest Land	547 130 km²
Wildland	2 735 485 km²
Agriculture	6 989 km²
Freshwater	133 300 km²

Communications

Railways: Yukon	93 km
N.W.T.	208 km
Highways	5 477 km

of which 2% hardsurfaced
Motor vehicles Yukon 56
N.W.T. 34 per 100 people
includes snowmobiles
Telephones Yukon 46
N.W.T. 34 per 100 people

Population
1976: Yukon 21 392
(0.04/km² : 1/2.5 km²)
N.W.T. 42 237
0.01/km² : 1/80 km²)

	Yukon	N.W.T.
1871		56 446*
1891		98 967
1911	8 512	6 507
1931	4 230	9 316
1951	9 096	16 004
1961	14 628	22 998
1971	18 390	34 805

*includes Saskatchewan
& Alberta

of which		
Rural non-farm	39%	52%
Urban	61%	48%

1976

Yukon:	Whitehorse	13 045
N.W.T.:	Yellowknife	8 195
	Hay River	3 222
	Inuvik	3 039
	Fort Smith	2 268

Production
1973: $ 166 000 000
(value added)

Electrical Power	8%
Trapping	1%
Manufactures	2%

of which

Paper & Pulp	30%
Food & Beverages	13%
Wood products	7%
Mining	89%

of which
Yukon

Zinc	40%
Lead	25%
Silver	10%
Copper	10%
Asbestos	9%

N.W.T.

Zinc	53%
Lead	19%
Gold	15%
Silver	8%

Metres
5000
3000
2000
1000
500
300
200
Sea level
Land
depression
Spot heights
in metres

The Territories
Scale 1:8 000 000
0   100   200 km
For legend see p.24

Conical Orthomorphic Projection

Urban Land Use

These urban land use maps show only a simplified land use pattern. Their primary intent is to illustrate the overall relationships of land use and transportation systems. Therefore, much detail has been omitted.

The built-up area where the major use of land is for residential purposes

Central business core

Lesser but significant commercial centres

Industrial districts

Major parks and open spaces

Major military and naval installations

Boundaries

International

Provincial or State

County

Highways

Limited access & rapid transit

Other main highways

Tunnels

Railroads and transportation yards

Airports and airfields

Scale 1:400 000

0   5   10   15 km

Montréal map

Dorval Airport

	Temp. °C	Rain mm
J	−9.9	76
F	−8.8	71
M	−2.3	70
A	5.9	74
M	12.8	83
J	18.5	87
J	21.2	85
A	19.9	87
S	15.3	80
O	9.4	75
N	2.3	87
D	−6.6	86
Year 6.5	941
Height 30 m	

Île Ste. Thérèse, Boucherville, Îles de Boucherville, CO. CHAMBLY, St-Hubert, St-Lambert, Longueuil, JACQUES CARTIER, CO. LAPRAIRIE, Laprairie, AUTOROUTE DES CANTONS DE L'EST, ST. LAWRENCE SEAWAY, Pointe-aux-Trembles, Montréal Est, Montréal Nord, MONTRÉAL NORD, ST. MICHEL, Olympic Stadium, SHERBROOKE ST, Île Ste Hélène, St-George, Sir Williams Univ., McGill University, Outremont, Mont Royal, VERDUN, Westmount, La Salle, Caughnawaga, LACHINE, VILLE DE LAVAL, Île Jésus, Ste. Rose, Ste. Thérèse, Ste. Dorothée, Laval-des-Rapides, Pont-Viau, Chomedey, CO. TERREBONNE, St. Eustache, Île Bizard, Ste. Geneviève, Ste-Anne-de-Bellevue, Pierrefonds, Beaconsfield, Pointe-Claire, Dorval, MONTRÉAL INTERNATIONAL, Lac St. Louis, CO. DEUX MONTAGNES, Deux-Montagnes, Lac des Deux Montagnes, St. Laurent Fleuve, Rivière des Prairies, LAURENTIAN AUTOROUTE, MÉTROPOLITAIN BLVD.

Toronto map

	Temp. °C	Rain mm
J	−6.3	56
F	−5.8	49
M	−0.9	60
A	6.4	64
M	12.2	67
J	18.2	67
J	20.7	73
A	19.7	79
S	15.7	63
O	9.8	59
N	3.4	67
D	−2.5	58

Toronto International Airport

Markham, Unionville, Richmond Hill, Buttonville, Thornhill, REGIONAL MUNICIPALITY OF YORK, METROPOLITAN TORONTO, SCARBOROUGH, EAST YORK, NORTH YORK, Don Mills, Leaside, Forest Hill, Rouge River, Highland Creek, Don River, Downsview, YORK, TORONTO, University of Toronto, GARDINER EXPRESSWAY, Kleinburg, Maple, Woodbridge, Humber River, Islington, Mimico, New Toronto, Long Branch, ETOBICOKE, Humber Bay, TORONTO ISLANDS, Port Credit, Etobicoke Creek, PEEL COUNTY, MACDONALD CARTIER FREEWAY

Ottawa map

	Temp. °C	Rain mm
J	−10.9	60
F	−9.5	57
M	−7.7	61
A	5.6	68
M	12.4	70
J	18.2	73
J	20.7	87
A	19.3	81
S	14.6	76
O	8.1	66
N	1.4	77
D	−7.7	78
Year 5.8	851
Height 104 m	

Ottawa International Airport

Cumberland, Sarsfield, Department of National Defence, Bear Brook, Carlsbad Springs, CARLTON CO., RUSSELL CO., Russell, CTE PAPINEAU, Queenswood Heights, Orléans, Blackburn, CFS Leitrim, North Gloucester, South Gloucester, Greely, Castor River, Ottawa River, Templeton, Gatineau, GATINEAU, CFB Rockcliffe, Beacon Hill, EASTVIEW, Rockcliffe Park, Ottawa, University of Ottawa, Parliament Buildings, OTTAWA, Carleton University, Gloucester, Rideau River and Canal, Central Experimental Farm, City View, Merivale, HULL, HULL CO., CTE GATINEAU, Pointe Gatineau, Kettle Island, Rivière Gatineau, Biscuit Gatineau, Chelsea Brook, Aylmer, Graham Bay, Kingsmere Lake, Crystal Bay, Bells Corner, Kanata, Shirleys Bay, Lac Deschênes, National Park, QUEBEC, ONTARIO, Old Stittsville, Stittsville, Manotick

©Oxford University Press

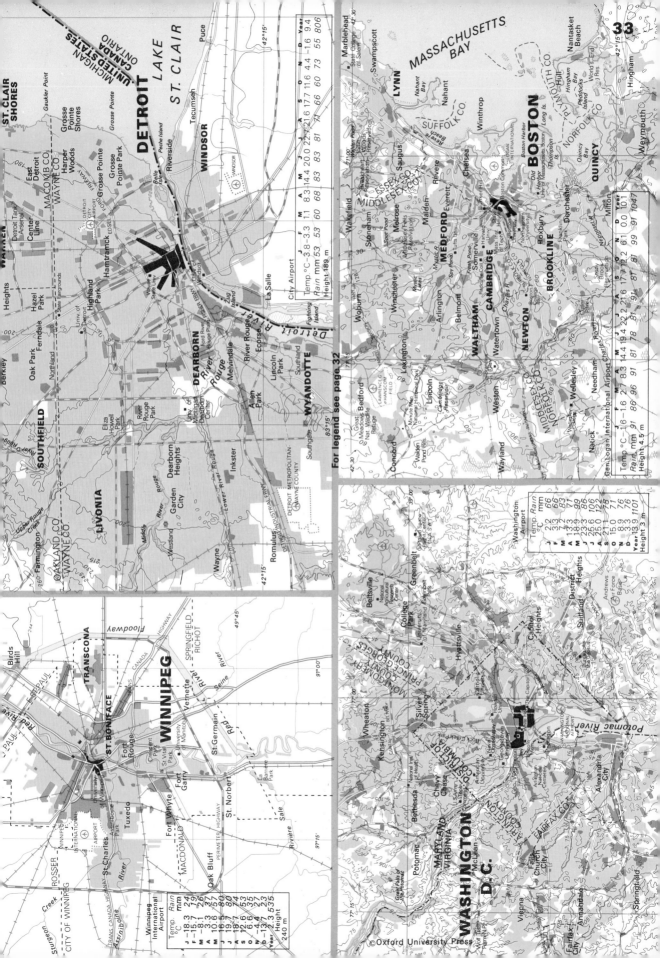

LAKE ST. CLAIR — DETROIT — WINDSOR

City Airport

	J	F	M	A	M	J	J	A	S	O	N	D	Year
Temp. °C	-3.8	-3.3	1.1	8.3	14.4	20.0	22.7	21.6	17.7	11.6	4.4	-1.6	9.4
Rain mm	53	53	60	68	83	83	81	66	60	73	55		806

Height 189 m

For legend see page 32

BOSTON — Gen. Logan International Airport Charles R.

	J	F	M	A	M	J	J	A	S	O	N	D	Year
Temp. °C	-1.6	-1.6	2.7	8.3	14.4	19.4	22.2	21.7	17.1	12.6	7.2	0.0	10.1
Rain mm	91	86	91	81	78	81	81	87	91	99	91		1047

Height 4.5 m

WASHINGTON D.C. — Washington Airport

	Temp. °C	Rain mm
J	2.2	66
F	3.3	66
M	7.2	83
A	13.3	71
M	18.9	99
J	23.3	86
J	26.0	106
A	25.0	122
S	21.1	78
O	15.0	76
N	8.9	76
D	3.3	76
Year	13.9	1101

Height 3 m

WINNIPEG — Winnipeg International Airport

	Temp. °C	Rain mm
J	-18.3	24
F	-15.7	19
M	-8.1	26
A	2.5	37
M	10.6	57
J	16.5	80
J	19.6	69
A	18.7	74
S	12.6	53
O	5.7	35
N	-4.4	27
D	-13.7	23
Year	2.3	535

Height 240 m

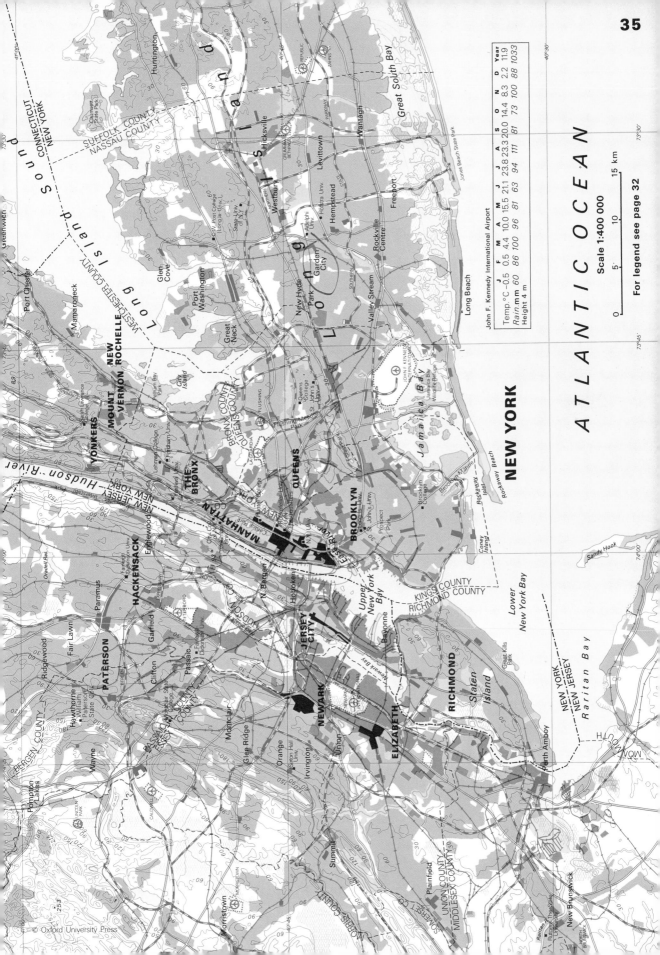

NEW YORK

ATLANTIC OCEAN

John F. Kennedy International Airport

	J	F	M	A	M	J	J	A	S	O	N	D	Year
Temp.°C	-0.5	0.5	4.4	10.0	15.5	21.1	23.8	23.3	20.0	14.4	8.3	2.2	11.9
Rain mm	60	86	100	96	81	63	94	111	81	73	100	88	1033

Height 4 m

Scale 1:400 000

0   5   10   15 km

For legend see page 32

© Oxford University Press

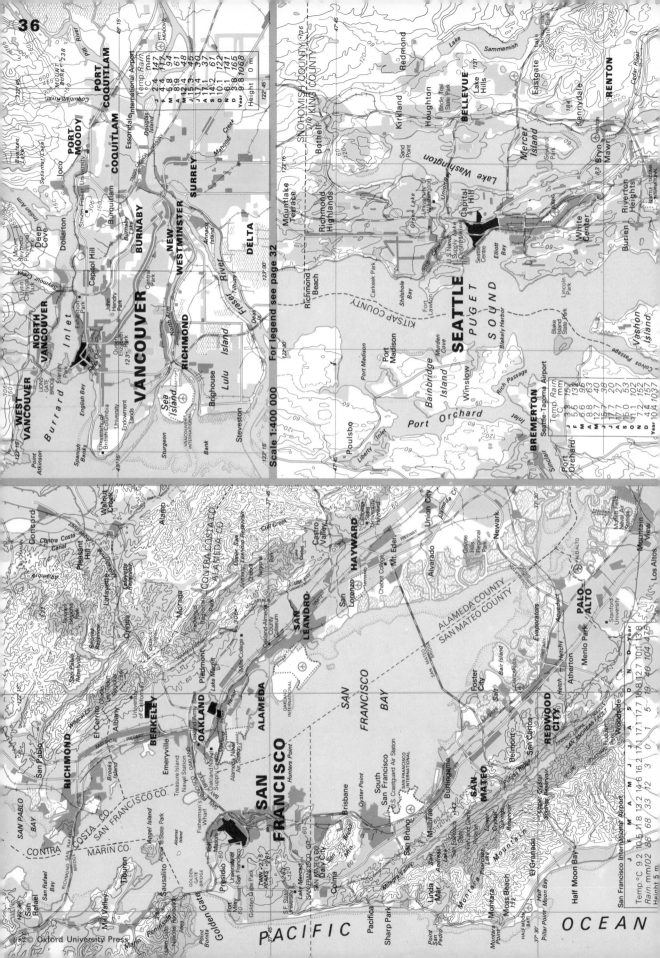

PACIFIC OCEAN

© Oxford University Press

Scale 1:400 000   For legend see page 32

	Temp.	Rain
	°C	mm
J	12.7	60
F	13.3	68
M	13.8	45
A	15.5	25
M	17.2	2
J	18.3	0
J	20.5	0
A	20.5	2
S	20.0	7
O	18.3	7
N	15.5	38
D	13.3	55
Year	16.3	302

Los Angeles International   Height 29 m

SAN GABRIEL MOUNTAINS

ANGELES NATIONAL FOREST

CLEVELAND NATIONAL FOREST

SAN BERNARDINO COUNTY
ORANGE COUNTY

LOS ANGELES COUNTY
ORANGE COUNTY

SANTA MONICA MOUNTAINS

SAN FERNANDO VALLEY

PALOS VERDES HILLS

San Pedro Bay

San Pedro Channel

RIVERSIDE

LOS ANGELES

POMONA

PASADENA

GLENDALE

BURBANK

ALHAMBRA

FULLERTON

ANAHEIM

GARDEN GROVE

SANTA ANA

NORWALK

LAKEWOOD

DOWNEY

SOUTH GATE

COMPTON

TORRANCE

INGLEWOOD

LONG BEACH

SANTA MONICA

Ontario

Upland

Chino

Corona

Claremont

Glendora

Covina

Azusa

West Covina

La Puente

Baldwin Park

Arcadia

Altadena

La Canada

El Monte

Temple City

San Gabriel

Rosemead

Monterey Park

Montebello

Pico Rivera

Whittier

La Habra

Brea

Orange

Buena Park

Westminster

Huntington Harbor

Bellflower

Gardena

Carson

Manhattan Beach

Redondo Beach

Culver City

Hollywood

North Hollywood

Beverly Hills

Van Nuys

Reseda

Sunland

Tujunga

San Fernando

Marina del Rey

Disneyland

Knott's Berry Farm

California State University, Fullerton

California State University, Long Beach

University of California, Los Angeles

University of Southern California

California Institute of Technology

San Gabriel Mission

Hollywood Bowl

Rose Bowl

Mount Wilson Observatory

East Los Angeles

Santa Fe Flood Control Basin

Whittier Narrows Dam Reservoir Area

Hansen Flood Control Basin

Prado Flood Control Basin

Sepulveda Dam Recreational Area

Los Angeles River

San Gabriel River

Rio Hondo

Los Angeles River

Coyote Creek

Santa Ana River

Cogswell Reservoir

Morris Reservoir

San Gabriel Reservoir

Big Dalton Reservoir

San Dimas Reservoir

Big Santa Anita Reservoir

Sawpit Reservoir

Eaton Wash Reservoir

Devils Gate Reservoir

Big Tujunga Reservoir

Hollywood Reservoir

Silver Lake Reservoir

Encino Reservoir

Franklin Canyon Reservoir

Stone Canyon Reservoir

Fullerton Reservoir

Brea Reservoir

Carbon Canyon Reservoir

Yorba Linda Reservoir

Arnold Reservoir

Villa Park Reservoir

Peters Canyon Reservoir

Santiago Reservoir

Featherly Regional Park

Marshall Canyon Regional Park

Thompson Regional Park

San Antonio Regional Park

Los Angeles Fairgrounds

Claremont Colleges

Occidental College

Huntington Library

Los Angeles State College

Elysian Park

Griffith Park

Will Rogers State Historic Park

Marina of the Pacific

Mainland of the San Pedro

Los Angeles International

Ontario International

San Antonio International

Los Alamitos

Long Beach Municipal

Torrance Municipal

Fullerton Municipal

Santa Monica Municipal

Los Angeles International Airport

U.S. Naval Weapons Station

U.S. Naval Air Station

U.S. Naval Air Station

U.S. Marine Corps

Santa Ana Marine Corps

Van Norman Lake

San Fernando

Santa Monica Freeway

Santa Ana Freeway

San Bernardino Freeway

Pomona Freeway

Long Beach Freeway

Harbor Freeway

San Diego Freeway

Golden State Freeway

Hollywood Freeway

Ventura Freeway

Riverside Freeway

San Gabriel River Freeway

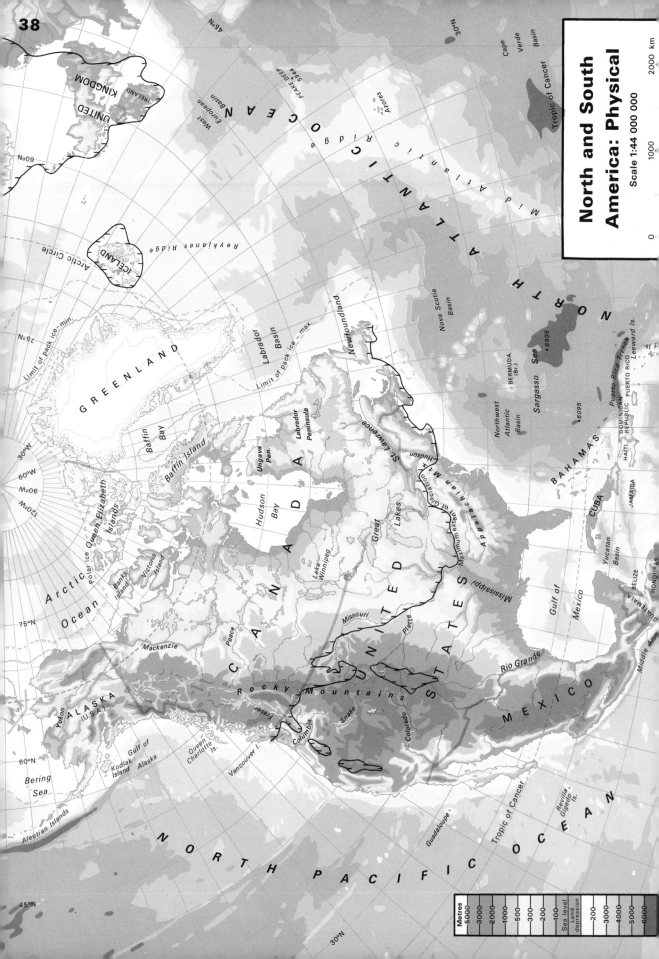

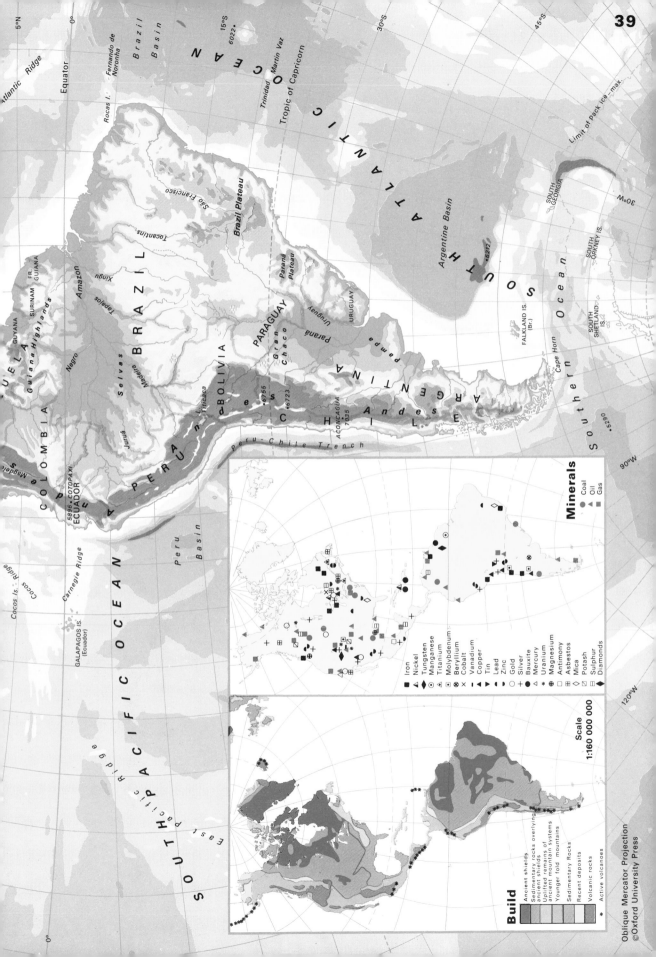

39

ATLANTIC OCEAN

SOUTH

Mid-Atlantic Ridge
Equator
Fernando de Noronha
Rocas I.
Trinidad *Martin Vaz*
Tropic of Capricorn
Brazil Basin
6022

Argentine Basin
6212

Limit of pack ice—max.

SOUTH GEORGIA

Southern Ocean

FALKLAND IS. (Br.)
SOUTH ORKNEY IS.
SOUTH SHETLAND IS.

Cape Horn
30°W

VENEZUELA
COLOMBIA
GUYANA
SURINAM
FR. GUIANA
Guiana Highlands
Galapagos
Negro
Juruá
Madeira
Amazon
Xingu
Tapajós
selvas
Tocantins
São Francisco
Brazil Plateau
BRAZIL
B O L I V I A
PERU
Titicaca
6755
6723
Gran Chaco
PARAGUAY
Paraná Plateau
Uruguay
Paraná
URUGUAY
Pampa
ARGENTINA
CHILE
Andes
ACONCAGUA
7035
Peru-Chile Trench

Magdalena
5896 COTOPAXI
ECUADOR
COTOPAXI
Peru Basin

Cocos Is.
Cocos Ridge
Carnegie Ridge
GALAPAGOS IS. (Ecuador)

SOUTH PACIFIC OCEAN

East Pacific Ridge

5290

90°W
120°W

0°
15°S
30°S
45°S
5°N

Minerals

- ● Coal
- ● Oil
- ▲ Gas

■ Iron	◆ Molybdenum	◖ Copper	● Silver
◀ Nickel	⊗ Beryllium	+ Tin	* Mercury
◉ Manganese	× Cobalt	◗ Lead	□ Magnesium
◢ Titanium	◀ Vanadium	✦ Zinc	⊡ Antimony
		⊞ Bauxite	△ Mica
		✳ Uranium	◇ Asbestos
			⬘ Potash
			⬠ Sulphur
			◆ Diamonds
		● Gold	

Build

	Ancient shields
	Sedimentary rocks overlying ancient shields
	Uplifted remains of ancient mountain systems
	Younger fold mountains
	Sedimentary Rocks
	Recent deposits
	Volcanic rocks
*	Active volcanoes

Scale
1:160 000 000

Oblique Mercator Projection
©Oxford University Press

North and South America: Vegetation

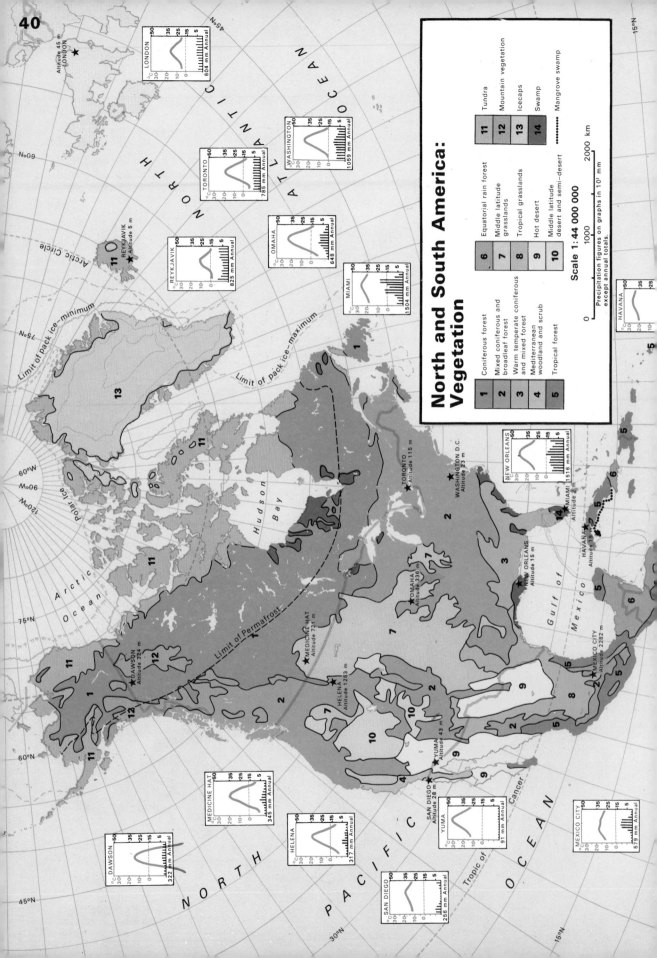

Scale 1:44 000 000

1	Coniferous forest	6	Equatorial rain forest	11	Tundra
2	Mixed coniferous and broadleaf forest	7	Middle latitude grasslands	12	Mountain vegetation
3	Warm temperate coniferous and mixed forest	8	Tropical grasslands	13	Icecaps
4	Mediterranean woodland and scrub	9	Hot desert	14	Swamp
5	Tropical forest	10	Middle latitude desert and semi-desert		Mangrove swamp

0   1000   2000 km

Precipitation figures on graphs in 10¹ mm except annual totals.

Climate graphs: LONDON (Altitude 45 m, 604 mm Annual), WASHINGTON (1059 mm Annual), TORONTO (785 mm Annual), REYKJAVIK (Altitude 5 m, 825 mm Annual), OMAHA (648 mm Annual), MIAMI (1504 mm Annual), HAVANA, NEW ORLEANS (1516 mm Annual), DAWSON (322 mm Annual), MEDICINE HAT (345 mm Annual), HELENA (317 mm Annual), SAN DIEGO (256 mm Annual), YUMA (91 mm Annual), MEXICO CITY (579 mm Annual)

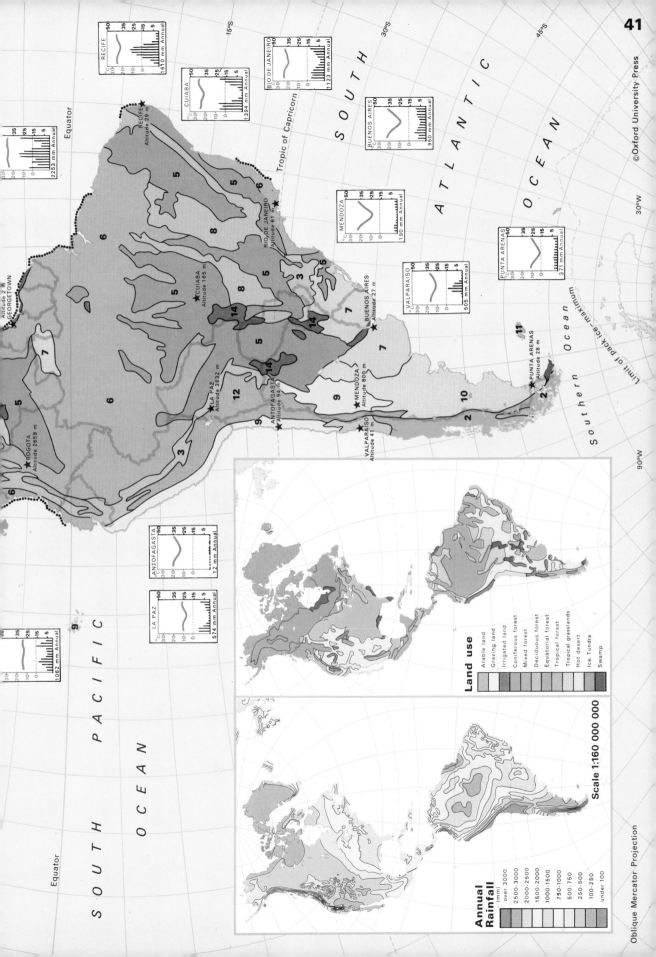

RECIFE
1610 mm Annual

CUIABA
1394 mm Annual

RIO DE JANEIRO
1123 mm Annual

BUENOS AIRES
950 mm Annual

MENDOZA
190 mm Annual

VALPARAISO
505 mm Annual

PUNTA ARENAS
371 mm Annual

ANTOFAGASTA
12 mm Annual

LA PAZ
574 mm Annual

2253 mm Annual

1062 mm Annual

Equator

15°S

30°S

45°S

Tropic of Capricorn

S O U T H

A T L A N T I C   O C E A N

Southern Ocean

Limit of pack ice—maximum

S O U T H   P A C I F I C   O C E A N

Equator

30°W

90°W

★ RECIFE
Altitude 29 m

★ CUIABA
Altitude 165 m

★ RIO DE JANEIRO
Altitude 61

★ BUENOS AIRES
Altitude 27 m

★ MENDOZA
Altitude 800

★ VALPARAISO
Altitude 4 m

★ PUNTA ARENAS
Altitude 28 m

★ ANTOFAGASTA
Altitude 94 m

★ LA PAZ
Altitude 3632 m

★ BOGOTA
Altitude 2859 m

★ GEORGETOWN
Altitude 2 m

Land use

Arable land
Grazing land
Irrigated land
Coniferous forest
Mixed forest
Deciduous forest
Equatorial forest
Tropical forest
Tropical grasslands
Hot desert
Ice, Tundra
Swamp

Scale 1:160 000 000

**Annual
Rainfall**
(mm)

over 3000
2500-3000
2000-2500
1500-2000
1000-1500
750-1000
500-750
250-500
100-250
under 100

Oblique Mercator Projection

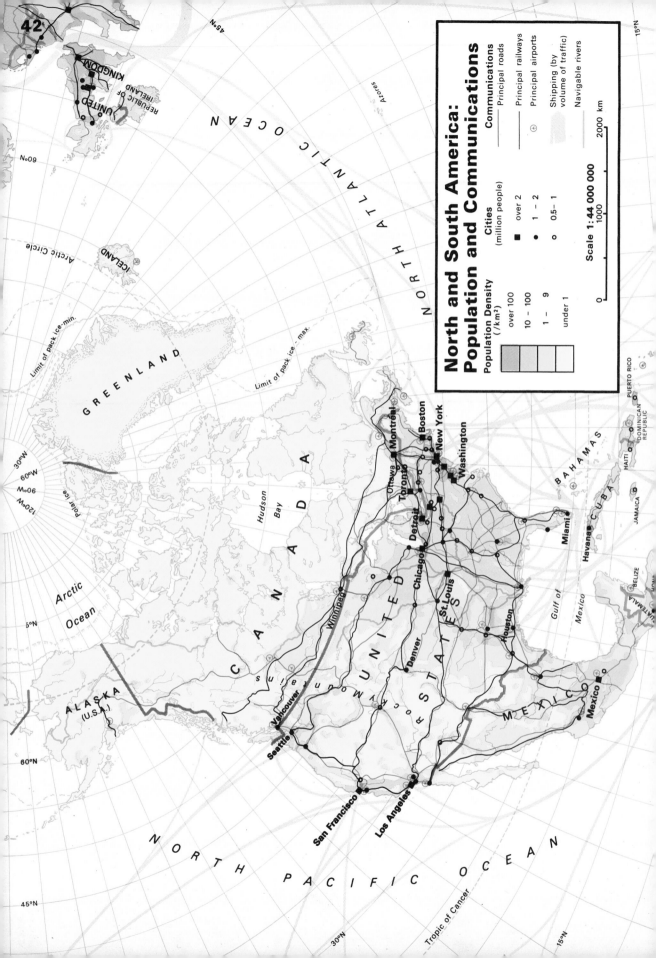

North and South America: Population and Communications

Communications
Principal roads
Principal railways
Principal airports
Shipping (by volume of traffic)
Navigable rivers

Cities
(million people)
- over 2
- 1 – 2
- 0.5 – 1

Population Density
(/km²)
- over 100
- 10 – 100
- 1 – 9
- under 1

Scale 1:44 000 000

0   1000   2000 km

Map labels:

NORTH ATLANTIC OCEAN

NORTH PACIFIC OCEAN

GREENLAND

CANADA

UNITED STATES

ALASKA (U.S.A.)

MEXICO

Arctic Ocean

Hudson Bay

Gulf of Mexico

Rocky Mountains

ICELAND

Azores

BAHAMAS

CUBA

HAITI

JAMAICA

DOMINICAN REPUBLIC

PUERTO RICO

BELIZE

GUATEMALA

UNITED KINGDOM

REPUBLIC OF IRELAND

Arctic Circle

Limit of pack ice - min.
Limit of pack ice - max.

Polar ice

Tropic of Cancer

Cities: Montréal, Boston, New York, Ottawa, Toronto, Washington, Detroit, Chicago, St. Louis, Denver, Houston, Winnipeg, Miami, Havana, Mexico, Vancouver, Seattle, San Francisco, Los Angeles

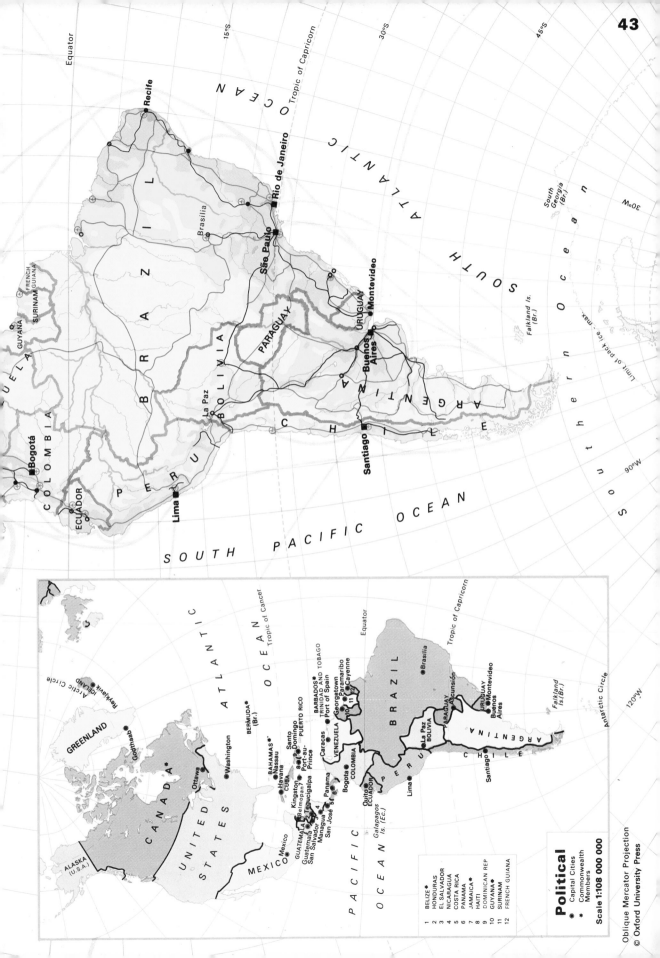

Equator

15°S

30°S

45°S

Tropic of Capricorn

N O R T H

A T L A N T I C

O C E A N

Recife

Rio de Janeiro

Brasília

São Paulo

B R A Z I L

FRENCH
GUIANA

SURINAM

GUYANA

ZUELA

COLOMBIA

Bogotá

ECUADOR

P E R U

Lima

La Paz

B O L I V I A

P A R A G U A Y

C H I L E

A R G E N T I N A

URUGUAY

Montevideo

Buenos
Aires

Santiago

S O U T H   A T L A N T I C   O C E A N

South
Georgia
(Br.)

Falkland Is.
(Br.)

30°W

90°W

S o u t h e r n   O c e a n

Limit of pack ice – max.

S O U T H   P A C I F I C   O C E A N

Tropic of Cancer

Equator

Tropic of Capricorn

A T L A N T I C

O C E A N

ICELAND

Reykjavik

Arctic Circle

GREENLAND

Godthaab

CANADA*

Ottawa

UNITED

STATES

Washington

BERMUDA*
(Br.)

ALASKA
(U.S.A.)

MEXICO

Mexico

GUATEMALA
Guatemala 3
San Salvador
Managua
San José 5 6
BAHAMAS*
Nassau
Havana
CUBA
Kingston
Belmopan 7
Tegucigalpa
Panama
2
8
4
9
Santo
Domingo
PUERTO RICO
Port-au-
Prince
Caracas
VENEZUELA
Bogotá
COLOMBIA
Quito
ECUADOR
Galapagos
Is. (Ec.)
PACIFIC
OCEAN
Lima
PERU
La Paz
BOLIVIA
BARBADOS*
TRINIDAD AND TOBAGO
Port of Spain
Georgetown
Paramaribo
Cayenne
10 11 12
BRAZIL
Brasília
PARAGUAY
Asunción
CHILE
Santiago
ARGENTINA
URUGUAY
Montevideo
Buenos
Aires
Falkland
Is.(Br.)
Antarctic Circle
120°W

Political

● Capital Cities

✳ Commonwealth
Members

Scale 1:108 000 000

1 BELIZE*
2 HONDURAS
3 EL SALVADOR
4 NICARAGUA
5 COSTA RICA
6 PANAMA
7 JAMAICA*
8 HAITI
9 DOMINICAN REP
10 GUYANA*
11 SURINAM
12 FRENCH GUIANA

Oblique Mercator Projection
© Oxford University Press

U.S.A. and Central America

Scale 1:19 000 000

0   200   400   600 km

Boundaries	International	(in sea)	(disputed)
	Internal		

Highways
Railways
Airports   International ⊕   Domestic ○
Canals
Seasonal rivers, lakes
Marshes   Salt pans   Ice cap
Sand desert limits   National Parks, etc.

The United States

Alabama 23, Arizona 44, Arkansas 30, California 48, Colorado 40, Connecticut 6, Delaware 10,
Florida 17, Georgia 16, Idaho 42, Illinois 28, Indiana 20, Iowa 27, Kansas 35, Kentucky 21,
Louisiana 31, Maine 1, Maryland 11, Massachusetts 4, Michigan 18, Minnesota 26,
Mississippi 24, Missouri 29, Montana 38, Nebraska 34, Nevada 47, New Hampshire 2,
New Jersey 8, New Mexico 41, New York 7, North Carolina 14, North Dakota 32,
Ohio 19, Oklahoma 36, Oregon 46, Pennsylvania 9, Rhode Island 5, South Carolina 15,
South Dakota 33, Tennessee 22, Texas 37, Utah 43, Vermont 3, Virginia 13,
Washington 45, West Virginia 12, Wisconsin 25, Wyoming 39.

Alaska became a state on January 3, 1959 and Hawaii on August 21, 1959

Zenithal Equidistant Projection

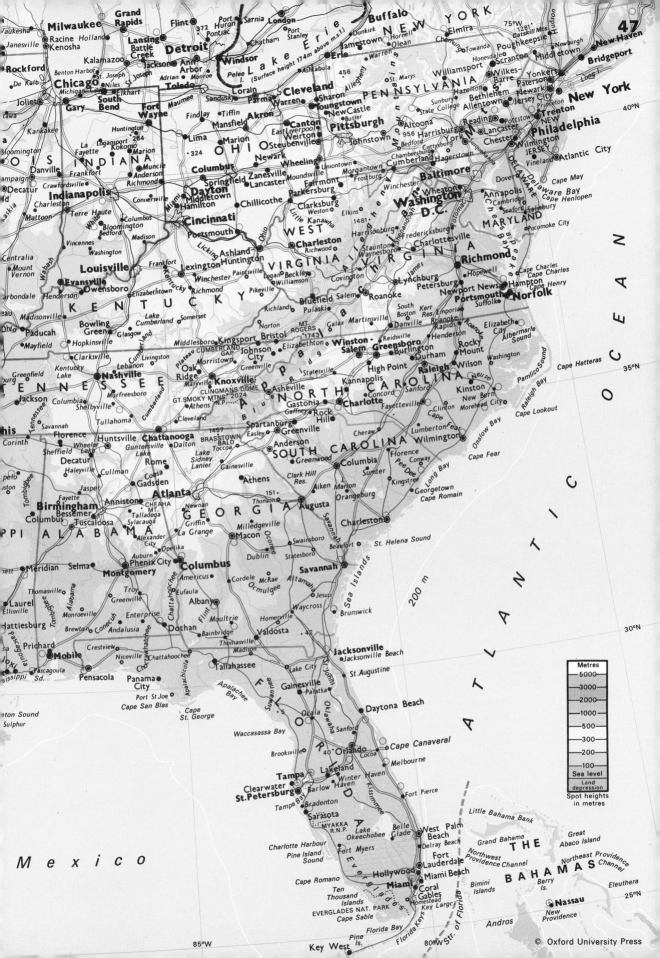

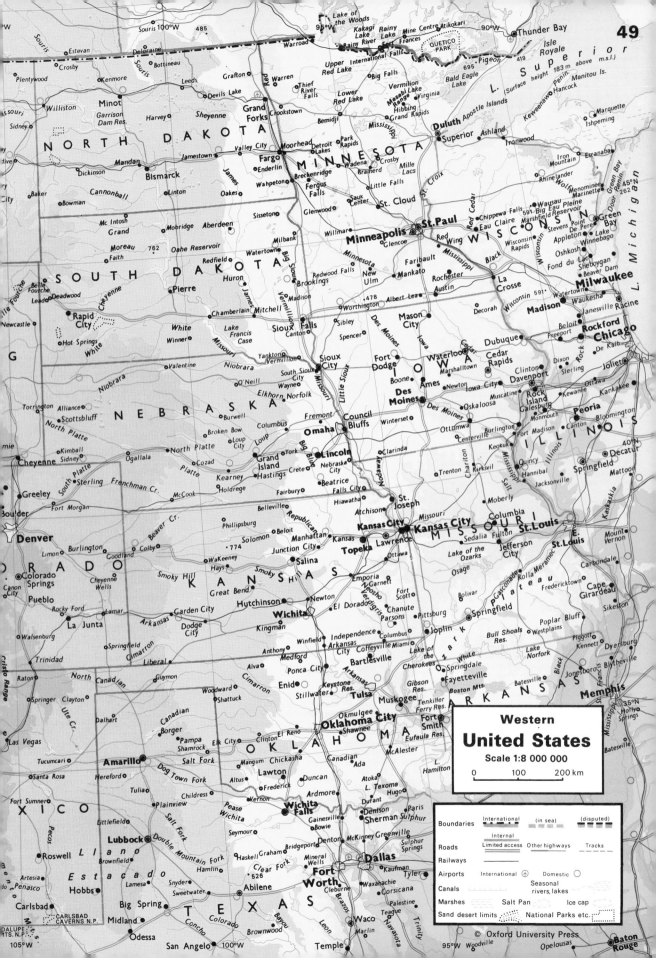

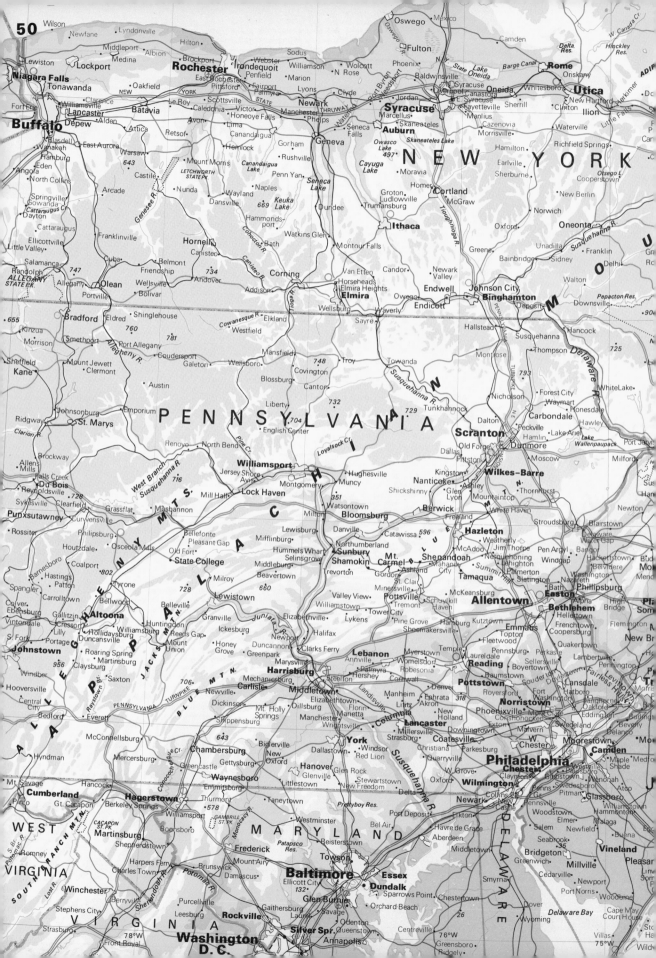

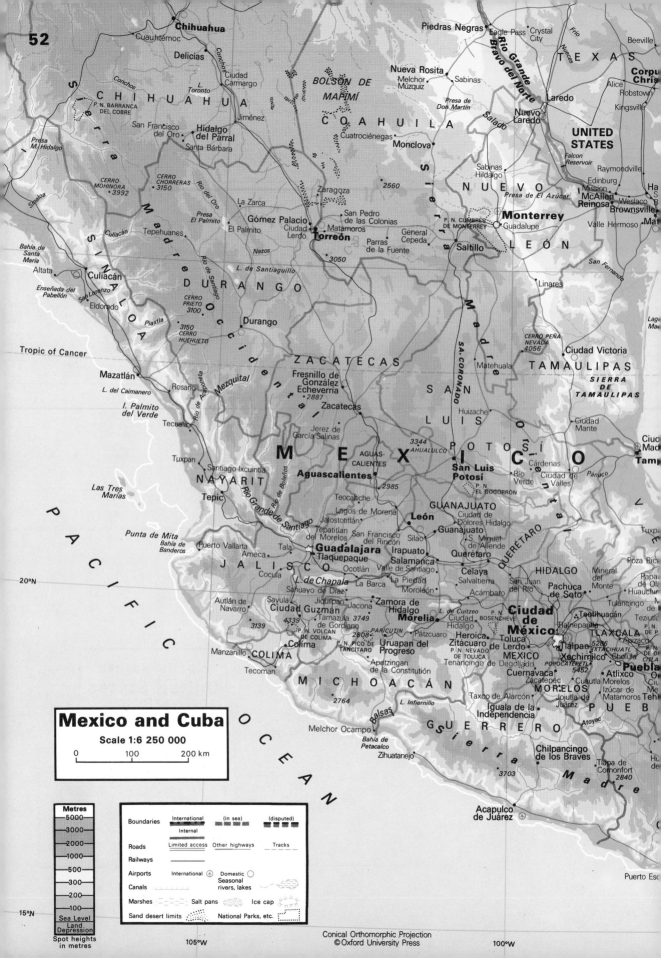

52

Mexico and Cuba

Scale 1:6 250 000

0   100   200 km

Conical Orthomorphic Projection
© Oxford University Press

Tropic of Cancer

20°N

15°N

105°W   100°W

Metres
—5000
—3000
—2000
—1000
—500
—300
—200
—100
Sea Level
Land
Depression

Spot heights
in metres

Boundaries — International — (in sea) — (disputed) — Internal
Roads — Limited access — Other highways — Tracks
Railways
Airports — International — Domestic / Seasonal rivers, lakes
Canals
Marshes — Salt pans — Ice cap
Sand desert limits — National Parks, etc.

PACIFIC OCEAN

TEXAS
UNITED STATES

Piedras Negras · Eagle Pass · Crystal City
Beeville
Nueces · Frio
Corpus Christi
Alice · Robstown
Kingsville
Raymondville
Edinburg · Mission
McAllen · Weslaco · Ha
Reinosa · Brownsville · Mat

CHIHUAHUA
Chihuahua
Cuauhtémoc
Delicias
Ciudad Camargo
L. Toronto
Conchos
Jiménez
San Francisco del Oro
Hidalgo del Parral
Santa Bárbara
CERRO MOHINORA · 3992
CERRO CHORRERAS · 3150
Rio del Oro
La Zarca
Presa El Palmito
El Palmito
Tepehuanes
Conchos
P. N. BARRANCA DEL COBRE
Sierra
Presa M. Hidalgo
Sinaloa
Culiacán

BOLSÓN DE MAPIMÍ

COAHUILA
Cuatrociénegas
Monclova
2560
Zaragoza
San Pedro de las Colonias
Gómez Palacio
Ciudad Lerdo
Torreón
Matamoros
Parras de la Fuente
General Cepeda
3050
Nazos

Nueva Rosita
Melchor Múzquiz
Sabinas
Presa de Don Martín
Saladо
Laredo
Nuevo Laredo
Falcon Reservoir
Presa de El Azúcar

NUEVO LEÓN
Monterrey
Guadalupe
P. N. CUMBRES DE MONTERREY
Saltillo
Sabinas Hidalgo
San Fernando
Linares

DURANGO
CERRO PRIETO · 3100
Durango
CERRO HUEHUETO · 3150
L. de Santiaguillo
Rio del Santiago

SINALOA
Bahía de Santa María
Altata
Ensenada del Pabellón
Eldorado
San Lorenzo
Culiacán
Piaxtla

Mazatlán
Rosario
L. del Caimanero
I. Palmito del Verde
Tecuala
Tuxpan

NAYARIT
Tepic
Santiago Ixcuintla
Rio Grande de Santiago

Las Tres Marías
Punta de Mita
Bahía de Banderas
Puerto Vallarta
Ameca

ZACATECAS
Fresnillo de González Echeverria · 2887
Zacatecas
Jerez de García Salinas
AHUALULCO · 3344
2985

SAN LUIS POTOSÍ
Matehuala
Huizache
Ciudad del Maíz
San Luis Potosí
Rio Verde
Cárdenas
Ciudad de Valles
P. N. EL GOGORRÓN
Pánuco

TAMAULIPAS
CERRO PEÑA NEVADA · 4056
Ciudad Victoria
Ciudad Mante
SIERRA DE TAMAULIPAS
Ciudad Madero
Tampico

MEXICO

AGUASCALIENTES
Aguascalientes
Teocaltiche

JALISCO
Guadalajara
Tlaquepaque
Tala
Ameca
Cocula
Ocotlán
L. de Chapala
Sahuayo de Díaz
La Barca
Autlán de Navarro
Sayula
Ciudad Guzmán
3139
4339
Tamazula de Gordiano · 3749
PARÍCUTIN · 2808
P. N. VOLCÁN DE COLIMA

Lagos de Moreno
Tepatitlán del Morelos
San Francisco del Rincón
Jalostotitlán

GUANAJUATO
León
Ciudad de Dolores Hidalgo
Guanajuato
S. Miguel de Allende
Silao
Irapuato
Salamanca
Valle de Santiago
La Piedad
Celaya
Salvatierra
Acámbaro
Morolеón

QUERÉTARO
Querétaro
San Juan del Río

HIDALGO
Pachuca de Soto
Mineral del Monte
Tulancingo
Huauchi

COLIMA
Manzanillo
Colima
Tecomán
P. N. PICO DE TANCÍTARO

MICHOACÁN
Zamora de Hidalgo
Jacona
Jiquilpan
Uruapan del Progreso
Pátzcuaro
Zitácuaro
Ciudad Hidalgo
Apatzingán de la Constitución
2764
L. Infiernillo
2808
L. de Cuitzeo
P. N. BOSENCHEVE
Morelia
Heroica Zitácuaro
P. N. NEVADO DE TOLUCA
Tenancingo de Degollado

Ciudad de México
Toluca
Ciudad de Lerdo
MEXICO
Teotihuacán
Tlalnepantla
Tlalpan
Xochimilco
POPOCATÉPETL · 5452
IXTACÍHUATL · 5286
Cuernavaca
Zacatepec

TLAXCALA
Cholula
Puebla
Atlixco
MORELOS
Cuautla Morelos
Izúcar de Matamoros
Jojutla de Juárez

PUEBLA

GUERRERO
Taxco de Alarcón
Iguala de la Independencia
Atoyac
Chilpancingo de los Bravos
Tlapa de Comonfort
2840
Melchor Ocampo
Bahía de Petacalco
Zihuatanejo
Balsas
3703
Sierra Madre
Acapulco de Juárez
Puerto Esc

Poza Rica
Tuxp
Papa de Ola

53

Tropic of Cancer

Arch. de Sabana

Great Bahama Bank

La Habana
Marianao
Guanabacoa
Matanzas
Guanajay
Artemisa
Güira
de
Melena
Cárdenas
Jovellanos
Colón
L A
H A B A N A Güines
M A T A N Z A S
Sagua la Grande
V I L L A
C L A R A
Remedios
Caibarién
Placetas
Cayo
Romano

P I N A R
D E L
R Í O
Santa Clara
Cruces
Cienfuegos
Cabaiguán
Morón
200 m
Arch. de Camagüey
Great
Ragged Is.

Pinar
del Río
Golfo de
Batabanó
Península
de Zapata
C I E N F U E G O S
SAN JUAN
1156
Sancti
Spíritus
Trinidad
SANCTI SPÍRITUS
C I E G O
D E
Á V I L A
Ciego
de Ávila
C A M A G Ü E Y
Nuevitas

La Fé
Santa Fé
Arch. de los Canarreos
Isla de Pinos
Florida
Camagüey
Golfo de
Ana Maria
Vertientes
San Pedro
Saramaguacán
Puerto Padre
Victoria
de las
Tunas
Gibara
Banes

C U B A
Cayos de los
12 Leguas
L A S
T U N A S
Holguín
HOLGUÍN
Sagua de Tánamo
Baracoa

Jardines de la Reina
Laberinto de los
12 Leguas
G R A N M A
Salado
Bayamo
S A N T I A G O
Guantánamo
GUANTÁNAMO
Guantánamo

Manzanillo
Palma Soriano
D E C U B A
San Luis

Sierra
Maestra
2005
**Santiago
de Cuba**
Guantánamo
Bay

C
A
R
I
B
B
E
A
N

Little Cayman
Cayman Brac
CAYMAN ISLANDS

Georgetown
Grand Cayman
C A Y M A N
T R E N C H
Jérémie

Montego Bay
Port Antonio
HAITI

Mandeville
May
Pen.
Blue Mts.
2256
Jamaica
Channel

S
E
A
Spanish
Town
Kingston

JAMAICA

Same scale as main map
80°W
75°W

G U L F   O F   M E X I C O

Cabo
Catoche

Progreso
Tizimín
Puerto
Juárez

Mérida
Y U C A T Á N
Muna
Mayapan
Chichén Itza

Campeche
Uxmal
Ticul
I. de Cozumel

Enríquez
Yucatán Península
Bahía de la
Ascensión

Veracruz
Llave
Bahía de Campeche
Q U I N T A N A
R O O

Alvarado
Ciudad del Carmen
L. de
Términos
C A M P E C H E
Escárcega
de Matamoros
Ciudad
Chetumal
Laguna
de
Bacalar
Banco
Chinchorro

Tierra Blanca
San Andrés Tuxtla
Candelaria
Hondo
Ambergris
Cay

Coatzacoalcos
T A B A S C O
Belize
Turneffe Is.

Minatitlán
Acayucan
Los Choapas
Villahermosa
Grijalva
Palenque
BELIZE
Belize
New
Belmopan

xaca
Juárez
I S T M O
D E
Presa de
Malpaso
Bonampak
Yaxchilán
L. Petén Itzá
Flores
Maya Mountains
Gulf of
Honduras

ablo Huixtepec
TEHUANTEPEC
Matías Romero
Tuxtla
Gutiérrez
San Cristóbal
de las Casas
Lacantún
Islas de la Bahía

Ixtepec
Juchitán de
Zaragoza
C H I A P A S
Venustiano
Carranza
Comitán de
Domínguez
San Pedro
Gulf of
Honduras

Sto. Domingo
Tehuantepec
L.
Superior
Mar
Muerto
Arriaga
Chixoy
GUATEMALA
Puerto Cortés
Puerto
Barrios
Tela
La Ceiba

3139
Salina
Cruz
Tonalá
Sierra
Altos
Cuchumatanes
3993
L. de
Izabal
San
Pedro
Sula
Olanchito

Golfo de
Tehuantepec
200 m
Madre
2948
Cobán
Sa. de Chuacús
Motagua
2858
Zacapa
Chiquimula
Santa Rosa de Copán
Yoro
Juticalpa

Puerto Ángel
Huixtla
Tapachula
Totonicapán
Quezaltenango
4210
Huehuetenango
Sololá
El Progreso
Antigua
Guatemala
Sa. de las Minas
El Progreso
Santa Bárbara
HONDURAS
Comayagua

95°W

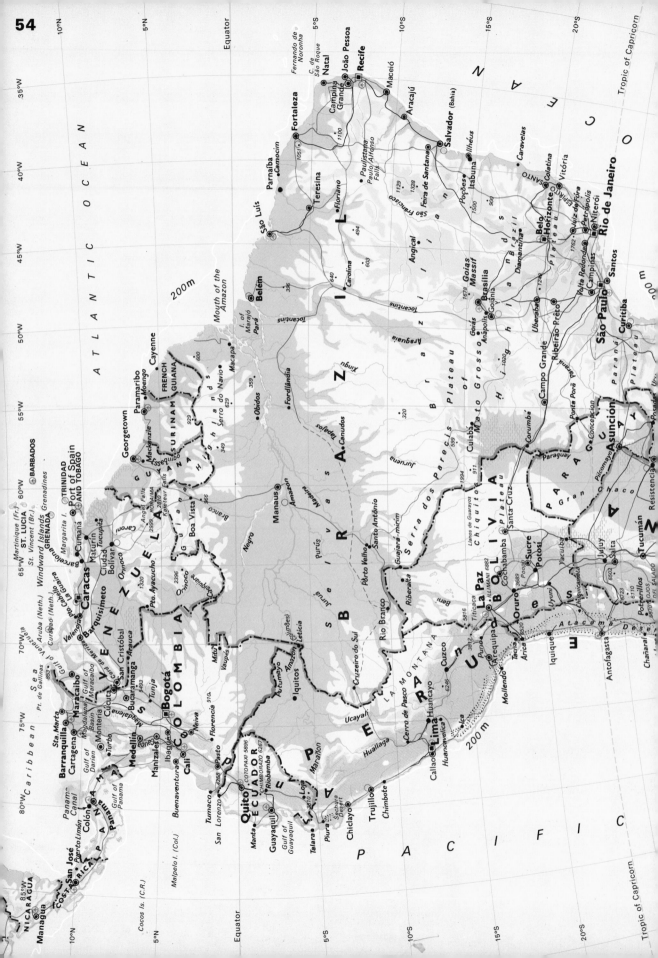

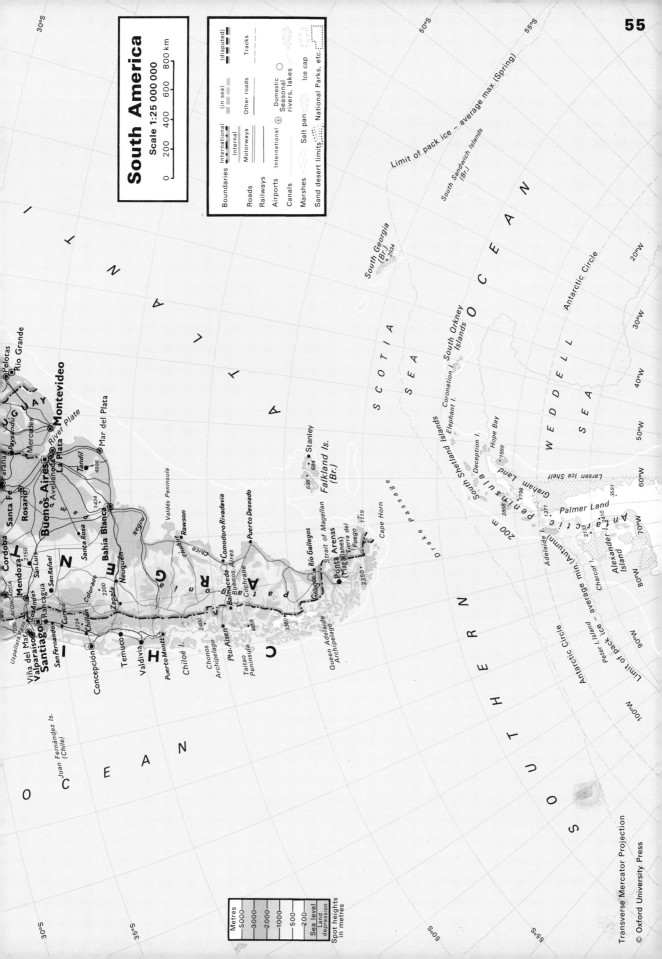

South America

Scale 1:25 000 000

0 200 400 600 800 km

Boundaries — International
— Internal
— (in sea)
— (disputed)

Roads — Motorways
— Other roads
— Tracks

Railways

Airports ⊕ International
⊕ Domestic

Canals

Marshes — Salt pan
— Seasonal rivers, lakes
○ Ice cap

Sand desert limits
National Parks, etc.

Pelotas
Rio Grande
Montevideo
Paysandú
Mercedes
La Plata
River Plate
Mar del Plata
Santa Fe
Córdoba
Rosario
Buenos Aires
Avellaneda
Tandil
4998
1434
Santa Rosa
San Luis
Mendoza
San Rafael
ACONCAGUA 7035
Uspallata Pass
Los Andes
Rancagua
Valparaíso
Viña del Mar
Santiago
San Fernando
Concepción
Chillán
Curicó
774
Talca
Temuco
Valdivia
Puerto Montt
Chiloé I.
Chonos Archipelago
Taitao Peninsula
Queen Adelaide Archipelago
Neuquén
Zapala
2150
2200
2400
Colorado
Negro
Chubut
Chico
Rawson
Valdés Peninsula
Comodoro Rivadavia
Puerto Deseado
Balmaceda
Pto. Aisén
L. Cochrane
4058
3380
2350
Río Gallegos
Gallegos
Strait of Magellan
Punta Arenas
(Magallanes)
Tierra del Fuego
1119
Cape Horn
Stanley
Falkland Is.
(Br.)
698
684
Drake Passage

PATAGONIA
ANDES

Juan Fernández Is.
(Chile)

OCEAN

SOUTHERN

SCOTIA SEA

OCEAN

South Georgia
(Br.)
2934

South Sandwich Islands
(Br.)

Limit of pack ice – average max. (Spring)

South Orkney Islands
Coronation I.
South Shetland Islands
Elephant I.
Deception I.
Hope Bay
1999

WEDDELL SEA

Larsen Ice Shelf
3587

Palmer Land

Graham Land
1798
2898

Antarctic Peninsula

Alexander Island
2133
Charcot I.
Adelaide I.
1371
210

200 m

Limit of pack ice – average min. (Autumn)

Peter I. Island

Antarctic Circle

Antarctic Circle

30°S
35°S

50°S
55°S
60°S

20°W
30°W
40°W
50°W
60°W
70°W
80°W
90°W
100°W

50°S
55°S

Metres
5000
3000
2000
1000
500
200
Sea level
Land depression

Spot heights in metres

Transverse Mercator Projection

© Oxford University Press

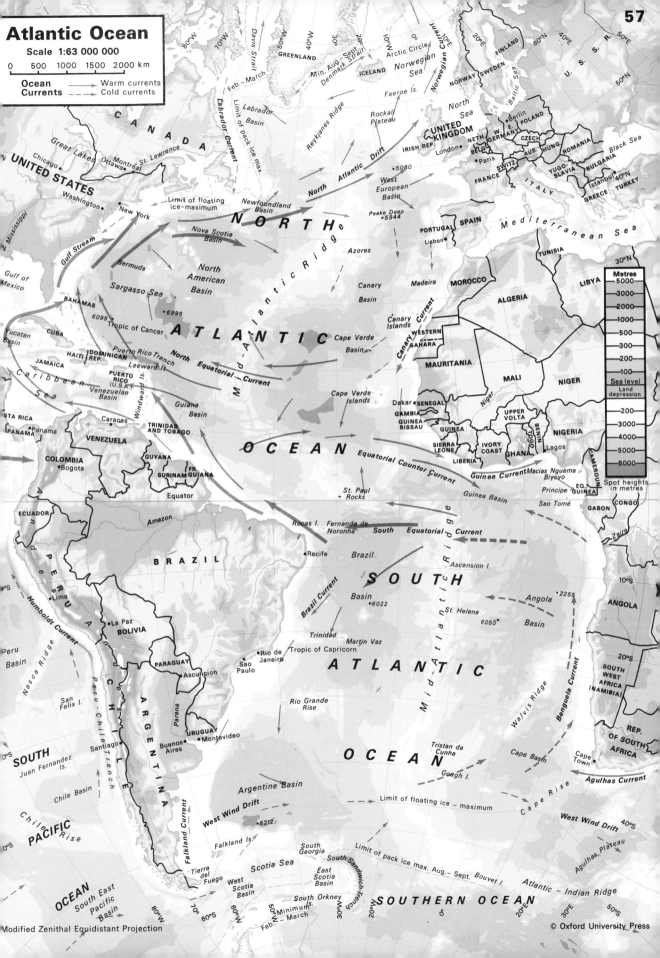

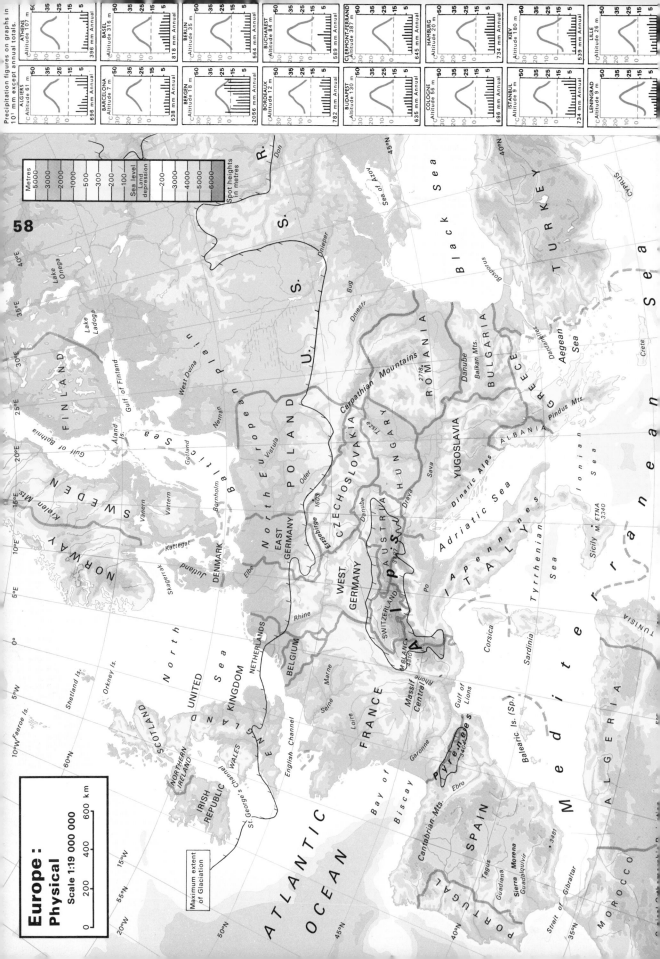

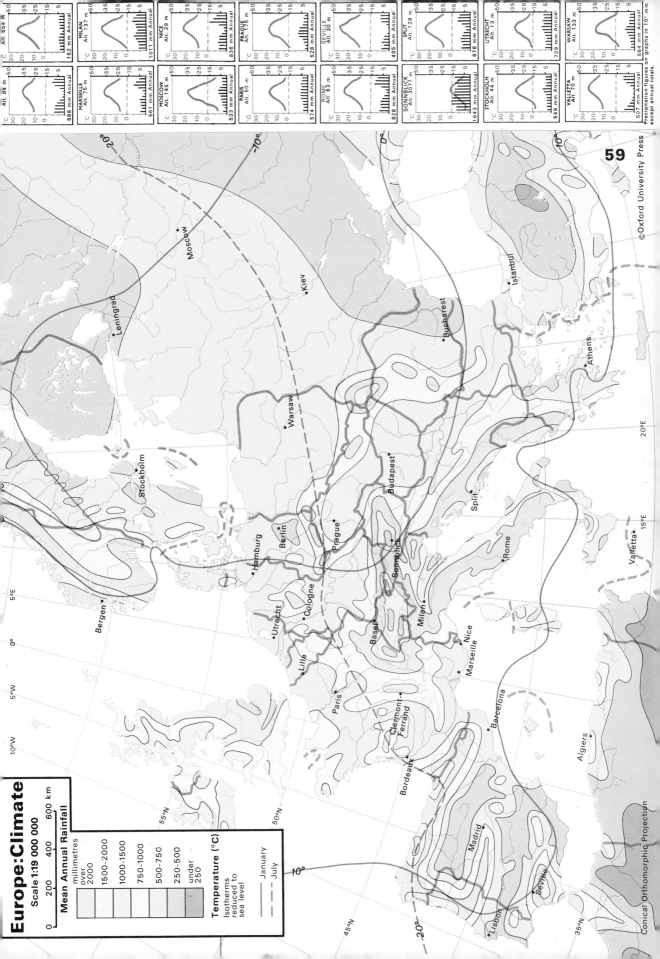

Europe:Climate
Scale 1:19 000 000

0 200 400 600 km

Mean Annual Rainfall

millimetres
- over 2000
- 1500–2000
- 1000–1500
- 750–1000
- 500–750
- 250–500
- under 250

Temperature (°C)

Isotherms reduced to sea level
- January
- July

Climate station graphs (altitude / mean annual precipitation):
- MILAN Alt. 137 m — 1011 mm Annual
- NICE Alt. 29 m — 836 mm Annual
- PRAGUE Alt. 175 m — 528 mm Annual
- SEVILLE Alt. 30 m — 495 mm Annual
- SPLIT Alt. 128 m — 876 mm Annual
- UTRECHT Alt. 13 m — 729 mm Annual
- WARSAW Alt. 133 m — 564 mm Annual
- (Alt. 654 m) — 162 mm Annual
- (Alt. 98 m) — 688 mm Annual
- MARSEILLE Alt. 75 m — 561 mm Annual
- MOSCOW Alt. 145 m — 533 mm Annual
- PARIS Alt. 50 m — 574 mm Annual
- ROME Alt. 8 m — 828 mm Annual
- SONNBLICK Alt. 3077 m — 1643 mm Annual
- STOCKHOLM Alt. 44 m — 549 mm Annual
- VALLETTA Alt. 70 m — 507 mm Annual

Precipitation figures on graphs in 10¹ mm except annual totals.

59

© Oxford University Press

Conical Orthomorphic Projection

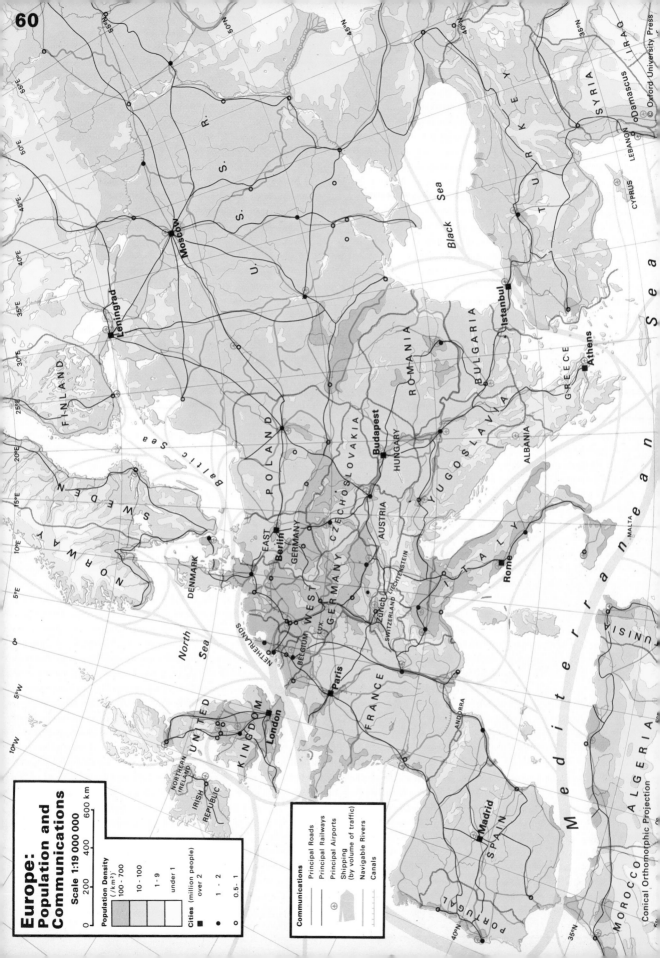

60

Europe: Population and Communications

Scale 1:19 000 000

0 200 400 600 km

Population Density (/km²)
- 100 - 700
- 10 - 100
- 1 - 9
- under 1

Cities (million people)
- ■ over 2
- ● 1 - 2
- ○ 0.5 - 1

Communications
- Principal Roads
- Principal Railways
- ⊕ Principal Airports
- Shipping (by volume of traffic)
- Navigable Rivers
- Canals

Conical Orthomorphic Projection

© Oxford University Press

Place names:

Moscow
Leningrad
Berlin
East Berlin
Budapest
Istanbul
Athens
Rome
Paris
London
Madrid
Zürich

FINLAND
SWEDEN
NORWAY
DENMARK
U. S. S. R.
POLAND
EAST GERMANY
WEST GERMANY
CZECHOSLOVAKIA
NETHERLANDS
BELGIUM
LUX.
FRANCE
SWITZERLAND
LIECHTENSTEIN
AUSTRIA
HUNGARY
ROMANIA
YUGOSLAVIA
BULGARIA
ALBANIA
GREECE
ITALY
SPAIN
PORTUGAL
ANDORRA
UNITED KINGDOM
NORTHERN IRELAND
IRISH REPUBLIC
TURKEY
SYRIA
LEBANON
CYPRUS
IRAQ
Damascus
MOROCCO
ALGERIA
TUNISIA
MALTA

North Sea
Baltic Sea
Black Sea
Mediterranean Sea

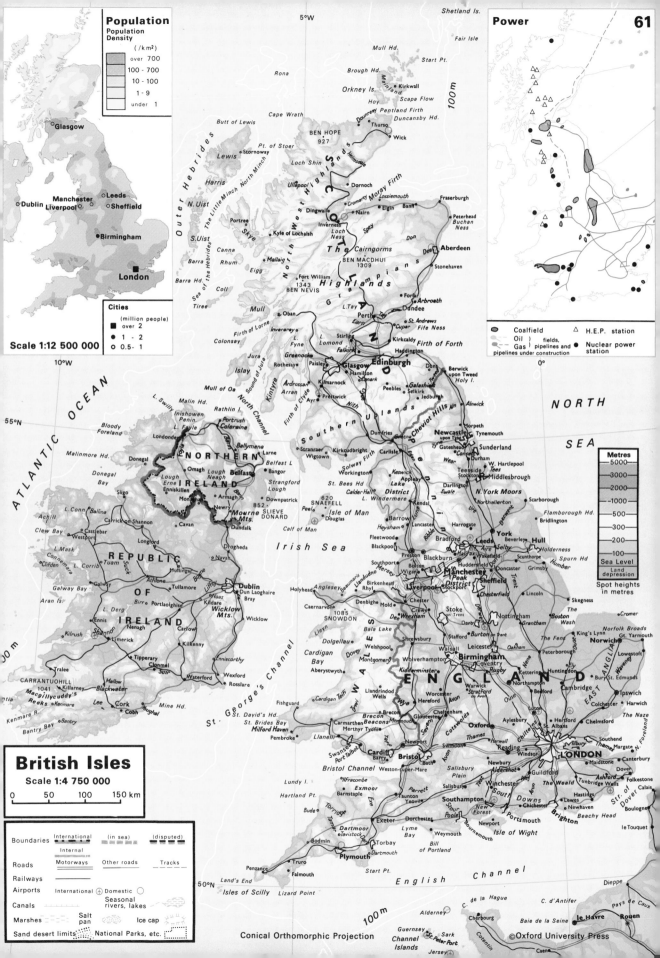

Great Britain

Scale 1:2 200 000

0   35   70 km

Metres
5000 · 3000 · 2000 · 1000 · 500 · 300 · 200 · 100 · Sea level · depression

Spot heights in metres

Boundaries
International
Internal (disputed)

Roads
Motorways
Other roads

Railways
International

Airports
Domestic

Canals
Seasonal rivers, lakes · Ice cap

Marshes
Salt pans

Sand desert limits
National Parks, etc.

North Sea

Irish Sea

North Channel

Firth of Clyde

Inner Hebrides

Map of Great Britain showing towns, counties, and physical features including: Aberdeen, Dundee, Perth, Stirling, Glasgow, Edinburgh, GRAMPIAN, Cairngorm Mts., Ben Macdhui 1309, Ben Nevis 1343, Fort William, Oban, Mull, Islay, Jura, Arran, Kintyre, LOTHIAN, FIFE, CENTRAL, STRATHCLYDE, DUMFRIES, GALLOWAY, BORDERS, Berwick upon Tweed, The Cheviot 816, NORTHUMBERLAND, Newcastle upon Tyne, TYNE & WEAR, Sunderland, DURHAM, Hartlepool, Middlesbrough, CLEVELAND, TEESSIDE, Carlisle, CUMBRIA, Lake District, Scafell 978, Helvellyn 950, Lancaster, LANCS, Blackpool, Preston, Blackburn, Bolton, Huddersfield, Leeds, Bradford, Wakefield, Halifax, York, NORTH YORKSHIRE, Yorkshire Dales, North York Moors, Harrogate, Ripon, Scarborough, Whitby, Bridlington, HUMBERSIDE, Hull, Kingston upon Hull, Scunthorpe, Grimsby, Flamborough Hd., Holderness, Humber, Spurn Hd., Isle of Man, Douglas, Snaefell 620, NORTHERN IRELAND, Belfast, ANTRIM, DOWN, Newry, Mourne Mts., Slieve Donard 852, Strangford Lough, Lough Neagh, Dundalk Bay, LOUTH, MEATH, Hamburg, Bergen & Oslo

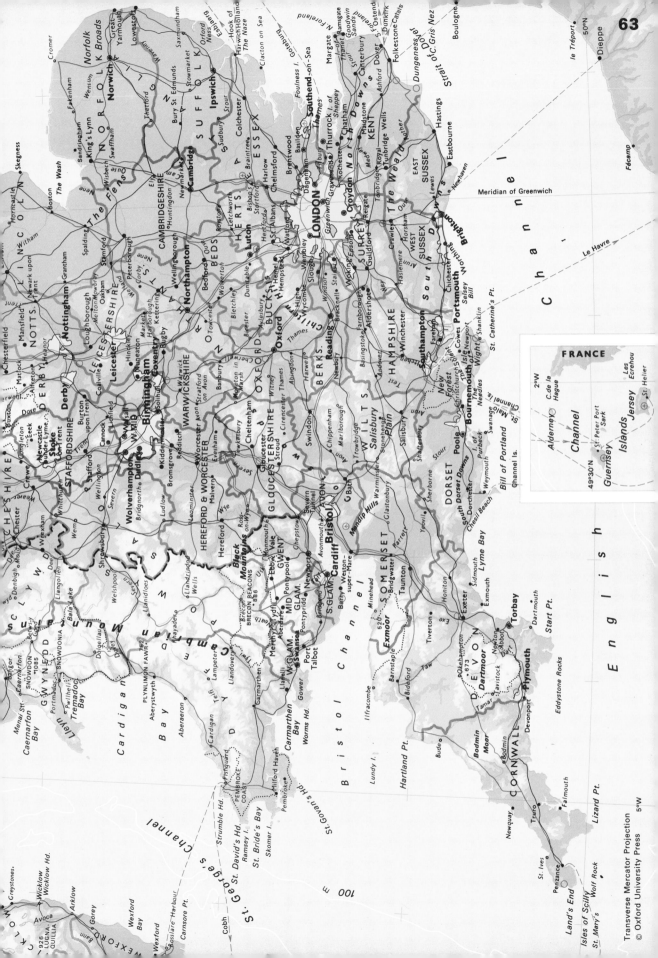

Transverse Mercator Projection
© Oxford University Press

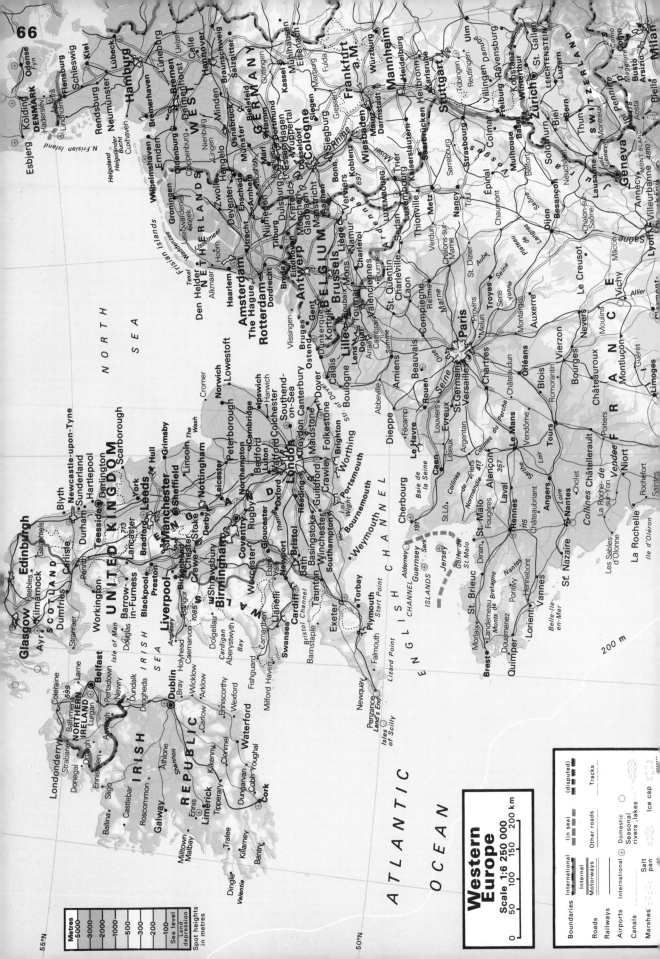

Conical Orthomorphic Projection

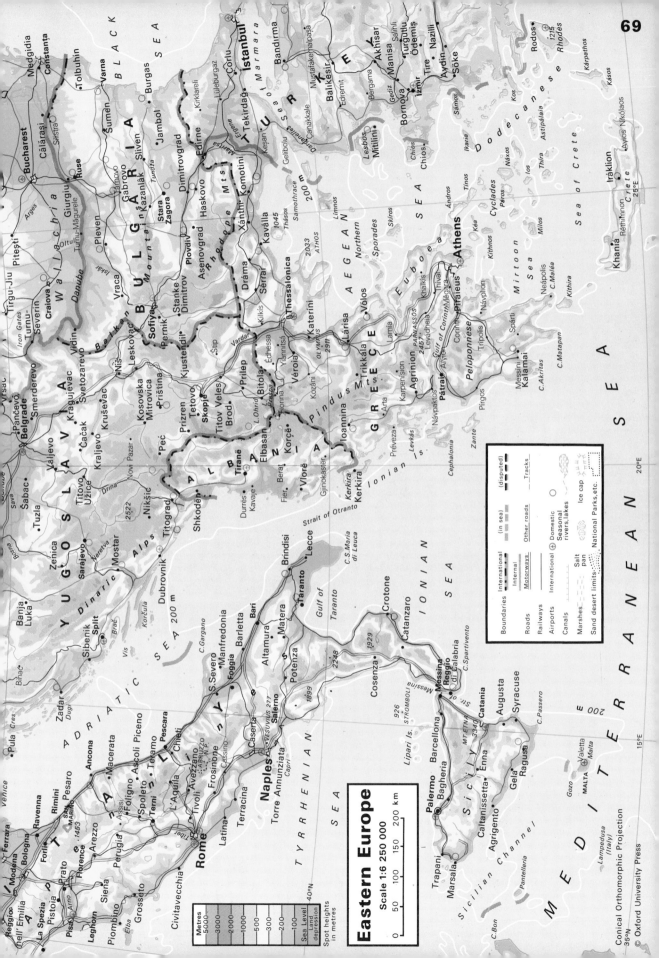

Eastern Europe

Scale 1:6 250 000

Conical Orthomorphic Projection

© Oxford University Press

Boundaries
International
Internal
(disputed)

Roads
Motorways
(in sea)
Other roads
Tracks

Railways
International

Airports
Domestic

Canals

Seasonal
rivers, lakes

Marshes
Salt pan
Ice cap

Sand desert limits
National Parks, etc.

Scandinavia and Iceland

Scale 1:6 250 000

0 50 100 150 200 km

Metres	
5000	
3000	
2000	
1000	
500	
300	
200	
100	
Sea level	
Land depression	
Spot heights in metres	

Boundaries	International	Internal	(disputed)
Roads	Motorways	Other roads	Tracks
Railways			
Airports	International	Domestic	
Canals		Seasonal rivers, lakes	
Marshes		Salt pan	
Sand desert limits		Ice cap	National Parks, etc.

BARENTS SEA

ARCTIC OCEAN

WHITE SEA

U. S. S. R.

R. S. F. S. R.

FINLAND

GULF OF BOTHNIA

NORWAY

SWEDEN

ICELAND

Greenland Sea

Severomorsk
Murmansk
Polyarnyy
Kirkenes
Monchegorsk 1120
Kirovsk
Apatity
Kandalaksha
Kola Pen.
Kola
Olenegorsk
955
1114
Lake Imandra
Tuoma
Pechenga
Rybachiy Pen.
Varangerfjorden
Vadsø
Vardø
637
Varanger Pen.
Tana
Laksefjorden
North Cape
Hammerfest
Nordkyn
Porsangerfjorden
Kvalsund
711
Sørøya
1067
Alta
Alta
Kautokeino
Finnmarks-vidda
Jies'- javr'i
1048
Inari
Inari
Ivalo
Lemmenjoen Nat. Park
Maanselka
Pallas Ounastunturin Nat. Park
Saariselka
Lokan Reservoir
Lokka
Portipahta
Maltion Nature Park
Ulangan Nat. Park
L. Vilikka
L. Kuusamo
432
Pyaozero
Pyavozero
L. Topozero
Voynitsa
Kalevala
Kuhmo
Lyeksa L.
409
Sortavala
Nurmes
Joensuu
Outokumpu
Pielinen
Lieksa
Pyhäselkä
Hauki L.
Savonlinna
Ori L.
Pihlaja L.
Sortavala

Rovaniemi
Kemijärvi
Kemi L.
Kemi
Sodankylä
Ounas
Muonio
Torne
Macmio
Kalix
Övertorneå
Haparanda
Torneå
Kemi
Tornio
355
Kuopio
Iisalmi
Suonenjoki
Varkaus
Pieksämäki
Mikkeli
Puula L.
Seinäjoki
Jyväskylä
210
Äänekoski
Kurikka
Näsi L.
Lapua
Kokkola
125
Pietarsaari
Vaasa
Ylivieska
Raahe
Oulu
Oulu
Oulujoki
Livo
Pudasjärvi
Iijo
Vaala
Vaala L.
Hailuoto
Pack ice – average Nov – May

Tromsø
Tromsøysund
Ringvass
Kvaløy
Vannøy
Senja
Andøya
Andfjorden
Harstad
Vesterfjorden
1117
Narvik
1740
1901
2117
Kiruna
Malmberget
Gällivare
697
Muddus Nationalpark
Jokkmokk
Stora Lule L.
2090
2042
Sarek Nationalpark
1915
Peljekaise Nationalpark
1694
1738
Lapland
Lofoten Islands
2000 Islands
Bodø
Bodin
Rausjen
1754
Skjerstad
Mo i Rana
Mosjøen
1912
Arvidsjaur
Arjeplog
L. Hornan
Storuman L.
Vinde
Sorsele
Skellefte
Storuman
Ume
Lycksele
Vilhelmina
Åsele
1588
Angerman
Junsele
1703
Draggan
1337
Strömsund
Stor L.
577
Östersund
1010
Skellefteå
Skellefteå
Burträsk
Umeå
Vännäs
Vindeln
Nordmaling
Örnsköldsvik
Kramfors
Sollefteå
Härnösand
Indal
Ljungan
Sundsvall
Ljus
Stor L.
Åreskutan
Sånfjället Nationalpark
Grong
Namsos
676
Vikna
Rørvik
Vega
Vega
Dønna
Arctic Circle
Sandnessjøen

Trondheim
Orkanger
Levanger
Steinkjer
Verdal
1459
Stjørdalshalsen
Snåsavatn
Berkåk
Røros
Femund
Femunden L.
1332
Kali L.
1667
Sundalsøra
Dovre-fjell
1883
Dombås
2083
2470
Andalsnes
Molde
Ålesund
Borgund
Kristiansund
Smøla
Hitra
Frøya
Frohavet
Froøya
Trollheimen
Reinen
Oppdal

Iceland

Reykjavík
Keflavík
Hafnarfjordhur
Kópavogur
Akranes
Faxa Bay
Stykkisholmur
Breidha Fjord
Ísafjördhur
Grimsey
Húsavík
Akureyri
Siglufjördhur
Seydhisfjördhur
Neskaupstadhur
Höfn
Vatnajökull
Langjökull
Hofsjökull
1765
Thjorsa
Hekla 1491
Mýrdalsjökull
Vestmannaeyjar
Surtsey
Kópavogur
Arctic Circle

ARCTIC OCEAN

70°N
65°N
65°N
35°E
30°E
25°E
20°E
15°E
20°W
15°W

Leningrad
Pushkin
Kronstadt
Gatchina
Siverskiy
Luga
Slantsy
Pskov
Ostrov
Plyussa
Lake
Pskov
Lake
Peipus
Tartu
318
271
Aluksne
Valga
Viljandi
Pärnu
Kingisepp
Gulf
of
Riga

R. S. F. S. R.
Opochka
Veltkya
Drissa
Novopolotsk
Polotsk
West. Dvina
Lepel
Borisov
Minsk
S. S. R.
Slutsk
Soligorsk
Molodechno
BYELORUSSIAN
Baranovichi
Slonim
Pinsk
Sarny
Lutsk

Helsinki
(Helsingfors)
Hyvinkää
Karhula
Kotka
Hamina
Rihimäki
Kerava
Porvoo
Järvenpää
Espoo
Turku
Salo
Lohja
Forssa
Pälsiö
Hanko
Maarianhamina
Mariehamn
Åland
Islands

G U L F   O F   F I N L A N D
Kotkla Yarve Sillamäe
Yarve
Rakvere Kiviili
Tallinn
Paide
Haapsalu
Kärdla
Hiiumaa
Viljandi
Võru
Avinekste
Cēsis
Valmiera
Vidzeme

E S T O N I A N   S. S. R.
Saaremaa
Kingisepp
Riga
Yurmala
Jelgava
Tukums
Šiauliai
LATVIAN S. S. R.
Daugava
Jēkabpils
Daugavpils
Panevēžys
Ukmergė
Kaunas
Neman
LITHUANIAN S. S. R.
Plunge
Venta
Kuldīga
Liepāja
Ventspils
Klaipeda
Kurškiy Zaliv
Sovetsk
Chernyakhovsk
Gusev
Kaliningrad
R. S. F. S. R.
Kapsukas
Grodno

Vilnius
Vilnius
Lida
Ešua
Olsztyn
Ełk
L. Mamry
L. Śniardwy
Gusev
Narew
BIELIEJA
N.P.
Kobrin
Brest
Bug
Pripet
Chełm
Lublin
Narew
Hajnówka
Białystok
Siedlce
Grudziądz
Mława
Warta
Warsaw
Żyrardów
Pruszków
Łódź
Tomaszów
Mazowiecki
Radom
Starachowice
Radomsko

N O R T H   S E A

Bergen
Haugesund
Stavanger
Sandnes
Egersund
Farsund
Mandal
Kristiansand
Arendal
Grimstad
Risør
Flekkefjord
Otra
Sira
525
Dalane
Jæren
Oslo
Drammen
Kongsberg
1431
Skien
Porsgrunn
Horten
Tønsberg
Sandefjord
Larvik
Kragerø
Moss
Ski
Sarpsborg
Fredrikstad
Halden
Lillestrøm
Kongsvinger
Elverum
1876
Hamar
Gjøvik
Mjøsa
Gol
Gjøvik
Hønefoss
324
Glåma
1460
Geilo
Hardangervidda
Hardanger
vidda
Odda
Ulvik
Voss
642
Klar
Siljan
Falun
Borlänge
Ludvika
Avesta
Dal
Gävle
Sandviken
Uppsala
Norrtälje
Stockholm
Södertälje
Nynäshamn
Nyköping
Katrineholm
Eskilstuna
Enköping
Västerås
L. Mälar
424
Arboga
Örebro
Kumla
Finspång
Motala
Linköping
Norrköping
L. Vättern
378
Mjölby
Tranås
Nässjö
Vetlanda
Nybro
Oskarshamn
Kalmar
Västervik
Borgholm
Öland
Visby
Gotland
Fårön

Karlstad
Kristinehamn
Arvika
Säffle
Åmål
L. Vänern
Lidköping
Mariestad
Skövde
Falköping
Alingsås
362
Trollhättan
Vänersborg
Uddevalla
Göteborg
Mölndal
Borås
Jönköping
Värnamo
L. Bolmen
Ljungby
226
Halmstad
Falkenberg
Varberg
Kungälv
Kungsbacka
Ängelholm
Hässleholm
Helsingborg
Landskrona
Malmö
Lund
Trelleborg
Ystad
Kristianstad
Karlshamn
Karlskrona
Växjö
Åsnen
Hanö Bay
Bornholm

K a t t e g a t
Skagen
Hjørring
Frederikshavn
Læsø
Grenå
Randers
Aarhus
Skanderborg
Silkeborg
Herning
Viborg
Skive
Thisted
Mors
Nykøbing
Limfjorden
Løgstør
Ålborg
89
Holstebro
Ringkøbing
Ringkøbing
Fjord
Esbjerg
N. Frisian Islands
D E N M A R K
Vejle
Horsens
Fredericia
Kolding
Haderslev
Åbenrå
Sønderborg
Lillebælt
Als
Tønder
Flensburg
Schleswig
Rendsburg
Neumünster

Fyn
Odense
Svendborg
Nyborg
Store Bælt
Korsør
Slagelse
Holbæk
Roskilde
Copenhagen
Køge
Næstved
Vordingborg
Lolland
Falster
Nykøbing
Gedser

Sassnitz
Rügen
Stralsund
Rostock
Warnemünde
Wismar
Lübeck
Lübeck Bay
164
Schwerin
Neubrandenburg
Eberswalde
Neubrandenburg
Neumünster
Hamburg
Lüneburg
Heide
Lüneburger Heide
Harburg
Winsen
Lauenburg
Lübeck

B A L T I C   S E A
Gulf of Gdańsk
Gulf of Danzig
Pomeranian Bay
Hel
Wejherowo
Gdynia
Sopot
Gdańsk
Gdański
Tczew
Starogard Gdański
Elbląg
Malbork
Elbląg
223
Koszalin
Słupsk
Stupsk
Szczecinek
Piła
Notec
Bydgoszcz
Toruń
Włocławek
Płock
Kutno
Inowrocław
Gniezno
Żnin
Kalisz
Ostrów Wielkopolski

Świnoujście
L. Szczecin
Szczecin
Stargard
Szczeciński
Gorzów
Wielkopolski
Warta
Poznań
Leszno
Zielona Góra
P O L A N D
Nowa Sól
Żary
Legnica
Bolesławiec
Wrocław
Görlitz

Oder
Neubrandenburg
Berlin
Potsdam
Brandenburg
Frankfurt
a.d.O.
Wittenberge
Stendal
Neisse
Cottbus
Bautzen
Dresden
Görlitz
Karl-Marx-Stadt
Magdeburg
Halberstadt
Halle
Dessau
Leipzig
Gera
Erfurt
Weissenfels
HARZ
Nordhausen
Weimar
Eisenach
Gotha
Mühlhausen

E A S T   G E R M A N Y

Bremerhaven
Wilhelmshaven
Emden
Oldenburg
Wesermünde
Bremen
Delmenhorst
Verden
Hanover
Hildesheim
Salzgitter
Brunswick
Wolfsburg
Celle
Minden
Göttingen
Kassel
Marburg
Siegburg
Bonn
Siegen
Cologne
Düsseldorf
Wuppertal
Hagen
Essen
Dortmund
Bochum
Duisburg
Bielefeld
Hamm
Münster
Osnabrück
Rheine
Lingen
Nordhorn
Enschede
Hengelo
Almelo
Deventer
Zwolle
Emmen
Groningen
Arnhem
NETHERLANDS

W E S T   G E R M A N Y

Heligoland
Heligoländer Bight
Cuxhaven
Elbe
LÜNEBURGER HEIDE
SÜDHEIDE
Delmenhorst
Wildeshausen

60°N
55°N
Pack ice - average max.
Feb. - March
200 m

Modified Conical Orthomorphic Projection

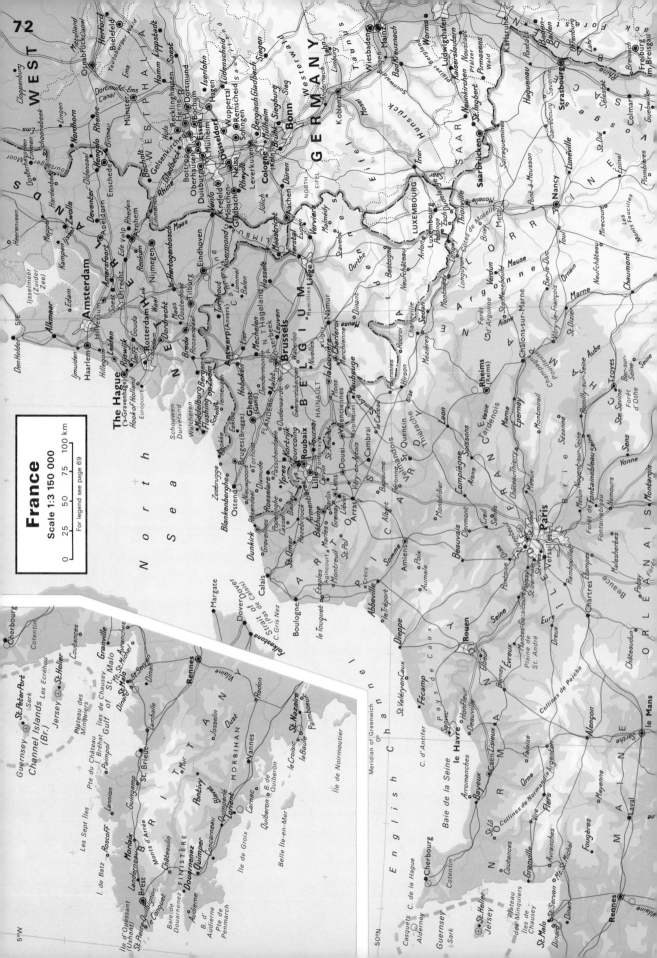

France

Scale 1:3 150 000

For legend see page 69

0   25   50   75   100 km

Conical Orthomorphic Projection

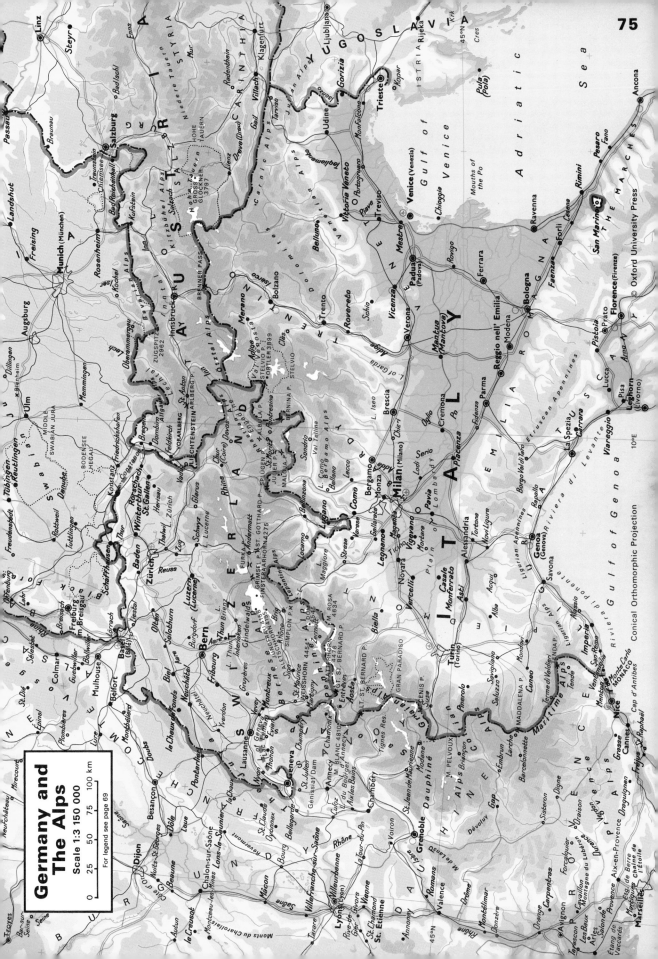

Germany and
The Alps

Scale 1:3 150 000

For legend see page 69

0   25   50   75   100 km

© Oxford University Press

Conical Orthomorphic Projection

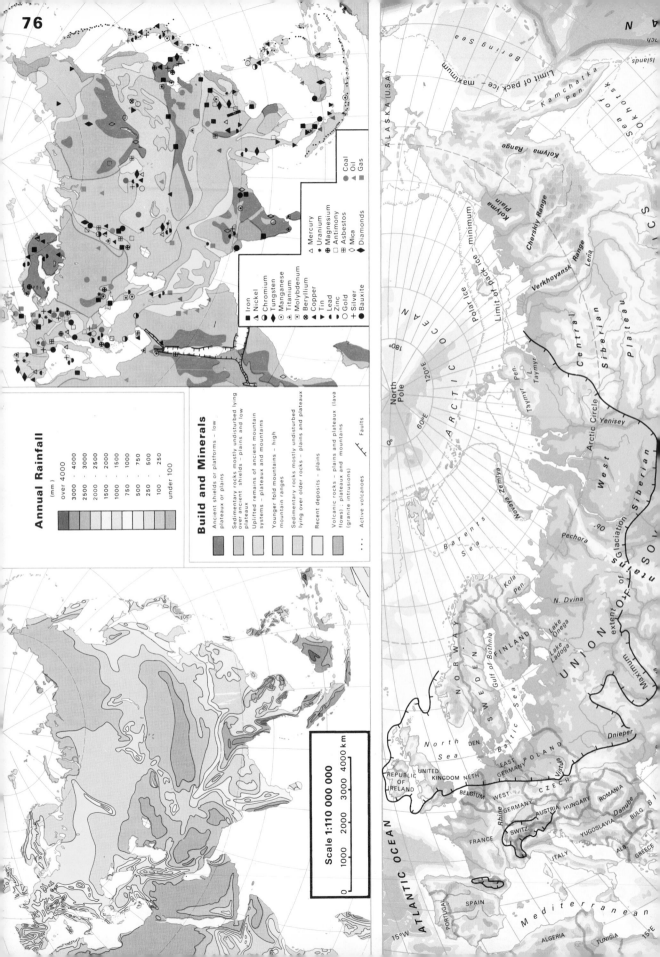

Coal ● **Oil** ▲ **Gas** ■

△ Mercury	△ Magnesium
✳ Uranium	⊕ Antimony
⊕ Magnesium	□ Asbestos
	⊞ Mica
	◆ Diamonds

■ Iron	◆ Molybdenum
◑ Nickel	⊗ Copper
◇ Chromium	▶ Tin
◆ Tungsten	▲ Lead
▲ Manganese	○ Zinc
▲ Titanium	○ Gold
	+ Silver
	● Bauxite

Annual Rainfall

(mm)

over 4000
3000 - 4000
2500 - 3000
2000 - 2500
1500 - 2000
1000 - 1500
750 - 1000
500 - 750
250 - 500
100 - 250
under 100

Build and Minerals

Ancient shields or platforms – low plateaux or plains

Sedimentary rocks mostly undisturbed lying over ancient shields – plains and low plateaux

Uplifted remains of ancient mountain systems – plateaux and mountains

Younger fold mountains – high mountain ranges

Sedimentary rocks mostly undisturbed lying over older rocks – plains and plateaux

Recent deposits – plains

Volcanic rocks – plains and plateaux (lava flows) ; plateaux and mountains (granite intrusions)

▲▲▲ Active volcanoes

⌐⌐⌐ Faults

Scale 1:110 000 000

0 1000 2000 3000 4000 km

ALASKA (U.S.A.)

ARCTIC OCEAN

North Pole

Polar ice – minimum

Limit of pack ice – minimum

Limit of pack ice – maximum

Bering Sea

Kamchatka Pen.

Sea of Okhotsk

Kolyma Range

Cherskiy Range

Verkhoyansk Range

Lena

Central Siberian Plateau

Kolyma Plain

Arctic Circle

Yenisey

West Siberian Plain

UNION OF SOV.

Maximum extent of Glaciation

Novaya Zemlya

Barents Sea

Pechora

N. Dvina

Kola Pen.

Lake Onega

Lake Ladoga

FINLAND

Gulf of Bothnia

NORWAY

SWEDEN

North Sea

Baltic Sea

DEN

POLAND

Dnieper

Vistula

EAST GERMANY

REPUBLIC OF IRELAND

UNITED KINGDOM

NETH

BELGIUM

WEST GERMANY

CZECH.

AUSTRIA

HUNGARY

ROMANIA

Rhine

SWITZ.

Danube

YUGOSLAVIA

BULG.

GREECE

FRANCE

ITALY

ALB.

PORTUGAL

SPAIN

Mediterranean

ATLANTIC OCEAN

ALGERIA

TUNISIA

15°W

15°E

L. Taymyr

Taymyr Pen.

0°

60°E

120°E

180°

Eurasia : Physical
Scale 1:44 000 000

0   1000   2000 km

Zenithal Equal Area Projection of Capricorn
© Oxford University Press

Japan Trench

P A C I F I C

J A P A N
Sea of Japan

Japan Trench

Ryukyu Trench

Ryukyu Is.

Philippine Sea

Philippine Trench

Philippines

Mindanao

Luzon

NORTH KOREA
SOUTH KOREA
KOREA
Yellow Sea
East China Sea
TAIWAN

Wuyi Shan

Si
Hainan

HONG KONG (Br.)

South China Sea

Hwang

Yangtze

C H I N A

Plateau of Tibet

M O N G O L I A

Gobi Desert

Altai Range

Turfan Depr. -154

Tsaidam Swamps

Altyn Tagh

Tien Shan

Lake Balkhash

Kazakh Uplands

Ust Urt Plateau

Aral Sea

Syr

Amu

Hindu Kush

AFGHANISTAN

PAKISTAN

Indus

EVEREST 8848

Himalaya

NEPAL

BHUTAN
Brahmaputra

BANGLADESH

BURMA

Salween

Irrawaddy

VIETNAM

LAOS

Mekong

CAMBODIA

THAILAND

Gulf of Siam

MALAYSIA

SINGAPORE

Malay Pen.

Sumatra

BRUNEI

Iran Mts.

Borneo

Celebes

Sulu Sea

Celebes Sea

Java Sea

I N D O N E S I A

Sunda Islands

Lesser Sunda Islands

Java

Java Trench

Seram Sea

Banda Sea

Halmahera

Timor Sea

Tropic of Cancer

I N D I A

Deccan

Eastern Ghats

Western Ghats

SRI LANKA

Bay of Bengal

Andaman Is.

Andaman Sea

Nicobar Is.

Cocos Basin

Cocos Is.

Lakshadweep

Maldives

Chagos - Laccadive Plateau

Cocos Is.

M I D   I N D I A N
Mid Indian Basin

Equator

I N D I A N   O C E A N

Arabian Sea

Arabian Basin

Carlsberg Ridge

I R A N

IRAQ

Tigris

Euphrates

SYRIA

CYPRUS

ISRAEL

JORDAN

LEB.

SAUDI ARABIA

KUWAIT

Persian Gulf

QATAR

UNITED ARAB EMIRATES

OMAN

Gulf of Aden

Red Sea

EGYPT

Lake Nasser

Nile

SUDAN

SOMALI REP.

Somali Basin

Amirante Islands

Seychelles

Seychelles - Mauritius Plateau

Aldabra Is.

Comoro Is.

MALAGASY REP.

Madagascar

Mauritius

Réunion

Mascarene Basin

Mid Indian Ridge

Tropic of Capricorn

30°N

30°E

90°E

75°E

60°E

Caspian Sea

Metres	
5000	
3000	
2000	
1000	
500	
300	
100	
Sea level	
Land depression	
200	
3000	
4000	
5000	
6000	

Spot heights in metres

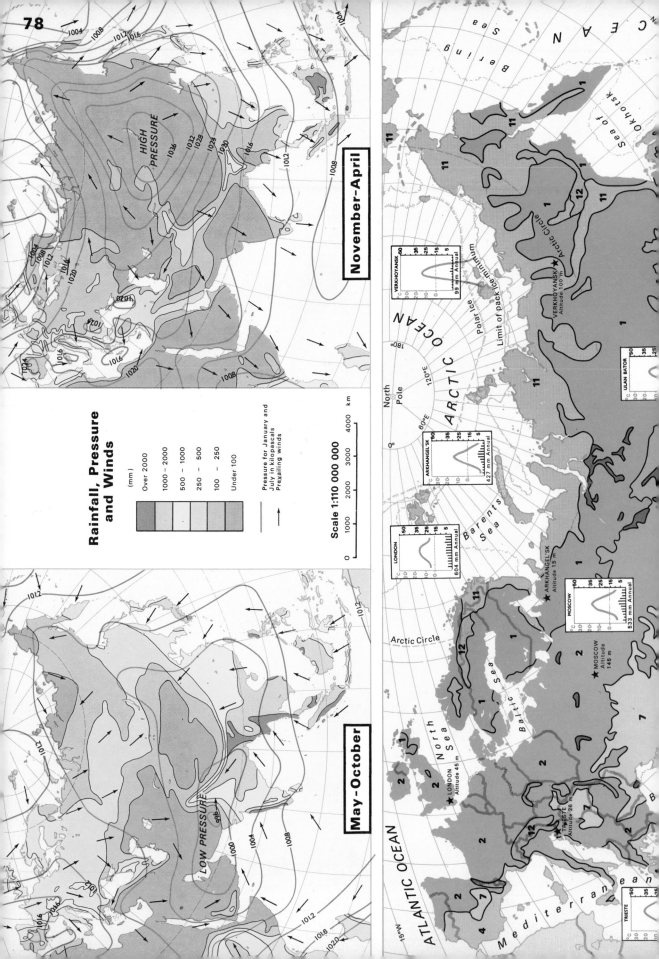

78

Rainfall, Pressure and Winds

November–April

May–October

HIGH PRESSURE

LOW PRESSURE

(mm)

Over 2000
1000 – 2000
500 – 1000
250 – 500
100 – 250
Under 100

Pressure for January and July in kilopascals
Prevailing winds

Scale 1:110 000 000

km

0   1000   2000   3000   4000

ARCTIC OCEAN

North Pole

Polar ice

Limit of pack ice minimum

Bering Sea

Sea of Okhotsk

Barents Sea

Baltic Sea

North Sea

ATLANTIC OCEAN

Mediterranean

Arctic Circle

VERKHOYANSK
VERKHOYANSK Altitude 100 m
99 mm Annual

ARKHANGEL'SK
ARKHANGEL'SK Altitude 15 m
427 mm Annual

LONDON
LONDON Altitude 45 m
604 mm Annual

MOSCOW
MOSCOW Altitude 145 m
533 mm Annual

ULAN BATOR

TRIESTE
TRIESTE Altitude 26 m

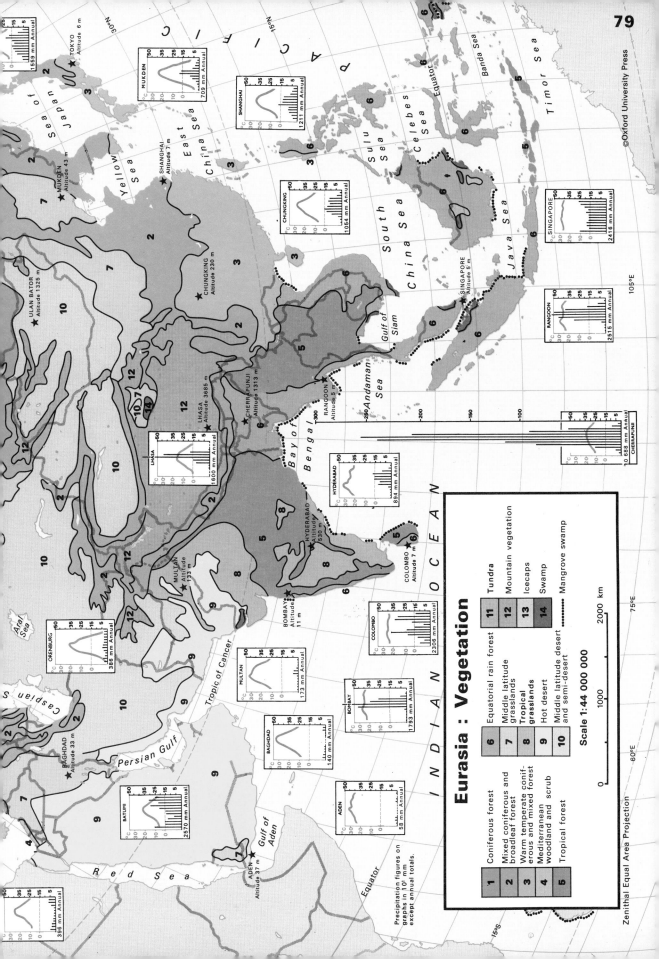

Eurasia : Vegetation

1	Coniferous forest	**6**	Equatorial rain forest	**11**	Tundra
2	Mixed coniferous and broadleaf forest	**7**	Middle latitude grasslands	**12**	Mountain vegetation
3	Warm temperate coniferous and mixed forest	**8**	Tropical grasslands	**13**	Icecaps
4	Mediterranean woodland and scrub	**9**	Hot desert	**14**	Swamp
5	Tropical forest	**10**	Middle latitude desert and semi-desert		Mangrove swamp

Scale 1:44 000 000

0   1000   2000 km

Precipitation figures on graphs in 10¹ mm except annual totals.

©Oxford University Press

Zenithal Equal Area Projection

Political

Membership of the European Economic Community (EEC)

Membership of the Council for Mutual Economic Aid (CMEA)

(1975) Date of independence

Scale 1:110 000 000

0 1000 2000 3000 4000 km

Land Use

Cultivated land
Grazing land
Cultivated land - paddy
Irrigated land
Coniferous forest
Mixed forest
Deciduous forest
Equatorial and Tropical forest
Marsh
Sand desert
Other hot desert
Tundra

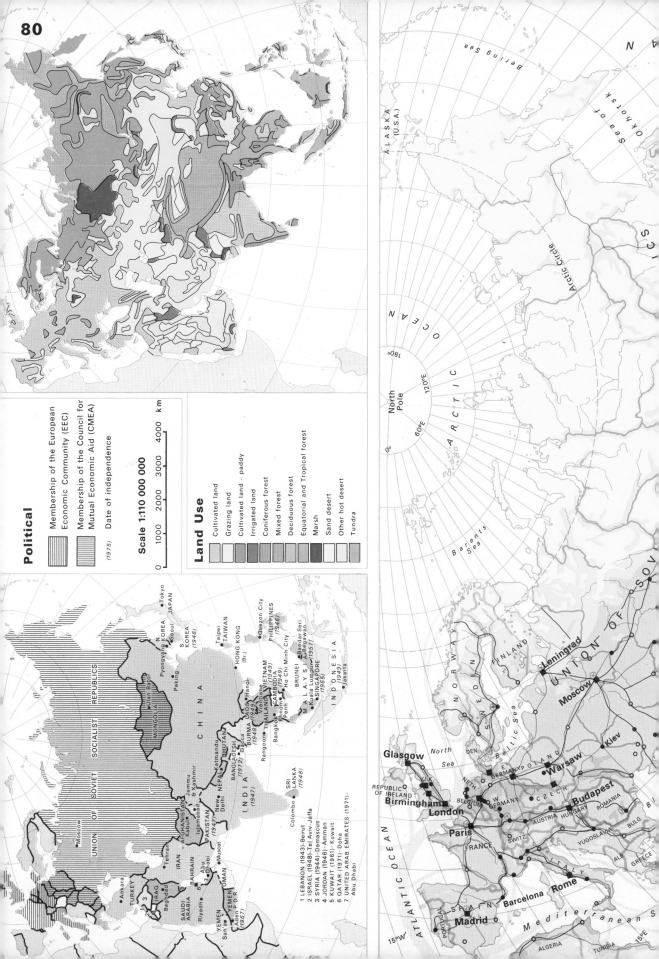

UNION OF SOVIET SOCIALIST REPUBLICS

Moscow
Tehran
IRAN
IRAQ
Baghdad
TURKEY
Ankara
SAUDI ARABIA
Riyadh
BAHRAIN
Abu Dhabi
OMAN
Muscat
YEMEN
San'a
YEMEN P.D.R.
Aden (1967)

AFGHANISTAN
Kabul
Islamabad
PAKISTAN (1947)
Jammu & Kashmir
New Delhi
INDIA (1947)
NEPAL
Katmandu
BHUTAN
BANGLADESH (1972)
Dacca
Colombo
SRI LANKA (1948)

MONGOLIA
Ulan Bator
CHINA
Peking
BURMA (1948)
LAOS
Rangoon
THAILAND
Vientiane
Bangkok
CAMBODIA (1949)
Phnom Penh
VIETNAM (1949)
Hanoi
Ho Chi Minh City

N. KOREA
Pyongyang
S. KOREA (1948)
Seoul
JAPAN
Tokyo
Taipei
TAIWAN
HONG KONG (Br.)
PHILIPPINES (1946)
Quezon City
BRUNEI
Bandar Seri Begawan
MALAYSIA (1957)
Kuala Lumpur
SINGAPORE (1965)
INDONESIA (1949)
Jakarta

1 LEBANON (1943)-Beirut
2 ISRAEL (1948)-Tel Aviv-Jaffa
3 SYRIA (1944)-Damascus
4 JORDAN (1946)-Amman
5 KUWAIT (1961)-Kuwait
6 QATAR (1971)-Doha
7 UNITED ARAB EMIRATES (1971)-Abu Dhabi

ALASKA (U.S.A.)

ARCTIC OCEAN

North Pole

Arctic Circle

Bering Sea
Sea of Okhotsk

Barents Sea

UNION OF SOV...

Leningrad
Moscow
Kiev
Warsaw

NORWAY
SWEDEN
FINLAND
North Sea
Baltic Sea
DEN.
POLAND
E. GERMANY
W. GERMANY
NETH.
BELGIUM
CZECH.
AUSTRIA
HUNGARY
Budapest
ROMANIA
SWITZ.
YUGOSLAVIA
BULG.
ALB.
GREECE
ITALY
Rome
FRANCE
Paris
SPAIN
PORTUGAL
Madrid
Barcelona
ATLANTIC OCEAN
Mediterranean Sea
ALGERIA
TUNISIA

Glasgow
U.K.
REPUBLIC OF IRELAND
Birmingham
London

15°W   15°E

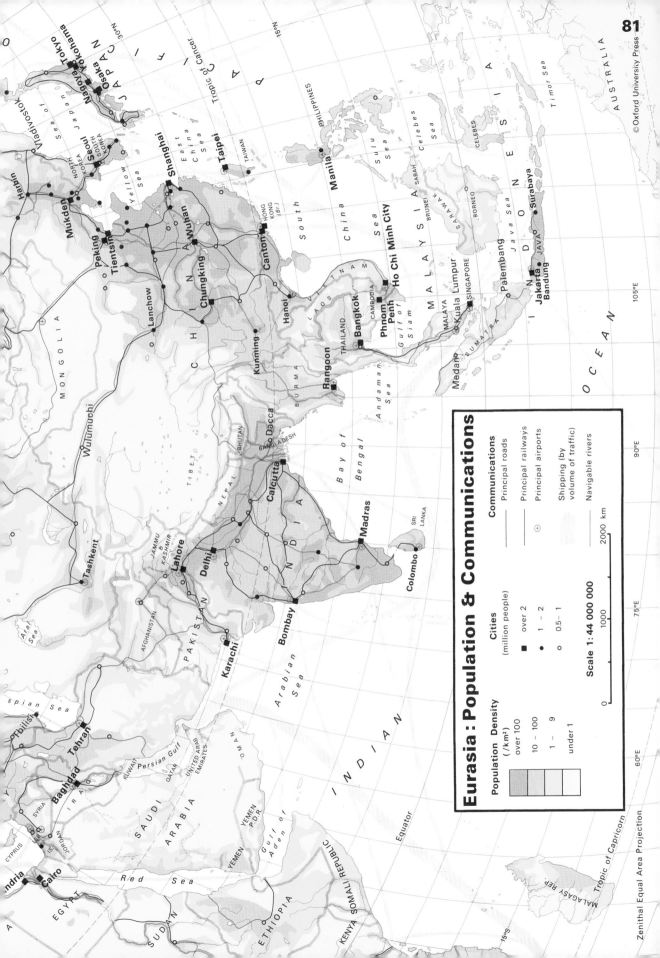

© Oxford University Press

Eurasia : Population & Communications

Communications

— Principal roads

— Principal railways

⊕ Principal airports

Shipping (by volume of traffic)

Navigable rivers

Cities
(million people)

■ over 2

● 1 – 2

○ 0.5 – 1

Scale 1:44 000 000

0   1000   2000 km

Population Density
(/km²)

over 100

10 – 100

1 – 9

under 1

Zenithal Equal Area Projection

North Pole

60°E
100°E

Boundaries   International   (in sea)   (disputed)
       Internal
Roads   Motorways   Other roads   Tracks
Railways
Airports   International   Domestic
Canals   Seasonal rivers, lakes
Marshes   Salt Pan   Ice cap
Sand desert limits   National Parks etc.

A L A S K A

140°E
80°N
180°
75°N
70°N
65°N

Chukchi Sea
C. Lisburne (U.S.)
Pt. Barrow
Bering Strait

Nome
Norton Sound
St Lawrence (U.S.)

B e r i n g   S e a

E a s t   S i b e r i a n   S e a
Wrangel I.
Ayon I.
Ambarchik •Ostrovnoye
•1624
Anadyr
Markovo
Kamenskoye
Korf
Kavecha

O C E A N
Wiese I. (Vize)
Bol'shevik I.
Severnaya Zemlya
C. Chelyuskin
Unnavigable Polar Ice
Novosibirskiye Ostrova
320
Lyakhov Islands
232
Laptev Str.
428

Taymyr Penin.
Taymyr
L. Taymyr •Nordvik
•Tiksi
•Kazachye
•1040
•914
•1847
Yukagir Plateau
Kolyma Plain
•819 Kolyma
Chelskiy Range
2498 3114 •2406
Susuman
Gydan (Kolyma) Range
•1381
•1739
•1850
Shelekov Bay
C.Tolstoy
•3607

Kamchatka
Kronotskiy Bay
Petropavlovsk-Kamchatskiy

Magadan
•Okhotsk
Sea of Okhotsk

Karaul
•Dudinka
•Noril'sk
•1500
Putoran Mts.
Igarka
•Khatanga
•601

Central
Siberian
Plateau

Verkhoyansk Range
•Verkhoyansk
Lena •Sangar

•1044
Vilyuy
Yakutsk
•El'gyey •190
Olekminsk
Dzherba
•Buyoga
Aldan •2101
•2481
•1418
Nikolayevsk
Sakhalin Bay
Sakhalin
Aleksandrovsk-Sakhalinskiy
Tarpeniya Bay
Yuzhno Sakhalinsk
Kholmsk
Wakkanai

F E D E R A T E D   S O C I A L I S T   R E P U B L I C

S. R.

Stony Tunguska
Lower Tunguska
92•
•920
•623
Yeniseysk
Angara
Chuna
Ust'-Kut
Tomsk
Kemerovo
•2178
•2216
Abakan •Minusinsk
Novokuznetsk
•Shalym
Biysk
Leninogorsk
3254

Vitim •Korshunova
Vitim
•812
Lena
•2332
•1728•
Bratsk
•1022
•Zhigalova
Cheremknovo •Usolye
Irkutsk
Lake Baykal
Ulan-Ude
•2248
Kyzyl
•3019
Selenga
Bulagan
Ulan Bator
•4116
Hovd
•2325
•Uliastay
•4030
Altai Range
•3791

•2800
Never
Zeya
Tygda
•Mogocha
Bukachacha
Shilka
Chekunda
•Blagoveshchensk
Bureya
Birobidzhan
Khabarovsk
Komsomolsk-na-Amur
Amgun •524
Amur
•2155
G.of Tartary
•1840

Soviet Harbour
Sikhote Alini Range
1868 •1853

Chita
Aksha
Erensab
Hulun
Nerchinsk
Sherlovaya Gora
Shihchan
Nunkiang
Sitsihar (Tsitsihar)
Chuho
Mutankiang
Harbin (Pinkiang)
Kirin
Changchun
Ch'angch'un
Mukden
Shenyang
Anshan

Khingan
Great
Ussuri
Ussuriysk
Partizansk
Vladivostok

S e a   o f   J a p a n
Sapporo
Muroran
Hakodate
Aomori

H O N S H U

M O N G O L I A
•2505
Aksha
Uldze
Choibalsan
Tamsag Bulag
Sayn Shanda
•3810
Gobi Desert
•2838

Wulumuchi (Urumchi)
•3962 •4252
Hami (Qomul)
Turfan depr. -154
•2809
Ansi
Ala Shan
Yinchwan (Ninghsia)
•2300

I N N E R   M O N G O L I A
Changkiakow (Kalgan)
•716
Huhehot
Paotow
Peking (Peiping)
Tientsin
Shihkiachwang
Taiyuan
Anyang
Loyang
Hwang
Kaifeng
Nanking

NORTH KOREA
•2505
Pyongyang
Nampo
SOUTH KOREA
•1914
Seoul (Kyongsong)
•1573
•1742
Lü-ta
Yentai
Tsingtao
Yellow Sea
East China Sea

Pusan
Hiroshima
Shimonoseki
Kitakyushu
Nagasaki
Kyoto
Kobe
Ryuku Is.
Shikoku
Kyushu

U I G H U R
•3962
Altyn Tagh
Tsaidam Swamps
•6346
•4298
•4194
Lanchow (Kaolan)
Sining
•2530
•4298

U S S U
REGION
C H
90°E
100°E
110°E
115°E
120°E

Chengteh (Jehol)
Yingkow
Po Hai (G.of Chihli)
Süchow (Tungshan)
Hwang
Tsinan
Shanghai

Berezovo · | West · | Ob' · Faktoriye · | Vakh · Yenisey · | Yeniseysk · | Angara 95°E

Polunochnoye · | Khanty-Mansiysk · | Surgut · | Vasyugan · | Asino · Chulym · | Mariinsk Achinsk · | 246 · | Krasnoyarsk

Ivdel' · 151 · | S O C I A L I S T   R E P U B L I C · | Tomsk · Anzhero-Sudzhensk · | Kemerovo · | Chernogorsk · | Minúsinsk

Severoural'sk · | Serov · Tavda · Sos'va · | Tobol'sk · Tavda · | Plain · | Irtysh · | 155 · | Kolyvan' · | Leninsk-Kuznetskiy · | Prokop'yevsk · 2178 · | Novo-kuznetsk · | Abakan · | Western Sayan Mts · 2248

Alapayevsk · Artemovskiy · Kamyshlov · Tyumen' · | Tara · | Kuybyshev · 134 · | Novosibirsk · | Barnaul · | Shalym · | 2930 · Western Yenisey

rdlovsk · Kamensk-Uralskiy · | Omutinskoye · | Novonazyvayevka · Omsk · Tatarsk · | Lake Chany · Ob' · | Biysk · 618 · | Gorno-Altaysk

Kasli · | Kurgan · Makushino · | Kalachinsk · · 117 · | L. Kulundinskoye · | Kosh-Agach · | MONGOLIA

1178 · Zlatoust · Chelyabinsk · Petropavlovsk · Petukhovo · | Ust'Uyskoye · | Kulunda · Pavlodar · | Rubtsovsk · Kolyvan' · | Leninogorsk · 4620 · Žyryanovsk · | Altai

Troitsk · | Kokchetav · 887 · Lake Selety-Tengiz · Danilovka · | Steppe · 351 · | Belousovka · Cherdoyak · | Kosh

Magnitogorsk · Kustanay · | Semiozernoye · Spasskoye · | Irtysh · | Semipalatinsk · Ust'-Kamenogorsk · | L.Zaysan · Black Irtysh

Kartaly · Bredy · Dzhetygara · | Atbasar · | Tselinograd · | 1085 · | Zharma · 386 · | Ulyungur Nor

aymak · | Turgay · | Temir-Tau · Karaganda · | Kazakh Uplands · 1301 · S.S.R. · Ayaguz · | Chuguchak · 2530

Orsk · | Turgay · Ulu-tau · Lake Tengiz · | 1621 · | Andreyevka · Ala Kul' · | Yamatu · | Dzungarian · Dzungaria · 45°N

Khrom-Tau · | Marganets · Atasuskiy · Uspenskiy · | Mointy · Kounradskiy · | 3380 · | Gate · | 5500

t'abr'sk · Emba · | L.Chelkar-Tengiz · | 1137 · Dzhezkazgan · | Balkhash · | Lake Balkhash · | Ebi Nor · | C H I N A

Z A K · | Baykonur · | Hunger Steppe · | 5044 · | Tekely

Aral'sk · | · 59 · | Chu · | Ili · | KHAN TENGRI 7200 · | Tien Shan · Tarim

Aral Sea Surface height 48 m above m.s.l. · | Kazalinsk · | Kzyl-Orda · | Suzak Muyun-Kum · Chu · | Alma-Ata · | 40°N

Turanian Plain · | Syr Darya (Jaxartes) · Kara-tau · | Turkestan · Chulak-Tau · | Frunze · Issyk-Kul' · Rybach'ye · | KIRGIZ S.S.R.

Kyzyl - Kum · | 1029 · | Arys' · Chimkent · | Dzhambul

Khodzheyli · | Tashkent · Namangan Andizhan · Osh · | Tien Shan

Khiva · | · 1923 · Begovat · Angren Kokand · Fergana · | Alai Range · LENIN PEAK 7127 · MT COMMUNISM 7495

Bukhara · Samarkand · | Leninabad · | 5487 · TADZHIK S.S.R. · | Khorog · Pamirs

Chardzhou · · 132 · | Dyushanbe · | 7010 · | TIBET

Ashkhabad · | Kerki · 3342 · | Termez · Faizabad · 1690 · | Hindu Kush

Dâgh · 3414 · Mashhad · | Mary (Merv) · Kirovsk · | Mazar-i-Sharif · | 5203 · Chitral

Kushka · | Maimana · | AFGHANISTAN · 5075 · | Kabul · Jalalabad · | Peshawar · | KASHMIR · 7315

Western U.S.S.R.

Scale 1:12 500 000

0 · 100 · 200 · 300 · 400 km

© Oxford University Press

India, Pakistan, Bangladesh and Sri Lanka

Scale 1:12 500 000

0   100   200   300   400 km

AFGHANISTAN

Hindu Kush

5143 7690

Chitral
Dir
Kunar
Malakand
Kabul
Jalalabad
KHYBER PASS
Peshawar
Kohat
Abbottabad
Islamabad
Rawalpindi
3725
Gilgit
7788
861?
K2
8068 GASHERBRUM
NANGA PARBAT
8126
KARAKORAM PASS
J A M M U
LANAK PASS
Pangong Range
Rudok
ALING KANGRI

Kargil
7154
Srinagar
K A S H M I R
Leh
Ladakh Range
Indus
and
7315
GARTOK

Miram Shah
3788
Bannu
Salt Range
Jhelum
Jammu
Dalhousie
Chamba
Pathankot
HIMACHAL
PRADESH
Indus
SHIPKI
PASS
MANA PASS
Kailas Range
Nyenc

P A K I S T A N
Sulaiman Range
Dera Ismail Khan
Gujranwala
Sialkot
Amritsar
Beas
Ravi
Kailas
Range
Shige

3725
Kandahar
Gardez
Chaman
2707
Qila Saifullah
Quetta
BOLAN PASS
Sibi
Jacobabad
Sukkur
Khairpur
Kalat
2772
Kharan
Khuzdar
Bela
Hyderabad
Karachi
Mouths of the Indus
Rann of Kutch
Tropic of Cancer
G. of Kutch
Okha
Kandla
Bhuj

Quetta
Kohat
Multan
Dera Ghazi Khan
Bahawalpur
Bikaner
Jaisalmer
Jodhpur
Pokaran
R A J A S T H A N
Ajmer
Jaipur
Abu
Udaipur

Lahore
Lyallpur
Kapurthala
Jullundur
Ludhiana
Ambala
Patiala
P U N J A B
Simla
Mussoorie
Dehra Dun
HARIYANA
Saharanpur
Meerut
Delhi
New Delhi
DELHI
Rewari
Alwar
Mathura
Agra

KAMET 7756
NANDA DEVI
7816
1728
7132
Naini Tal
Moradabad
Rampur
Bareilly
Shahjahanpur
Lakhimpur
Bahraich
Sitapur
ANNAPURNA
8078
N E P A L
Kathmandu
MT. EVEREST
8848
KANGCHENJUNGA 8585
Sik
Darjeeling
Birganj
Gorakhpur
Muzaffarpur
Chapra
Purnea
Tsangpo

C H I N
T I B E T

Tanot
Jodhpur
Umarkot
Bela
Kotri

Kota
U.P.
Etawah
Kanpur
Lucknow
Ghaghara
Ganga (Ganges)
Ghazipur
Varanasi
Allahabad
Gaya
Patna
Bhagalpur
Ganga (Ganges)
B I H A R

Ahmedabad
Rajkot
Jamnagar
Porbandar
KATHIAWAR
Bhavnagar
Baroda
Cambay
G. of Cambay

I N D I A
Mandsaur
Ratlam
Ujjain
Indore
Narbada
M A D H Y A
Bhopal
Vindhya Range
Hoshangabad
Satpura Range
Khandwa
Khargon
P R A D E S H
Jabalpur
Saugor
Jhansi
Betwa
Gwalior
Chambal
Parbati
Son
1225
Hazaribagh
Daltonganj
Bokaro
Asansol
Raniganj
Damodar
Ranchi
Rourkela
Jamshedpur
WEST BENGAL
Krishna
Barrackpore
Midnapore
Kharagpur
Howrah
Calc

Arabian
Sea
200 m
20°N
75°E

DAMAN
DADRA AND
NAGAR HAVELI
Surat
Dhulia
Tapti
Nasik
Bandra
Bombay
Ahmadnagar
Poona
Satara
Ratnagiri
M A H A R A S H T R A
Godavari
Aurangabad
Parbhani
Penganga
B E R A R
Akola
Amraoti
Nagpur
Wardha
Chhindwara
Balaghat
Bilaspur
Mahanadi
Raipur
Sambalpur
Brahmani
Cuttack
Bhubaneswar
Puri
Chatrapur
200 m

BALUCHISTAN
30°N
Mastung
Nushki
Dalbandin
Kharan
Kalat
Mashkel
Khuzdar
2030
Dasht
MAKRAN
965
Turbat
Pasni
Bela
Gwadar
Hab
Same scale
65°E
Karachi

Osmanabad
Manjra
Bhima
Sholapur
Kolhapur
Bhima
H Y D E R A B A D
Warangal
Godavari
1680
Vizianagaram
Vishakhapatnam
85°E

Malvan
Panjim
GOA
Dharwar
Hubli
Karwar
Belgaum
Tungabhadra
Raichur
Krishna
Kurnool
Bellary
Cuddapah
Nellore
Rajahmundry
Kakinada
Vijayawada
Bandar
Guntur
A N D H R A P R A D E S H
Coromandel Coast
Laccadive

Mangalore
Shimoga
Tumkur
1467
Hassan
Bangalore
Vellore
Madras
Mercara
Mysore
Cauvery
Salem
Mettur
Pondicherry
Cuddalore
Nilgiri Hills
Ootacamund
Calicut
Coimbatore
Tiruchirapalli
Thanjavur
Nagapattinam
Palghat
ANAI MUDI
2695
Madurai
Palk Str.
Pt. Pedro
Jaffna
Cochin
Alleppey
Danushkodi
Adam's Bridge
G. of
Mannar
Tirunelveli
SRI LANKA
C. Comorin
Trincomalee
Trivandrum

Sri Lanka
80°E
INDIA
Palk Str.
Pt. Pedro
Jaffna
Danushkodi
Manaar
Adam's Bridge
G. of Mannar
Mullaittivu
Mankulam
Vavuniya
Trincomalee
Kathiraveli
Anuradhapura
Gal Oya
Puttalam
Dambulla
Chilaw
Kurunegala
Matale
Batticaloa
Kalmunai
Kandy
Negombo
Gampola
Badulla
Colombo
Nuwara Eliya
Mt. Lavinia
Ratnapura
Opanake
Moratuwa
Ambalangoda
Tissamaharar
Galle
Dondra Head
Matara
Hambantota
6°
10
Scale 1:7 750 000

Boundaries
International   (in sea)   (disputed)
Internal
Roads   Roads   Tracks
Railways   Metre   Broad   Narrow
Airports   International ⊕   Domestic ○
Canals   Seasonal rivers, lakes
Marshes   Salt pan   Ice cap
Sand desert limits   National Parks, etc.

Conical Orthomorphic Projection

Metres
5000
3000
1000
500
300
200
100
Sea Level
Land
depression

Spot heights
in metres

Metres
5000
3000
1000
500
300
200
100
Sea Level
Land
depression
200
3000
4000
5000
6000

Spot heights
in metres

Indian Ocean

Scale 1:63 000 000

0 500 1000 1500 2000 km

**Ocean
Currents**   → Warm
             --→ Cold

ITALY GREECE Black Sea U. S. S. R.
Istanbul
Athens Ankara Baku Tashkent
TURKEY
LEB. SYRIA Tehran CHINA
Mediterranean Sea ISRAEL JORDAN Baghdad IRAN AFGHANISTAN Kabul 30°N
LIBYA Cairo IRAQ Lahore PAKISTAN Delhi
EGYPT Tropic of Cancer SAUDI Riyadh Karachi NEPAL Ganga BANGLA-DESH HONG KONG (Br.)
SUDAN ARABIA Indus Delhi Dacca BURMA South
Nile Persian Gulf G. of Oman I N D I A Calcutta LAOS China Sea
YEMEN A.R. OMAN Bombay Rangoon Vientiane THAI-LAND
Aden YEMEN P.D.R. Arabian Madras Bangkok
G. of Aden Socotra Sea MALAYSIA 10°N
SOMALI REP. Arabian Basin SRI LANKA Andaman Is. (India) Ho Chi Minh City (Saigon) BRUNEI
Monsoon Lakshadweep Colombo Nicobar Is. (India) Kuala Lumpur
Mombasa Somali Basin MALDIVES Equator SINGAPORE
Mogadiscio Carlsberg Ridge INDONESIA Jakarta
5340 SEYCHELLES Cocos Basin Surabaya
Amirante Is. (Seychelles) Chagos - Laccadive Plateau Mid - Indian Java Trench
Zanzibar TANZANIA Seychelles Mauritius Plateau I N D I A N Christmas I. (Austl.) 7125
Dar es Salaam Aldabra Is. (Seychelles) Basin Cocos Is. (Austl.)
Comoro Is. Mascarene Basin Wharton Basin
MALAWI Mid South Equatorial Current West Australian Basin 6459
Mascarene Basin O C E A N Réunion (Fr.) MAURITIUS 3069 Tropic of Capricorn
Mozambique Channel Madagascar Basin 6400 Indian AUSTRALIA
Salisbury RHODESIA (ZIMBABWE) Broken Ridge Perth
BOTSWANA MALAGASY REP. 2644 Southeast Indian Basin
Gaborone Maputo Ridge
Johannesburg LESOTHO Mozambique Basin 5778 Southwest Indian Ridge New Amsterdam St. Paul (Fr.) South Australian Basin
REPUBLIC OF SOUTH AFRICA Durban Madagascar Ridge Crozet Basin 5440 West Wind Drift
Cape Town Agulhas Current West Wind Drift Crozet Is. (Fr.) Southeast Indian Ridge
Agulhas Basin Prince Edward Is. (S.A.) Kerguelen Is. (Fr.) South Australian Basin
Heard I. (Aust.)
Kerguelen Plateau 6089 Limit of icebergs - average max.
South Indian Basin Limit of pack ice - average . max. South Indian Basin Aug.-Sept.
Limit of pack ice - average min. Feb.-March
Antarctic Circle

A N T A R C T I C A

30°E 50°E 70°E 90°E 110°E 130°E

**Modified Zenithal
Equidistant Projection**

S O U T H E R N   O C E A N

Inset (lower left)

LOW PRESSURE
Punjab 1st July
Delhi 25th June
Bengal 15th June
Bombay 5th June

**Rainfall during the
Summer Monsoon**

over 2000 mm
1000 - 2000
500 - 1000
250 - 500
under 250 mm

Main S.W.
Monsoon currents

Dates show the approx.
arrival of the Monsoon

Distance tables

		km
Karachi to Aden		2750
" " Basra		2750
" " Bombay		900
" " Chittagong		4800
" " Colombo		2400
" " Durban		7200
" " Fremantle		8300
" " Hong Kong		8150
" " Jidda		4050
" " Mombasa		4450
" " Rangoon		4800
" " Singapore		5350
" " Suez		5150

		km
Chittagong to Aden		6300
" " Bombay		4050
" " Calcutta		550
" " Colombo		2400
" " Durban		9050
" " Fremantle		6850
" " Hong Kong		5700
" " Jidda		7600
" " Madras		2000
" " Mombasa		7000
" " Rangoon		1100
" " Singapore		2950
" " Suez		8700

		km
Aden to Colombo		3850
" " Jakarta		7200
" " Durban		5900
" " Mombasa		2950
" " Suez		2400
Durban to Bombay		7200
" " Fremantle		7750
" " Mombasa		3300
" " Shanghai		12 950
Colombo to Hong Kong		5500
Madras to Rangoon		1800
Mombasa to Singapore		7600
" " Fremantle		8850

© Oxford University Press

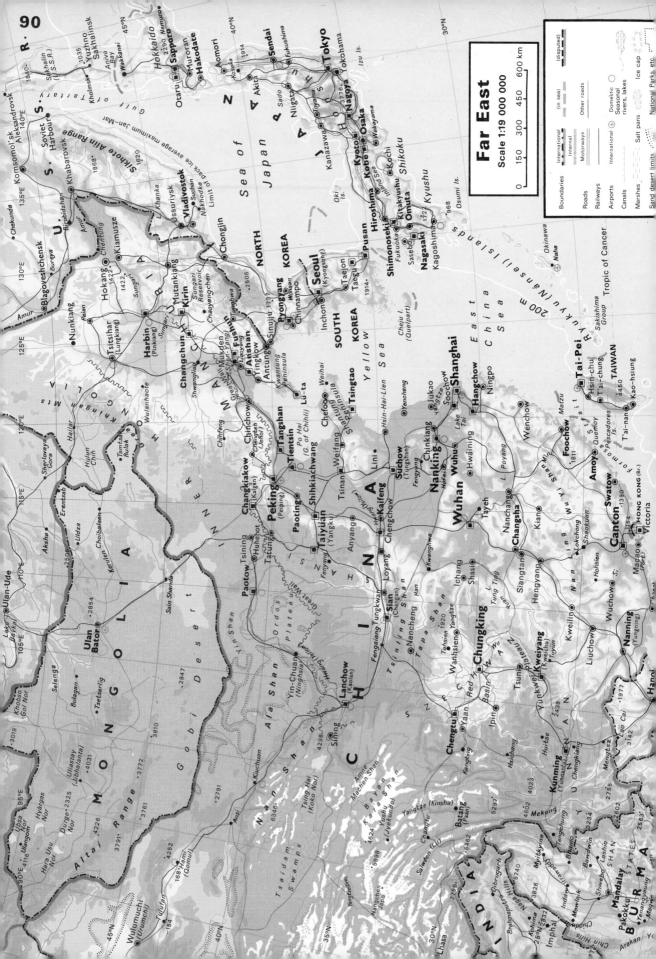

Eastern China

Scale 1:6 250 000

0 50 100 150 200 km

Metres	
5000	
3000	
2000	
1000	
500	
300	
200	
100	
Sea level	
Land depression	

Gobi Desert

INNER MONGOLIA

Yin Shan

Lang Shan

Ordos Plateau

NINGSIA HUI

Yinchwan (Ningsia)
Wuchung
Lingwu
Tung-hsin
Pinglo

Paotow
Wuta
Shenmu
Yulin
Hengshan

Great Wall

Huhehot
Salachi
Tokoto
Tatung
Hoku

SHENSI

Yenan
Yenchang
Ichwan
Huanglung
Fuping
Weinan
Sian
Sienyang
Sanyuan
Hanchung

Tsingling Shan

Taiyuan
SHANSI
Yutze
Pingyao
Fenyang
Linfen

Paoteh
Kolan
Hinghsien
Kiahsien

Shangtu
(L. Chahan)
Changkiakow (Kalgan)
Suanhwa
Huaian
Hunyuan

PEKING SHIH
Peking (Peiping)
Chohsien
Paoting (Chingyuan)
Shihkiachwang
Tinghsien
Chengting
Yenchiang
Singtai
HOPEH

Tientsin
TIENTSIN
Tangshan
Tangchow
Tungchow
Wuching
Taku

Gulf of Chihli

Liaotung Peninsula
Mukden (Shenyang)
Liaoyang
Anshan
Yingkow
LIAONING
Chaoyang (Jehol)
Chengteh (Jehol)
Lushun
Luta

Liaotung Bay

Shanhaikuan
Chinwangtao
Changli
Lulung

Luan

Yentai
Weihai
Laiyang
Tsingtao
Kiaohsien
Weifang
SHANTUNG
Shantung Pen.
Tsinan
Poshan
Tzepo
Taian
Feicheng
Liaocheng
Lintsing
Tehchow
Potow

Yellow Sea

Laichow Bay

HONAN
Kaifeng
Chengchow
Loyang
Lushan
Nanyang
Hsinhsiang
Anyang
Puyang
Hsuchang

KIANGSU
Suchow
Hwainan
Pengpu
Fowyang
Fangcheng
Yencheng
Yangchow
Taichow

Hwang (Yellow R.)

KANSU
Paoki

ANHWEI

Grand Canal

Tsinling Shan
Taipai Shan 4107

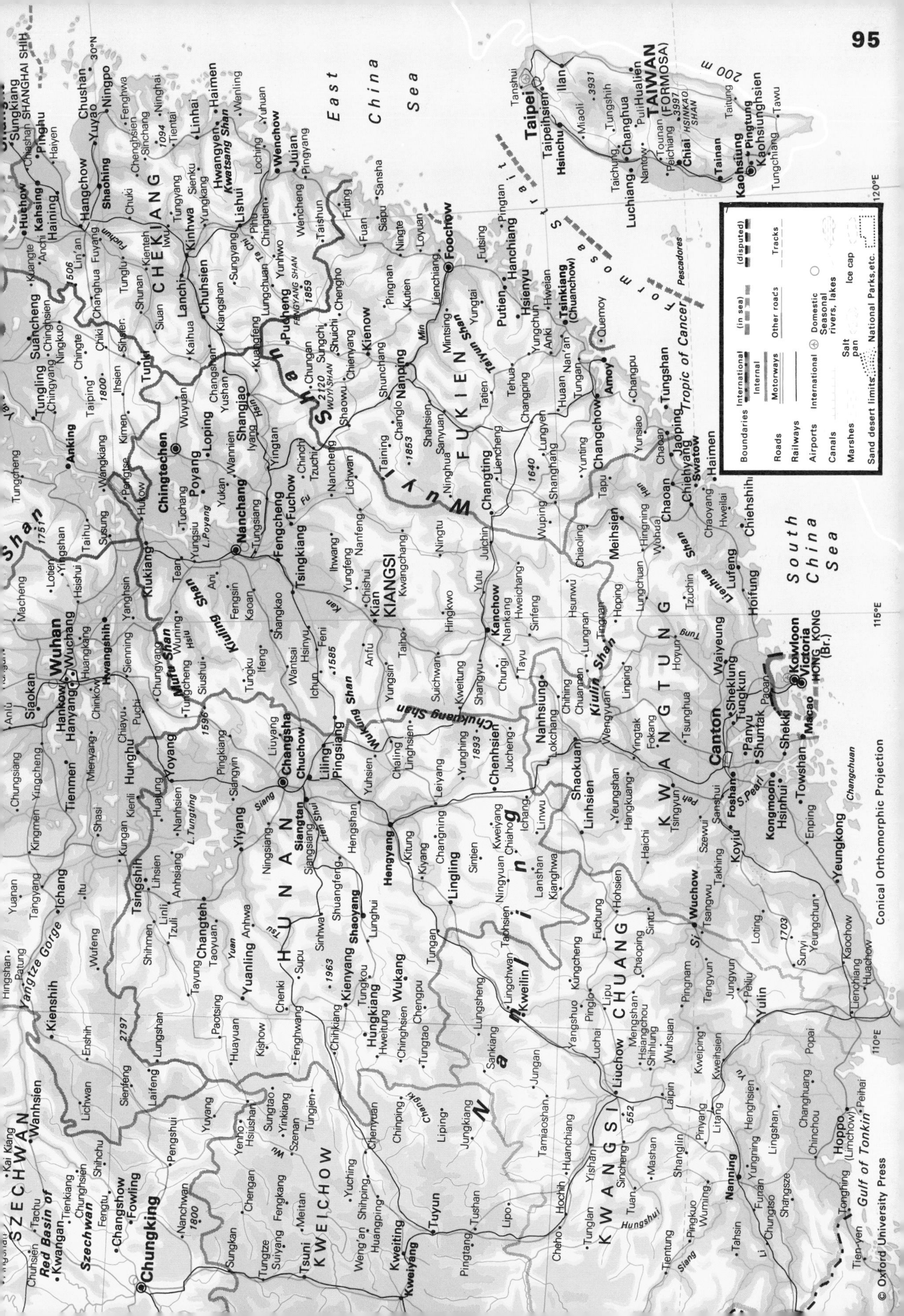

East China Sea

South China Sea

CHEKIANG
FUKIEN
KIANGSI
HUNAN
KWANGTUNG
KWEICHOW
KWANGSI CHUANG
SZECHWAN
TAIWAN (FORMOSA)

Wuhan · Hankow · Hanyang · Wuchang
Nanchang
Changsha
Foochow
Taipei
Canton
HONG KONG (Br.)
Macao
Chungking
Nanning
Kweiyang
Amoy
Swatow
Hengyang
Lingling
Kaohsiung
Tainan

Tropic of Cancer

Conical Orthomorphic Projection

© Oxford University Press

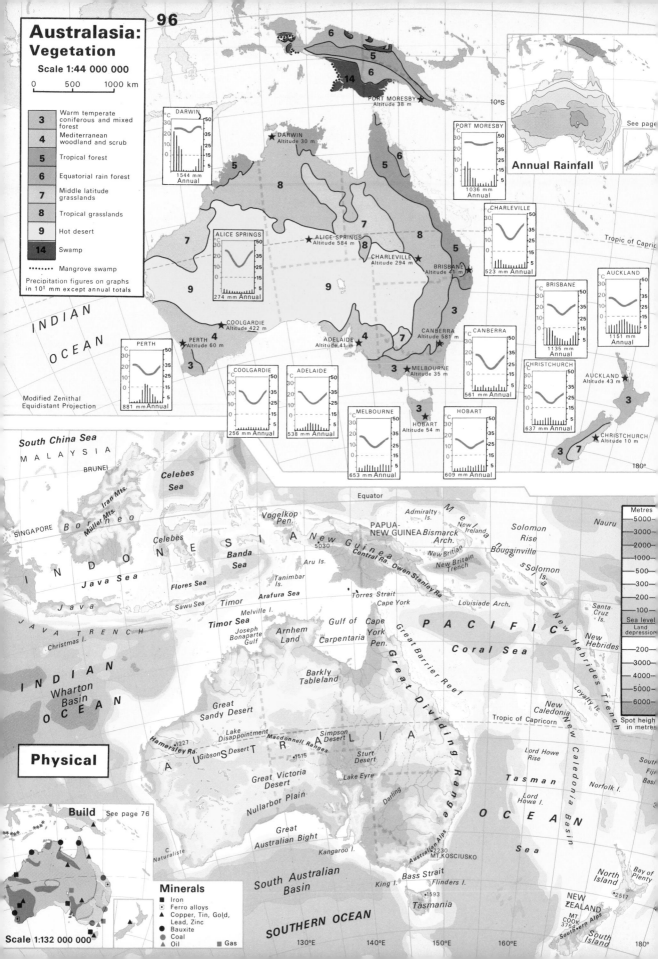

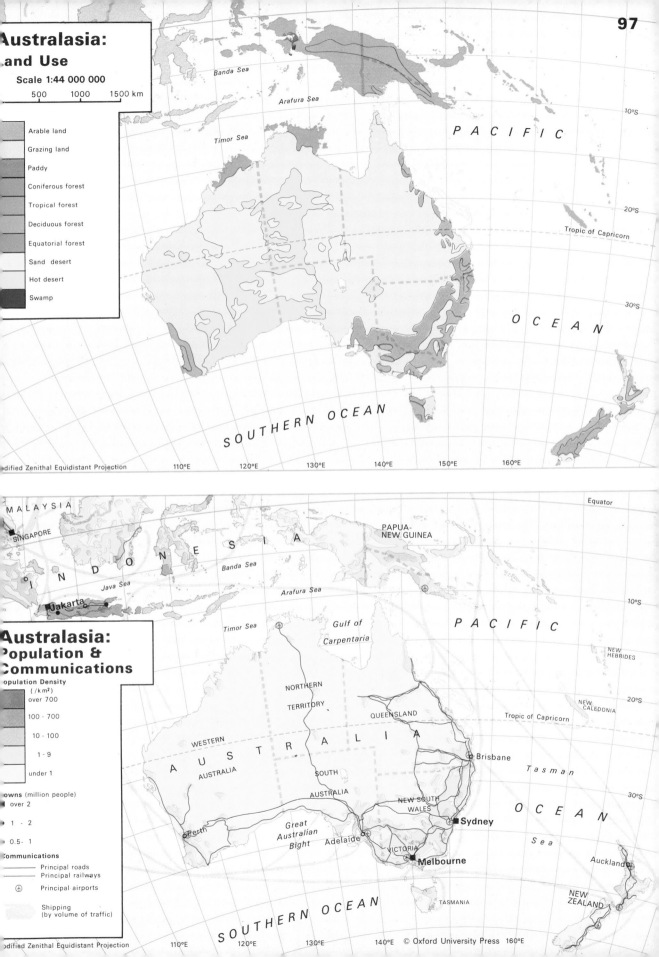

Australasia: Land Use

Scale 1:44 000 000

	500	1000	1500 km

Arable land
Grazing land
Paddy
Coniferous forest
Tropical forest
Deciduous forest
Equatorial forest
Sand desert
Hot desert
Swamp

Banda Sea

Arafura Sea

Timor Sea

PACIFIC

OCEAN

Tropic of Capricorn

SOUTHERN OCEAN

Modified Zenithal Equidistant Projection

110°E 120°E 130°E 140°E 150°E 160°E

10°S
20°S
30°S

MALAYSIA

SINGAPORE

INDONESIA

Java Sea

Banda Sea

Jakarta

Australasia: Population & Communications

Population Density (/km²)
over 700
100 - 700
10 - 100
1 - 9
under 1

Towns (million people)
over 2
1 - 2
0.5 - 1

Communications
—— Principal roads
—— Principal railways
⊕ Principal airports

Shipping
(by volume of traffic)

Equator

PAPUA-
NEW GUINEA

Arafura Sea

Timor Sea

Gulf of
Carpentaria

PACIFIC

NEW
HEBRIDES

NEW
CALEDONIA

Tropic of Capricorn

NORTHERN

TERRITORY

QUEENSLAND

WESTERN

AUSTRALIA

A U S T R A L I A

SOUTH

AUSTRALIA

Brisbane

Tasman

Perth

Great
Australian
Bight

Adelaide

NEW SOUTH
WALES

VICTORIA

Sydney

Melbourne

OCEAN

Sea

Auckland

TASMANIA

NEW
ZEALAND

SOUTHERN OCEAN

Modified Zenithal Equidistant Projection

110°E 120°E 130°E 140°E © Oxford University Press 160°E

10°S
20°S
30°S

Kota Kinabalu Tawitawi
BRUNEI Bandar Seri Begawan THE PHILIPPINES Caroline Is.
Kota Sandakan
Bharu SABAH Talaud Is.
5°N 110°E 120°E 125°E 130°E 135°E

MALAYA M A L A Y S I A EAST Celebes Morotai
Natuna Is. SARAWAK Sea Manado Halmahera
WEST (Indon.) •1840 Ternate
Kuantan Anambas S A 1970 Molucca Sea
Is.(Indon.) Sibu 2707 Sula Is. Manokwari
Malacca Kuching B o r n e o Gulf of 2279 Obi Is. Doberai 2940 Biak
Johore Bahru Serian Müller Mts. Tomini 990 Misool Peninsula Japen
SINGAPORE Pontianak (Kalimantan) Samarinda Molucca (Maluku) 3016. 3019 WEST 2239 New
Bintan 1755• •2278 Balikpapan Celebes Gulf 1731. Seram IRIAN Nassau Mts. 503
Lingga 189 (Sulawesi) of Buru Ambon Kai
0° Tolo Is. Aru
Jambi Bangka Belitung Gulf of Butung Tanimbar Is. Is.
3800 (Billiton) Bone Muna B a n d a S e a Dolak I.
Palembang Bandjarmasin 2871 Kabaena C. Vals
I N D O N E S I A
3159 Java Ujung Pandang Kangean L o m b l e n A r a f u r a S e a
2232 Telukbetung Sea Is. F l o r e s S e a Wetar
Jakarta Semarang 1602 Madura Bali Flores Alor Dili
Enggano Bandung Jogjakarta Madiun 3726 Sea 2851 2300 Pantar Timor 2920
Sunda Str. 3265 3142 Sumbawa 999 Sawu Sea Melville
J a v a Malang 3332 Bali Sumba Waingapu Kupang Bathurst I.
5°S Lombok Str. Lombok Sawu Roti Darwin
Christmas I. Timor S e a Rum Jungle
(Austl.) Arnhem Land Katherine
10°S C. Talbot Joseph Daly Birdum
Bonaparte Victoria Daly Waters
INDIAN Gulf Barkly
Wyndham Tableland
Yampi Sound Halls Creek NORTHERN Tennant Creek
C. Leveque Fitzroy 711 TERRITORY
Dampier Derby
15°S Land Broome Great Alice Springs
200 m Sandy Desert L. Mackay Macdonnell Ranges
80 Mile Beach Stuart Simp
Monte Port Marble Bar Desert 1515 SOUTH
Bello Is. Hedland Fortescue Lake Disappointment 707 Oodnadatta
Dampier Hamersley Ra. Gibson Desert AUSTRALIA
Exmouth Ashburton 1226 WESTERN AUSTRAL
Gulf 342 •994 Great Victoria Desert Mt. Eba
20°S Carnarvon AUSTRALIA 564 594 Nullarbor Plain Gairdner
Murchison Wiluna 565 Forrest Ceduna Port Aug
Dirk Mt. Magnet 707 Oldea Iron K
Hartog I. Laverton Great Eucla Wh
585 Kalgoorlie Australian Bight Po
25°S Geraldton Coolgardie Zanthus Port Lincoln
Southern C. Catastrophe
Northam Cross Recherche
Perth Esperance Arch.
Fremantle Great
C. Naturaliste 1109
30°S Bunbury Albany
C. Leeuwin

Australasia
Scale 1:22 000 000
0   350   700 km

Boundaries	International	(in sea)	(disputed)
Roads	Internal		
Railways			
Airports	International ⊕	Domestic ○	
Canals		Seasonal rivers, lakes	
Marshes	Salt pans	Ice cap	
Sand desert limits	National Parks, etc.		

Metres
5000
3000
2000
1000
500
300
200
100
Sea level
Land depression
Spot heights in metres

Zenithal Equidistant Projection
100°E 40°S 110°E 115°E 120°E 45°S 125°E 130°E

145°E 150°E 155°E 160°E 165°E 170°E 175°E

P A C I F I C

Equator

Tarawa Gilbert

Nauru Ocean I. Islands
(Br.) (Br.)

0°

Pura
Aitape Manus Admiralty Kavieng
Wewak Is.

Bismarck New
Archipelago Ireland Rabaul

PAPUA – NEW GUINEA

Madang New Britain

Lae Finschhafen

3106· Solomon Islands
Bougainville Choiseul Santa (Br.)
Shortland Is. New Isabel Stewart Is.
Ganongga Georgia
Vangunu Malaita
Central Ra. Honiara Ulawa
·3993 Guadalcanal 2440
D'Entrecasteaux Is. San Cristobal
Gulf of 3422 Rennell I. Santa Cruz Is.
Papua Port Cherry I.
Moresby Louisiade Arch. Mitre I.

5°S

Tuvalu

Funafuti

C. York
714· 595·
Cape
York 586·
Peninsula Cooktown 1387·
Mitchell Cairns
Gilbert Herberton

10°S

New Hebrides
(Br.-Fr. Condominium)

Espiritu
Santo

Malekula

Vila Efate

Erromanga

15°S

Fiji Is

Vanua Levu

Viti Levu
Suva Lau Group

C o r a l

S e a

Forsayth
Norman
Townsville
Charters 1055
Towers
Hughenden Mackay
Winton 628
Longreach Rockhampton
Barcoo Mt. Morgan· Gladstone
Yaraka ·738 Bundaberg
Quilpie Maryborough
394· Charleville
Cunnamulla Darling
Toowoomba **Brisbane**
Downs Ipswich
Bourke Lismore
·1555
Darling Grafton
·1615
Tamworth
·520 Maitland
Dubbo **Newcastle**
Broken Hill 1274·
Orange Lithgow
Katoomba □**Sydney**
Wollongong
Goulburn
Murray **Canberra**
Swan Hill Albury
Riverina MT. KOSCIUSKO
Echuca 2230
·1167
Bendigo
Ballarat Gippsland Orbost Cape Howe
Geelong
Melbourne

Chesterfield Is.
(Fr.)

L o y a l t y   I s.

New
Caledonia
(Fr.) Nouméa

20°S

Tropic of Capricorn

O C E A N

25°S

Norfolk I.
(Austl.)

T a s m a n

S e a

30°S

North Cape

Kaikohe
771·
Auckland
Hamilton
NORTH ISLAND 819·
New Plymouth ·1754
2517· ·279
Gisborne
Napier
1213· Palmerston N.
NEW
Westport Nelson
Greymouth 2338· **Wellington**
SOUTH ISLAND **ZEALAND**
MT. COOK
3764·
3035· Southern Alps **Christchurch**
2027 170°E

35°S

King I. Bass Furneaux
Strait Group

Burnie ·1573
Mt. Lyell St. Marys
TASMANIA Launceston
·1439
Hobart

40°S

165°E
Invercargill **Dunedin**
Stewart I.

45°S

© Oxford University Press

140°E 145°E 150°E 155°E 160°E

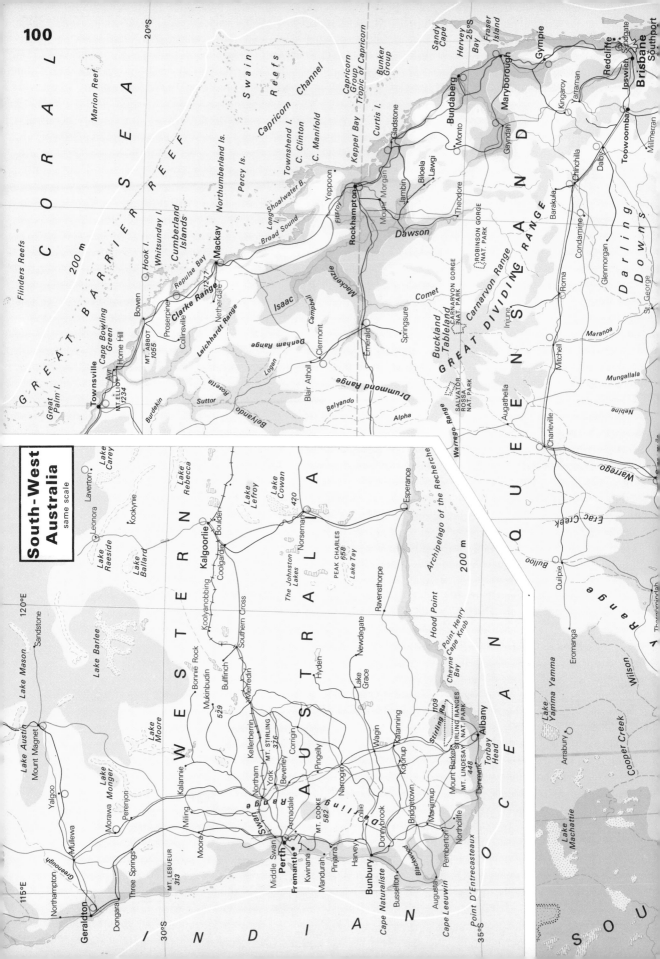

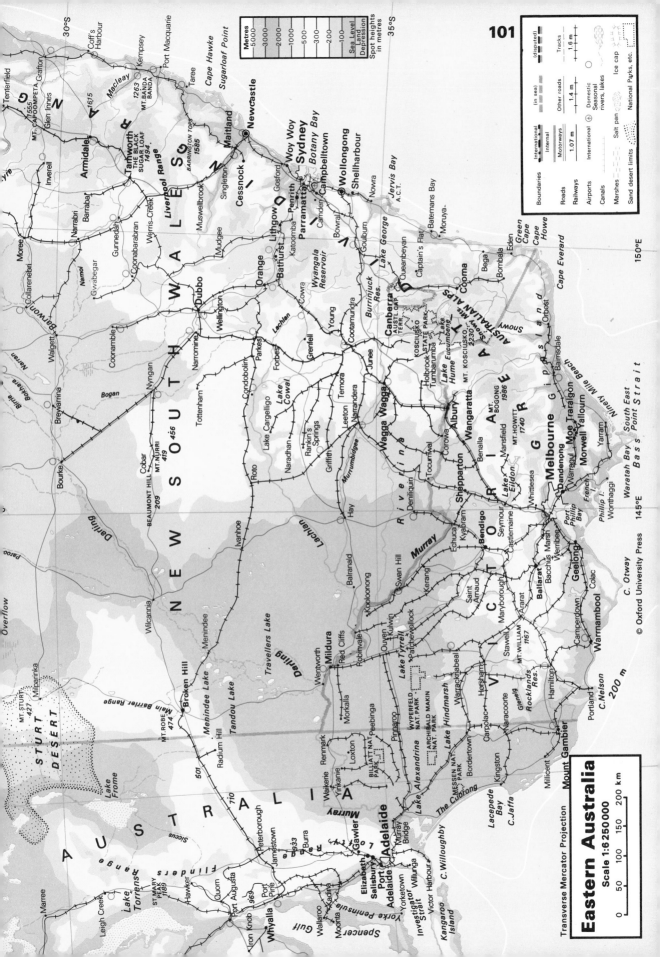

Eastern Australia

Transverse Mercator Projection

Scale 1:6 250 000

0 50 100 150 200 km

© Oxford University Press

101

Boundaries		
Roads		
Railways		
Airports		
Canals		
Marshes		
Sand desert limits		

International
Internal
(disputed)
(in sea)
Other roads
Motorways
International
1.07 m
1.4 m
1.6 m
Tracks
Domestic
Seasonal rivers, lakes
Salt pan
Ice cap
National Parks, etc.

Metres
5000
3000
2000
1000
500
300
200
Sea Level
Land Depression
Spot heights in metres

30°S
35°S
150°E
145°E
200 m

NEW SOUTH WALES

VICTORIA

GIPPSLAND

AUSTRALIA

STURT DESERT

Sydney
Newcastle
Wollongong
Canberra
Melbourne
Adelaide
Broken Hill
Mount Gambier

Coff's Harbour
Kempsey
Port Macquarie
Cape Hawke
Sugarloaf Point
Taree
Grafton
Glen Innes
Inverell
Tenterfield
Armidale
Tamworth
Cessnock
Maitland
Woy Woy
Botany Bay
Campbelltown
Shellharbour
Nowra
Jervis Bay
A.C.T.
Batemans Bay
Moruya
Eden
Green Cape
Cape Howe
Cape Everard

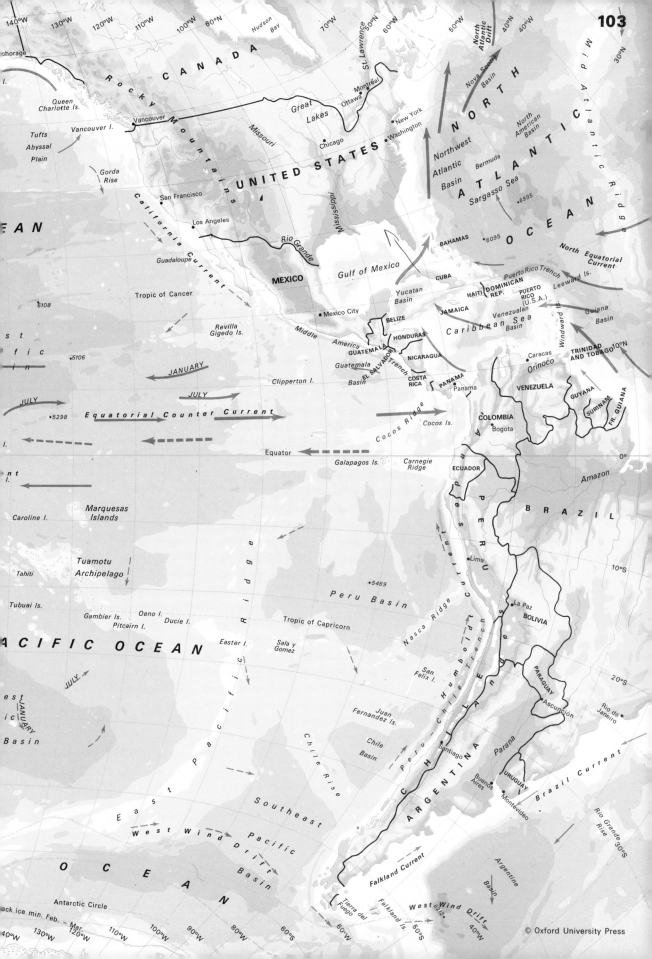

140°W 130°W 120°W 110°W 100°W 60°N Hudson Bay 70°N 50°N 60°N 50°W 40°W 40°N 30°N

Anchorage

CANADA

Rocky Mountains

Queen Charlotte Is.

Vancouver Vancouver I.

Tufts Abyssal Plain

Gorda Rise

St. Lawrence

Montréal

Ottawa

Great Lakes

Missouri

Chicago

New York

Washington

UNITED STATES

North Atlantic Drift

Nova Scotia Basin

NORTH

Northwest Atlantic Basin

North American Basin

Bermuda

ATLANTIC

Mid Atlantic Ridge

•6995

San Francisco

Los Angeles

California Current

Guadaloupe Current

Rio Grande

MEXICO

Gulf of Mexico

BAHAMAS

•6095

OCEAN

Sargasso Sea

North Equatorial Current

Tropic of Cancer

•6108

CUBA

Yucatan Basin

HAITI DOMINICAN REP.

PUERTO RICO (U.S.A.)

Puerto Rico Trench

Leeward Is.

Guiana Basin

JAMAICA

Revilla Gigedo Is.

•5106

Mexico City

Middle

America

Trench

BELIZE

GUATEMALA

HONDURAS

Caribbean Sea

Venezuelan Basin

Windward Is.

Guiana Basin

TRINIDAD AND TOBAGO

10°N

st

fic

n

JANUARY

Guatemala Basin

NICARAGUA

EL SALVADOR

COSTA RICA

PANAMA

Caracas

Orinoco

VENEZUELA

GUYANA

SURINAM

FR. GUIANA

JULY

•5298

JULY

Equatorial Counter Current

Clipperton I.

Cocos Ridge

Cocos Is.

Panama

COLOMBIA

Bogota

I.

Equator

Galapagos Is.

Carnegie Ridge

ECUADOR

Amazon

0°

nt

I.

Caroline I.

Marquesas Islands

•5469

Peru Basin

Lima

PERU

BRAZIL

10°S

Tahiti

Tuamotu Archipelago

La Paz

BOLIVIA

Tubuai Is.

Gambier Is. Oeno I. Ducie I.

Pitcairn I.

Tropic of Capricorn

Nasca Ridge

PARAGUAY

Ascunción

Rio de Janeiro

20°S

PACIFIC OCEAN

Easter I.

Sala y Gomez

San Felix I.

Parana

JULY

st

ic

JANUARY

Basin

Juan Fernandez Is.

Chile Basin

Peru-Chile Trench

Humboldt Current

Santiago

Andes

Parana

Buenos Aires

ARGENTINA

URUGUAY

Montévideo

Brazil Current

Rio Grande Rise

30°S

East

Pacific

Southeast

Chile Rise

CHILE

West Wind Drift

Basin

Falkland Current

Argentine Basin

OCEAN

Antarctic Circle

pack ice min. Feb. - Mar.

140°W 130°W 120°W 110°W 100°W 90°W 80°W Tierra del Fuego 60°W Falkland Is. West Wind Drift 50°W 40°W

© Oxford University Press

New Zealand

Scale 1:6 250 000

0 50 100 150 200 km

Boundaries
International | (in sea) | (disputed)

Roads | Motorways | Other roads | Tracks

Railways

Airports | International ⊕ | Domestic ○

Canals

Seasonal rivers, lakes

Marshes | Salt Pan | Ice cap

Sand desert limits | National Parks etc.

Three Kings Is.
C. Maria Van Diemen
North Cape

Kaitaia *751
Waitangi *Russell
Bay of Islands
Kaikohe *481
Hokianga Harbour
Whangarei
*771
Dargaville
*221
Great Barrier I.
Kaipara Harbour

NORTHLAND

Helensville
Hauraki Gulf
Devonport

Auckland
*819
Papakura
Thames
Coromandel
Pukekohe
Paeroa
*404
Huntly
*953

NORTH ISLAND

Bay of Plenty
Tauranga
Cambridge
Whakatane
Hamilton
Karapiro
Kawerau
Opotiki
Te Awamutu
*962
Raukumara Ra.
*1754
Te Kuiti
Rotorua
*808
Kinleith
*822
Volcanic Plateau
Wairakei
Murupara
*1213
Taupo
Te Karaka
Waikaremoana
L. Taupo
UREWERA N.P.
Taumarunui
*1087
Waikaremoana
*1383
Gisborne
New Plymouth
Waitara
NGAURUHOE *2291
Wairoa
Poverty Bay

TARANAKI
MT.EGMONT N.P.
TONGARIRO N.P.
RUAPEHU
Mahia Penin.
*2517
Stratford
*2797
Ohakune
Kaimanawa Mts.
Opunake
Ruahine Ra.
*743
Hawke Bay
Hawera
Taihape
Napier
Waipawa
Hastings
Wanganui
Marton
Dannevirke
Feilding
*803
Woodville
Palmerston North
C. Turnagain

C. Farewell
Golden Bay
Takaka
*1671
Masterton
Tasman Bay | D'Urville I.
ABEL *1213
TASMAN N.P.
The Sounds
Tararua Ra.
Motueka
Tasman Mts.
Cook Strait
Rimutaka Tunnel
Petone
*536
Hutt *663
Nelson
Picton
*1760 *Wairau
Blenheim
Wellington
MT.OWEN
*1876
C. Palliser

Westport
C.Foulwind

BULLER
Buller
NELSON LAKES N.P.
*1501
Reefton
Spenser Mts.
TAPUAENUKU
*2338
*2885
Kaikoura Ra.
LEWIS P.
*1875
Kaikoura
Waiau
*965
Greymouth
Hurunui
Hokitika
Waiau
OTIRA Tunnel
ARTHURS PASS N.P.
Waipara
*2400
ARTHURS PASS
*1935
Pegasus Bay

W E S T L A N D
WESTLAND N.P.
MT.TASMAN
*3498
MT.ARROWSMITH
*2795
Christchurch
*1951
MT.COOK
*3764 N.P.
*2330
Riccarton
Lyttelton
Hermitage
Akaroa
Banks Peninsula

Jackson Bay
Haast
Canterbury Plains
Ashburton
MT.ASPIRING
*2508
*1322
HAAST P.
Timaru
*3035
SOUTH ISLAND

Milford Sound
Canterbury Bight
L. Wanaka
*1871
Kurow
FIORDLAND
Queenstown
Oamaru
N.P.
L. Wakatipu
Cromwell
*945
*1855
Te Anau
Alexandra
*1679
Doubtful Sound
Kingston
*1449
Roxbury
Manapouri
*1067
*1694
Lumsden
*777
Port Chalmers
Dusky Sound
Ohai
Edievale
Otago Peninsula
*1018
Gore
Dunedin
C.Providence
Tuatapere
*869
Balclutha
Kaitangata
*720

SOUTHLAND
Invercargill
Bluff
*980
Foveaux Strait

Stewart Island
Southwest Cape

T a s m a n   S e a

S O U T H   P A C I F I C   O C E A N

200 m

Metres
5000
3000
2000
1000
500
300
200
100
Sea level
Land depression

Spot heights in metres

170°E | 175°E

©Oxford University Press

Bounty Is. (N.Z.)

35°S | 40°S | 45°S

170°E | 175°E

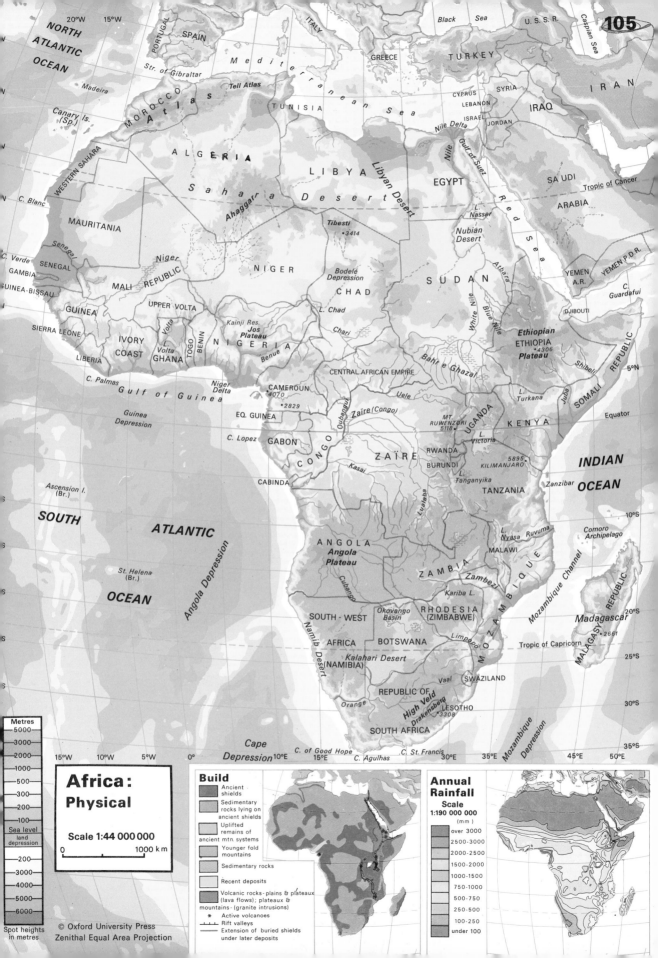

NORTH ATLANTIC OCEAN

Madeira

Canary Is. (Sp.)

C. Blanc

C. Verde

GAMBIA

GUINEA-BISSAU

SIERRA LEONE

LIBERIA

C. Palmas

SOUTH ATLANTIC OCEAN

Ascension I. (Br.)

St. Helena (Br.)

PORTUGAL

SPAIN

Str. of Gibraltar

MOROCCO

Tell Atlas

Atlas

WESTERN SAHARA

MAURITANIA

SENEGAL

Senegal

MALI

GUINEA

IVORY COAST

Guinea Depression

Mediterranean Sea

ALGERIA

Sahara

Ahaggar

Niger

NIGER REPUBLIC

UPPER VOLTA

Volta

L. Volta

GHANA

TOGO

BENIN

Niger Delta

Gulf of Guinea

C. Lopez

Desert

ITALY

GREECE

TUNISIA

LIBYA

Libyan Desert

Tibesti
•3414

Bodélé Depression

CHAD

L. Chad

Chari

Kainji Res.

Jos Plateau

NIGERIA

Benue

CAMEROUN
4070

•2829

EQ. GUINEA

GABON

CABINDA

CONGO

Kasai

ANGOLA

Angola Plateau

Angola Depression

Namib Desert

SOUTH-WEST AFRICA (NAMIBIA)

Kalahari Desert

Cape Depression

Cape of Good Hope

Black Sea

TURKEY

CYPRUS

LEBANON

ISRAEL

JORDAN

EGYPT

Nile Delta

Gulf of Suez

L. Nasser

Nubian Desert

SUDAN

White Nile

Blue Nile

Bahr e Ghazal

Uele

Oubangui

Zaïre (Congo)

ZAÏRE

RWANDA

BURUNDI

MT. RUWENZORI 5118

Lualaba

L. Tanganyika

L. Nyasa

ZAMBIA

Kariba L.

Zambezi

RHODESIA (ZIMBABWE)

Limpopo

BOTSWANA

SWAZILAND

Vaal

REPUBLIC OF SOUTH AFRICA

Orange

High Veld

Drakensberg
•3308

LESOTHO

C. of Good Hope

C. Agulhas

C. St. Francis

SYRIA

IRAQ

U.S.S.R.

Caspian Sea

IRAN

Tropic of Cancer

SA UDI

ARABIA

Red Sea

YEMEN A.R.

YEMEN P.D.R.

C. Guardafui

DJIBOUTI

Atbara

Ethiopian

ETHIOPIA

Plateau
•4306

Shibeli

Juba

SOMALI REPUBLIC

5°N

L. Turkana

UGANDA

KENYA

Equator

L. Victoria

KILIMANJARO
5895

TANZANIA

Zanzibar

INDIAN OCEAN

10°S

Ruvuma

Comoro Archipelago

MALAWI

MOZAMBIQUE

Mozambique Channel

Madagascar

MALAGASY REPUBLIC
•2661

20°S

Tropic of Capricorn

Mozambique Depression

25°S

30°S

35°S

CENTRAL AFRICAN EMPIRE

Chad

Okovango Basin

Cubango

Cuanza

Mozambique Channel

20°W 15°W 10°W 5°W 0° 10°E 15°E 30°E 35°E 45°E 50°E

Cape Depression

Metres
- 5000
- 3000
- 2000
- 1000
- 500
- 300
- 200
- 100

Sea level
land depression

- 200
- 2000
- 3000
- 4000
- 5000
- 6000

Spot heights in metres

Africa:
Physical

Scale 1:44 000 000

0 1000 km

© Oxford University Press

Zenithal Equal Area Projection

Build

Ancient shields

Sedimentary rocks lying on ancient shields

Uplifted remains of ancient mtn. systems

Younger fold mountains

Sedimentary rocks

Recent deposits

Volcanic rocks - plains & plateaux (lava flows); plateaux & mountains - (granite intrusions)

✱ Active volcanoes

✲ Rift valleys

Extension of buried shields under later deposits

Annual Rainfall
Scale 1:190 000 000

(mm)

- over 3000
- 2500-3000
- 2000-2500
- 1500-2000
- 1000-1500
- 750-1000
- 500-750
- 250-500
- 100-250
- under 100

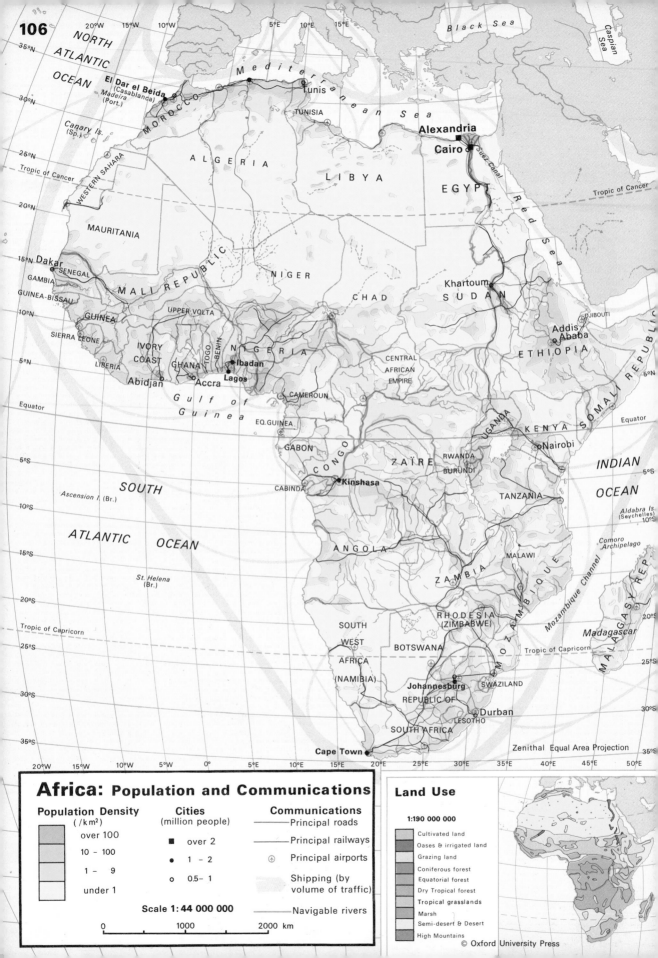

Africa: Population and Communications

Population Density
(/km²)

over 100

10 – 100

1 – 9

under 1

Cities
(million people)

■ over 2

● 1 – 2

⊙ 0.5 – 1

Communications

—— Principal roads

—— Principal railways

⊕ Principal airports

Shipping (by
volume of traffic)

—— Navigable rivers

Scale 1 : 44 000 000

0   1000   2000 km

Land Use

1 : 190 000 000

Cultivated land
Oases & irrigated land
Grazing land
Coniferous forest
Equatorial forest
Dry Tropical forest
Tropical grasslands
Marsh
Semi-desert & Desert
High Mountains

© Oxford University Press

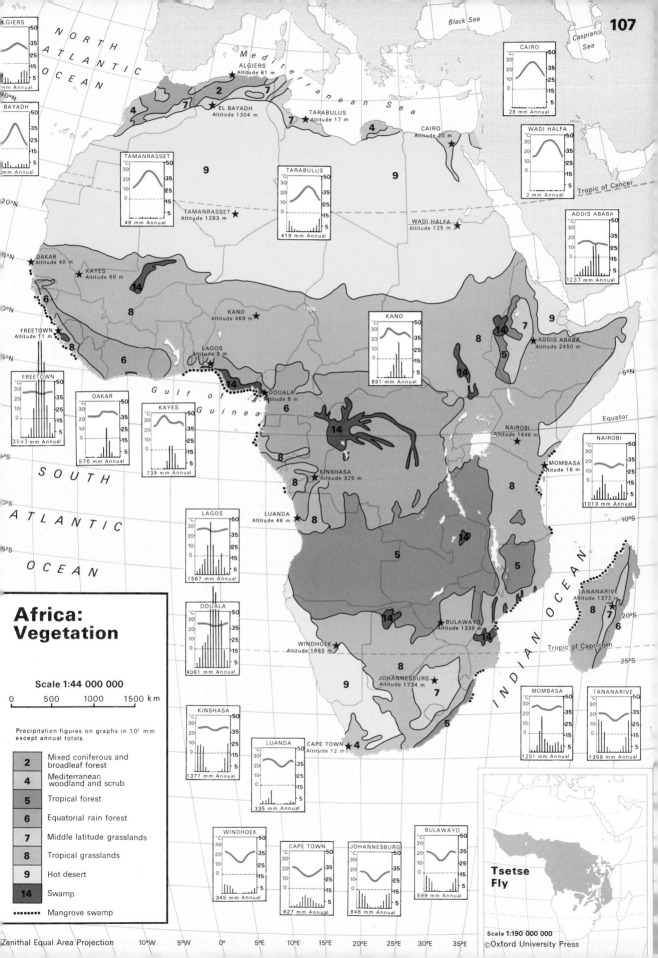

Africa: Vegetation

Scale 1:44 000 000

0   500   1000   1500 km

Precipitation figures on graphs in 10¹ mm except annual totals.

2	Mixed coniferous and broadleaf forest
4	Mediterranean woodland and scrub
5	Tropical forest
6	Equatorial rain forest
7	Middle latitude grasslands
8	Tropical grasslands
9	Hot desert
14	Swamp
••••••	Mangrove swamp

Tsetse Fly

Scale 1:190 000 000

©Oxford University Press

Zenithal Equal Area Projection

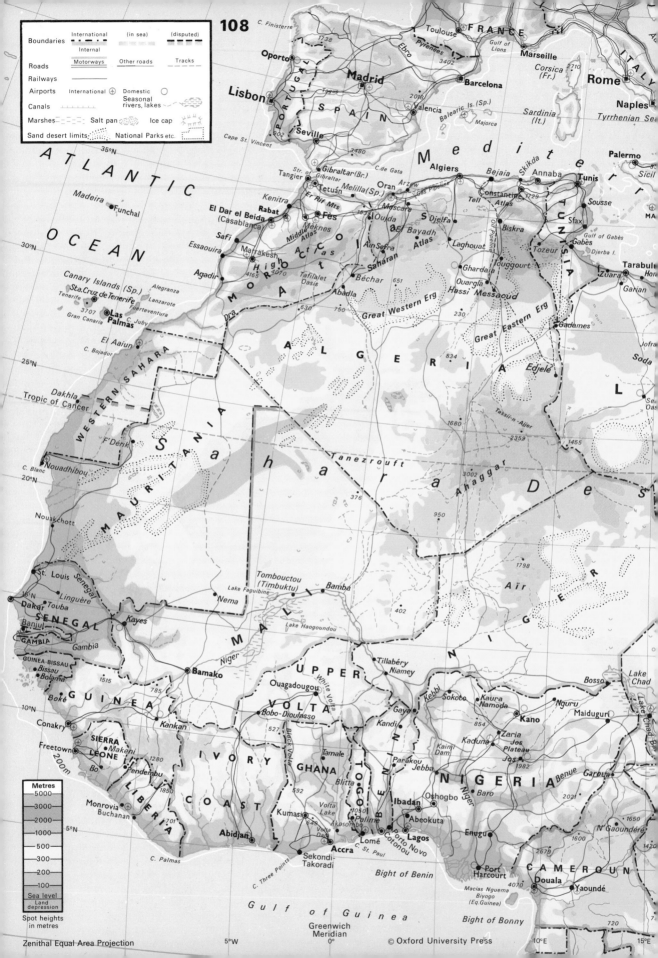

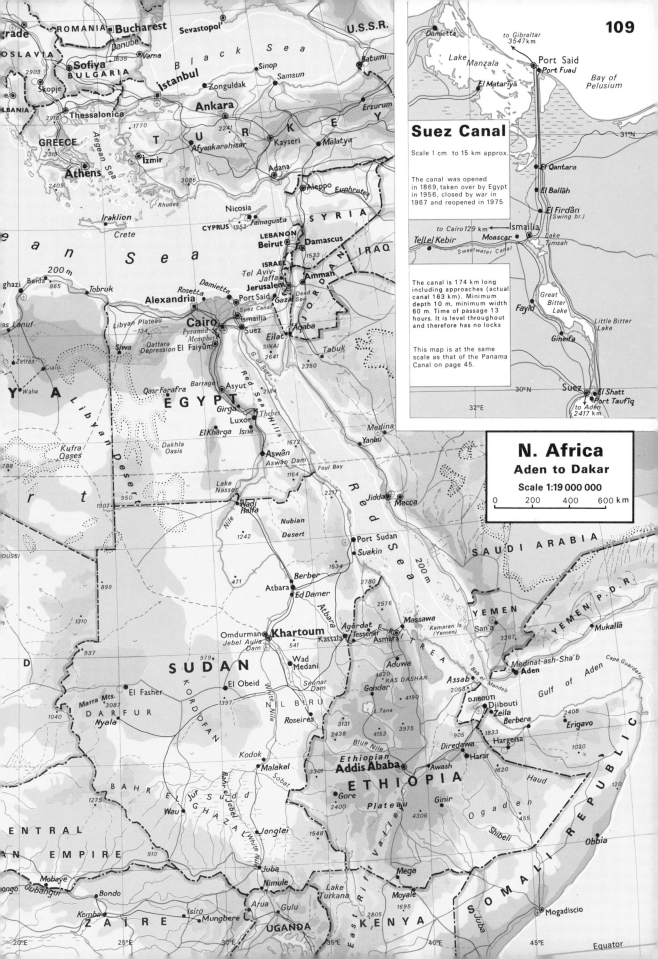

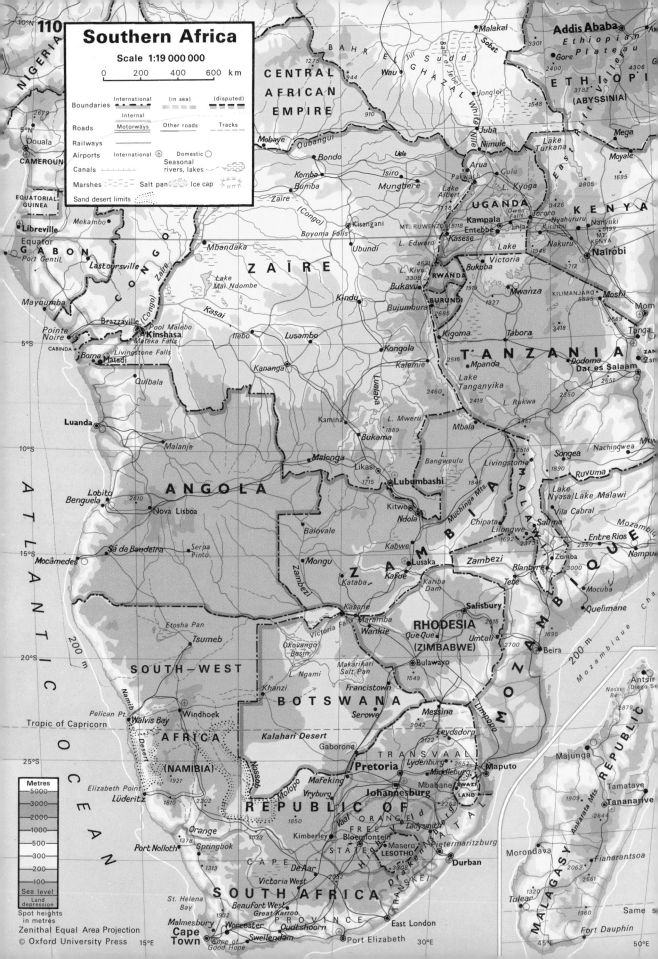

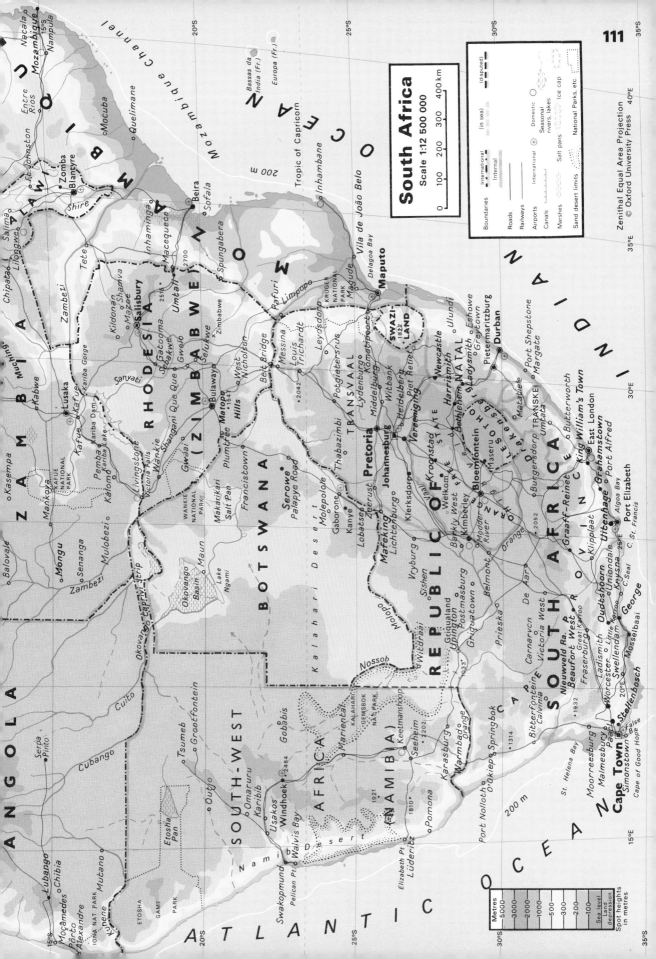

South Africa

Scale 1:12 500 000

Boundaries		
International	—·—·—	(disputed) ▦▦▦
Internal	▒▒▒	(in sea)
Roads		
Railways		
Airports	International ✈	Domestic ○
Canals		Seasonal rivers, lakes
Marshes		Salt pans
Sand desert limits	··········	National Parks, etc.

0 100 200 300 400 km

Zenithal Equal Area Projection
© Oxford University Press

Metres
5000
3000
2000
1000
500
300
200
100
Sea level
Land
depression

Spot heights in metres

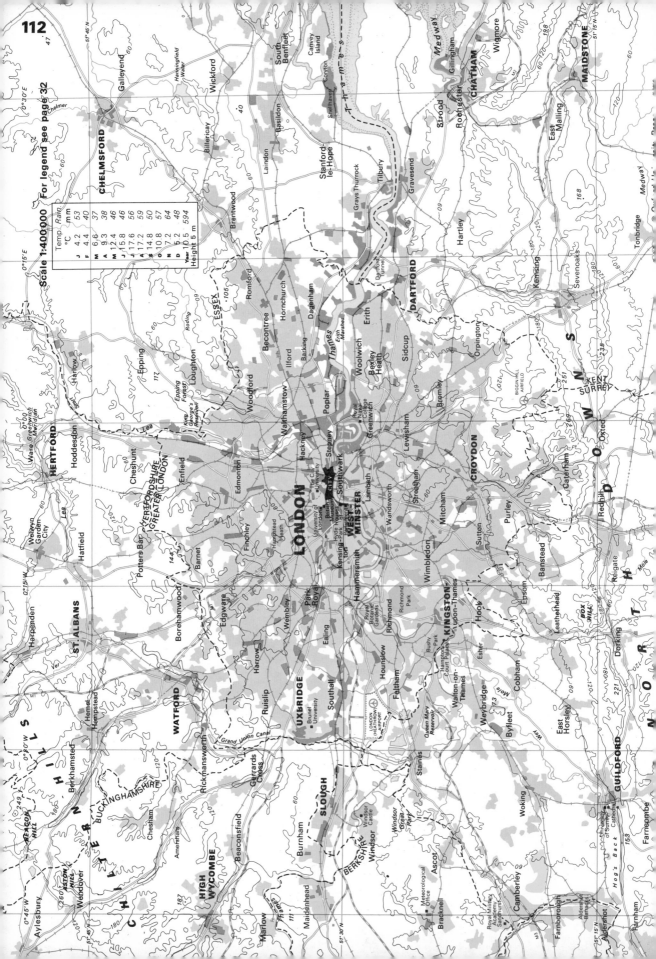

Scale 1:400,000 For legend see page 32

CHELMSFORD

Temp.	Rain.	
°C	mm	
J	4.2	53
F	4.4	40
M	6.6	37
A	9.3	38
M	12.4	46
J	15.8	46
J	17.6	56
A	17.2	59
S	14.8	50
O	10.8	57
N	7.2	64
D	5.2	48
Year	10.5	594
Height 5 m		

Galleyend

Chelmer

Wickford

Hanningfield Water

South Benfleet

Carvey Island

Canvey Island

Coryton

Shellhaven

Medway

Wigmore

CHATHAM

Gillingham

MAIDSTONE

Billericay

Laindon

Basildon

Stanford-le-Hope

Grays Thurrock

Tilbury

Gravesend

Strood

Rochester

East Malling

Brentwood

Romford

ESSEX

Roding

Hartley

Kemsing

Tonbridge

DARTFORD

Dartford Tunnel

Sevenoaks

Epping

Loughton

Epping Forest

King George's Reservoir

Woodford

Ilford

Barking

Dagenham

Thames

Erith Marshes

Erith

Woolwich

Bexley Heath

Sidcup

BIGGIN HILL AIRFIELD

KENT

SURREY

HERTFORD

Ware

Hoddesdon

Cheshunt

Enfield

Edmonton

Walthamstow

Hackney

Poplar

Royal Naval College Greenwich

Lewisham

Bromley

Orpington

Welwyn Garden City

Hatfield

Potters Bar

HERTFORDSHIRE
GREATER LONDON

Barnet

Finchley

Hampstead Heath

University of London

LONDON

The City
British Museum

CITY

Southwark

WEST MINSTER

Lambeth

Wandsworth

Streatham

Mitcham

CROYDON

Caterham

Redhill

DOWNS

Oxted

Harpenden

ST. ALBANS

Borehamwood

Edgware

Wembley

Park Royal

Hyde Park
Kensing-ton

Hammersmith

Wimbledon

Sutton

Purley

Banstead

Reigate

Mole

Berkhamsted

Hemel Hempstead

Rickmansworth

Grand Union Canal

Harrow

Ruislip

Southall

Ealing

Hounslow

Richmond

Richmond Park

Bushy Park

KINGSTON upon-Thames

Hook

Esher

Epsom

Leatherhead

BOX HILL

Dorking

NORTH

WATFORD

Gerrards Cross

UXBRIDGE

Brunel University

LONDON (HEATHROW) AIRPORT

Feltham

Queen Mary Reservoir

Walton-on-Thames

Weybridge

Byfleet

Cobham

East Horsley

Wey

BEACON HILL

Aston Wendover

High Wycombe

Marlow

Maidenhead

BUCKINGHAMSHIRE

Chesham

Amersham

Beaconsfield

Burnham

SLOUGH

BERKSHIRE

Windsor

Windsor Castle

Windsor Great Park

Ascot

Bracknell

Meteorological Office

Royal Military Academy Sandhurst

Camberley

Farnborough

Aldershot Barracks

Aldershot

Woking

Staines

University of Surrey

GUILDFORD

Hog's Back

Hog's Back Catterick

CHILTERN HILLS

WESTERN HILLS

Aylesbury

Farnham

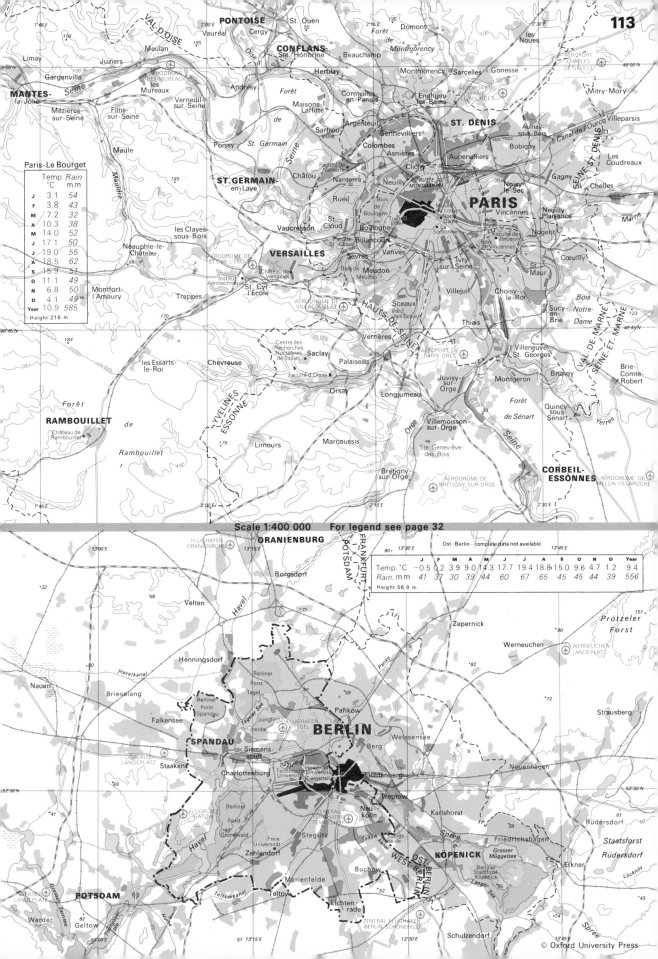

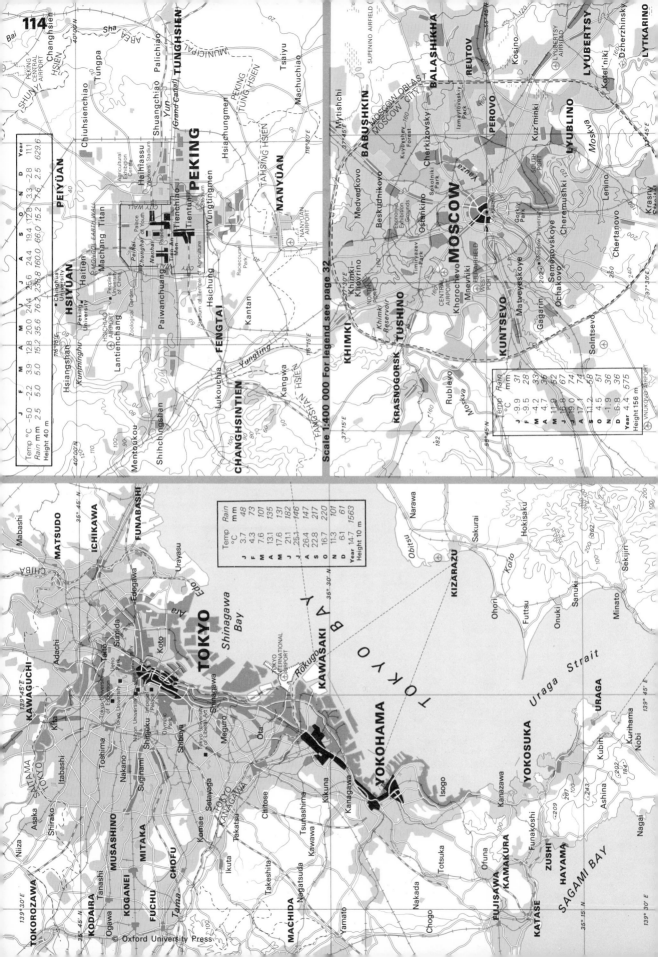

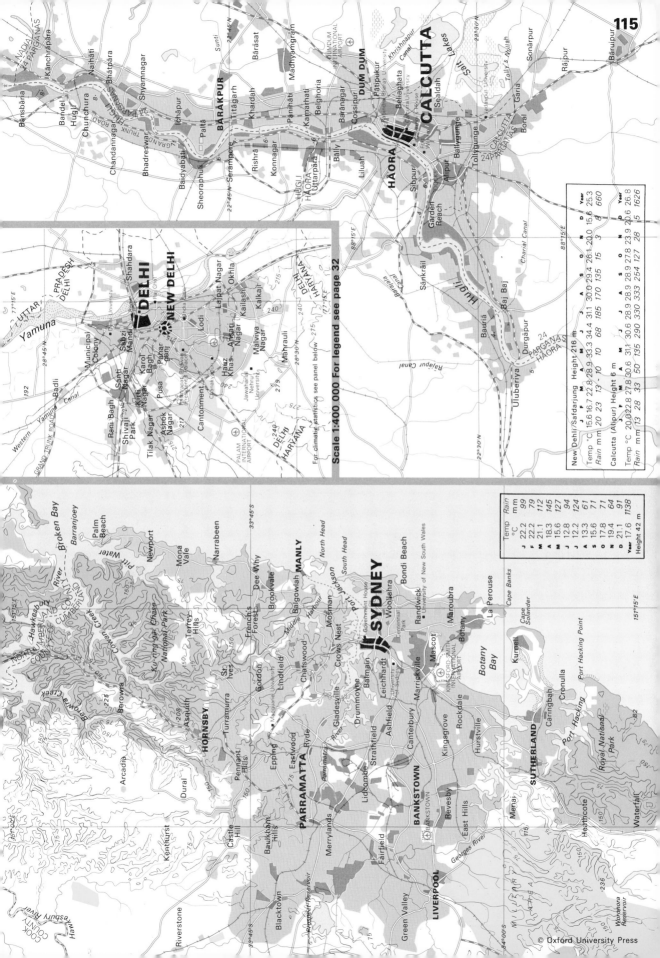

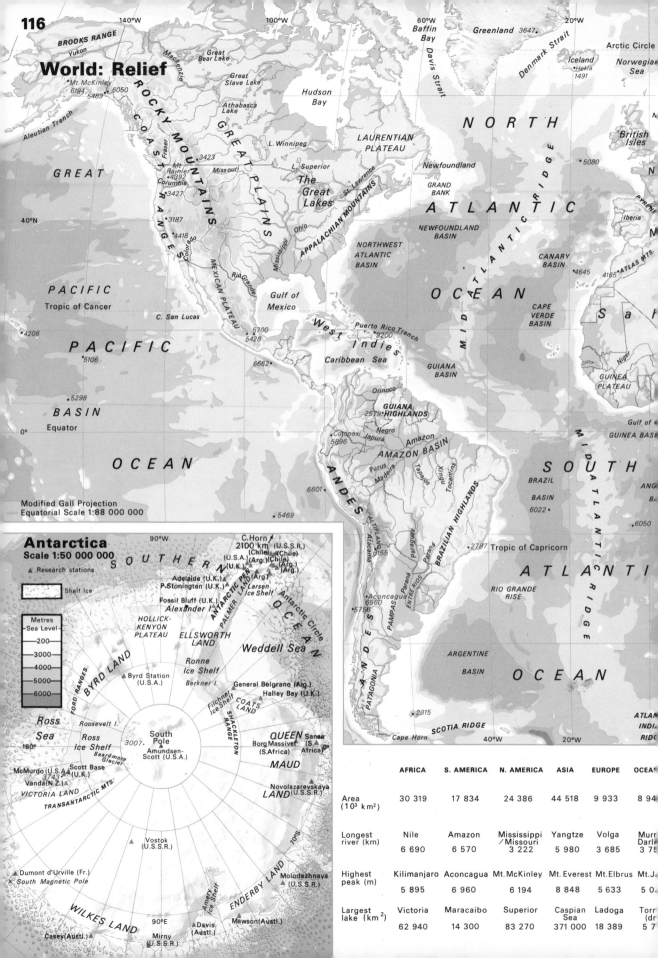

World: Relief

Modified Gall Projection
Equatorial Scale 1:88 000 000

Antarctica
Scale 1:50 000 000

▲ Research stations

Shelf Ice

Metres
Sea Level
-200
-3000
-4000
-5000
-6000

	AFRICA	S. AMERICA	N. AMERICA	ASIA	EUROPE	OCEA
Area (10³ km²)	30 319	17 834	24 386	44 518	9 933	8 94
Longest river (km)	Nile 6 690	Amazon 6 570	Mississippi /Missouri 3 222	Yangtze 5 980	Volga 3 685	Murr Darli 3 75
Highest peak (m)	Kilimanjaro 5 895	Aconcagua 6 960	Mt.McKinley 6 194	Mt.Everest 8 848	Mt.Elbrus 5 633	Mt.J. 5 0.
Largest lake (km²)	Victoria 62 940	Maracaibo 14 300	Superior 83 270	Caspian Sea 371 000	Ladoga 18 389	Torr (dr 5 7

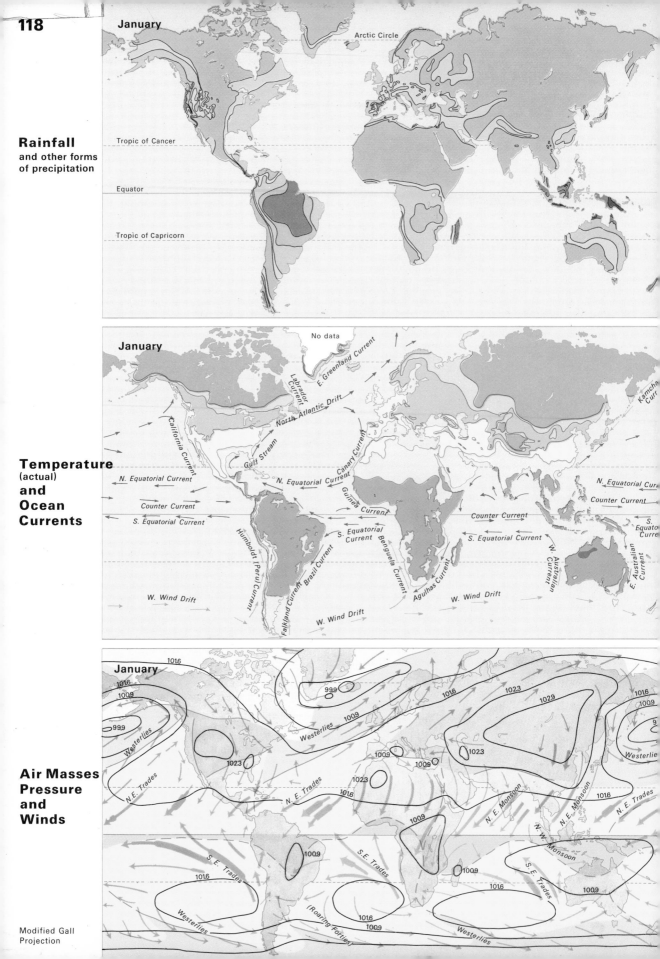

118

Rainfall
and other forms
of precipitation

January

Arctic Circle

Tropic of Cancer

Equator

Tropic of Capricorn

Temperature
(actual)
**and
Ocean
Currents**

January

No data

E. Greenland Current

Labrador Current

Kamcha Curr

California Current

North Atlantic Drift

Gulf Stream

Canary Current

N. Equatorial Current

N. Equatorial Current

N. Equatorial Cure

Counter Current

Counter Current

Guinea Current

S. Equatorial Current

Humboldt (Peru) Current

Falkland Current

Brazil Current

S. Equatorial Current

Benguela Current

Agulhas Current

Counter Current

S. Equatorial Current

S. Equato Curre

W. Australian Current

E. Australian Current

W. Wind Drift

W. Wind Drift

W. Wind Drift

**Air Masses
Pressure
and
Winds**

January

101.6

101.6

100.9

99.9

99.9

Westerlies

Westerlies

1009

1016

1023

1029

1016

1009

N.E. Trades

1023

1009

1009

1009

Westerlie

9

1023

1023

N.E. Trades

N.E. Trades

101.6

N.E. Monsoon

N.E. Monsoon

101.6

N.E. Trades

1009

N.W. Monsoon

S.E. Trades

100.9

S.E. Trades

100.9

100.9

S.E. Trades

101.6

Westerlies

(Roaring Forties)

101.6

100.9

101.6

Westerlies

Modified Gall
Projection

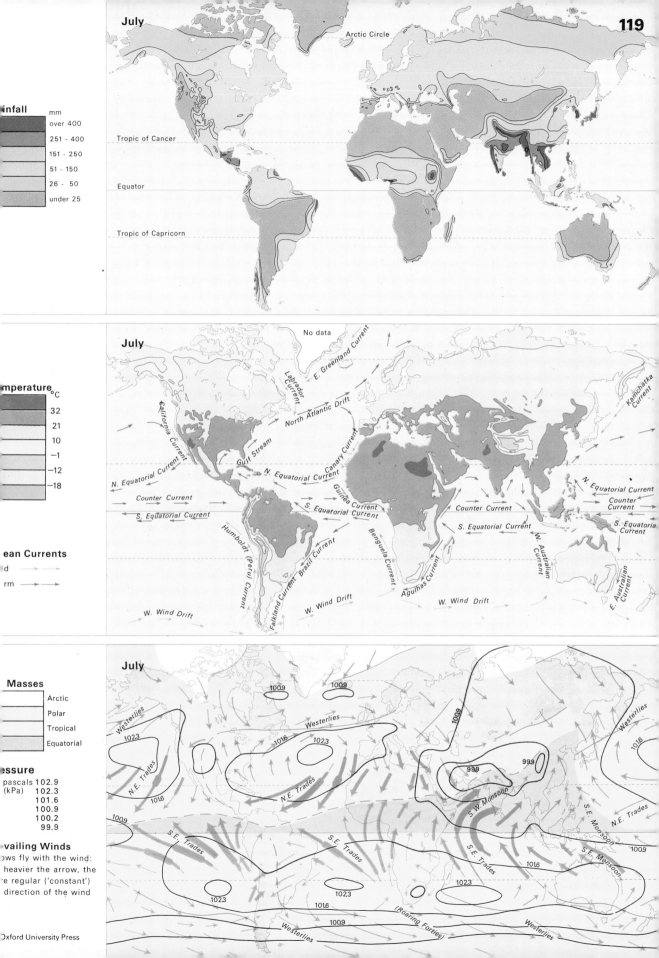

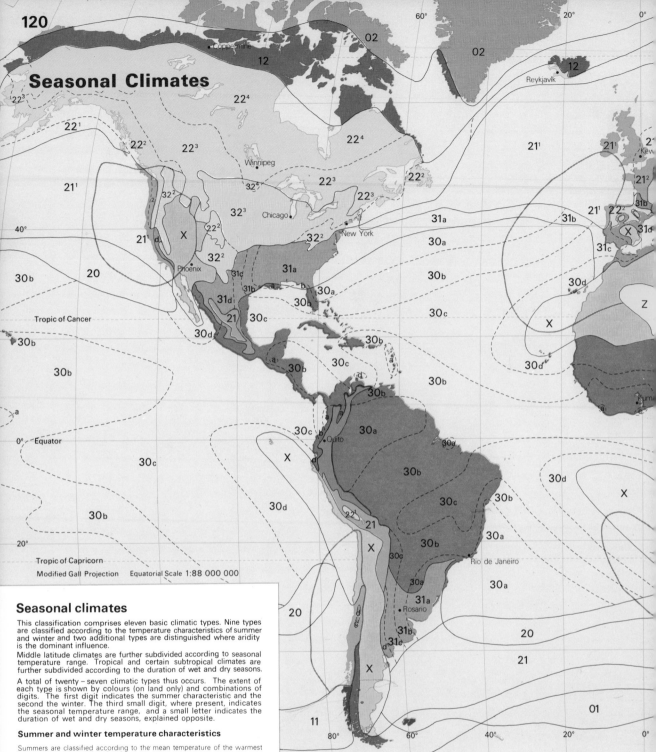

Seasonal Climates

Seasonal climates

This classification comprises eleven basic climatic types. Nine types are classified according to the temperature characteristics of summer and winter and two additional types are distinguished where aridity is the dominant influence.

Middle latitude climates are further subdivided according to seasonal temperature range. Tropical and certain subtropical climates are further subdivided according to the duration of wet and dry seasons.

A total of twenty – seven climatic types thus occurs. The extent of each type is shown by colours (on land only) and combinations of digits. The first digit indicates the summer characteristic and the second the winter. The third small digit, where present, indicates the seasonal temperature range, and a small letter indicates the duration of wet and dry seasons, explained opposite.

Summer and winter temperature characteristics

Summers are classified according to the mean temperature of the warmest month and designated 0, 1, 2 or 3.

		MEAN TEMPERATURE OF THE WARMEST MONTH
0	No summer	6°C and under.
1	Very cool summer	6-10°C
2	Cool summer	10-20°C
3	Full summer	over 20°C

Winters are classified according to the mean temperature of the coldest month and designated 0, 1 or 2.

		MEAN TEMPERATURE OF THE COLDEST MONTH
0	No winter	over 13°C
1	Mild winter	2-13°C
2	Cold winter	below 2°C

Combinations of summer and winter conditions are used to indicate climatic types. These are shown on land areas by colour and by figures and on sea areas by figures only. The digit for summer is always given first. Thus 02 indicates no summer, cold winter.

Combinations of summer and winter conditions

02	No summer / Cold winter		20	Cool summer / No winter
12	Very cool summer / Cold winter		32	Full summer / Cold winter
11	Very cool summer / Mild winter		31	Full summer / Mild winter
22	Cool summer / Cold winter		30	Full summer / No winter
21	Cool summer / Mild winter			

Arid climates

X	Arid

Arid climates are those climates middle and low latitudes in which month receives as much as 50 r rainfall.

Z	Extremely arid

Extremely arid climates are per nially rainless with no more th 2.5 mm rainfall per month for at least 10 months of the year.

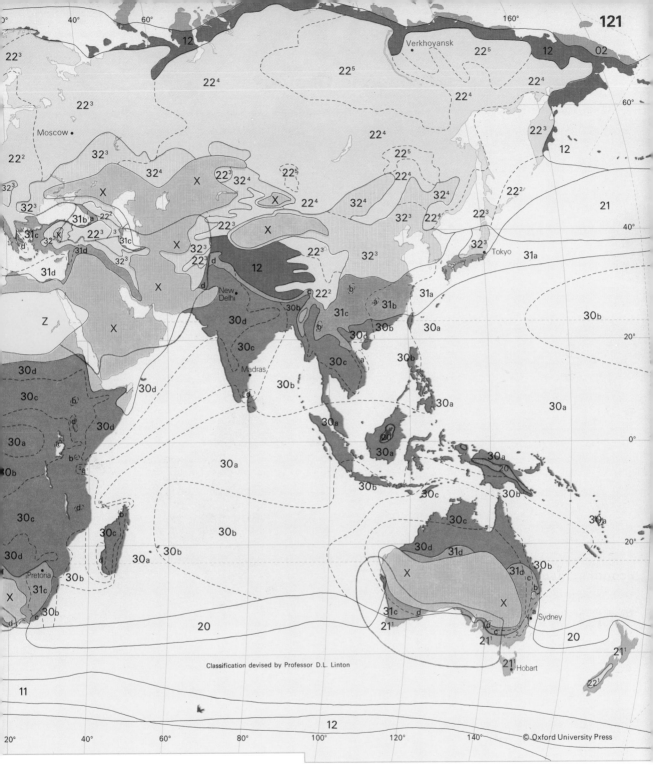

Verkhoyansk

Moscow

New Delhi

Madras

Tokyo

Sydney

Hobart

Pretoria

Classification devised by Professor D.L. Linton

© Oxford University Press

Seasonal temperature range

areas 21, 22 and 32 outside the tropics

Oceanic
Seasonal range under 12°C

Sub Continental
Seasonal range 12 -24°C

Continental
Seasonal range 24-36°C

Very Continental
Seasonal range 36-48°C

Extremely Continental
Seasonal range over 48°C

Duration of wet and dry seasons

For areas 30 and 31 only

a   All months rainy
  i.e. with over 50 mm rainfall

b   Rainy season predominant
  8-11 months with over 50 mm

c   Rainy and dry seasons approx. equal
  5, 6 or 7 months with over 50 mm

d   Dry season predominant
  1-4 months with over 50 mm

Winter rain regions

Boundary of region where
rainfall occurs predominantly
in winter

Mean monthly temperatures for January and July

Selected stations (with altitude in metres)

	Jan. °C	July °C		Jan. °C	July °C
Coppermine (0)	−28.6	9.3	Chicago (190)	−3.3	24.3
Verkhoyansk (137)	−46.8	15.7	New York (16)	0.9	24.9
Winnipeg (240)	−17.7	20.2	Sydney (42)	21.9	12.3
Moscow (156)	−9.9	19.0	Rosario (27)[1]	23.8	9.9
Berlin (50)	−0.5	19.4	Pretoria (1400)[2]	21.0	10.3
Reykjavík (16)	−0.4	11.2	Rio de Janeiro (27)	26.0	20.8
Kew (5)	4.2	17.6	Kumasi (293)[1]	25.2	24.2
Hobart (54)	16.3	7.8	Madras (16)	24.5	30.7
Quito (2812)	13.0	12.9	New Delhi (216)[1]	14.3	31.2
Tokyo (6)	3.7	25.1	Phoenix (337)	10.4	32.9

Temperatures decrease with increasing altitude at a rate of about 2°C for every 300 m
Location, season and time of day all influence the actual rate.

[1]1941–60   [2]1951–60

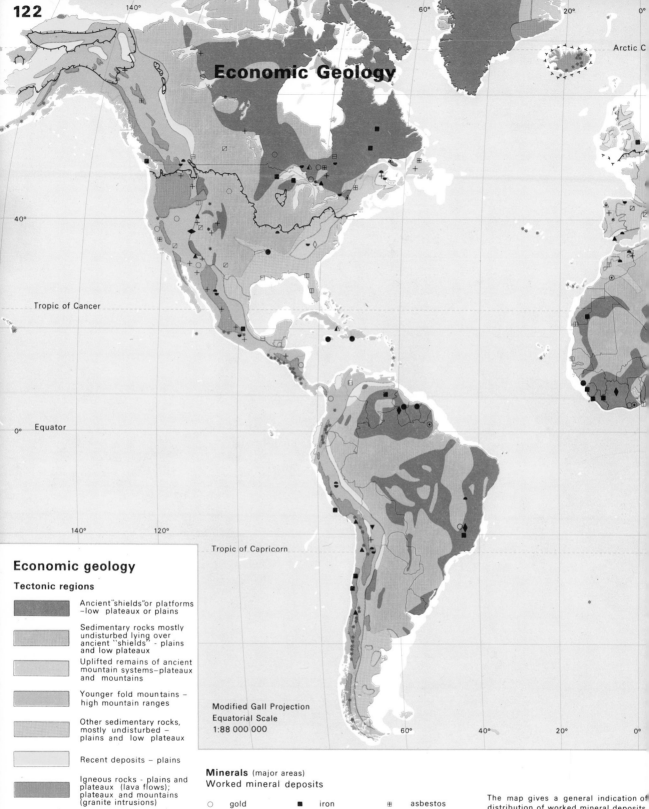

Economic Geology

Arctic C

Tropic of Cancer

Equator

Tropic of Capricorn

Economic geology

Tectonic regions

Ancient "shields" or platforms
– low plateaux or plains

Sedimentary rocks mostly
undisturbed lying over
ancient "shields" – plains
and low plateaux

Uplifted remains of ancient
mountain systems – plateaux
and mountains

Younger fold mountains –
high mountain ranges

Other sedimentary rocks,
mostly undisturbed –
plains and low plateaux

Recent deposits – plains

Igneous rocks – plains and
plateaux (lava flows);
plateaux and mountains
(granite intrusions)

＊＊＊＊＊ Active volcanoes

Volcanoes which have shown no major
activity during this century are not shown

Continental shelf/ocean shallows

White areas represent those regions lying
between 0 and 200 m below sea level

Pleistocene glaciation

Approximate limit of maximum
extent of Pleistocene glaciation

Modified Gall Projection
Equatorial Scale
1:88 000 000

Minerals (major areas)
Worked mineral deposits

○	gold	■	iron	⊕	asbestos
+	silver	⬣	nickel	◆	diamond
▲	copper	⊖	chrome	◇	mica
▼	tin	⊙	manganese	▥	phosphate
⬟	lead	⬤	titanium	▨	potash
⬗	zinc	＊	uranium	⊟	sulphur
●	bauxite				

The distribution of Fossil Fuels is
shown on pages 124–5

The map gives a general indication of
distribution of worked mineral deposits
their relationship with the structure of
earth's crust. Only the major areas of wo
deposits of a selection of minerals are i
cated.

It is important to note that lack of min
workings does not necessarily indicate
of deposits. Some areas remain unwo
either because of insufficient knowledg
the geology or inaccessibility of deposit
because the deposits are uneconomica
work given present day levels of technol

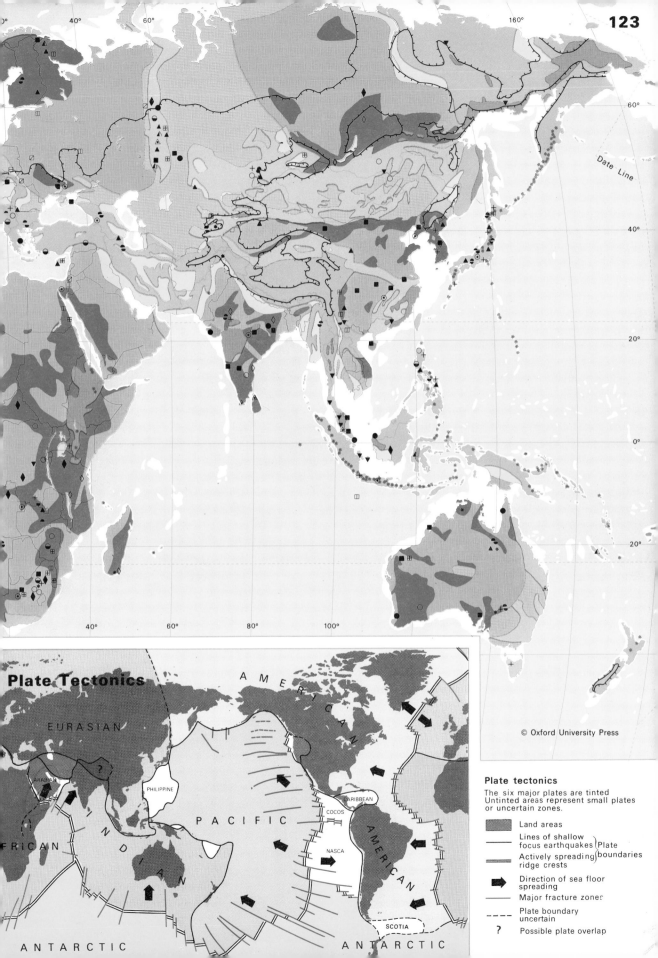

© Oxford University Press

Plate tectonics

The six major plates are tinted
Untinted areas represent small plates
or uncertain zones.

- Land areas
- Lines of shallow focus earthquakes ⎫ Plate
- Actively spreading ridge crests ⎭ boundaries
- ➤ Direction of sea floor spreading
- Major fracture zones
- - - Plate boundary uncertain
- ? Possible plate overlap

Plate Tectonics

AMERICAN

EURASIAN

ARABIAN

PHILIPPINE

AFRICAN

INDIAN

PACIFIC

CARIBBEAN

COCOS

NASCA

AMERICAN

SCOTIA

ANTARCTIC   ANTARCTIC

Date Line

Energy

Natural gas reserves have been found in the Canadian Arctic Islands.

Arctic Circle

140°   60°   20°

Prudhoe Bay
Mackenzie/Beaufort

WESTERN EUROPE 3 1 225

Brent

Gordon M. Shrum
Alberta
La Grande
Churchill Falls

NORTH AMERICA 6 8 373

Colombia River
Monticello

North America (bar graph)
1200 / 1000 / 800 / 600 / 400 / 200

Western Europe (bar graph)
1000 / 800 / 600 / 400 / 200

FROM INDONESIA
Los Angeles

Panhandle
Brown's Ferry
Oconee
Houston
Port Arthur
Freeport
Gulf
Turkey Point

Tropic of Cancer

Tabasco

CARIBBEAN 4 2 6

Virgin Is.
Amuay
Bolivar/Maracaibo

Hass Mess

Energy

Producing areas
oil   oilshale   gas   coal
(Offshore: oil   gas   oil and gas)

Reserves by region (1976)
region name: **NORTH AMERICA**
OIL thousand million tonnes (Gt)
GAS million million cubic metres (10^{12} m³)
COAL thousand million tonnes (Gt)

Crude oil movements (million tonnes 1975)
Every 30 Mt is shown by 0.5 mm width, thus:

represents 60 Mt   →   represents 1–15 Mt

Movements of below a million tonnes are not shown

Oil refining (1975)
Crude oil capacity by refining centre (million tonnes per year)

○ 5 – 25   ◯ OVER 25

Hydro-electric power
Station capacity (MW)
· 500 – 3500
● 3500 – 5000
⬤ OVER 5000

Nuclear power
Station capacity (MW)
○ 500 – 2000
◯ OVER 2000
★ under construction

Fuel and energy by region (1975)
Graphs show regional production and consumption in tonnes coal equivalent

	Liquid fuel	Natural gas	Solid fuel	H.E.P./Nuclear energy
Production				
Consumption				

The energy value of 1 kg of hard coal is equal to that of 3.5 kg lignite, 0.7 kg crude oil, 0.71 kg fuel oil, 0.91 kg natural gas, and 2.5 kW·h electricity.

Caribbean (bar graph)
400 / 200

Other America (bar graph)
200

OTHER AMERICA 1 1 4

Bolivar/Maracaibo

Ilha Solteira

Africa (bar graph)
400 / 200

Modified Gall Projection
Equatorial Scale 1:88 000 000

60°   40°   20°   0°

Crude oil production
2 630 million tonnes 1975
1 830 million tonnes 1967

	PERCENTAGE 1975	1967
U.S.S.R.	18	16
U.S.A.	16	26
Saudi Arabia	13	7
Iran	10	7
Venezuela	4	10
Iraq	4	3
Kuwait	3	6
Nigeria	3	1
China	3	—
Canada	3	3
Others	23	21
	100	100

Natural gas production
1 353 780 million cubic metres 1975
821 650 million cubic metres 1967[1]

	PERCENTAGE 1975	1967
U.S.A.	43	63
U.S.S.R.	21	19
Canada	7	6
Netherlands	7	1
Iran	4	1
China	3	1
U.K.	3	1
Romania	2	2
Mexico	2	2
West Germany	1	—
Others	7	6
	100	100

[1] Excl. China

Coal production

Anthracite/Bituminous 2 227 300 tonnes 1974		Lignite 842 140[1]	
PERCENTAGE 1974		PERCENTAGE 1974	
—	East Germany	29	
24	U.S.A	2	
21	U.S.S.R.	19	
5	West Germany	15	
19	China	1	
1	Czechoslovakia	10	
7	Poland	5	
5	U.K.	—	
—	Yugoslavia	4	
4	India	—	
14	Others	16	
100		100	

[1] Excl. China

A

Montréal
Bruce   Pickering
Zion   Monroe   Indian Point
Bridgman   Perth Amboy
Pennsylvania   Philadelphia
Robinson   N. Anna
Wood River   West Virginia
Kentucky

Scale 1:29 000 0

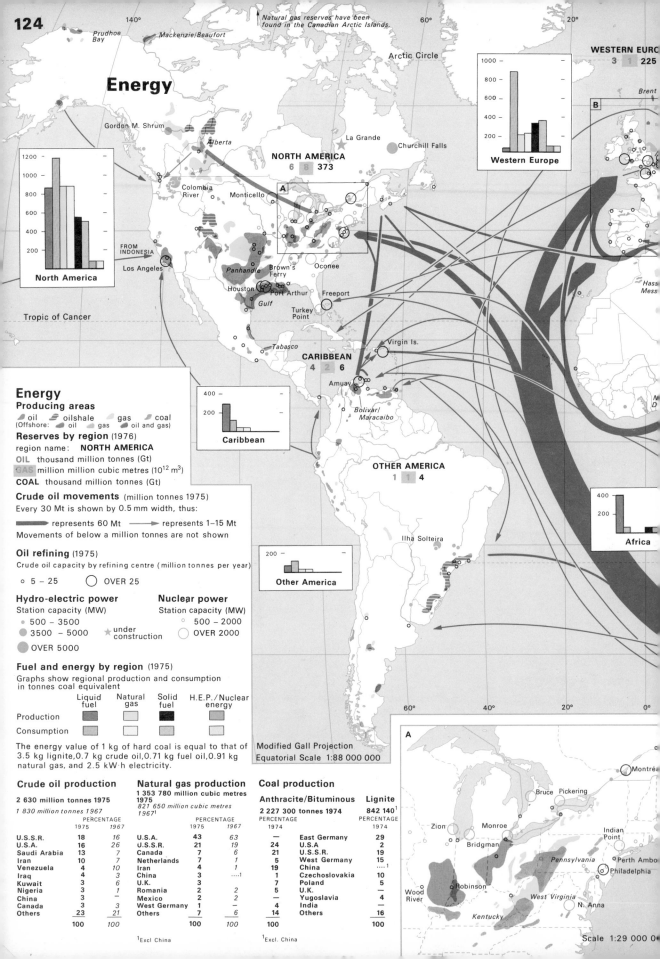

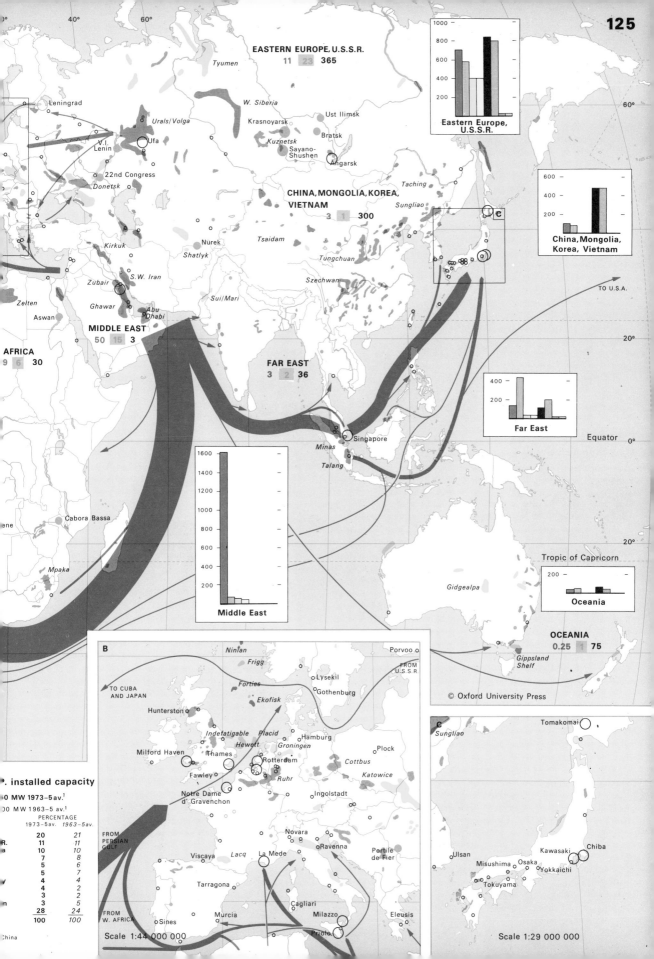

Iron and Steel

Trondheim

Tasu
Harbour

Edmonton

Bruce
Lake

Steep Rock Lake
Marquette Range

Scefferville

Labrador City

Wabash
Gagnon

Haulbowline

Regina

Sault St.
Marie

Selkirk
Mesabi Range

Wawa

Kirkland Lake
Timagami &
Moose Mt.
Montreal

Mondeville

Seattle

Portland
McMinnville

Iron
Mt.

Bilbao

Aviles/Oviedo

Norfolk

Peoria

Bridgeport

Madrid

Fo

Sayreville

Seixal

Sa
M

Union City

Geneva

Kansas
City

Los Angeles

Pueblo

Sand
Springs

Grahite
City

Gadsden

Roanoke
Georgetown

Nadar

Ann

Ou
Bou K

Fontana

Tempe

Fort
Worth

Lone
Star

Atlanta

Eagle
Mt.

Ciudad
Camargo

Birmingham

Tampa

Houston

Indiantown

Fort-Gouraun

Monclova

Monterrey

Victoria de Durango

Pihuamo

Mexico City

Pena Colorado
Las Truchas

Veracruz

Tropic of Cancer

Caracas

El Pao

Marampo
Nimba

Boyaca

Cerro Bolivar

Conakry

Mano
River

Mt.Klah

Belencito

Bomi
Hills

Bong

Chimbote

Iron and steel

Iron ore production (1972–4av.)

thousand tonnes iron content

25 000
AND OVER
15 000 –
25 000
5 000 –
15 000
2 500 –
5 000
1 000 –
2 500
100 –
1 000

+ Data not available for known producing centres, but where
regional data are known the appropriate symbol is enclosed
in a box

☆ Major area of development

Steel production centres (1976)

thousand tonnes crude steel capacity

32 000
AND OVER
16 000 –
32 000
8 000 –
16 000
4 000 –
8 000
2 000 –
4 000
1 000 –
2 000
150 –
1 000

Where iron ore mine and steel works are coincident the
locational name is underlined, for example Maanshan

Marcona
Acari

Belo Horizonte/
Itabira

Belo Horizonte

Piracicaba

Juiz de Fora

Palpalá

Zapla

Barra Mansa

São Paulo

Rio de Janeiro

El Romeral

Atacama

Sapucaia do Sul

Algarrobo

Rosario

San Nicolas de los Arroyos

Buenos Aires

Huachipato

Modified Gall Projection
Equatorial Scale 1:88 000 000

Inset A

Hamilton

Welland

Auburn

Nanticoke

Lackawanna/Buffalo

Detroit

Trenton

Erie

Dunkirk

Chicago
E.Chicago

Warren

Burns
Harbor

Cleveland

Youngstown

Fairless
Hills

Gary

Lorain

Farrell
Butler

Milton

Mansfield

Canton
Brackenridge

Bethlehem

Kokomo

Midland

Johnstown

Weirton/Steubenville

Monessen

Steelton

Aliquippa

Conshohocken

Middletown

Pittsburgh

Wilder

Baltimore

Portsmouth

Sparrows
Point

Ashland

Owensboro

Scale 1:13 000 000

Iron ore production[1]

477 533 000*   tonnes 1972–4av.
309 707 000*   1963–5av.

Steel production

674 067 000*
428 044 000*

PERCENTAGE			PERCENTAGE	
1963–5av.	1972–4av.		1972–4av	1963–5av.
28	25	U.S.S.R.	19	20
15	10	U.S.A.	19	26
—	—	Japan [2]	16	9
1	10	Australia [2]	1	1
3	8	Brazil [2]	1	1
1	—	W. Germany [2]	7	8
8	7	China*	4	3
6	6	Canada [2]	2	2
6	3	France*[2]	4	4
32	31	Others	27	26
100	100		100	100

*Estimate [1]Iron content. [2]The inclusion of countries whose
ratings for the commodity are not greybacked, is based on their
production of the other commodity.

Inset B

Glasgow

Motherwell

Glengarnock

Hartle

Trenton

Consett

Middlesborough

Manchester

Scunth

Birkenhead

Deeside

Sheffiel
Stoke

Wrexham

Wolverhampton

Corb

Ebbw Vale

Llanwern

Llanelli
Port
Talbot

Cardiff

Sheer

Scale 1:22 000 000

Sydney

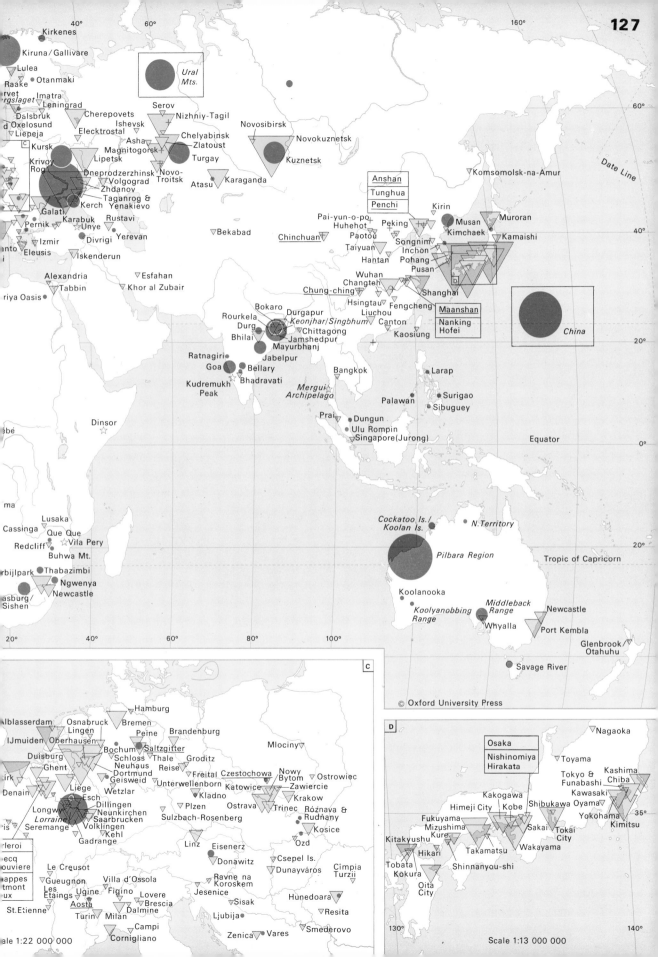

40° 60° 160°

● Kirkenes
● Kiruna/Gallivare
● Lulea
● Otanmaki
● Raake
rvet
●rgslaget
● Imatra
● Leningrad
Dalsbruk ● Cherepovets
d Oxelosund
▽ Liepeja
Ishevsk
● Elecktrostal
C
● Kursk
● Krivoy
Rog
Asha
▽ Magnitogorsk
Lipetsk
Dneprodzerzhinsk
▽ Volgograd
Zhdanov
Taganrog &
● Galati Yenakievo
Kerch
● Pernik Karabuk
Unye
▽ Izmir
Eleusis Divrigi
anto
● Yerevan
i
riya Oasis ●
● Alexandria
▽ Tabbin

Serov
Nizhniy-Tagil
▽ Chelyabinsk
Zlatoust
Novo- Turgay
Troitsk
Atasu Karaganda

Novosibirsk
Novokuznetsk
Kuznetsk

▽ Komsomolsk-na-Amur

Date Line

60°

▽ Bekabad

Ural
Mts.

Rustavi

▽ Esfahan
▽ Khor al Zubair

Pai-yun-o-po
Huhehot Kirin
Paotou Musan
Chinchuan Songnim Kimcheak Kamaishi
Taiyuan Inchon
Hantan Pohang
Wuhan Pusan
Changteh
Hsingtau Fengcheng
Liuchou Shanghai
Canton Maanshan
Kaosiung Nanking
Hofei

Peking Muroran

Anshan
Tunghua
Penchi

40°

China

20°

Bokaro
Rourkela Durgapur
Durg Keonjhar/Singbhum
Bhilai Chittagong
Jamshedpur
Mayurbhanj
Jabelpur
Ratnagiri
Goa Bellary
Kudremukh Bhadravati
Peak

Bangkok
Larap

Surigao
Palawan Sibuguey

Mergui
Archipelago

Dinsor

Prai Dungun
Ulu Rompin
Singapore(Jurong)

Equator 0°

bé

ma
Lusaka
Cassinga Que Que
Redcliff Vila Pery
Buwha Mt.
rbijlpark Thabazimbi
asburg/ Ngwenya
Sishen Newcastle

Cockatoo Is./
Koolan Is. N.Territory

Pilbara Region

Tropic of Capricorn 20°

Koolanooka

Koolyanobbing
Range Middleback
Range Newcastle
Whyalla Port Kembla

Glenbrook/
Otahuhu

© Oxford University Press

Savage River

20° 40° 60° 80° 100°

Iblasserdam Hamburg
Osnabruck
IJmuiden Lingen Bremen
Oberhausen Peine Brandenburg
Duisburg Bochum Saltzgitter
Ghent Schloss Mlociny
irk Neuhaus Thale Groditz
Denain Dortmund Reise
Liege Geisweid Unterwellenborn Nowy
Longwy Wetzlar Freital Czestochowa Bytom Ostrowiec
Lorraine Esch Dillingen Kladno Katowice Zawiercie
Seremange Neunkirchen Plzen Krakow
Volklingen Saarbrucken Ostrava Trinec Róznava &
leroi Kehl Sulzbach-Rosenberg Rudnany
ecq Gadrange Kosice
ouviere Linz Eisenerz Ozd
appes Le Creusot Donawitz Csepel Is. Cimpia
mont Gueugnon Ravne na Dunayváros Turzii
ux Les Villa d'Ossola Koroskem
Etaings Ugine Figino Lovere Jesenice Hunedoara
St.Etienne Aosta Dalmine Sisak Resita
Turin Milan Ljubija
Campi Zenica Vares Smederovo
Cornigliano

C

Scale 1:22 000 000

D

Nagaoka
Osaka Toyama
Nishinomiya Tokyo & Kashima
Hirakata Funabashi Chiba
Kawasaki
Kakogawa Oyama
Himeji City Kobe Shibukawa Yokohama
Fukuyama Sakai Kimitsu
Mizushima Tokai
Kitakyushu Kure City
Tobata Takamatsu Wakayama
Kokura Hikari
Shinnanyou-shi
Oita
City

35°

130° 140°

Scale 1:13 000 000

Economic Regions

140°   60°   20°   0°

Arctic C

40°

Tropic of Cancer

0° Equator

20°

Tropic of Capricorn

40°

Modified Gall Projection   Equatorial Scale 1:88 000 000   80°   60°   20°   0°

Economic regions (by predominant activity)

Little or no economic activity	Subsistence agriculture: rice dominant	Other commercial crops: grain dominant
Nomadic herding	Subsistence agriculture: rice unimportant	Commercial agriculture: mixed crop and livestock
Hunting, gathering, fishing and primitive cultivation	Subsistence agriculture: mixed crop and livestock	Dairy farming
Shifting and marginal cultivation	Mediterranean agriculture	Manufacturing and service industries
Commercial forestry	Plantation crops	
Extensive grazing or stock raising	Specialized horticulture	Mining and extractive industries

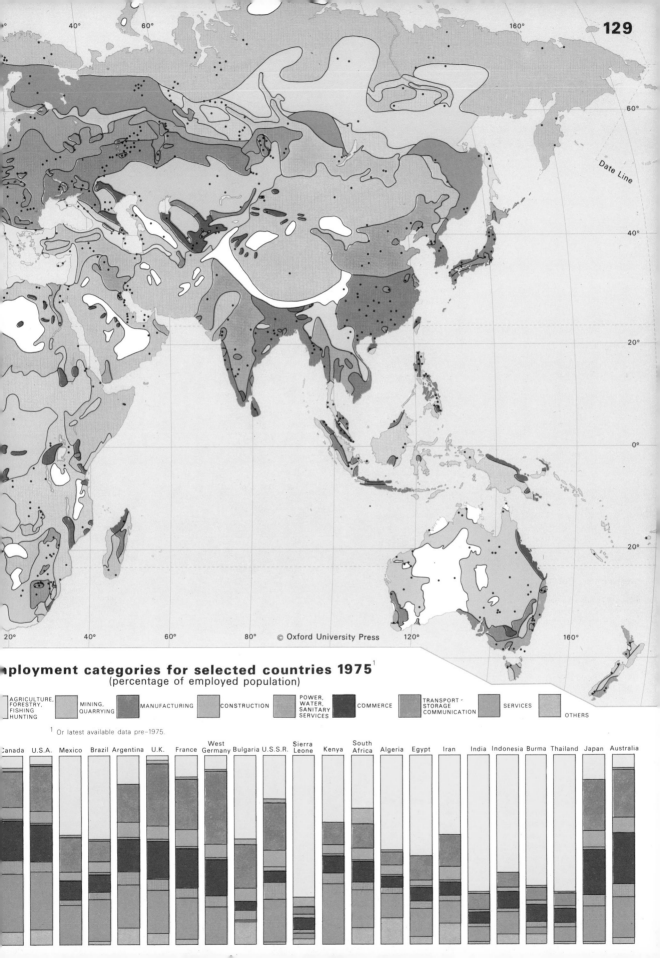

60°

40°

20°

0°

20°

Date Line

40° 60° 160°

20° 40° 60° 80° © Oxford University Press 120° 160°

ployment categories for selected countries 1975[1]
(percentage of employed population)

AGRICULTURE, FORESTRY, FISHING HUNTING | MINING, QUARRYING | MANUFACTURING | CONSTRUCTION | POWER, WATER, SANITARY SERVICES | COMMERCE | TRANSPORT STORAGE COMMUNICATION | SERVICES | OTHERS

[1] Or latest available data pre-1975.

Canada U.S.A. Mexico Brazil Argentina U.K. France West Germany Bulgaria U.S.S.R. Sierra Leone Kenya South Africa Algeria Egypt Iran India Indonesia Burma Thailand Japan Australia

World Political

140° 60° 20° 0°

Arctic Cir

GREENLAND (Den.)

• Godthaab

ICELAND
Reykjavik

FAEROE ISLANDS (Den.)

C A N A D A

REP. OF IRELAND — UNITED KINGDOM
Dublin • London
Brusse
Paris • FRAN

• Ottawa

U. S. A.

40°

• Washington

Cuba claims that the treaty allowing the U.S.A. to establish a naval base at Guantánamo Bay is void and that occupation of the territory by the U.S.A. is therefore illegal.

Spain claims sovereignty over Gibraltar, a U.K. dependency.

PORTUGAL • Madrid
Lisbon • SPAIN

• Rabat

MOROCCO

CANARY ISLANDS (Sp.)

ALGEF

• BERMUDA

Algeria does not accept the agreement of Nov.1975 providing for the transfer of power in Western Sahara from Spain to Morocco and Mauritania, affirming the right of the territory as a whole to self-determination.

WESTERN SAHARA

• El Aaiûn

MEXICO

Tropic of Cancer

HAWAIIAN ISLANDS (U.S.A.)

Nassau • BAHAMAS

Havana CUBA

Mexico City

DOMINICAN REP.
HAITI PUERTO RICO
Port- Santo (U.S.A.)
au- Domingo
Prince West Indies

Guatemala claims sovereignty over Belize, a U.K. dependency.

BELIZE JAMAICA
Belmopan Kingston
GUATEMALA
Guatemala City HONDURAS
San Salvador Tegucigalpa
EL SALVADOR NICARAGUA
Managua

BARBADOS
• Bridgetown
TRINIDAD AND TOBAGO
Port of Spain

MAURITANIA
• Nouakchott

CAPE VERDE ISLANDS
• Praia

MALI REPUBLIC

SENEGAL
Dakar • Banjul Bamako UPPER
GAMBIA VOLTA
GUINEA-BISSAU Bissau GHANA
GUINEA Oua
Freetown • Conakry IVORY
SIERRA LEONE COAST
Monrovia Abidjan Acc
LIBERIA

COSTA RICA
San José PANAMA
Panama City

Caracas

VENEZUELA GUYANA
Georgetown • Paramaribo
Bogota • SURINAM
COLOMBIA Cayenne
FR. GUIANA

EQ. GUINEA

SAO AND PRINC

Abbreviations
.DEN. Denmark
N. Netherlands
B. Belgium
LUX. Luxembourg
W. GER West Germany
E.GER East Germany
AUS. Austria
SW. Switzerland
CZECH. Czechoslovakia
ALB. Albania
LEB. Lebanon
T. Togo

0° Equator

GALAPAGOS ISLANDS (Ec.)

ECUADOR

• Quito

B R A Z I L

Ecuador ceded a large area to Peru in 1942 after invasion, but denounced the peace treaty in 1961.

• Lima

P E R U

BOLIVIA
La Paz

• Brasilia

20°

140° 120°

Tropic of Capricorn

PARAGUAY
Asunción

A R G E N T I N A
C H I L E

URUGUAY
Buenos Montevideo
Aires

Santiago

South West Africa (Namibia) is administered by South Africa des the U.N. General Assembly resolu reaffirming the right of South We Africa to self-determination and independence, and despite the decision of the International Cour Justice and the U.N. that South Africa's presence there is illegal.

• Capital cities (1976)

Nigeria — it was announced in February 1976 that the Federal Capital would be moved inland from Lagos to a new site north of Lokoja.

✱✱✱✱✱✱ Unsettled boundaries (1976)

This includes active and latent disputes over exact positioning of boundaries whether demarcated, delimited, provisional or undefined.

Modified Gall Projection
Equatorial Scale
1:88 000 000

Argentina claims sovereignty over the Falkland Islands, a U.K. dependency.

20° 0°

FALKLAND ISLANDS (U.K.)
• Stanley

Membership of International Organizations (1976)

● Full Member
○ Associate Member

	Canada	U.S.A.	Mexico	Belize	Guatemala	Honduras	El Salvador	Nicaragua	Costa Rica	Panama	Cuba	Jamaica	Haiti	Dominican R.	St. Kitts[1,2]	Antigua[2]	Montserrat[2]	Dominica[2]	St. Lucia[2]	St Vincent[2]	Barbados[2]	Grenada[2]	T. & T.[3]	Guyana	Venezuela	Colombia	Ecuador	Peru	Brazil	Bolivia	Paraguay	Uruguay	Chile	Argentina		Norway	Sweden	Denmark	Finland	Iceland	U.K.	Ireland	W. Germany	Netherlands	Belgium	Luxembourg	France	Switzerland	Austria	Italy	Spain
OAS (Organization of American States)	●	●	●		●	●	●	●	●	●		●	●	●							●		●		●	●	●	●	●	●	●	●	●	●	1																
LAFTA (Latin American Free Trade Association)			●																						●	●	●	●	●	●	●	●	●	●	2																
CARICOM (Caribbean Free Trade Area)				●								●			●	●	●	●	●	●	●	●	●	●											3																
NATO (North Atlantic Treaty Organization)	●	●																																	4	●		●		●	●		●	●	●	●	●			●	
EEC (European Economic Community)																																			5			●			●	●	●	●	●	●	●			●	
OECD (Org. for Econ. Cooperation & Development)	●	●																																	6	●	●	●	●	●	●	●	●	●	●	●	●	●	●	●	●
COMECON/CMEA (Council for Mutual Econ. Aid)[4]											●																								7																
OAU (Organization of African Unity)																																			8																
ECOWAS (Econ. Community of W African States)																																			9																
OCAM (Common African & Mauritian Organization)																																			10																
Arab League																																			11																
CENTO (Central Treaty Organization)		●																																	12						●										
SEATO (South East Asia Treaty Organization)		●																																	13						●						●				

[1] Includes St.Kitts -Nevis-Anguilla   [2] Islands of the West Indies   [3] Trinidad & Tobago

India claims sovereignty over the state of Jammu and Kashmir. This has been disputed by Pakistan and armed conflict has ensued on several occasions since 1947. The state is now divided by a "control line" agreed in 1972.

Turkey invaded Cyprus in 1974 in support of the Turkish Cypriot minority. As a result a Turkish Cypriot state was established in the northern part of the island, despite the opposition of the U.N.

Japan claims sovereignty over southern Kurile Islands.

China regards Taiwan as a province of China.

The Somali Republic claims sovereignty over Djibouti.

Indonesia does not accept the union of Sabah and Sarawak with Malaya to form Malaysia, affirming that they should be independent. The Philippines claims sovereignty over Sabah.

Rhodesia (Zimbabwe), although legally a self-governing colony within the British Commonwealth, declared unilateral independence in 1965. Consequently most of the U.N. member states broke off economic relations. Repeated but unsuccessful attempts have been made to resolve the constitutional problem, notably in 1966, 1968, 1972 and 1976.

© Oxford University Press

MECON members except Mongolia and Cuba are members of the Warsaw Pact, as is Albania. China, North Korea and North Vietnam are "observers" to COMECON

140°　　　　　　　　　　60°　　　　　　20°　　　　0°

Population Distribution and Growth

Arctic

40°

Tropic of Cancer

Equator

Tropic of Capricorn

40°

Population distribution and growth

Population distribution

Towns of at least 100 000 population

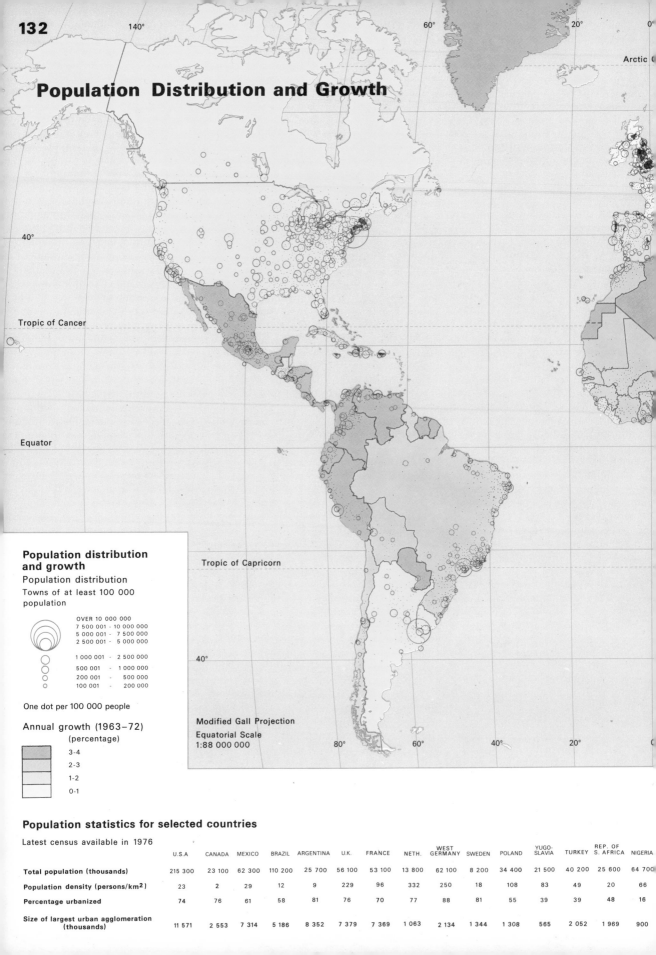

OVER 10 000 000
7 500 001 - 10 000 000
5 000 001 - 7 500 000
2 500 001 - 5 000 000

1 000 001 - 2 500 000
500 001 - 1 000 000
200 001 - 500 000
100 001 - 200 000

One dot per 100 000 people

Annual growth (1963–72)

(percentage)

3-4
2-3
1-2
0-1

Modified Gall Projection
Equatorial Scale
1:88 000 000

80°　　　　　60°　　　　　40°　　　　　20°

Population statistics for selected countries

Latest census available in 1976

	U.S.A	CANADA	MEXICO	BRAZIL	ARGENTINA	U.K.	FRANCE	NETH.	WEST GERMANY	SWEDEN	POLAND	YUGO-SLAVIA	TURKEY	REP. OF S. AFRICA	NIGERIA
Total population (thousands)	215 300	23 100	62 300	110 200	25 700	56 100	53 100	13 800	62 100	8 200	34 400	21 500	40 200	25 600	64 700
Population density (persons/km²)	23	2	29	12	9	229	96	332	250	18	108	83	49	20	66
Percentage urbanized	74	76	61	58	81	76	70	77	88	81	55	39	39	48	16
Size of largest urban agglomeration (thousands)	11 571	2 553	7 314	5 186	8 352	7 379	7 369	1 063	2 134	1 344	1 308	565	2 052	1 969	900

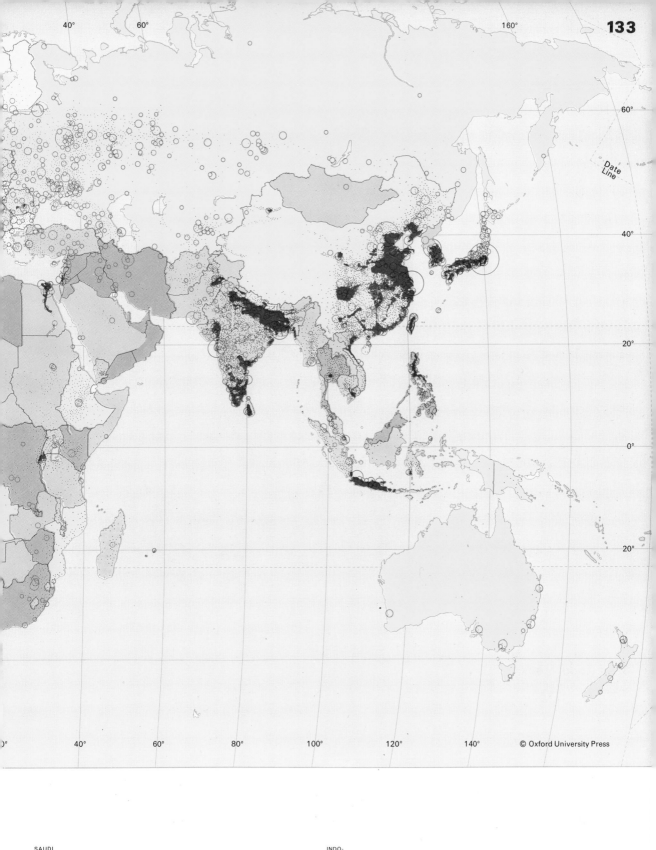

40° 60° 160°

60°

Date Line

40°

20°

0°

20°

© Oxford University Press

40° 60° 80° 100° 120° 140°

	EGYPT	SAUDI ARABIA	ISRAEL	IRAQ	INDIA	BURMA	THAILAND	CAMBODIA	MALAYSIA	INDO-NESIA	PHILIPPINES	CHINA	TAIWAN	JAPAN	U.S.S.R.	AUSTRALIA
	38 100	6 400	3 500	11 400	620 700	31 200	43 300	8 300	12 400	134 700	44 000	836 800	16 300	112 300	257 000	13 800
	36	4	159	25	178	45	80	44	35	86	138	86	433	295	12	2
	43	18	86	61	20	19	13	19	27	18	32	23	63	72	60	86
	4 961	225	838	1 657	7 005	1 718	1 867	1 800	452	4 576	1 377	10 820	1 155	11 454	7 172	2 717

Nutrition

Modified Gall Projection   Equatorial Scale 1:88 000 000

Basic food crops

Production   areas of production of selected crops

Rice, Wheat, Corn,
Barley, Rye, Millet, Teff.   (one dot:100 000 t)

Cassava, Yams, Potatoes.   (one dot:100 000 t)
Sugar, Plantains, Fruit.   (one dot:20 000 t)

Consumption   estimated domestic consumption from
national production of those crops shown
(kilojoules per capita per day)

| 0–1900 | 1900–3800 | 3800–5700 | 5700–7600 |

For each country are shown per capita domestic consumption
and areas of production for one or more basic food crop. The
crops selected are those carbohydrates which contribute the
highest number of kilojoules per capita of any home-grown crop.
Selection has been based on national averages, and does not
take account of regional or other variations.
Further crops are shown for a country if the contribution to the
national average kilojoule intake is at least 75% of that of the
first crop selected. When this occurs, the consumption category
is based on the aggregate for all crops shown; for example, in
Brazil rice provides 2000 kJ/d and sugar 1660 (83% of the rice).
Both crops are mapped and kilojoule intake is given as
3650 kJ/d

Fat levels per capita

Selected countries
(grams per day)

West Germany	163.6
U.S.A.	159.2
Canada	147.2
U.K.	142.3
Argentina	129.5
U.S.S.R.	74.5
South Africa	66.2
Venezuela	63.3
Japan	51.9
Nigeria	48.7
Iraq	36.7
Bolivia	33.9
Algeria	28.7
India	25.9
Laos	13.6

In general there are two methods
employed in increasing food production. The first is to improve the
existing methods of husbandry at a
minimal cost. The second, which is
used to raise the levels of yield
further, entails the breeding and
selection of seeds or crops best
fitted to the environment coupled
with the efficient use of fertilizers,
pesticides and farm mechanization. Increased productivity of the
agrarian labour force is also a requirement. In some areas a high
level of mechanization is essential
to ensure that the crops are sown
and harvested at the right times, as
in the Canadian wheat belt. In
other regions where, as a conse-
quence of industrialization, farm
workers must be paid high wages,
mechanization is essential to keep

down costs of production. Trac
are only a part of mechaniza
but the following table gives
idea of one aspect of the lab
mechanization balance.

	Agrarian labour as % of total	Tractors arable 10 (
India	72.0	11
Thailand	71.8	10
Ghana	58.4	11
Bulgaria	44.4	160
Brazil	44.3	55
Peru	40.6	41
Kenya	34.8	33
Jordan	33.7	24
U.S.S.R.	26.3	94
Japan	12.8	536
New Zealand	11.8	1 177
Netherlands	8.1	2 031
Canada	6.0	143
U.S.A.	4.0	215
U.K.	2.5	634

40° 60° 160°

Date line

60°

Wheat

Wheat *Wheat* *Wheat*

Wheat *Wheat* *Wheat* *Wheat*

40°

Wheat *Wheat* *Wheat* *Rice* *Rice*

Wheat *Wheat* *Rice* *Rice*

Wheat *Wheat* *Rice*

at *Wheat*

Wheat *Fruit* *Wheat* *Wheat* *Rice*

Wheat *Corn* *Wheat* *Rice* *Rice* *Rice* *Rice*

Millet *Rice* *Rice* *Rice* *Rice*

20°

Rice *Rice* *Rice* *Rice*

Millet *let* *Millet* *Rice* *Rice* *Rice* *Rice*

Teff *Rice* *Rice* *Rice* *Rice*

Cassava *Millet/Corn* *Rice*

Plantains *Rice* *Rice*

a *Corn* *Rice* 0°

Millet *Rice* *Rice*

Corn *Corn* *Rice*

Corn *Rice* 20°

Corn

Wheat

Wheat *Wheat* *Wheat*

Wheat

Wheat

© Oxford University Press

40° 60° 80° 100° 120° 140°

---

mated megajoules per capita per day

Estimated minimum megajoule requirement to avoid malnutrition, by region

Europe[1]	10.8
North America	10.8
Latin America	10.1
Middle East	10.0
Africa	9.8
Asia[2]	9.6

Estimated grams per day of protein available, by region

North America	93
Europe[1]	88
Middle East	76
Latin America	67
Africa	61
Asia[2]	56

[1]Incl. U.S.S.R. [2]Incl. China

Estimated protein per capita (grams per day)

86–110
76–86
66–76
56–66
UNDER 56

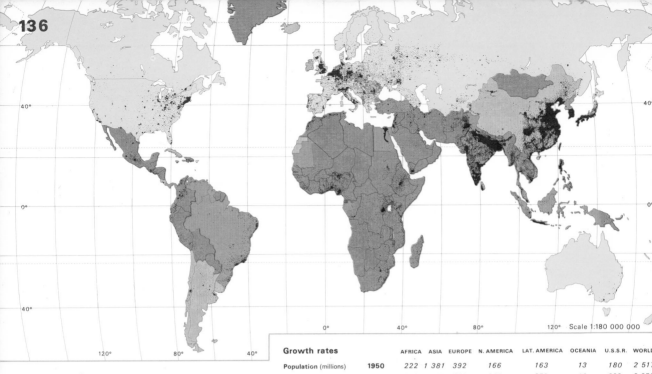

Crude birth rate

Annual rate per thousand people
(latest available data pre-1975)

40 & OVER	20 – 30
30 – 40	10 – 20

One dot to 100 000 population

Data for much of Asia, Africa, Latin America and Oceania are of dubious reliability. Comparison between *any* countries should be treated with care. The extent and type of survey, variation in basis and year of data will all affect the rate.

Growth rates		AFRICA	ASIA	EUROPE	N. AMERICA	LAT. AMERICA	OCEANIA	U.S.S.R.	WORLD
Population (millions)	1950	222	1 381	392	166	163	13	180	2 512
	1960	318	1 868	449	217	253	18	233	3 356
	1976	413	2 287	476	239	326	22	257	4 019
Av. annual birth rate (‰)	1960–66	46	38	18	22	41	26	22	34
	1970–75	46	33	15	15	37	22	18	30
Av. annual death rate (‰)	1960–66	23	18	10	9	13	11	7	16
	1970–75	20	13	10	9	9	10	9	12
Av. rate of population increase (%)	1960–66	2.3	2.3	0.9	1.5	2.8	2.1	1.4	1.9
	1970–75	2.6	2.0	0.6	0.8	2.8	1.8	0.9	1.8

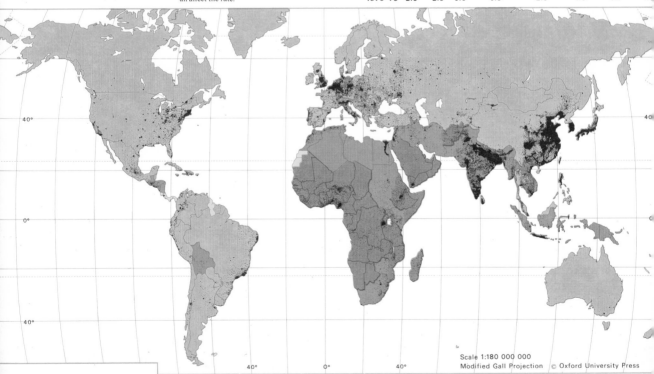

Scale 1:180 000 000
Modified Gall Projection © Oxford University Press

Crude death rate

Annual rate per thousand people
(latest available data pre–1975)

18 & OVER	6 – 12
12 – 18	UNDER 6

One dot to 100 000 population

There are many difficulties in obtaining accurate mortality statistics. A major problem is the variation among countries in the basis of tabulation, that is, by date of occurrence or by date of registration. If registration is prompt the difference is slight, but if registration is delayed internationally comparable data will not be produced, especially since the number of events registered may vary due to temporary incentives to encourage registration. There is also a real danger of excluding the deaths of infants who died before registration of their births. Large areas of Latin America, North Africa, the Middle East and Asia are particularly suspect.

Although death rates are still high in many developing nations, great advances are being made with the introduction of advanced medical methods such as in the campaign to fight malaria in Ceylon which started in 1946. The rapidly falling death rates, which are linked with medical technology and socio-political organization, are not matched by equally declining birth rates, which are more responsive to cultural conditions.

Ceylon
Death

1921–25
1940–44
1946
1948
1955
1965
1975

Gazetteers

Notes

This atlas has two gazetteers. The Gazetteer of Canada, which covers the topographical maps of Canada (pages 12-31) and the urban plans of Montréal, Ottawa and Toronto (page 32), Winnipeg (page 33) and Vancouver (page 36), is exhaustive and lists all the names shown on the maps. Entries without page numbers are places which do not appear on the maps but their location may be deduced from their latitude and longitude or found by reference to the *Canadian Oxford Atlas*. The World Gazetteer is selective and only lists the more important places and features so the absence of a name in the gazetteer does not necessarily mean that the place or feature is not shown on the map.

All entries are gazetteered to the largest scale map on which the feature appears in its entirety. The geographical co-ordinates are given to the nearest whole degree, thus:

Åland Is.: Finland. Co-ordinates to degrees and minutes: 60°15′N 20°00′E. Gazetteered to 60N 20E.

Port Elizabeth: S.Africa. Co-ordinates to degrees and minutes: 33°58′S 25°36′E. Gazetteered to 34S 26E.

Entries in capital letters denote provincial capitals in Canada (thus: TORONTO) or country capitals in the rest of the world.

Entries in bold face capitals denote countries (thus: **JAPAN**).

Abbreviations

The following abbreviations have been used on the maps and in the gazetteers.

A.C.T. — Australian Capital Territory
admin. — administrative
Afghan. — Afghanistan
Afr. — Africa
Ala. — Alabama
Alg. — Algeria
Alta. — Alberta
Antarc. — Antarctica
A.R. — Autonomous Republic
Arch. — Archipelago
Arab. Sea — Arabian Sea
Arg. — Argentina
Ariz. — Arizona
Ark. — Arkansas
Atl. O. — Atlantic Ocean
Aust. — Austria
Austl. — Australia
B., b. — Baie, Bay
Bangl. — Bangladesh
B.C. — British Columbia
Beds. — Bedfordshire
Belg. — Belgium
Berks. — Berkshire
Bol. — Bolivia
Bots. — Botswana
Br. — British
Braz. — Brazil
Bucks. — Buckinghamshire
Bulg. — Bulgaria
C., c. — Cape, Cabo
Calif. — California
Can. — Canada
cap. — capital
Carib. Sea — Caribbean Sea
Chan. — Channel
Co. — County
Col. — Colombia
Colo. — Colorado
Conn. — Connecticut
C.R. — Costa Rica
Cumb. — Cumbria
Czech. — Czechoslovakia
D.C. — District of Columbia
Del. — Delaware
Den. — Denmark
dep. — depression
Derby. — Derbyshire
dist. — district
Dom. Repub. — Dominican Republic
Dumfr. & Gall. — Dumfries and Galloway
E. — East, Eastern
Ec. — Ecuador
Eng. — England
Eq. — Equatorial
Eth. — Ethiopia
Eur. — Europe
Fd. — Fjord
Fed. — Federal, Federation
Fin. — Finland
Fla. — Florida
Fr. — France, French
Ft. — Fort
G. — Gulf
Ga. — Georgia (U.S.A.)
geog. — geographical
Ger. — German, Germany
Gl. — Glacier
Glos. — Gloucestershire
Gramp. — Grampian

Grnld. — Greenland
Gt. — Great, Greater
Hd. — Head
Herts. — Hertfordshire
Har., Harb. — Harbour
hist. — historical
Hond. — Honduras
Hung. — Hungary
I.(s), i.(s) — island(s)
Ice. — Iceland
Ill. — Illinois
Ind. — Indiana
Ind. O. — Indian Ocean
Indon. — Indonesia
Int. — International
Irel. — Ireland
Jam. — Jamaica
Kans. — Kansas
Ky. — Kentucky
L. — Lago, Lake, Loch
La. — Louisiana
Labr. — Labrador
Lag. — Lagoon
Lancs. — Lancashire
Les. — Lesotho
Lux. — Luxembourg
Mal. — Malaysia
Malag. — Malagasy
Man. — Manitoba
Mass. — Massachusetts
Maur. — Mauritania
Md. — Maryland
Medit. — Mediterranean
Mex. — Mexico
Mich. — Michigan
Minn. — Minnesota
Miss. — Mississippi
Mo. — Missouri
Mong. — Mongolia
Mont. — Montana
Mor. — Morocco
Moz. — Mozambique
Mt.(n) — Mount, Mountain
Mtns. — Mountains
N. — North, Northern
N.B. — New Brunswick
N.C. — North Carolina
N. Dak. — North Dakota
Nebr. — Nebraska
Neth. — Netherlands
Nev. — Nevada
Nfld. — Newfoundland
N.H. — New Hampshire
Nic. — Nicaragua
Nig. — Nigeria
N.J. — New Jersey
N.M. — New Mexico
Nor. — Norway
Northants. — Northhamptonshire
Notts. — Nottinghamshire
N.S. — Nova Scotia
N.W.T. — Northwest Territories
N.Y. — New York
N.Z. — New Zealand
O. — Ocean
Okla. — Oklahoma
Ont. — Ontario
Oreg. — Oregon
P. — Pass

Pa. — Pennsylvania
Pac. O. — Pacific Ocean
Pak. — Pakistan
P.E.I. — Prince Edward Island
Penin. — Peninsula
Phil. — Philippines
Pk. — Peak
Plat. — Plateau
Pol. — Poland
Port. — Portugal, Portuguese
Prov. — Province
Pt.(e) — Point (e)
Pto. — Puerto
Qué. — Québec
R., r. — River, rivière
R., Rep., Repub. — Republic
Reg. — Region
Res. — Reservoir
Rhod. — Rhodesia
R.I. — Rhode Island
Rom. — Romania
R.S.F.S.R. — Russian Soviet Federated Socialist Republic
S. — South, Southern
S. Am. — South America
Sask. — Saskatchewan
Sau. Arab. — Saudi Arabia
S.C. — South Carolina
Scot. — Scotland
Sd. — Sound
S. Dak. — South Dakota
sett. — settlement
Som. Rep. — Somali Republic
Sp. — Spain, Spanish
S.S.R. — Soviet Socialist Republic
St.(e) — Saint (e)
Str. — Strait
Sud. — Sudan
Suff. — Suffolk
Swed. — Sweden
Switz. — Switzerland
Tanzan. — Tanzania
Tenn. — Tennessee
Territ. — Territory
Tex. — Texas
Thai. — Thailand
Tur. — Turkey
U.A.E. — United Arab Emirates
U.S.A. — United States of America
U.S.S.R. — Union of Soviet Socialist Republics
Va. — Virginia
Venez. — Venezuela
volc. — volcano
Vt. — Vermont
W. — West, Western
Wash. — Washington
W. Ind. — West Indies
Wilts. — Wiltshire
Wisc. — Wisconsin
Worcs. — Worcestershire
W. Va. — West Virginia
Wyo. — Wyoming
Yemen A.R. — Yemen Arab Republic
Yemen P.D.R. — Yemen People's Democratic Republic
Yorks. — Yorkshire
Yugo. — Yugoslavia
Zim. — Zimbabwe

Gazetteer of Canada

Canada

Clarence, Cape — English

	Page	N	W
Clarence, Cape: N.W.T.	**31**	74	90
Clarence Creek: *town*, Ont.	**23**	45	75
Clarenville: Nfld.		48	54
Claresholm: Alta.	**26**	50	114
Clark Point: Ont.	**20**	44	82
Clarke City: Qué.	**16**	50	67
Clarks Harbour: N.S.	**17**	43	66
Clayoquot Sound: B.C.	**29**	49	126
Clear, Lake: Ont.	**22**	45	77
Clear Hills: Alta.	**26**	57	119
Clearwater: *riv.*, Sask./Alta.	**26**	57	109
Clearwater Lake: B.C.	**29**	52	120
Clearwater Lake Prov. Park: Man.	**27**	54	102
Clearwater Station: B.C.	**29**	51	120
Clermont: Qué.	**21**	48	70
Clinton: B.C.	**29**	51	121
Clinton: Ont.	**20**	43	82
Clinton-Colden Lake: N.W.T.	**31**	64	107
Clo-oose: B.C.	**28**	49	125
Close Lake: Sask.	**27**	58	105
Clova: Qué.	**21**	48	75
Clute: Ont.		49	81
Clyde: *riv.*, N.S.	**17**	44	65
Clyde: *riv.*, Ont.	**21**	45	76
Coaldale: Alta.	**26**	50	113
Coalhurst: Alta.	**26**	50	113
Coalspur: Alta.		53	117
Coast Mtns.: B.C.	**28**	30	124
Coaticook: Qué.	**21**	45	72
Coats I.: N.W.T.	**14**	62	83
Cobalt: Ont.	**20**	47	80
Cobden: Ont.	**21**	46	77
Cobequid Bay: N.S.	**17**	45	64
Cobequid Mtns.: N.S.	**17**	45	64
Coboconk: Ont.	**22**	45	79
Cobourg: Ont.	**22**	44	78
Cochrane: Alta.	**26**	51	114
Cochrane: Ont.	**19**	49	81
Cochrane: *riv.*, Man.	**27**	58	102
Cockburn, Cape: N.W.T.	**31**	75	100
Cockburn I.: Ont.	**20**	46	83
Cockram Strait: N.W.T.	**14**	68	75
Cod I.: Nfld.	**14**	58	62
Coe Hill: *town*, Ont.	**22**	45	78
Coffin I.: Magdalen Is.	**17**	47	61
Cognac, Lac: Qué.		55	70
Colborne: Ont.	**22**	44	78
Cold Lake: *& town*, Alta.	**26**	54	110
Coldspring Head: N.S.	**17**	46	64
Cold Spring Pond: Nfld.		48	56
Coldwater: Ont.	**22**	45	80
Coleman: Alta.	**26**	50	115
Colinet: Nfld.		47	54
Collingwood: Ont.	**20**	44	80
Collins Bay: Ont.	**22**	44	77
Collins Mt.: Ont.	**20**	48	81
Colombier, Cap: Qué.		49	69
Colonsay: Sask.	**27**	53	105
Columbia: *riv.*, Can./U.S.A.	**29**	51	117
Columbia, Cape: N.W.T.	**13**	83	70
Columbia, Mt.: Alta.	**26**	52	117
Columbia Mtns.: B.C.	**29**	52	120
Colville Bay: N.W.T.	**31**	68	88
Colville Lake: Nfld.		54	66
Colville Lake: N.W.T.	**30**	67	125
Comber: Ont.	**20**	42	82
Combermere: Ont.		45	78
Comfort, Cape: N.W.T.	**14**	65	83
Comfort Bight: Nfld.		53	56
Commissaires, Lac des: Qué.	**21**	48	72
Committee Bay: N.W.T.	**31**	68	87
Como, Lake: Ont.	**20**	48	83
Comox: B.C.	**28**	50	125
Comox Lake: B.C.	**28**	50	125
Conception Bay: Nfld.	**17**	48	53
Conception Harbour: Nfld.		47	53
Conche: Nfld.		51	56
Conestogo: *riv.*, Ont.	**20**	43	81
Coniston: Ont.	**20**	46	81
Conklin: Alta.	**26**	56	111
Connors: N.B.		47	69
Conrad: Yukon		60	134
Consecon: Ont.	**22**	44	77
Consort: Alta.	**26**	52	111
Contrecoeur: Qué.	**23**	46	73
Contwoyto Lake: N.W.T.	**31**	66	111
Cook, Cape: B.C.		50	128
Cook, Mt.: U.S.A./Can.		60	140
Cook Bay: Lake Simcoe	**22**	44	79
Cookshire: Qué.	**21**	45	72
Co-op Point: Sask.	**27**	57	102
Coppell: Ont.		50	84
Copper Cliff: Ont.	**20**	46	81
Coppermine: *& riv.*, N.W.T.	**30**	67	115
Copper Mountain: *town*, British Columbia	**28**	49	120
Coquitlam: *riv.*, B.C.	**36**	49	123
Coral Harbour: *town*, N.W.T.	**18**	64	83
Coral Rapids: *town*, Ont.		50	82
Corbeil Point: Ont.		47	85
Corbett Inlet: N.W.T.	**31**	62	92
Cormac: Ont.		45	77
Cormack, Mt.: Nfld.	**17**	48	56
Cormorant: *& lake*, Man.	**27**	54	101

	Page	N	W
Cornelius Grinnell Bay: N.W.T.	**14**	63	65
Corner Brook: Nfld.	**17**	49	58
Cornwall: Ont.	**23**	45	75
Cornwall I.: N.W.T.	**13**	77	95
Cornwallis I.: N.W.T.	**31**	75	95
Coronation: Alta.	**26**	52	111
Coronation Gulf: N.W.T.	**31**	68	110
Cortes I.: B.C.	**28**	50	125
Corunna: Ont.	**20**	43	82
Corvette, Lac: *& riv.*, Qué.		53	74
Côteau Station: Qué.	**23**	45	74
Cottel I.: Nfld.		49	54
Couchiching, Lake: Ont.	**22**	45	79
Coulonge: *riv.*, Qué.	**20**	47	77
Coulonge Est: *riv.*, Qué.	**21**	46	76
Courtenay: B.C.	**28**	49	125
Coutts: Alta.	**26**	49	112
Couture, Lac: Qué.		60	75
Cove I.: Ont.	**20**	45	82
Cowansville: Qué.	**21**	45	73
Cox's Cove: Nfld.		49	58
Crabtree: Qué.	**23**	46	73
Cracroft I.: B.C.		50	126
Craik: Sask.	**27**	52	105
Cramolet, Lac: Qué.		56	68
Cranberry Portage: Man.	**27**	55	101
Cranbrook: B.C.	**29**	49	116
Crane Lake: Sask.	**26**	50	109
Crauford, Cape: N.W.T.	**31**	74	84
Cree: *riv.*, Sask.	**27**	58	106
Cree Lake: Sask.	**26**	57	107
Creighton: Ont.	**20**	46	81
Creighton: Sask.	**27**	55	102
Creston: Nfld.		47	55
Creswell Bay: N.W.T.	**31**	73	94
Croche: *riv.*, Qué.	**21**	48	73
Crofton: N.S.	**28**	49	123
Croix, Lac à la: Qué.		51	70
Croker, Cape: Ont.	**20**	45	81
Croker Bay: N.W.T.	**31**	75	83
Crooked Lake: Nfld.	**17**	48	56
Crosby: Ont.		45	76
Crossfield: Alta.	**26**	51	114
Cross Lake: Ont.	**22**	45	77
Cross Lake: *& town*, Man.	**27**	55	98
Crown Prince Frederick I.: N.W.T.	**31**	70	87
Crowsnest Pass: B.C./Alta.	**29**	50	115
Crozier Chan.: N.W.T.	**30**	76	118
Crystal Falls: *town*, Ont.	**20**	46	80
Crysler: Ont.	**23**	45	75
Cudworth: Sask.	**27**	52	106
Cumberland: B.C.	**28**	50	125
Cumberland: *penin. & sound*, N.W.T.	**14**	66	65
Cumberland: Ont.	**32**	46	75
Cumberland Bay: *town*, N.B.	**17**	46	66
Cumberland Lake: Sask.	**27**	54	102
Cupar: Sask.	**27**	51	104
Cutknife: Sask.	**26**	53	109
Cuvillier, Lac: Qué.		49	77
Cypress Hills: *& park*, Sask.	**26**	50	109
Dalhousie: N.B.	**16**	48	66
Dalhousie: Qué.	**15**	48	66
Dalhousie, Cape: N.W.T.	**30**	70	130
Dalmas, Lac: Qué.		53	72
Dalmeny: Sask.	**26**	52	107
Dalquier: Qué.		48	78
Dalton: Ont.		48	84
Dalton Mills: Ont.	**20**	48	84
Daly Bay: N.W.T.	**31**	64	90
Dana, Lac: Qué.		51	77
Dane: Ont.	**20**	48	80
Daniels Harbour: Nfld.	**17**	50	58
Danville: Qué.	**21**	46	72
Darnley Bay: N.W.T.	**30**	70	124
Dartmouth: N.S.	**17**	45	64
Dauphin: Man.	**27**	51	100
Dauphin: *riv.*, Man.	**27**	52	99
Dauphin Lake: Man.	**27**	51	100
Davangus: Qué.		48	79
Davidson: Sask.	**27**	51	106
Davidson Mtns.: Can./U.S.A.	**30**	68	142
Davieau I.: N.W.T.		57	77
Davis Inlet: *settlement*, Newfoundland	**15**	56	61
Davis Str.: Can./Grnld.	**13**	67	58
Davy Lake: Sask.	**26**	59	108
Dawson: Yukon	**30**	64	139
Dawson, Mt.: B.C.	**29**	51	117
Dawson Bay: Man.	**27**	53	101
Dawson Creek: *town*, B.C.	**29**	56	120
Dawson Inlet: N.W.T.	**31**	62	93
Dawson Range: Yukon	**30**	62	139
Daysland: Alta.	**26**	53	112
Dayton: Ont.		46	83
Deadman Bay: Nfld.		49	54
Dean: *riv.*, B.C.	**29**	53	126
Deans Dundas Bay: N.W.T.	**30**	72	119
Dease: *riv.*, B.C.		59	129
Dease Arm: Great Bear Lake, N.W.T.	**30**	67	120
Dease Lake: *& settlement*, British Columbia	**24**	58	130

	Page	N	W
Dease Plateau: B.C.		60	128
Dease Str.: N.W.T.	**31**	69	107
Déception: Qué.	**18**	63	75
Deep River: *town*, Ont.		46	77
Deer Hill: *town*, Alta.	**26**	56	118
Deer I.: N.B.		45	67
Deer Lake: *town*, Ont.	**27**	53	94
Deer Lake: *town & lake*, Newfoundland	**17**	49	58
Deer Pond, Nfld.		48	55
Defot: B.C.		59	130
Delhi: Ont.	**20**	43	80
Delisle: Sask.	**26**	52	107
Deloraine: Man.	**27**	49	100
Delorme, Lac: Qué.	**15**	54	70
Deloro: Ont.	**22**	44	78
Delson: Qué.	**23**	45	74
Denholm: Sask.		53	108
Denman I.: B.C.	**28**	50	125
Departure Bay: B.C.	**28**	53	124
De Pas: *riv.*, Qué.	**15**	56	65
Depot Harbour: Ont.	**20**	45	80
De Salis Bay: N.W.T.	**30**	72	122
Desbarats: Ont.	**20**	46	84
Desbiens: Qué.	**21**	48	72
Deschaillons: Qué.	**21**	47	72
Deschambault Lake: Sask.	**27**	55	103
Deschênes: *lake & town*, Québec	**32**	45	75
Deseronto: Ont.	**22**	44	77
Desmaraisville: Qué.	**15**	49	76
Desolation Lake: Nfld.		55	63
Detah: N.W.T.	**31**	62	114
Detroit: *riv.*, Can./U.S.A.	**20**	42	83
Deux Montagnes: *town*, Québec	**32**	46	74
Deux Montagnes, Lac des: Québec	**32**	45	74
Deux Rivières: *town*, Ont.	**20**	46	78
Devenyns, Lac: Qué.	**21**	47	74
Devon: Alta.	**26**	53	114
Devon I.: N.W.T.	**31**	75	85
Dezadeash Lake: Yukon		60	137
D'Iberville, Lac: Qué.	**15**	56	73
Dickson Lake: Ont.		46	78
Dickson Peak: B.C.	**28**	51	123
Didsbury: Alta.	**26**	52	114
Didyme: Qué.		49	73
Diefenbaker, Lake: Sask.	**26**	51	107
Digby: N.S.	**17**	45	66
Digby Neck: *penin.*, N.S.	**17**	44	66
Digges Is.: Qué.	**14**	62	68
Dihourse, Lac: Qué.		56	64
Dildo: Nfld.		47	54
Dingwall: N.S.	**17**	47	60
Disappointment Lake: Newfoundland		54	62
Disaster Rapids: Nfld.		53	64
Dismal Lakes: N.W.T.	**30**	67	117
Disraeli: Qué.	**21**	46	71
Dix: Qué.	**21**	48	76
Dixon Entrance: *str.*, U.S.A./Canada	**28**	54	132
Doating Cove: Nfld.		49	54
Doda, Lac: Qué.		49	75
Dodge Lake: Sask.	**27**	60	106
Dodsland: Sask.	**26**	52	109
Doe Lake: Ont.	**22**	46	79
Dog Creek: *town*, B.C.	**29**	52	122
Dog Lake: Man.	**27**	51	98
Dog Lake: Ont.		49	89
Dog Lake: Ont.		48	84
Dolbeau: Qué.	**21**	49	72
Dolphin & Union Str.: N.W.T.	**30**	69	115
Dome Peak: N.W.T.		61	127
Domes, The: *mtn.*, Nfld.		58	63
Dominion, Cape: N.W.T.	**14**	66	74
Dominion Lake: Nfld.		53	62
Don: *riv.*, Ont.	**32**	44	79
Donald Lake: Ont.	**27**	51	95
Donjek: *riv.*, Yukon	**30**	62	140
Donkin: N.S.	**17**	46	60
Donnacona: Qué.	**21**	47	72
Dorchester: N.B.	**17**	46	64
Dorchester, Cape: N.W.T.	**14**	65	78
Doré, Lac: Qué.	**21**	47	75
Doré Lake: Sask.	**26**	55	107
Dorion: Qué.	**23**	45	74
Dorset: Ont.	**20**	45	79
Dorset, Cape: N.W.T.	**14**	64	77
Dorval: Qué.	**32**	45	74
Dosquet: Qué.	**21**	46	71
Dot: B.C.	**28**	50	121
Double Mer.: *inlet*, Nfld.		54	59
Douglas Point: Ont.	**20**	44	82
Dowling Lake: Alta.	**26**	52	112
Downton, Mt.: B.C.	**29**	53	125
Dozois, Réservoir: Qué.	**20**	47	77
Drayton Valley: *town*, Alta.	**26**	54	115
Dresden: Ont.	**20**	43	82
Driftwood: Ont.		49	81
Drumbo: Ont.	**20**	43	81
Drumheller: Alta.	**26**	51	113
Drummondville: Qué.	**21**	46	72
Dryden: Ont.	**19**	50	93
Dubawnt: *riv.*, N.W.T.	**31**	62	103
Dubawnt Lake: N.W.T.	**31**	63	102
Dubuisson: Qué.	**20**	48	78
Duck Bay: *town*, Man.	**27**	52	100
Duck I.: Ont.	**22**	44	77

	Page	N	W
Duck Lake: *town*, Sask.	**26**	53	106
Duck Mt.: *& Prov. Pk.*, Manitoba	**27**	51	101
Duffey Lake: B.C.		50	122
Du Gué: *riv.*, Qué.	**15**	57	72
Duke of York Bay: N.W.T.	**14**	65	85
Du Lièvre: *riv.*, Qué.	**23**	46	75
Du Loup: *riv.*, Qué.	**21**	46	73
Dumoine: *riv. & lake*, Qué.	**20**	47	78
Duncan: B.C.	**28**	49	124
Duncan, Cape: Akimiski I.		53	81
Duncan Dam: B.C.	**29**	50	117
Duncan Lake: B.C.	**29**	51	117
Duncan, Lac: Qué.	**18**	53	78
Dundalk: Ont.	**20**	44	80
Dundas: Ont.	**20**	43	80
Dundas I.: B.C.	**28**	55	131
Dundas Penin.: N.W.T.	**31**	75	112
Dunkirk: Sask.	**27**	50	106
Dunnville: Ont.	**20**	43	80
Dunville: Nfld.		47	54
Duparquet: Qué.	**20**	49	79
Dupuy: Qué.		49	79
Durham: Ont.	**20**	44	81
Duvernay: Alta.		54	112
Dyer, Cape: N.W.T.	**14**	67	61
Dyer Bay: N.W.T.	**30**	76	122
Dyer Bay: *town*, Ont.		45	81
Dyke Lake: Nfld.		54	66
Eabamet Lake: Ont.	**19**	52	88
Eagle: *riv.*, Nfld.		53	58
Eagle Lake: Ont.	**19**	50	93
Ear Falls: Ont.	**19**	51	93
Earlton: Ont.	**20**	48	80
East Angus: Qué.	**21**	45	71
East Bay: Nfld.		47	55
East Broughton: Qué.	**21**	46	71
East Chezzetcook: N.S.	**17**	45	63
East Cub I.: N.W.T.		54	80
Eastend: Sask.	**26**	49	109
East Jordan: N.S.	**17**	44	65
Eastmain: *& riv.*, Qué.	**15**	52	78
Eastman: Qué.	**21**	45	72
East Point: P.E.I.	**17**	46	62
Eastport: Nfld.		49	54
East Thurlow I.: B.C.		50	125
Eastview: Ont.	**32**	45	76
East York: Ont.	**32**	44	79
Eatonia: Sask.	**26**	51	110
Ebbegunbaeg Lake: Nfld.		48	56
Echo Bay: *town*, Ont.	**20**	46	84
Eclipse: *riv & chan.*, Nfld.		60	64
Eclipse Sound: N.W.T.	**31**	73	79
E. C. Manning Prov. Park: British Columbia	**28**	49	121
Ecum Secum: N.S.	**17**	45	62
Edehon Lake: N.W.T.	**31**	60	97
Edgell I.: N.W.T.	**14**	62	65
Edgewood: B.C.	**29**	50	118
EDMONTON: Alta.	**26**	54	114
Edmund Lake: Man.	**27**	55	93
Edmundston: N.B.	**16**	47	68
Edson: Alta.	**26**	54	116
Eduni, Mt.: N.W.T.	**30**	64	128
Edziza Peak: B.C.	**28**	58	131
Edzo: N.W.T.	**30**	63	116
Eganville: Ont.	**20**	45	77
Egmont: B.C.	**27**	50	124
Egmont Bay: P.E.I.	**18**	46	64
Eileen Lake: N.W.T.	**31**	62	107
Eisenhower, Mt.: Alta.	**26**	51	116
Ekwan Point: Ont.		53	82
Eldorado: Sask.	**26**	58	109
Eldridge Bay: N.W.T.	**31**	76	110
Elgin: N.B.	**17**	46	65
Elgin: Ont.	**23**	45	76
Eliot, Mt.: Nfld.		59	64
Elkhorn: Man.	**27**	50	101
Elk Lake: *town*, Ont.	**20**	48	80
Elk Point: *town*, Alta.	**26**	54	111
Ell Bay: N.W.T.	**18**	64	87
Ellef Ringnes I.: N.W.T.	**12**	78	103
Ellesmere I.: N.W.T.	**13**	80	80
Ellice: *riv.*, N.W.T.	**31**	67	104
Elliot I.: N.W.T.	**30**	69	136
Elliot Lake: *town*, Ont.	**19**	46	83
Elliston: Nfld.		49	53
Elmira: Ont.	**20**	43	80
Elmira: P.E.I.	**17**	46	62
Elmsdale: N.S.	**17**	45	63
Elmvale: Ont.	**22**	45	80
Elrose: Sask.	**26**	51	108
Elsas: Ont.		48	83
Elsie I.: N.W.T.		59	79
Elu Inlet: N.W.T.	**31**	68	106
Elvira, Cape: N.W.T.	**31**	74	107
Embarras Portage: Alta.		58	111
Embrun: Ont.	**23**	45	75
Emerald I.: N.W.T.	**31**	76	114
Emerson: Man.	**27**	49	97
Emo: Ont.	**27**	49	93
Emsdale: Ont.	**22**	46	79
Enderby: B.C.	**29**	50	119
Enfield: N.S.	**17**	45	64
Engineer: B.C.		59	134
Englee: Nfld.	**15**	51	56
Englehart: Ont.	**20**	48	80
Englewood: B.C.		51	127
English: *riv.*, Ont.	**19**	50	95

Kilmar — Manitowaning

Canada

	Page	N	W
Kilmar: Qué.	23	46	75
Kimakto Penin.: N.W.T.	31	70	88
Kimberley: B.C.	29	49	116
Kincardine: Ont.	20	44	82
Kindersley: Sask.	26	51	109
Kingcome Inlet: *& town,* British Columbia	29	51	126
King Cove: Nfld.		49	53
King George, Mt.: B.C.	29	51	115
King George IV Lake: Newfoundland		48	58
King George Is.: N.W.T.	18	57	79
King I.: B.C.	28	52	127
King Kirkland: Ont.	20	48	80
Kings Point: *town,* Nfld.	17	50	56
Kingston: Ont.	23	44	76
Kingsville: Ont.	20	42	83
Kingurutik Lake: Nfld.		57	63
King William I.: N.W.T.	31	69	97
Kinistino: Sask.	27	53	105
Kinnaird: B.C.	29	49	118
Kinojevis, Lac: Qué.	20	48	79
Kinosis: Alta.		56	111
Kinsella: Alta.		53	112
Kiosk: Ont.	20	46	79
Kipahigan Lake: Sask./Man.	27	55	102
Kipawa: *town & lake,* Qué.	20	47	79
Kipawa, Parc de: Qué.	20	47	79
Kipling: Sask.	27	50	102
Kirkfield: Ont.	22	45	79
Kirkland Lake: *town,* Ont.	20	48	80
Kirkpatrick Lake: Alta.	26	52	111
Kirkpatrick Lake: Ont.	20	47	83
Kirton: B.C.		50	120
Kisgegas: B.C.	28	56	128
Kississing Lake: Man.	27	55	101
Kistigan Lake: Man.	27	55	92
Kitchener: Ont.	20	43	80
Kitimat: B.C.	28	54	129
Kittigazuit: N.W.T.	30	69	134
Klappan: *riv.,* B.C.	28	57	129
Kleinburg: Ont.	32	44	80
Klinaklini: *riv.,* B.C.	29	51	126
Klondike, *riv.,* Yukon	30	64	138
Kluane Lake: Yukon	30	61	138
Kluane Nat. Park: N.W.T.	30	61	140
Klukshu: Yukon		60	137
Knee Lake: Man.	27	55	95
Knight Inlet: B.C.	29	51	126
Knob Lake, *see* Schefferville			
Knowlton: Qué.	21	45	72
Knox, Cape: B.C.	28	54	133
Koch I.: N.W.T.	14	70	78
Kogaluc: *riv.,* Qué.	14	59	77
Kogaluc, Baie: Qué.	14	59	78
Kokanee Park: B.C.	29	50	117
Koksoak: *riv.,* Qué.	14	58	69
Kootenay: *riv.,* Can./U.S.A.	29	49	115
Kootenay Lake: B.C.	29	49	117
Kootenay Nat. Park: B.C.	29	51	116
Koraluk: *riv.,* Nfld.	15	56	63
Koruk: *riv.,* Qué.		59	66
Kotcho Lake: B.C.		59	121
Koukdjuak: *riv.,* N.W.T.	14	67	72
Kovik, Baie: Qué.	14	62	78
Kowkash: Ont.		50	87
Kugmallit Bay: N.W.T.	30	70	133
Kunghit I.: B.C.	28	52	131
Kusawa Lake: Yukon		60	136
Kwadacha Wilderness Prov. Park: B.C.	29	58	125
Kyle: Sask.	26	51	108
Kynocks: Yukon		61	136
Labelle: Qué.	21	46	75
Laberge, Lake: Yukon	30	61	135
Labrador: Nfld.	15	—	—
Labrador City: Nfld.	15	53	67
Labrador Sea: Atl. O.	14/15	—	—
Lac aux Sables: Qué.	21	47	72
La Cave: Ont.	20	46	79
Lac Baker: N.B.		47	69
Lac Bouchette: Qué.	21	48	72
Lac Castagnier: Qué.		49	78
Lac Decelles: Qué.	20	48	78
Lac de l'Est: Qué.	21	47	70
Lac du Bonnet: Man.	27	50	96
Lac Edouard: Qué.	21	48	72
Lac Etchemin: Qué.	16	46	70
Lac Frontière: Qué.	16	47	70
Lachine: *& rapids,* Qué.	32	45	74
Lac Humqui: Qué.		48	68
Lachute: Qué.	23	46	74
Lac la Biche: Alta.	26	55	112
Lac La Marie: N.W.T.	30	53	117
Lac La Ronge Prov. Park: Saskatchewan	27	55	105
Lac Mégantic: *town,* Qué.	21	45	71
Lacolle: Qué.	23	45	73
Lacombe: Alta.	26	52	114
Lacoste: Qué.		46	75
Lac Rémi: Qué.	23	46	75
La Croche: Qué.	16	48	73
Lac St. Paul: Qué.		47	75
Ladner: B.C.	28	49	123
Lady Evelyn Falls: N.W.T.		61	117
Lady Evelyn Lake: Ont.	20	47	80
Ladysmith: B.C.	28	49	124
Laflèche: Sask.	26	50	107

	Page	N	W
Laforest: Ont.		47	81
La Grande: *riv.,* Qué.	15	54	77
Lahave: *riv.,* N.S.	17	45	65
La Hune, Cap: Nfld.		48	57
Lake Cowichan: *& lake,* British Columbia	29	49	124
Lakefield: Ont.	22	44	78
Lake Harbour: N.W.T.	14	63	70
Lake Louise: Alta.	26	51	116
Lake River: Ont.	18	54	82
Lake St. Peter: Ont.	22	45	78
Lake Superior Prov. Park: Ontario	20	48	85
La Loche: Sask.	26	56	109
La Malbaie: Qué.	21	48	70
Lamaline: Nfld.		47	56
Lamartine: Qué.		47	70
La Martre, Lac: N.W.T.	30	63	118
Lambeth: Ont.	20	43	81
Lambton: Qué.	16	46	71
Lambton, Cape: N.W.T.	30	71	123
La Moinerie, Lac: Qué.		57	67
Lamorandière: Qué.	20	49	77
La Motte: *& lake,* Qué.	20	48	78
Lampman: Sask.	27	49	103
Lanark: Ont.	23	45	76
Lancaster: N.B.	17	45	66
Lancaster: Ont.	23	45	75
Lancaster Sound: N.W.T.	31	74	85
Lance Point: Nfld.		47	54
Langenburg: Sask.	27	51	101
Langham: Sask.	26	52	107
Langlade: Qué.	21	48	76
Langley: *town,* B.C.	28	49	123
Laniel: Qué.	20	47	79
Lanigan: Sask.	27	52	105
Lanoraie: Qué.	23	46	73
Lansdowne: Ont.	23	44	76
Lansdowne House: Ont.		52	88
L'Anse au Loup: Nfld.		51	57
L'Anse-aux-Meadows: Nfld.	15	52	55
L'Anse St. Jean: Qué.	21	48	70
Lantzville: B.C.	28	49	124
Lapêche, Lac: Qué.	23	46	76
La Perade: Qué.	21	46	72
La Plonge, Lac: Sask.	26	55	107
La Pocatière: Qué.	21	47	70
La Poile Bay: Nfld.	17	48	58
Lapointe, Lac: Qué.		53	69
La Potherie, Lac: Qué.	14	59	72
Laprairie: Qué.	32	45	73
La Providence: Qué.	21	46	73
Larder Lake: *town,* Ont.	20	48	80
L'Ardoise: N.S.	17	46	61
La Reine: Qué.		49	79
Larive, Lac: Qué.	20	47	77
Lark Harbour: Nfld.	17	49	58
La Ronge: *& lake,* Sask.	27	55	105
Larry's River: *town,* N.S.	17	45	61
Larus Lake: Ont.	27	51	95
La Salle: Qué.	32	45	74
La Sarre: Qué.	15	49	79
L'Ascension: Qué.		49	72
La Scie: Nfld.	17	50	55
Lashburn: Sask.	26	53	110
Lasqueti I.: B.C.	28	49	124
L'Assomption: Qué.	23	46	73
L'Assomption: *riv.,* Qué.	21	46	74
Last Mountain Lake: Sask.	27	51	105
Latchford: Ont.	20	47	80
La Tuque: Qué.	21	47	73
Laurentides, Parc des: Qué.	20	47	71
Lauzon: Qué.	21	47	71
Laval-des-Rapides: Qué.	32	46	74
Lavaltrie: Qué.	23	46	73
Lavant Station: Ont.		45	77
La Vérendrye, Parc de: Qué.	20	47	77
Lavieille, Lac: Ont.	20	46	78
Lawn: Nfld.		47	56
Lawrencetown: N.S.	17	45	65
Leader: Sask.	26	51	110
Leamington: Ont.	20	42	83
L'Eau Claire, Lac à: Qué.	15	56	74
L'Ecorce, Lac de: Qué.	21	47	76
Leduc: Alta.	26	53	114
Lefroy: Ont.	22	44	80
Lemieux Is.: N.W.T.	14	64	65
Lennoxville: Qué.	21	45	72
Lenore Lake: Sask.	27	52	105
Leopold I.: N.W.T.	14	65	64
Leoville: Sask.	26	54	108
L'Epiphanie: Qué.	23	46	73
Lepreau, Pointe: N.B.	17	45	66
Léry: Qué.	23	45	74
L'Escalier, Lac: Qué.	21	46	76
Les Escoumains: Qué.	16	48	69
Les Etroits: Qué.		47	69
Lesser Slave Lake: Alta.	26	55	115
L'Est, Pointe de: Qué.	17	49	62
Lethbridge: Alta.	26	50	113
Lethbridge: Nfld.		48	54
Levack: Ont.	20	47	81
Level Mt.: B.C.		58	131
Lévis: Qué.	21	47	71
Lewisporte: Nfld.	17	49	55
Leyson Point: N.W.T.	14	63	81
Liard: *riv.,* B.C./N.W.T.	30	61	123
Liard Plain: Yukon/B.C.		60	126

	Page	N	W
Liard Range: N.W.T.	30	61	123
Liddon Gulf: N.W.T.	31	75	114
Lillooet: B.C.	28	51	122
Lillooet: *riv.,* B.C.	28	50	122
Lillooet Lake: B.C.	28	50	122
Lime Ridge: *town,* Qué.		46	72
Limoges: Ont.	23	45	75
Lindsay: Ont.	22	44	79
Lingman Lake: *town,* Ont.	27	54	93
Linton: Qué.	21	47	72
Linzee, Cape: N.S.	17	46	62
Liot Point: N.W.T.	30	74	125
Lipton: Sask.	27	51	104
Lismore: N.S.	17	46	62
Listowel: Ont.	20	44	81
Little Bay I.: *& town,* Nfld.		50	56
Little Current: Ont.	20	46	82
Little Dover: N.S.	17	45	61
Little Grand Lake: Nfld.		49	58
Little Grand Rapids: *town,* Manitoba	27	52	95
Little Longlac: Ont.		50	87
Little Missinaibi Lake: Ont.	20	48	84
Little Narrows: N.S.	17	46	61
Little Pic: *riv.,* Ont.		49	86
Little Smoky: *riv.,* Alta.	26	54	117
Little Vermilion Lake: Ont.	27	51	94
Lively: Ont.	20	46	81
Liverpool: N.S.	17	44	65
Liverpool, Cape: N.W.T.	31	74	78
Liverpool Bay: N.W.T.	30	70	130
Lizotte: Qué.		48	72
Lloyd George, Mt.: B.C.	29	58	125
Lloyd Lake: Sask.	26	57	109
Lloydminster: Alta./Sask.	26	53	110
Lobstick Lake: Nfld.	15	54	65
Lochalsh: Ont.		48	84
Lock Barrage: Qué.	21	48	75
Lockeport: N.S.	17	44	65
Logan, Mt.: Qué.	16	49	67
Logan, Mt.: Yukon	30	60	140
Logan Mts.: Yukon/N.W.T.	30	62	128
Logan Point: N.S.	17	46	63
Loks Land: *i.,* N.W.T.	14	63	65
London: Ont.	20	43	81
Lonely I.: Ont.	20	45	81
Lone Star: Alta.		57	118
Long Harbour: B.C.	26	49	123
Long I.: Nfld.		48	56
Long I.: Nfld.		50	56
Long I.: Nfld.		47	54
Long I.: N.W.T.	18	55	80
Long I.: N.S.	17	44	66
Longlac: Ont.	19	50	86
Long Lake: N.B.	16	47	67
Long Lake: Ont.		50	87
Long Point: Man.	27	53	98
Long Point: *& bay,* Ont.	20	43	80
Long Pond: Nfld.		48	56
Long Range: Nfld.	17	48	59
Long Range: Nfld.	17	50	57
Long Sault: Ont.	23	45	75
Longueuil: Qué.	32	46	73
Lookout, Cape: Ont.		55	84
Lookout Mt.: Nfld.		53	64
Loon Lake: *town,* Sask.	26	54	109
Lord Mayor Bay: N.W.T.	31	70	92
Lord's Cove: Nfld.		47	56
Loretteville: Qué.	21	47	71
L'Orignal: Ont.	23	46	75
Lorrainville: Qué.	20	47	79
Lotbinière: Qué.	21	47	72
Loughborough Inlet: B.C.	28	50	125
Louisbourg: N.S.	17	46	60
Louise I.: B.C.	28	53	132
Louis XIV, Pointe: Qué.	15	55	80
Louiseville: Qué.	21	46	73
Low: Qué.	23	46	76
Low, Cape: N.W.T.	18	63	85
Low Bush: Ont.		49	80
Lower Arrow Lake: B.C.	29	49	118
Lower Foster Lake: Sask.	27	57	105
Lower Post: B.C.	24	60	128
Lowther: Ont.		50	83
Lowther I.: N.W.T.	31	75	93
Lubicon Lake: Alta.	26	56	116
Lucan: Ont.	20	43	81
Lucania, Mt.: Yukon		61	140
Lucas Channel: Ont.	20	45	82
Luceville: Qué.	16	48	68
Ludgate: Ont.		46	80
Lulu I.: B.C.	36	49	123
Lumière, Cap: N.B.	17	47	65
Lumsden: Nfld.		49	54
Lumsden: Sask.	27	51	105
Lund: B.C.	28	50	125
Lundar: Man.	27	51	98
Lunenburg: N.S.	17	44	64
Luseland: Sask.	26	52	109
Lyall, Mt.: B.C./Alta.	29	50	115
Lynn Lake: Man.	27	57	101
Lynx Lake: N.W.T.	31	62	106
Lyon, Cape: N.W.T.	30	70	123
Lyon Inlet: N.W.T.	14	66	84
Lyster Station: Qué.	21	46	72
Lytton: B.C.	28	50	122
Mabel Lake: B.C.	29	50	119
Mabou: N.S.	17	46	61

	Page	N	W
McAdam: N.B.	16	45	67
MacAlpine Lake: N.W.T.	31	67	103
Macamic: *& lake,* Qué.		49	79
Mcbeth Fiord: N.W.T.	14	69	69
McBride: B.C.	29	53	120
Maccan: N.S.	17	46	64
Maccles Pond: Nfld.		49	54
McClintock: Man.	27	58	94
McClintock Chan.: N.W.T.	31	73	104
McClure, Cape: N.W.T.	30	75	121
McClure Str.: N.W.T.	30	75	118
McConnell Creek: *town,* British Columbia	29	57	126
McConnell Range: N.W.T.	30	64	124
McDame: B.C.		59	129
Macdougall Lake: N.W.T.	31	66	99
MacDowell Lake: Ont.	27	52	92
Macduff: Ont.		49	84
McFarlane: *riv.,* Sask.	26	58	108
McGillivray: B.C.	28	51	122
McGivney: N.B.	16	46	66
MacGregor: Man.	27	50	99
McGregor Lake: Alta.	26	50	113
McGuire: B.C.	28	50	123
McInnes Lake: Ont.	27	52	94
MacKay Lake: N.W.T.	31	64	112
Mackenzie: B.C.	29	56	124
Mackenzie: *riv.,* N.W.T.	30	67	133
Mackenzie, District of: N.W.T.	30/31	—	—
Mackenzie Bay: Yukon	30	69	138
Mackenzie Bison Sanctuary: N.W.T.	30	62	117
Mackenzie Highway: Alta.	26	57	118
McKenzie Island: *town,* Ontario	27	51	94
Mackenzie Mtns.: Yukon/N.W.T.	30	64	130
Mackies: Ont.		48	90
Macklin: Sask.	26	52	110
McLellan Strait: Nfld.		60	64
McLennan: Alta.	26	55	117
Macleod Bay: N.W.T.	31	63	110
McLeod Lake: B.C.	29	55	125
McLoughlin Bay: N.W.T.	31	67	99
McMasterville: Qué.	23	46	73
Macmillan: *riv.,* Yukon	30	63	133
McNamee: N.B.	16	46	66
McNaughton Lake: B.C.	29	52	118
McNutt I.: N.S.	17	44	65
Macoun Lake: Sask.	27	56	104
MacRae: Yukon		61	135
Mactaquac: N.B.	17	46	67
McTavish Arm: Great Bear Lake, N.W.T.	30	66	118
MacTier: Ont.	22	45	80
McVicar Arm: Great Bear Lake, N.W.T.	30	65	120
Madawaska: *& riv.,* Ont.	20	45	78
Madeleine, Îles de la: Qué.	15	47	61
Madoc: Ont.	22	45	77
Madsen: Ont.	19	51	94
Magaquadavic: *riv.,* N.B.		45	67
Magnet: Man.	27	51	99
Magnetawan: Ont.	22	46	80
Magog: Qué.	21	45	72
Magpie: *riv.,* Ont.	20	48	84
Magpie: Qué.	16	50	65
Magpie, Lac: Qué.	15	51	65
Magrath: Alta.	26	49	113
Maguse Lake: N.W.T.	31	62	95
Maguse Point: N.W.T.		61	94
Maguse River: *town,* N.W.T.	31	61	94
Maher: Ont.		49	81
Mahone Bay: *& town,* N.S.	17	44	64
Maidstone: Sask.	26	53	109
Main Brook: *town,* Nfld.		51	56
Maitland: *riv.,* Ont.	20	44	81
Makkovik: Nfld.	15	55	59
Makobe Lake: Ont.	20	47	80
Malartic: Qué.	20	48	78
Malaspina Strait: B.C.	28	50	124
Malbaie: *riv.,* Qué.		48	70
Malcolm I.: B.C.	28	51	127
Mallery Lake: N.W.T.	31	64	98
Mallorytown: Ont.	23	44	76
Malpeque Bay: P.E.I.	17	47	64
Mamainse-Hill: Ont.	20	47	84
Mamainse Point: Ont.		47	85
Mamette Lake: *town,* B.C.		50	121
Mammamattawa: Ont.		50	84
Manicouagan: Qué.	15	51	69
Manicouagan: *riv.,* Qué.	15	50	68
Manicouagan: *penin.,* Qué.		49	68
Manicouagan, Réservoir: Qué.	15	51	68
Manigotagan Lake: Man.	27	51	95
Manitoba: *Prov. (cap.* Winnipeg)	27	—	—
Manitoba, Lake: Man.	27	51	99
Manito Lake: Sask.	26	53	110
Manitou: Man.	27	49	98
Manitou, Lac: Qué		51	65
Manitou Lake: Ont.	20	46	82
Manitou Lakes: Ont.		49	93
Manitoulin I.: Ont.	20	46	82
Manitouwadge: Ont.	19	49	86
Manitowaning: *& bay,* Ont.	20	46	82

Norris Arm — Pouce Coupé

Canada

	Page	N	W
Norris Arm: Nfld.		49	55
North: *riv.*, Nfld.	14	57	63
North, Cape: N.S.	17	47	60
North Aulatsivik I.: Nfld.	14	60	64
North Battleford: Sask.	26	53	108
North Bay: *riv.*, Nfld.		48	55
North Bay: *town*, Ont.	20	46	79
North Cape: P.E.I.	17	47	64
North Caribou Lake: Ont.	18	53	90
North Channel: Ont.	20	46	83
Northern Bay: Nfld.		48	53
Northern Indian Lake: Manitoba	27	57	97
North Gower: Ont.	23	45	76
North Head: Nfld.		49	58
North Head: *town*, Great Manan I.		45	67
North Henik Lake: N.W.T.	31	62	98
North Knife: *riv.*, Man.	27	59	96
North Knife Lake: Man.	27	58	97
North Magnetic Pole: N.W.T.	31	76	101
North Payne: *riv.*, Qué.	14	60	73
North River: *settlement*, Newfoundland		54	57
North River: *town*, Man.	27	59	95
North River Bridge: N.S.	17	46	61
North Saskatchewan: *riv.*, Alberta/Saskatchewan	26	53	107
North Saugeen: *riv.*, Ont.		44	81
North Seal: *riv.*, Man.	27	59	100
North Sydney: N.S.	17	46	60
North Thames: *riv.*, Ont.	20	43	81
North Thompson: *riv.*, British Columbia	29	52	120
Northumberland Strait: Canada	17	46	64
North Vancouver: B.C.	36	49	123
North Wabiskaw Lake: Alberta	26	56	114
North West River: *settlement*, Nfld.	15	53	60
Northwest Territories: (*seat of Govt.* Yellowknife)	30/31	—	—
North York: Ont.	32	44	79
Norton: N.B.	17	46	66
Norway Bay: N.W.T.	31	71	105
Norway House: Man.	27	54	98
Norway I.: N.W.T.	30	74	125
Norwich: Ont.	20	43	81
Norwood: Ont.	22	44	78
Notre Dame: N.B.	17	46	65
Notre Dame Bay: Nfld.	17	50	55
Notre-Dame-de-la-Paix: Québec	23	46	75
Notre-Dame-de-la-Salette: Québec		46	76
Notre Dame du Lac: Qué.		48	69
Notre-Dame-du-Laus: Québec	21	46	76
Notre-Dame-du-Nord: Québec	20	48	80
Notre Dame Junction: Nfld.		49	55
Notre Dame, Monts: Qué.	16	48	67
Notta: *riv.*, Ont.	22	44	80
Nottawasaga Bay: Ont.	20	45	80
Nottaway: *riv.*, Qué.		51	79
Nottingham I.: *& town*, N.W.T.	14	63	78
Nouveau Comptoir: Qué.	18	53	78
Nouvelle France, Cap de: Qué.	14	63	74
Nova Scotia: *Prov.* (*cap.* Halifax)	17	—	—
Novar: Ont.	22	45	79
Noyan: Qué.	23	45	73
Nueitin Lake: N.W.T.	31	60	100
Nungesser Lake: Ont.	27	51	93
Nutak: Nfld.	14	58	62
Nut Mountain: *town & mt.*, Saskatchewan	27	52	103
Nwabasca Lake: B.C.	29	50	122
Oak Bluff: Man.	33	50	97
Oak Lake: Man.	27	50	101
Oakville: Ont.	22	43	80
Obalski, Lac: Qué.		49	78
Oban: Sask.	26	52	108
Obatogameau, Lac: Qué.	16	50	74
Observatory Inlet: B.C.	28	55	130
Ocean Falls: *town*, B.C.	28	52	128
Odessa: Ont.	22	44	77
O'Donnell Point: Ont.	20	45	80
Ogahalla: Ont.		50	86
Ogilvie Mtns.: Yukon	30	65	138
Ogoki: Ont.		52	86
Ogoki: *riv.*, Ont.	19	51	88
Ogoki Reservoir: Ont.		51	88
Oka: Qué.	23	45	74
Okak Is.: Nfld.		58	62
Okanagan Lake: B.C.	29	50	120
Okotoks: Alta.	26	51	114
Old Crow: *& riv.*, Yukon	30	68	140
Oldman: *riv.*, Alta.	26	50	114
Old Perlican: Nfld.		48	53
Olds: Alta.	26	52	114
Old Wives Lake: Sask.	27	50	106
Oliver: B.C.	29	50	120
Olomanc: *riv.*, Qué.		51	61

	Page	N	W
Omemee: Ont.	22	44	79
Omineca: *riv.*, B.C.	29	56	125
Omineca Mtns.: B.C.	28	57	127
Ommanney Bay: N.W.T.	31	73	101
Onaman Lake: Ont.		50	87
Onaping Lake: *& riv.*, Ont.	20	47	81
Onistagan, Lac: Qué.		51	71
Ontario: *Prov.* (*cap.* Toronto)	18/19	—	—
Ontario, Lake: Can./U.S.A.	20	44	78
Ootsa Lake: *town*, B.C.	29	54	126
Opasatica, Lac: Qué.	20	48	79
Opasatika: Ont.		50	83
Opataca, Lac: Qué.		50	75
Opawica: *lake & riv.*, Qué.		50	76
Opeongo Lake: Ont.	20	46	78
Opinaca: *riv.*, Qué.		53	77
Opinnagau Lake: Ont.		54	84
Opiscotéo, Lac: Qué.	15	53	68
Orange Bay: Nfld.		50	56
Orangeville: Ont.	20	44	80
Ordale: Sask.	26	53	107
Orillia: Ont.	22	45	79
Orleans: Ont.	32	45	76
Orleans, Île d': Qué.	21	47	71
Ormstown: Qué.	23	45	74
Oromocto: N.B.	17	46	66
Orono: Ont.	22	44	79
Osgoode: Ont.	23	45	75
Oshawa: Ont.	22	44	79
Oskélanéo: Qué.	21	48	75
Osnadorgh House: Ont.		51	90
Osoyoos: B.C.	29	49	120
Ospika: *riv.*, B.C.	29	57	124
Osprey Lake: *town*, B.C.		50	120
Ossokmanuan Lake: Nfld.	15	53	65
Otelnuk Lake: Qué.		56	68
Otish Mts.: Qué.	15	52	70
Otoskwin: *riv.*, Ont.	19	51	89
OTTAWA: Ontario	32	45	75
Ottawa: *riv.*, Qué./Ont.	23	46	75
Ottawa Is.: N.W.T.	18	59	80
Otter: Qué.	16	50	64
Otter Head: Ont.		48	86
Otter Lake: Ont.	22	45	80
Otter Lake: Sask.	27	55	104
Ouest, Pointe: Qué.	16	50	65
Ouimet: Ont.		49	89
Oureau: *riv.*, Qué.	21	46	74
Outlook: Sask.	26	51	107
Outremont: Qué.	32	46	74
Owen Sound: *& town*, Ont.	20	45	81
Owl: *riv.*, Man.	27	58	93
Oxbow: Sask.	27	49	102
Oxford: N.S.	17	46	64
Oxford House: Man.	27	55	95
Oxford Junction: N.S.	17	46	64
Oxford Lake: Man.	27	55	95
Oyen: Alta.	26	51	110
Pacific: B.C.	28	55	128
Packenham: Ont.	23	45	76
Pack's Harbour: Nfld.		54	57
Paddle Prairie: *town*, Alta.	26	58	117
Paddockwood: Sask.	27	53	105
Padlei: N.W.T.	31	62	97
Pagwa River: *town*, Ont.	19	50	85
Pakenham: Ont.	23	45	76
Pakowki Lake: Alta.	26	49	111
Pakwash Lake: Ont.	27	51	93
Palling: B.C.	29	54	126
Palmarolle: Qué.		48	79
Palmer Point: N.W.T.	31	75	108
Palmerston: Ont.	20	44	81
Panache, Lake: Ont.	20	46	81
Pancake Point: Ont.		47	85
Pangnirtung: N.W.T.	14	66	66
Papineau, Lac: Qué.	23	46	75
Papineauville: Qué.	23	46	75
Paradis: Qué.	21	48	77
Paradise: *riv.*, Nfld.		53	58
Paradise Sound: Nfld.		47	55
Parc, Lac du: Qué.		57	67
Parent, Lac: Qué.	20	48	77
Parent, Pointe: Qué.	16	50	62
Paris: Ont.	20	43	80
Parisienne, I.: Ont.		46	84
Park Head: *town*, Ont.		45	81
Park Hill: *town*, Ont.	20	43	82
Parksville: B.C.	28	49	124
Parrsboro: N.S.	17	45	64
Parry, Cape: N.W.T.	30	70	125
Parry Bay: N.W.T.	14	68	82
Parry Is.: N.W.T.	31	76	110
Parry Sound: *town*, Ont.	22	45	80
Parsnip: *riv.*, B.C.	29	55	123
Partridgeberry Hills: Nfld.		48	56
Pascalis, Lac: Qué.	20	48	77
Pasfield Lake: Sask.	27	58	105
Pashkokogan Lake: Ont.		51	90
Pasley Bay: N.W.T.	31	71	97
Pasqua: Sask.	27	50	105
Pasquia Hills: Sask.	27	53	103
Passamaquoddy Bay: N.B.	17	45	67
Pattullo, Mt.: B.C.	28	56	130
Paulatuk: N.W.T.	30	69	123
Paul I.: Nfld.	15	56	62
Pavilion: B.C.		51	122
Payne: *riv.*, Qué.	14	60	72

	Page	N	W
Payne, Baie: Qué.	14	60	70
Payne, Lac: Qué.	14	59	74
Peace: *riv.*, B.C./Alta.	26	58	114
Peace River: *town*, Alta.	26	56	117
Peachland: B.C.		50	120
Pearl I.: Nfld.		49	58
Peary Chan.: N.W.T.	13	79	100
Peel: *plat. & riv.*, Yukon	30	67	134
Peel Point: N.W.T.	31	73	115
Peel Sound: N.W.T.	31	73	97
Peerless Lake: Alta.	26	57	114
Pefferlaw: Ont.	22	44	79
Peggy's Cove: *town*, N.S.	17	44	64
Pelee Island: *town & i.*, Ont.	20	42	83
Pelee Passage: *chan.*, Ont.	20	42	83
Pelee Point, Ont.	20	42	83
Pélican, Lac: Qué.		60	74
Pelican Bay: Man.	27	53	100
Pelican Lake: Man.	27	52	100
Pelican Mtns.: Alta.	26	56	114
Pelican Narrows: *town*, Saskatchewan	27	55	103
Pelly: *riv.*, Yukon	30	62	133
Pelly Bay: *& settlement*, N.W.T.	31	69	90
Pelly Lake: N.W.T.	31	66	102
Pelly Mtns. Yukon	30	62	133
Pemberton: B.C.	28	50	123
Pembina: Alta.	26	53	115
Pembina: *riv.*, Alta.	26	53	116
Pembroke: Ont.	20	46	77
Penetanguishene: Ont.	22	45	80
Penguin Is.: Nfld.		45	57
Penhold: Alta.	26	52	114
Pennant Point: N.S.	17	44	64
Pennask Lake: B.C.		50	120
Pennfield: N.B.	17	45	67
Penny Highland: N.W.T.	14	67	66
Penticton: B.C.	29	49	120
Penzance: Sask.	27	51	105
Percé: Qué.	16	49	64
Perdu, Lac: Qué.		51	70
Perdue: Sask.	26	52	108
Péribonca: Qué.		49	72
Péribonca: *riv.*, Qué.	15	49	71
Péribonca, Lac: Qué.		50	71
Perow: B.C.	29	54	126
Perrault Lake: Ont.	27	50	93
Perron: Qué.	20	48	78
Perrot, Île: Qué.	23	45	74
Perry River: *town*, N.W.T.	31	67	103
Perth: Ont.	23	45	76
Perth-Andover: N.B.	16	47	68
Petawawa: Ont.	20	46	78
Peterbell: Ont.		48	83
Peterborough: Ont.	22	44	78
Peter Pond Lake: Sask.	26	56	109
Peters Arm: Nfld.		49	55
Petitcodiac: N.B.	17	46	65
Petite Rivière de la Baleine: Québec	15	56	76
Petit Etang: *town*, N.S.	17	47	61
Petit Mécatina, R. du: Qué.	15	52	62
Petit Nord Penin.: Nfld.		51	57
Petitot: *riv.*, B.C.	24	60	121
Petitsikapau Lake: Nfld.	15	54	66
Petre, Point: Ont.	22	44	77
Petries: Nfld.		49	58
Petrolia: Ont.	20	43	82
Peyton, Mt.: Nfld.		49	55
Philomena: Alta.		55	112
Piacoudie, Lac: Qué.		51	71
Pickering: Ont.	22	44	79
Pickle Lake: Ont.	19	51	90
Picton: Ont.	22	44	77
Pictou: *& i.*, N.S.	17	46	63
Picture Butte: Alta.	26	50	113
Piedmont: Qué.	23	46	74
Pie I.: Ont.		48	89
Pierrefonds: Qué.	32	45	74
Pierreville: Qué.	21	46	73
Pigeon: *riv.*, Can./U.S.A.		48	90
Pigeon Bay: Man.	27	52	97
Pigeon Bay: Ont.	20	42	83
Pigeon Lake: Alta.	26	53	114
Pigeon Lake: Ont.	22	44	78
Pikangikum Lake: Ont.	19	52	94
Pike: B.C.		59	133
Pikwitonei: Man.	27	56	97
Pilley's I.: Nfld.		50	56
Pilot Mound: Man.	27	49	99
Pinawa: Man.	27	51	96
Pincher Creek: *town*, Alta.	26	49	114
Pinchi Lake: B.C.	29	55	124
Pine, Cape: Nfld.	17	47	54
Pine Falls: *town*, Man.	27	51	96
Pine Pass: B.C.	29	55	122
Pine Point: N.W.T.	30	61	114
Pine River: *town*, Sask.	26	56	107
Pins, Pte. aux: Ont.	20	42	82
Pinto Butte: *mtn.*, Sask.	26	49	107
Pipestone: *riv.*, Ont.		52	90
Pipmuacan, Lac: Qué.	19	49	70
Piscatosin Lac: Qué.	21	47	75
Pistolet Bay: Nfld.		51	56
Pitt: *riv. & lake*, B.C.	28	49	123
Pitt I.: B.C.	28	53	130
Pitt Sound: Nfld.		49	54
Placentia: *& bay*, Nfld.	17	47	54
Plaisance: Qué.	23	46	75

	Page	N	W
Plantagenet: Ont.	23	45	75
Plaster Rock: N.B.	16	47	67
Plate Cove: Nfld.		49	53
Playgreen Lake: Man.	27	54	98
Pledger Lake: Ont.		50	84
Plessisville: Qué.	21	46	72
Plétipi, Lac: Qué.	15	51	70
Plonge, Lac la: Sask.	26	55	107
Plum Coulee: Man.	27	49	98
Pointe-aux-Trembles: Qué.	32	46	74
Pointe-Claire: Qué.	32	45	74
Pointe Fortune: Ont.	23	46	74
Pointe-Gatineau: Qué.	32	45	76
Pointe Le Bel: Qué.		49	68
Point Lake: N.W.T.	31	65	113
Point Leamington: Nfld.		49	55
Poisson Blanc, Lac: Qué.	23	46	76
Polaris, Lac: Qué.		53	73
Poltimore: Qué.	23	46	76
Pomquet: N.S.	17	46	62
Pond Inlet: *& settlement*, N.W.T.	31	73	78
Ponds, I. of: Nfld.		53	56
Ponoka: Alta.	26	53	114
Pons: *riv.*, Qué.		56	69
Pontax: *riv.*, Qué.		52	77
Ponteix: Sask.	26	50	108
Pont Rouge: Qué.	21	47	72
Pontypool: Ont.	22	44	79
Poplar: *riv.*, Man./Ont.	27	53	97
Poplar Hill: *town*, Ont.	27	52	94
Porcher I.: B.C.	28	54	130
Porcupine: Ont.	20	48	81
Porcupine: *riv.*, U.S.A./Can.	30	67	138
Porcupine, Cape: Nfld.		54	57
Porcupine Hills: Sask./Man.	27	52	101
Porcupine Plain: *town*, Sask.	27	53	103
Porquis Junction: Ont.		48	81
Portage Bay: Man.	27	51	99
Portage-du-Fort: Qué.		46	77
Portage la Prairie: Man.	27	50	98
Port Alberni: B.C.	28	49	125
Port Alfred: Qué.	21	48	71
Port Alice: B.C.	28	50	127
Port Anson: Nfld.		50	56
Port Arthur: Ont. *see* Thunder Bay			
Port-au-Port: *penin. & bay*, Newfoundland	17	49	59
Port Bolster: Ont.	22	44	79
Port Burwell: Ont.	20	42	81
Port Carling: Ont.	22	45	80
Port Cartier: Qué.	15	50	67
Port Cartier, Parc de: Qué.	15	51	67
Port Clements: B.C.	28	53	132
Port Colborne: Ont.	22	43	79
Port Coquitlam: B.C.	36	49	123
Port Credit: Ont.	32	44	80
Port Daniel: Qué.	16	48	65
Port Dover: Ont.	20	43	80
Port Edward: B.C.	28	54	130
Port Edward: Ont.	20	43	82
Port Elgin: N.B.	17	46	64
Port Elgin: Ont.	20	44	81
Porter: B.C.		58	130
Porter Lake: Sask.	26	56	107
Port Essington: B.C.	28	54	130
Port Hardy: B.C.	28	51	128
Port Hawkesbury: N.S.	17	46	61
Port Hood: N.S.	17	46	62
Port Hope: Ont.	22	44	78
Port Hope Simpson: Nfld.		53	56
Portland: Ont.	23	45	76
Portland Canal: B.C.	28	55	130
Portland Inlet: B.C.	28	55	130
Portland Promontory: Qué.		58	78
Port Logan: N.W.T.	31	72	93
Port Loring: Ont.	20	46	80
Port McNeill: B.C.	28	51	128
Port McNicoll: Ont.	22	45	80
Port Maitland: N.S.	17	44	66
Port Mellon: B.C.	28	49	123
Port Menier: Qué.	16	50	64
Port Moody: B.C.	29	49	123
Port Morien: N.S.	17	46	60
Port Mouton: N.S.	17	44	65
Port Nelson: Man.	27	57	93
Portneuf, Parc de: Qué.	16	48	73
Portneuf: *& riv.*, Qué.	21	47	72
Portneuf sur Mer: Qué.		48	69
Port Neville: B.C.		50	126
Port-Nouveau-Québec: Qué.	14	58	66
Port Perry: Ont.	22	44	79
Port Radium: N.W.T.	30	66	118
Port Renfrew: B.C.	28	49	124
Port Rexton: Nfld.		48	53
Port Rowan: Ont.	20	43	80
Port Royal: N.S.	17	44	66
Port Saunders: Nfld.	15	51	57
Port Severn: Ont.		45	80
Port Simpson: B.C.	28	55	130
Port Stanley: Ont.	20	43	81
Port Viau: Qué.	23	46	74
Poste-de-la-Baleine: Qué.	15	55	78
Poste-Mistassini: Qué.	15	50	74
Postville: Nfld.		55	60
Pouce Coupé: B.C.	29	55	120

	Page	N	W
Walton: N.S.	17	45	64
Wanapitei: *lake & riv.*, Ont.	20	47	81
Wanapitei Prov. Forest: Ontario	20	47	81
Wanham: Alta.	24	56	118
Wanless: Man.	27	54	101
Wanup: Ont.		46	81
Wapawekka Hills: & *lake*, Saskatchewan	27	54	105
Wapella: Sask.	27	50	102
Wapesi Lake: Ont.		51	92
Wapiti: *riv.*, B.C./Alta.	26	55	120
Wardlow: Alta.	26	51	112
Ware: B.C.	29	58	126
Warkworth: Ont.	22	44	78
Warman: Sask.	26	52	106
Warner: Alta.	26	49	112
Warren: Ont.	20	46	80
Warren Landing: Man.	27	54	98
Warwick: Qué.	21	46	72
Wascana Creek: Sask.	30	50	105
Wasekamio Lake: Sask.	26	57	109
Washagami: Ont.		47	80
Washago: Ont.	22	45	79
Washburn Lake: N.W.T.	31	70	107
Washow Bay: Man.	27	51	97
Waskesiu: Sask.	26	54	106
Waskigomog Lake: Ont.		46	79
Waswanipi: & *lake*, Qué.		50	76
Watabeag Lake: & *riv.*, Ont.	20	48	80
Watcomb: Ont.		50	91
Waterbury Lake: Sask.	27	58	104
Waterdown: Ont.	22	43	80
Waterford: Ont.	20	43	80
Waterhen: *riv.*, Sask.	26	54	109
Waterhen Lake: Man.	27	52	99
Waterloo: Ont.	20	43	81
Waterloo: Qué.	21	45	73
Waterton Glacier Int. Peace Park: Can./U.S.A.	48	49	114
Waterton Lakes Nat. Park: Alberta	26	49	114
Watford: Ont.	20	43	82
Wathaman: *riv.*, Sask.	27	57	104
Watino: Alta.		56	118
Watrous: Sask.	27	52	105
Watson: Sask.	27	52	104
Watson Lake: *town*, Yukon	30	60	129
Waubaushene: Ont.	22	45	80
Waugh: N.B.	16	47	66
Wawa: Ont.	19	48	85
Wawaitin Falls: Ont.	20	48	81
Wawota: Sask.	27	50	102
Weagamow Lake: Ont.		53	91
Weaver Lake: Man.	27	53	97
Webbwood: Ont.	20	46	82

	Page	N	W
Wedge Mt.: B.C.	28	50	123
Wedgeport: N.S.	17	44	66
Weedon: Qué.	21	46	71
Wekusko: & *lake*, Man.	27	55	100
Welland: & *canal*, Ont.	22	43	79
Welland: *riv.*, Ont.	22	43	80
Wellington: Nfld.		49	54
Wellington: Ont.	22	44	77
Wellington Chan.: N.W.T.	31	75	93
Wellington Station: N.S.	17	45	64
Wellington Station: P.E.I.	17	46	64
Wells: B.C.	29	53	122
Wells Gray Prov. Park: British Columbia	29	52	120
Welsford: N.B.	17	45	66
Wembley: Alta.	26	55	119
Wenebegon: *lake & riv.*, Ontario	20	47	83
Wernecke Mts.: Yukon	30	65	133
Weslemkoon Lake: Ont.	20	45	77
Wesleyville: Nfld.	17	49	54
West Club I.: N.W.T.		54	81
Westfield: N.B.	17	45	66
West Fiord: N.W.T.		76	90
Westlock: Alta.	26	54	114
West Lorne: Ont.	20	43	82
Westmount: Qué.	32	45	74
West Point: P.E.I.	17	47	64
Westport: N.S.	17	44	66
Westport: Ont.	23	45	76
Westree: Ont.		47	82
West Road: *riv.*, B.C.	29	53	123
West Vancouver: B.C.	36	49	123
Westville: N.S.	17	46	63
Westwold: B.C.		50	120
Wetaskiwin: Alta.	26	53	113
Weyburn: Sask.	27	50	104
Weymouth: N.S.	17	44	66
Whale Cove: Ont.	18	63	92
Wharton Lake: N.W.T.	31	64	100
Wheatley: Ont.	20	42	82
Wheeler: *riv.*, Qué.	15	56	67
Wheeler: *riv.*, Sask.	27	57	105
Whipple Point: N.S.	17	44	66
Whiskey Lake: Ont.	20	46	82
Whitby: Ont.	22	44	79
White: *riv.*, Ont.	19	48	85
White: *riv.*, Yukon	30	63	140
White Bay: Nfld.	17	50	57
White Bear: *riv.*, Nfld.		48	57
Whitecap Mt.: B.C.	28	51	123
Whiteclay Lake: Ont.		51	89
Whitecourt: Alta.	26	54	116
Whitefish Bay: Can./U.S.A.		46	84
Whitefish Lake: N.W.T.	31	63	107
Whitegull, Lac: Qué.	15	55	64
WHITEHORSE: Yukon	30	61	135
White I.: N.W.T.	14	66	85
White Lake: Ont.	21	45	76

	Page	N	W
White Lake: Ont.		49	86
Whitemouth: Man.	27	50	96
Whitemouth Lake: Man.	27	49	96
White Otter Lake: Ont.		49	92
White Pass: *town*, B.C.		60	135
White Rock: B.C.	28	49	123
Whitesail Lake: B.C.	28	53	127
Whiteshell Prov. Park: Manitoba	27	50	95
Whitewater Lake: Ont.		51	89
Whitewood: Sask.	27	50	102
Whitney: Ont.	20	45	78
Whittle, Cap: Qué.	17	50	60
Whitworth: Qué.		48	69
Wholdaia Lake: N.W.T.	31	60	104
Whycocomagh: N.S.	17	46	61
Wiarton: Ont.	20	45	81
Widdifield: Ont.		46	79
Wignes Lake: N.W.T.		60	106
Wikwemikong: Ont.	20	46	82
Wilberforce Falls: N.W.T.	31	67	109
Wilderness Area: *park*, Newfoundland	17	47	53
Wilderness Area: *park*, Newfoundland	17	48	57
Wildwood: Alta.	26	54	115
Wilkie: Sask.	26	52	109
Will, Mt.: B.C.	28	58	129
Willet: Ont.		50	88
William: *riv.*, Sask.	26	59	109
Williamsburg: Ont.	23	45	75
Williams Lake: *town*, B.C.	29	52	122
Willis I.: Nfld.		49	54
Williston Lake: B.C.	29	56	124
Willmore Wilderness Prov. Park: Alta.	26	53	118
Willowbunch Lake: Sask.	27	49	106
Willow Lake: N.W.T.	31	62	119
Wilson, Cape: N.W.T.	14	67	81
Wilson, Mt.: Qué.		48	74
Winchester: Ont.	23	45	75
Windermere Lake: Ont.	20	48	84
Windigo: *riv.*, Qué.		48	73
Windigo Lake: & *riv.*, Ont.	18	53	92
Windsor: Nfld.	17	49	56
Windsor: N.S.	17	45	64
Windsor: Ont.	20	42	83
Windsor: Qué.	21	46	72
Windy Tickle: *str.*, Nfld.		56	60
Winefred Lake: Alta.	26	55	111
Wingham: Ont.	20	44	81
Winisk: & *riv.*, Ont.	18	55	85
Winisk Lake: Ont.	18	53	87
Winkler: Man.	27	49	98
WINNIPEG: Manitoba	33	50	97
Winnipeg: *riv.*, Man.	27	50	95
Winnipeg, Lake: Man.	27	52	98
Winnipeg Beach: Man.	27	51	98
Winnipegosis: Man.	27	52	100

	Page	N	W
Winnipegosis, Lake: Man.	27	52	100
Winokapau Lake: Nfld.		53	63
Winter Harbour: N.W.T.	31	75	110
Winter I.: N.W.T.	14	66	83
Winterton: Nfld.		48	53
Witless Bay: *town*, Nfld.		47	53
Wolfe, Cape: P.E.I.	17	47	65
Wolf Island: & *i.*, Ont.	23	44	76
Wolf I.: Magdalen Is., Qué.	16	47	62
Wolfville: N.S.	17	45	64
Wollaston, Cape: N.W.T.	30	71	118
Wollaston Lake: Sask.	27	58	103
Wollaston Penin.: N.W.T.	30	70	115
Wolseley: Sask.	27	50	103
Wood Buffalo Park: N.W.T./Alberta	26	59	113
Woodbridge: Ont.	32	44	80
Woodfibre: B.C.	28	50	123
Wood Is.: P.E.I.	17	46	63
Wood Mt.: Sask.	26	49	106
Woods, Lake of the: Canada/U.S.A.	19	49	94
Woods I.: Nfld.		49	58
Woods Lake: Nfld.		54	65
Woodstock: N.B.	16	46	68
Woodstock: Ont.	20	43	81
Woodville: Ont.	22	44	79
Woody Island: *town*, Nfld.		48	54
Wrigley: N.W.T.	30	63	124
Writing on Stone Park: Alberta	26	49	112
Wrong Lake: Man.	27	53	96
Wrottesley Inlet: N.W.T.		72	96
Wunnummin Lake: Ont.	18	53	89
Wurtele: Ont.		49	81
Wynniatt Bay: N.W.T.		72	111
Wynyard: Sask.	27	52	104
Yale: B.C.	28	50	121
Yamaska: Qué.	21	46	73
Yarker: Ont.	22	44	77
Yarmouth: N.S.	17	44	66
Yathkyed Lake: N.W.T.	31	63	98
Yellow Grass: Sask.	27	50	104
Yellowhead Pass: B.C./Alta.	29	53	119
YELLOWKNIFE: N.W.T.	30	62	114
Yellowknife: *riv.*, N.W.T.	31	63	114
Yoho Nat. Park: B.C.	29	51	117
York: Ont.	32	44	79
York, Cape: N.W.T.	31	74	87
York Factory: Man.	27	57	92
Yorkton: Sask.	27	51	102
Youbou: B.C.	28	49	124
Young: Sask.	27	52	106
Yukon: *riv.*, U.S.A./Can.	30	62	137
Yukon: *Territ.* (*cap.* Whitehorse)	30	—	—

Gazetteer of the World

	Page	Lat.	Long.
Aachen: W. Germany	74	51N	6E
Aalst: Belgium	72	51N	4E
Aare: *r.*, Switzerland	75	47N	7E
Ābādān: Iran	87	30N	48E
Abadla: Algeria	108	31N	2W
Abakan: U.S.S.R.	85	54N	91E
Åbenrå (Aabenraa): Denmark	71	55N	9E
Abbeville: France	72	50N	2E
Abbeville: U.S.A.	46	30N	92W
Abbottabad: Pak.	88	34N	73E
Abd al Kuri: *i.*, Indian O.	87	12N	52E
Abeokuta: Nigeria	108	7N	3E
Aberaeron: Wales	63	52N	4W
Abercorn: see Mbala			
Aberdare: Wales	63	52N	4W
Aberdeen: Scotland	62	57N	2W
Aberdeen: S. Dak., U.S.A.	49	45N	99W
Aberdeen: Wash., U.S.A.	48	47N	124W
Aberfeldy: Scotland	62	57N	4W
Aberystwyth: Wales	63	52N	4W
ABIDJAN: Ivory Coast	108	5N	4W
Abilene: U.S.A.	46	32N	100W
Abingdon: England	63	52N	1W
Abqaiq: Saudi Arabia	87	26N	49E
Absaroka Range: U.S.A.	48	45N	110W
Abu: India	88	25N	73E
ABU DHABI: United Arab Emirates	87	24N	54E
ABYSSINIA: see **ETHIOPIA**			
Acapulco de Juárez: Mexico	52	17N	99W
ACCRA: Ghana	108	5N	0
Achill I.: R. of Ireland	61	54N	10W
Achinsk: U.S.S.R.	85	56N	90E
Acklins I.: The Bahamas	45	22N	74W
Aconcagua: *mtn.*, Argentina	55	33S	70W

	Page	Lat.	Long.
Acqui: Italy	75	44N	8E
Acre: *see* Akko			
Ada: U.S.A.	49	35N	97W
Adam's Bridge: India/Sri Lanka	88	9N	80E
Adana: Turkey	86	37N	35E
Adapazarı: Turkey	86	41N	30E
Adda: *r.*, Italy	75	46N	9E
ADDIS ABABA: Ethiopia	109	9N	39E
Adelaide: Australia	101	35S	139E
Adelaide I.: Antarctica	116	*Inset*	
ADEN: Yemen P.D.R.	87	13N	45E
Aden: *gulf*, Arabian Sea	87	13N	47E
Adige: *r.*, Italy	75	46N	11E
Adirondack Mts.: U.S.A.	51	43N	75W
Admiralty Is.: Papua New Guinea	99	2S	147E
Adour: *r.*, France	73	44N	1W
Adrian: U.S.A.	47	42N	84W
Adriatic Sea	69	43N	15E
Aduwa: Ethiopia	109	14N	39E
Aegean Is.: & *sea*	69	38N	26E
AFGHANISTAN: *cap.* Kabul	88	—	—
Afyonkarahisar: Turkey	86	39N	30E
Agadir: Morocco	108	30N	10W
Agartala: India	89	24N	91E
Agde, Cap d': France	73	43N	4E
Agen, France	73	44N	1E
Agenais: *reg.*, France	73	44N	1E
Agincourt: *hist.*, France	72	51N	2E
Agordat: Ethiopia	109	15N	37E
Agra: India	88	27N	78E
Agrigento: Sicily	69	37N	14E
Aguascalientes: Mexico	52	22N	102W
Agulhas Basin: Southern Ocean	89	44S	20E

	Page	Lat.	Long.
Ahaggar: *mtns.*, Algeria	108	23N	6E
Ahmedabad: India	88	23N	73E
Ahvāz: Iran	87	31N	49E
Aigues-Mortes: & *gulf*, France	73	44N	4E
Ailsa Craig: *i.*, Scot.	62	55N	5W
Aïn Sefra: Algeria	108	33N	1W
Aïr: *mtns.*, Niger	108	18N	8E
Aire: *r.*, England	62	54N	1W
Aisne: *r.*, France	72	49N	3E
Aitape: Papua New Guinea	99	3S	142E
Aix-en-Provence: Fr.	73	44N	5E
Aix-les-Bains: France	73	46N	6E
Aizuwakamatsu: Japan	93	34N	135E
Ajaccio: Corsica	67	42N	9E
Ajmer: India	88	27N	75E
Ajo: U.S.A.	48	32N	113E
Akaroa: N.Z.	104	44S	173E
Akashi: Japan	93	35N	135E
Akhisar: Turkey	69	39N	28E
Akita: Japan	93	40N	140E
Akko (Acre): Israel	86	32N	35E
Akola: India	88	21N	77E
Akritas, C.: Greece	69	37N	22E
Akron: U.S.A.	47	41N	82W
Aksha: U.S.S.R.	83	50N	113E
Aktyubinsk: U.S.S.R.	85	50N	57E
Akureyri: Iceland	70	66N	18W
Akyab: Burma	92	20N	92E
Alabama: *r.*, U.S.A.	47	32N	88W
Alabama: *State*, U.S.A.	47	33N	87W
Alai Range: U.S.S.R.	85	39N	71E
Ala Kul': *l.*, U.S.S.R.	85	46N	82E
Alameda: U.S.A.	48	43N	112W
Alamogordo: U.S.A.	49	33N	106W
Alamosa: U.S.A.	46	37N	106W
Åland Is.: Finland	71	60N	20E

	Page	Lat.	Long.
Alapayevsk: U.S.S.R.	85	58N	62E
Ala Shan: *desert*, China	90	40N	103E
Alaska: *State*, U.S.A.	12	65N	150W
Alaska, Gulf of: U.S.A.	12	58N	145W
Alaska Penin.: U.S.A.	12	56N	160W
Alaska Range: U.S.A.	12	64N	147W
Alaskan Highway: Canada/U.S.A.	12	—	—
Alassio: Italy	75	44N	8E
Alaverdi: U.S.S.R.	84	41N	45E
Alba: Italy	75	45N	8E
Albacete: Spain	67	39N	2W
ALBANIA: *cap.* Tiranë	69	41N	20E
Albany: Australia	100	35S	118E
Albany: Ga., U.S.A.	47	32N	84W
Albany: N.Y., U.S.A.	51	43N	74W
Albany: Oregon, U.S.A.	48	45N	123W
Albemarle Sd.: U.S.A.	47	36N	76W
Albert: France	72	50N	3E
Albert, Lake: Uganda	110	2N	31E
Albert Lea: U.S.A.	49	44N	93W
Albi: France	73	44N	2E
Ålborg (Aalborg): Denmark	71	57N	10E
Alborz Mts.: Iran	87	36N	52E
Albret, Pays d': Fr.	73	44N	1W
Albula Pass: Switz.	75	47N	10E
Albuquerque: U.S.A.	48	35N	107W
Albury: Australia	101	36S	147E
Alcázar de San Juan: Spain	67	39N	3W
Alcoy: Spain	67	39N	0
Aldan: U.S.S.R.	83	58N	125E
Alderney: *i.*, Channel Is.	63	*Inset*	

Name	Page	Lat.	Long.
cap. Nassau	**45**	25N	75W
Bahawalpur: Pak.	**88**	29N	72E
Bahia: *see* Salvador			
Bahia Blanca: Arg.	**55**	39S	62W
Bahraich: India	**88**	28N	82E
BAHRAIN: *cap.* Manama	**87**	26N	51E
Bahr el Ghazal: *r.*, Chad	**108**	14N	17E
Bahr el Ghazal: *Prov.*, Sudan	**109**	10N	27E
Bahr el Jebel: *see* White Nile			
Baia-Mare: Rom.	**68**	48N	24E
Bailleul: France	**72**	53N	1E
Bainbridge: U.S.A.	**47**	31N	85W
Bairnsdale: Australia	**101**	38S	148E
Baker: Mont., U.S.A.	**49**	46N	104W
Baker: Oreg., U.S.A.	**48**	45N	118W
Bakersfield: U.S.A.	**48**	35N	119W
Baku: U.S.S.R.	**84**	40N	50E
Balaghat: India	**88**	22N	80E
Balaklava: *hist.*, U.S.S.R.	**84**	45N	34E
Bala Lake: Wales	**62**	53N	4W
Balashikha: U.S.S.R.	**114**	55N	38E
Balashov: U.S.S.R.	**84**	51N	43E
Balasore: India	**88**	21N	87E
Balatón L.: Hungary	**68**	47N	18E
Balboa: Panama	**45**	*Inset*	
Balclutha: N.Z.	**104**	46S	170E
Bâle: *see* Basel			
Balearic, Islas: Spain	**67**	39N	3E
Balen: Belgium	**72**	51N	5E
Bali: *i.*, Indonesia	**91**	8S	115E
Balikesir: Turkey	**86**	40N	28E
Balikpapan: Indon.	**91**	1S	117E
Balkan Mts.: Bulgaria	**69**	43N	25E
Balkhash: & *l.*, U.S.S.R.	**85**	46N	75E
Ballarat: Australia	**101**	38S	144E
Ballater: Scotland	**62**	57N	3W
Ballina: Australia	**101**	29S	154E
Ballina: R. of Ireland	**61**	54N	9W
Ballymena: N. Ireland	**61**	55N	6W
Balmaceda: Chile	**55**	46S	72W
Balmoral: Scotland	**62**	57N	3W
Balovale: Zambia	**110**	14S	23E
Balranald: Australia	**101**	35S	144E
Balsas: *r.*, Mexico	**52**	18N	102W
Balta: U.S.S.R.	**68**	48N	30E
Baltic Sea	**71**	—	—
Baltimore: U.S.A.	**50**	39N	77W
Baltrum: *i.*, W. Ger.	**74**	54N	7E
Baluchistan: *reg.*, Pakistan	**88**	27N	65E
BAMAKO: Mali	**108**	13N	8W
Bamba: Mali	**108**	17N	2W
Bamberg: W. Germany	**74**	50N	11E
Banbury: England	**63**	52N	1W
Banchory: Scotland	**62**	57N	2W
Banda Aceh: Indon.	**92**	5N	95E
Bandar: India	**88**	16N	81E
Bandar Abbās: Iran	**87**	27N	56E
Bandar-e-Shāh: Iran	**87**	37N	54E
Bandar-e-Shāhpūr: Iran	**87**	30N	49E
BANDAR SERI BEGAWAN: Brunei	**91**	5N	115E
Banda Sea: Indon.	**91**	6S	127E
Banderas, Bahia de: Mexico	**52**	21N	106W
Bandırma: Turkey	**69**	40N	28E
Banja Luka: Yugo.	**69**	45N	17E
Ban Me Thuot: Vietnam	**92**	12N	108E
Bandjarmasin: Indon.	**91**	3S	115E
Bandra: India	**88**	19N	73E
Bandung: Indonesia	**91**	7S	107E
Bangalore: India	**88**	13N	78E
Bangka: *i.*, Indonesia	**91**	2S	106E
BANGKOK: Thailand	**92**	14N	100E
Bangor: N. Ireland	**62**	55N	6W
Bangor: U.S.A.	**19**	45N	69W
Bangor: Wales	**63**	53N	4W
BANGUI: Central African Empire	**109**	4N	18E
Bangweulu, L.: Zambia	**110**	11S	31E
Ban Houei Sai: Laos	**92**	20N	100E
Baniâs: Syria	**86**	35N	36E
Banja Luka: Yugo.	**69**	45N	17E
BANJUL: The Gambia	**108**	13N	17W
Banks Penin.: N.Z.	**104**	44S	173E
Bankstown: Australia	**115**	34S	151E
Bann: *r.*, N. Ireland	**62**	55N	7W
Bannu: Pakistan	**88**	33N	71E
Bantry: & *bay*, R. of Ireland	**61**	52N	9W
Bapaume: France	**72**	50N	3E
Bārākpur (Barrackpore): India	**115**	23N	88E
Baranof I.: U.S.A.	**24**	57N	135W
Baranovichi: U.S.S.R.	**84**	53N	26E
Barataria Bay: U.S.A.	**47**	29N	90W
BARBADOS: *cap.* Bridgetown	**45**	13N	60W
Barbuda: *i.*, W. Indies	**45**	18N	62W
Barce: Libya	**86**	33N	21E
Barcelona: Spain	**67**	41N	2E
Barcelona: Venezuela	**45**	10N	65W
Barcelonnette: Fr.	**73**	44N	7E
Barcoo: *r.*, Australia	**99**	24S	144E
Bardawīl, Lake: Egypt	**86**	31N	33E
Bardia: Libya	**86**	32N	25E
Bareilly: India	**88**	28N	80E
Barents Sea: U.S.S.R.	**82**	73N	40E
Bari: Italy	**69**	41N	17E
Barking: England	**112**	51N	0
Barkly Tableland: Australia	**98**	18S	136E
Barkly West: S. Africa	**111**	28S	25E
Bar-le-Duc: France	**72**	49N	5E
Barlee, L.: Australia	**100**	29S	119E
Barletta: Italy	**69**	41N	16E
Barlin: France	**72**	50N	3E
Barnaul: U.S.S.R.	**85**	53N	84E
Barnet: England	**112**	52N	0
Barnsley: England	**62**	54N	2W
Barnstaple: England	**63**	51N	4W
Baroda: India	**88**	22N	73E
Barquisimeto: Venez.	**45**	10N	69W
Barra: *i.* & *Hd.*, Scot.	**61**	57N	7W
Barraba: Australia	**101**	30S	151E
Barrackpore: *see* Bārākpur			
Barra do Pirai: Brazil	**56**	22S	44W
Barranquilla: Colombia	**45**	11N	75W
Barrow-in-Furness: England	**62**	54N	3W
Barrow, Point: U.S.A.	**12**	72N	156W
Barry: Wales	**63**	51N	3W
Barstow: U.S.A.	**48**	35N	117W
Bar-sur-Seine: France	**72**	48N	4E
Bartlesville: U.S.A.	**49**	37N	96W
Basel (Bâle): Switzerland	**75**	48N	7E
Basildon: England	**112**	51N	0
Basingstoke: England	**63**	51N	1W
Basra: Iraq	**87**	30N	48E
Bassein: Burma	**92**	17N	95E
Basse-Terre: Guadeloupe	**45**	16N	62W
Bass Strait: Australia	**99**	40S	146E
Bastogne: Belgium	**72**	50N	6E
Bastrop: U.S.A.	**46**	33N	92W
Bataan Penin.: Phil.	**91**	15N	120E
Batang: China	**90**	30N	99E
Batesville: Arkansas, U.S.A.	**46**	36N	92W
Batesville: Miss., U.S.A.	**47**	34N	90W
Bath: England	**63**	51N	2W
Bathurst: Australia	**101**	33S	150E
Bathurst I.: Australia	**98**	12S	130E
Baton Rouge: U.S.A.	**46**	31N	91W
Batticaloa: Sri Lanka	**88**	8N	82E
Battle Creek: *city*, U.S.A.	**47**	42N	85W
Battle Mountain: *city*, U.S.A.	**48**	41N	117W
Batu Is.: Indonesia	**91**	0	99E
Batumi: U.S.S.R.	**84**	42N	42E
Batz, I. de: France	**72**	49N	4W
Bautzen: E. Germany	**74**	51N	14E
Bavaria: *Prov.*, W. Ger.	**74/5**	49N	11E
Bavarian Forest: W. Germany	**74/5**	49N	13E
Bawdwin: Burma	**92**	23N	97E
Bayamo: Cuba	**53**	20N	77W
Bayan Kara Shan: *mtns.*, China	**90**	34N	99E
Bay City: Michigan, U.S.A.	**19**	44N	84W
Bay City: Texas, U.S.A.	**46**	29N	96W
Bayeux: France	**72**	49N	1W
Baykal, L.: U.S.S.R.	**83**	53N	107E
Baykonur: U.S.S.R.	**85**	48N	66E
Baymak: U.S.S.R.	**85**	53N	58E
Bayonne: France	**73**	43N	1W
Bayonne: U.S.A.	**35**	41N	74W
Bayreuth: W. Germany	**75**	50N	12E
Baytown: U.S.A.	**46**	29N	95W
Baza: Spain	**67**	37N	3W
Beachy Head: Eng.	**61**	51N	0
Beaconsfield: England	**112**	51N	0
Beardmore Glacier: Antarctica	**116**	*Inset*	
Bear I.: U.S.S.R.	**82**	74N	20E
Béarn: *Old Prov.*, Fr.	**73**	43N	1W
Beas: *r.*, India	**88**	32N	76E
Beatrice: U.S.A.	**49**	40N	97W
Beauce: *reg.*, France	**72**	48N	2E
Beaufort: U.S.A.	**47**	32N	81W
Beaufort Sea	**12**	73N	140W
Beaufort W.: S. Africa	**111**	32S	23E
Beaujolais, Mts. du: France	**73**	46N	4E
Beaumont: U.S.A.	**46**	30N	94W
Beaune: France	**73**	47N	5E
Beauvais: France	**72**	49N	2E
Beaver: *i.*, U.S.A.	**19**	45N	85W
Beaver Dam: *city*, U.S.A.	**49**	43N	89W
Béchar: Algeria	**108**	32N	2W
Beckley: U.S.A.	**47**	38N	81W
Bedford: & *Co.*, Eng.	**63**	52N	0
Bedford: Mass., U.S.A.	**33**	42N	71W
Bedford: Ind., U.S.A.	**47**	39N	86W
Bedford: Pa., U.S.A.	**50**	40N	79W
Beersheba: Israel	**86**	31N	35E
Beeville: U.S.A.	**46**	29N	97W
Bega: Australia	**101**	37S	150E
Begovat: U.S.S.R.	**85**	40N	69E
Beira: Mozambique	**110**	20S	35E
BEIRUT: Lebanon	**86**	34N	34E
Beit Bridge: Rhod. (Zimbabwe)	**111**	22S	30E
Beja: Portugal	**67**	38N	8W
Bejaïa: Algeria	**67**	36N	5E
Bela: Pakistan	**88**	26N	66E
Belaya: *r.*, U.S.S.R.	**84**	54N	56E
Belém: Brazil	**54**	1S	48W
Belen: U.S.A.	**48**	35N	107W
BELFAST: N. Ireland	**62**	55N	6W
Belfast L.: N. Ireland	**61**	55N	6W
Belfort: France	**73**	48N	7E
Belgaum: India	**88**	16N	75E
BELGIUM: *cap.* Brussels	**72**	51N	4E
Belgorod: U.S.S.R.	**84**	51N	36E
BELGRADE: Yugo.	**69**	45N	20E
Belitung: *i.*, Indon.	**91**	3S	108E
BELIZE: *cap.* Belmopan	**53**	17N	88W
Belize: Belize	**53**	17N	88W
Bellac: France	**73**	46N	1E
Bellary: India	**88**	15N	77E
Belle Fourche: & *r.*, U.S.A.	**49**	45N	104W
Bellegarde: France	**73**	46N	6E
Belle Glade: U.S.A.	**47**	27N	81W
Belle Île-en-Mer: Fr.	**72**	47N	3W
Belleville: Kansas, U.S.A.	**49**	40N	98W
Bellingham: U.S.A.	**48**	49N	122W
Bellinzona: Switz.	**75**	46N	9E
Belluno: Italy	**75**	46N	12E
Belmont: S. Africa	**111**	30S	24E
BELMOPAN: Belize	**53**	17N	88W
Belo Horizonte: Brazil	**54**	20S	44W
Beloit: Kans., U.S.A.	**49**	39N	98W
Beloit: Wisc., U.S.A.	**49**	43N	89W
Bel'tsy: U.S.S.R.	**69**	47N	28E
Belyando: *r.*, Australia	**100**	22S	146E
Belyy I.: U.S.S.R.	**83**	73N	70E
Bemidji: U.S.A.	**49**	47N	95W
Benalla: Australia	**101**	37S	146E
Bend: U.S.A.	**48**	44N	121W
Bendery: U.S.S.R.	**68**	47N	30E
Bendigo: Australia	**101**	37S	144E
Bengal, Bay of: Bangl./India	**89**	17N	87E
Benghazi: Libya	**109**	32N	20E
Benguela: Angola	**110**	13S	13E
Beni: *r.*, Bolivia	**54**	13S	67W
BENIN: *cap.* Cotonou	**108**	10N	3E
Benin, Bight of: Africa	**108**	4N	3E
Beni Saf: Algeria	**67**	35N	1W
Ben Macdhui: *mt.*, Scotland	**62**	57N	4W
Ben Nevis: *mt.*, Scot.	**62**	57N	5W
Bennington: U.S.A.	**19**	43N	74W
Bensenville: U.S.A.	**34**	42N	88W
Benton: U.S.A.	**46**	35N	93W
Benton Harbor: U.S.A.	**47**	43N	86W
Benue: *r.*, Africa	**108**	9N	12E
Berar: *reg.*, India	**88**	21N	77E
Berber: Sudan	**109**	18N	34E
Berbera: Somali Republic	**109**	10N	45E
Berdichev: U.S.S.R.	**84**	50N	29E
Berezovo: U.S.S.R.	**85**	64N	65E
Bergama: Turkey	**69**	39N	27E
Bergamo: & *Alps*, It.	**75**	46N	10E
Bergen: Norway	**70**	60N	5E
Bergen-op-Zoom: Netherlands	**74**	51N	4E
Bergerac: France	**73**	45N	0
Bergisch Gladbach: W. Germany	**74**	51N	7E
Berhampore: India	**88**	24N	88E
Bering Sea	**12**	61N	170W
Bering Str.: U.S.S.R./U.S.A.	**12**	65N	170W
Berkeley: U.S.A.	**36**	38N	122W
Berkley: U.S.A.	**33**	42N	83W
Berkhamsted: Eng.	**112**	51N	0
Berkshire: *Co.*, Eng.	**63**	51N	1W
BERLIN: E. & W. Ger.	**113**	—	—
Berlin: U.S.A.	**19**	45N	71W
Bermejo: *r.*, Arg.	**56**	26S	60W
Bermuda: *i.*, Atlantic Ocean	**57**	32N	65W
BERN: Switzerland	**75**	47N	7E
Bernay: France	**72**	49N	1E
Bernese Alps: Switz.	**75**	46N	7E
Berre, Étg. de: France	**73**	43N	5E
Berry: *Old Prov.*, Fr.	**73**	47N	2E
Berry Is.: The Bahamas	**47**	26N	78W
Berwick upon Tweed: England	**62**	56N	2W
Berwyn: U.S.A.	**34**	41N	88W
Besançon: France	**73**	47N	6E
Bessèges: France	**73**	44N	4E
Bessemer: U.S.A.	**47**	33N	87W
Bessines: France	**73**	46N	1E
Bethlehem: Jordan	**86**	31N	35E
Bethlehem: S. Africa	**111**	28S	28E
Bethlehem: U.S.A.	**50**	41N	75W
Béthune: France	**72**	51N	3E
Béticas, Cordillera: *mtns.*, Spain	**67**	38N	2W
Betwa: *r.*, India	**88**	26N	80E
Betws-y-Coed: Wales	**62**	53N	4W
Beuvron: *r.*, France	**73**	47N	2E
Beverley: England	**62**	54N	0
Beverly: U.S.A.	**51**	42N	71W
Beverly Hills: U.S.A.	**37**	34N	118W
Bexley Heath: England	**112**	51N	0
Bezhitsa: U.S.S.R.	**84**	53N	34E
Béziers: France	**73**	43N	3E
Bhagalpur: India	**88**	25N	88E
Bhamo: Burma	**92**	24N	97E
Bhavnagar: India	**88**	22N	72E
Bhima: *r.*, India	**88**	17N	76E
Bhopal: India	**88**	23N	77E
Bhubaneswar: India	**88**	20N	86E
Bhuj: India	**88**	23N	70E
BHUTAN: *cap.* Punakha	**89**	27N	90E
Biak: *i.*, Indon.	**91**	1S	136E
Białystok: Poland	**68**	53N	23E
Biarritz: France	**73**	43N	1W
Bicester: England	**63**	52N	1W
Biddeford: U.S.A.	**19**	43N	70W
Bideford: England	**63**	51N	4W
Biel: Switzerland	**75**	47N	7E
Bielefeld: W. Germany	**74**	52N	9E
Biella: Italy	**75**	46N	8E
Big Black: *r.*, U.S.A.	**46**	33N	90W
Big Blue: *r.*, U.S.A.	**46**	41N	97W
Big Falls: *city*, U.S.A.	**49**	48N	94W
Bighorn Mts.: & *r.*, U.S.A.	**48**	45N	108W
Big Spring: U.S.A.	**49**	32N	102W
Big Wood: *r.*, U.S.A.	**48**	43N	115W
Bihać: Yugoslavia	**69**	45N	16E
Bihar: *State*, India	**88**	25N	85E
Bikaner: India	**88**	28N	73E
Bilaspur: India	**88**	22N	82E
Bilbao: Spain	**67**	43N	3W
Billericay: England	**112**	51N	0
Billings: U.S.A.	**48**	46N	109W
Biloxi: U.S.A.	**47**	30N	89W
Bimini Is.: The Bahamas	**47**	26N	79W
Bingen: W. Germany	**74**	50N	8E
Binghamton: U.S.A.	**50**	42N	76W
Binjai: Indonesia	**92**	3N	98E
Birdum: Australia	**98**	16S	133E
Bīrjand: Iran	**87**	33N	59E
Birkenhead: England	**63**	53N	3W
Bîrlad: Romania	**69**	46N	28E
Birmingham: England	**63**	52N	2W
Birmingham: Ala., U.S.A.	**47**	33N	87W
Birmingham: Mich., U.S.A.	**20**	42N	83W
Birobidzhan: U.S.S.R.	**83**	49N	133E
Bisbee: U.S.A.	**48**	31N	110W
Biscay, Bay of: Atl. Ocean	**64**	45N	5W
Bishop's Stortford: England	**63**	51N	0
Biskra: Algeria	**108**	35N	6E
Bismarck: U.S.A.	**49**	47N	101W
Bismarck Arch.: Papua New Guinea	**99**	5S	150E
BISSAU: Guinea-Bissau	**108**	12N	16W
Bistrita: *r.*, Romania	**68**	47N	26E
Bitola: Yugoslavia	**69**	41N	21E
Bitterfeld: E. Germany	**74**	52N	12E
Bitterfontein: S. Africa	**111**	31S	18E
Bitterroot Range: U.S.A.	**48**	46N	115W
Biwa-ko: *l.*, Japan	**93**	35N	136E
Biysk: U.S.S.R.	**85**	53N	85E
Black: *r.*, Ark., U.S.A.	**46**	36N	91W
Black: *r.*, N.Y., U.S.A.	**19**	43N	75W
Black: *r.*, Wisc., U.S.A.	**49**	44N	91W
Blackburn: England	**62**	54N	2W
Blackfoot: U.S.A.	**48**	43N	112W
Black Forest: W. Ger.	**75**	48N	8E
Black Irtysh: *r.*, U.S.S.R./China	**85**	48N	85E
Black Mtns.: Wales	**63**	52N	3W
Blackpool: England	**62**	54N	3W
Black Sea: U.S.S.R.	**84**	43N	35E
Black Volta: *r.*, West Africa	**108**	10N	2W
Blackwater: *r.*, R. of Ireland	**61**	52N	8W
Blackwood: *r.*, Austl.	**100**	34S	115E
Blagoveshchensk: U.S.S.R.	**83**	50N	127E
Blanc, C.: W. Sahara	**108**	20N	17W
Blanc, Mt.: Fr./Italy	**73**	46N	7E
Blankenberghe: Belg.	**72**	51N	3E
Blantyre: Malawi	**110**	16S	35E
Blavet: *r.*, France	**72**	48N	3W
Blaye: France	**71**	45N	1W
Blenheim: *hist.*, W. Germany	**75**	49N	10E
Blenheim: N.Z.	**104**	42S	174E
Bletchley: England	**63**	52N	1W
Blida: Algeria	**67**	36N	3E
Bloemfontein: S. Africa	**111**	29S	26E
Blois: France	**71**	48N	1E
Bloody Foreland: R. of Ireland	**61**	55N	8W
Bloomington: Ill., U.S.A.	**49**	40N	89W
Bloomington: Ind., U.S.A.	**47**	39N	86W

The World

Bluefield — Capricorn Group

	Page	Lat.	Long.
Bluefield: U.S.A.	47	37N	81W
Blue Mts.: Jamaica	53	18N	76W
Blue Mts.: U.S.A.	48	45N	120W
Blue Nile: *r.*, Africa	109	10N	37E
Blue Ridge: *mts.*, U.S.A.	47	36N	81W
Bluff: N.Z.	104	46S	168E
Blumenthal: W. Ger.	74	53N	9E
Blythe: U.S.A.	48	34N	115W
Blytheville: U.S.A.	49	36N	90W
Bo: Sierra Leone	108	8N	12W
Boa Vista: Brazil	54	3N	61W
Bobo Dioulasso: Upper Volta	108	12N	4W
Bocholt: W. Germany	74	52N	7E
Bochum: W. Germany	64	51N	7E
Bodelé Depression: Chad	109	17N	17E
Boden: Sweden	70	66N	22E
Bodensee: *see* Constance, L.			
Bodmin: & *moor*, England	63	50N	5W
Bodø: Norway	70	67N	14E
Bogalusa: U.S.A.	47	31N	90W
BOGOTÁ: Colombia	54	5N	74W
Bohol: *i.*, Phil.	91	10N	124E
Boise: U.S.A.	48	44N	116W
Bojador, C.: W. Sahara	108	26N	15W
Boké: Guinea	108	11N	14W
Boknafjorden: Norway	70	59N	6E
Bolama: Guinea-Bissau	108	12N	15W
Bolan Pass: Pakistan	88	30N	68E
Bolivar: U.S.A.	49	38N	93W
BOLIVIA: *cap.* La Paz (government), Sucre (legal)	54	17S	65W
Bollwiller: France	72	48N	7E
Bologna: Italy	75	44N	11E
Bol'shevik I.: U.S.S.R.	83	78N	102E
Bolton: England	62	53N	2W
Bolzano: Italy	75	47N	11E
Boma: Zaïre	110	6S	13E
Bombay: India	88	19N	73E
Bon, C.: Tunisia	69	37N	11E
Bonaire: *i.*, Caribbean Sea	45	12N	98W
Bondo: Zaïre	110	4N	24E
Bone, G. of: Indon.	91	4S	121E
Bonin Is.: Pacific O.	102	27N	142E
BONN: W. Germany	74	51N	7E
Bonny, Bight of: Gulf of Guinea	108	3N	8E
Borås: Sweden	71	58N	13E
Bordeaux: France	73	45N	1W
Borders: *Reg.*, Scotland	62	55N	3W
Bordertown: Australia	101	36S	141E
Borehamwood: Eng.	112	52N	0
Borger: U.S.A.	49	36N	101W
Borgholm: Sweden	71	57N	17E
Borislav: U.S.S.R.	68	49N	23E
Borisoglebsk: U.S.S.R.	84	51N	42E
Borkum: *i.*, W. Ger.	74	54N	7E
Borlänge: Sweden	71	60N	15E
Borneo: *i.*, Indonesia	91	0	115E
Bornholm: *i.*, Den.	71	55N	15E
Bosporus: *str.*, Tur.	65	41N	29E
Bossier City: U.S.A.	46	33N	94W
Bosso: Niger	108	14N	13E
Boston: England	63	53N	0
Boston: U.S.A.	51	42N	71W
Botany Bay: Australia	115	34S	151E
Bothnia, Gulf of: Baltic Sea	70	63N	20E
Botosani: Romania	68	47N	26E
BOTSWANA: *cap.* Gaborone	110	22S	24E
Bottrop: W. Germany	64	51N	7E
Bougainville: *i.*, Papua New Guinea	99	6S	155E
Boulder: Australia	100	31S	122E
Boulder: U.S.A.	49	40N	105W
Boulder City: U.S.A.	48	36N	115W
Boulogne: France	72	51N	2E
Boulogne-Billancourt: France	113	49N	2E
Bourbonnais: *reg.*, Fr.	73	46N	3E
Bourg: France	73	46N	5E
Bourges: France	73	47N	2E
Bourget, Lac du: Fr.	73	46N	6E
Bourg Madame: Fr.	73	42N	2E
Bourke: Australia	101	30S	146E
Bournemouth: Eng.	63	51N	2W
Bourtanger Moor: Neth./W. Germany	74	53N	7E
Bou Saâda: Algeria	67	35N	4E
Boussac: France	73	46N	2E
Bowling Green: U.S.A.	47	37N	86W
Bowling Green C.: Australia	100	19S	147E
Bowman: U.S.A.	49	46N	103W
Box Hill: England	112	51N	0
Boyome Falls: Zaïre	110	0	25E
Boyne: *r.*, R. of Irel.	61	54N	6W
Bozeman: U.S.A.	48	46N	111W
Brabant: Belgium	72	51N	4E
Brač: *i.*, Yugoslavia	69	43N	16E
Bracknell: England	63	51N	0
Bradenton: U.S.A.	47	28N	83W
Bradford: England	62	54N	1W
Braga: Portugal	67	42N	8W
Brahmani: *r.*, India	88	22N	85E
Brahmaputra: *r.*, Bangl./India	89	26N	93E
Braila: Romania	69	45N	28E
Brainerd: U.S.A.	49	46N	94W
Braintree: England	63	52N	0
Braintree: U.S.A.	33	42N	71W
Branco: *r.*, Brazil	54	1N	62W
Brandenburg: E. Ger.	74	52N	13E
BRASÍLIA: Brazil	54	16S	48W
Braşov: Romania	68	46N	26E
Brasstown Bald: *mtn.*, U.S.A.	47	35N	84W
Bratislava: Czech.	68	48N	17E
Bratsk: U.S.S.R.	83	56N	102E
Braunau: Austria	75	48N	13E
Braunschweig: *see* Brunswick, W. Ger.			
Brawley: U.S.A.	48	33N	115W
Bray: R. of Ireland	63	53N	6W
BRAZIL: *cap.* Brasília	54/5	—	—
Brazil Basin: Atl. O.	57	10S	25W
Brazilian Highlands: Brazil	54	15S	50W
Brazos: *r.*, U.S.A.	46	29N	95W
Brazo Sur del Río Pilcomayo: *r.*, Arg./Paraguay	56	24S	59W
BRAZZAVILLE: Congo	110	4S	15E
Breckenridge: U.S.A.	49	46N	97W
Brecon: Wales	63	52N	3W
Brecon Beacons: *mtns.*, Wales	63	52N	3W
Breda: Netherlands	74	52N	5E
Bregenz: Austria	75	47N	10E
Bréhat, Î.: France	72	49N	3W
Breisach: W. Germany	75	48N	8E
Bremen: W. Germany	74	53N	9E
Bremerhaven: W. Germany	74	54N	9E
Bremerton: U.S.A.	48	47N	123W
Brenner Pass: Austria/Italy	75	47N	12E
Brentwood: England	112	51N	0
Brescia: Italy	75	46N	10E
Bressuire: France	73	47N	0
Brest: France	72	48N	4W
Brest: U.S.S.R.	68	52N	24E
Breton Sound: U.S.A.	47	30N	90W
Briançon: France	73	45N	7E
Bridgend: Wales	63	52N	4W
Bridgeport: Conn. U.S.A.	51	41N	73W
Bridgeport: Texas, U.S.A.	46	33N	99W
Bridgetown: Austl.	100	34S	116E
Bridgnorth: England	63	52N	2W
Bridgwater: England	63	51N	3W
Bridlington: England	62	54N	0
Brie: *reg.*, France	72	49N	3E
Brienz, Lake: Switz.	75	47N	8E
Briey: France	72	49N	6E
Brig: Switzerland	75	46N	8E
Brigham: U.S.A.	48	42N	112W
Brighton: England	63	51N	0
Brindisi: Italy	69	41N	18E
Brisbane: Australia	100	27S	153E
Bristol: England	63	51N	3W
Bristol: U.S.A.	47	37N	82W
Bristol Bay: U.S.A.	12	58N	160W
Bristol Channel: Eng.	63	51N	4W
British Isles: Europe	61	—	—
British Mts.: U.S.A./Canada	30	69N	140W
Brittany: *Old Prov.*, France	72	48N	3W
Brive: France	73	45N	2E
Brno: Czech.	68	49N	17E
Broadview: U.S.A.	34	42N	88W
Brockton: U.S.A.	51	42N	71W
Brockway: U.S.A.	49	47N	106W
Brod: Yugoslavia	69	45N	18E
Broken Bow: U.S.A.	49	41N	100W
Broken Hill: Australia	101	32S	141E
Bromley: England	112	51N	0
Bromsgrove: England	63	52N	2W
Bronx, The: U.S.A.	35	41N	74W
Brookfield: U.S.A.	34	43N	83W
Brookings: U.S.A.	49	44N	97W
Brookline: U.S.A.	33	43N	72W
Brooklyn: U.S.A.	35	41N	74W
Brooks Range: U.S.A.	12	68N	150W
Brooksville: U.S.A.	47	29N	82W
Broome: Australia	98	18S	122E
Brough Head: Scotland	61	59N	3W
Brownsville: U.S.A.	52	26N	97W
Brownwood: U.S.A.	49	32N	99W
Bruchsal: W. Germany	74	49N	9E
Bruges (Brugge): Belgium	72	51N	3E
Brühl: W. Germany	74	51N	7E
BRUNEI: *cap.* Bandar Seri Begawan	91	5N	115E
Brunswick: U.S.A.	47	31N	81W
Brunswick (Braunschweig): W. Ger.	74	52N	10E
BRUSSELS: Belgium	72	51N	4E
Bryan: U.S.A.	46	30N	96W
Bryansk: U.S.S.R.	84	53N	34E
Bucaramanga: Colombia	54	7N	73W
Buchan Ness: Scotland	61	57N	2W
BUCHAREST: Romania	69	44N	26E
Buckhaven: Scotland	62	56N	3W
Buckingham: *Co.*, England	63	52N	0
Buckland Tableland: Australia	100	25S	148E
BUDAPEST: Hungary	68	48N	19E
Bude: England	63	51N	5W
Büderich: W. Germany	64	51N	7E
Buenaventura: Colombia	54	4N	77W
BUENOS AIRES: Arg.	56	35S	58W
Buffalo: N.Y., U.S.A.	50	43N	79W
Buffalo: Wyo., U.S.A.	48	44N	107W
Bug: *r.*, Pol./U.S.S.R.	68	51N	24E
Bug: *r.*, U.S.S.R.	84	48N	31E
BUJUMBURA: Burundi	110	3S	30E
Bukachacha: U.S.S.R.	83	53N	117E
Bukama: Zaïre	110	9S	26E
Bukavu: Zaïre	110	2S	29E
Bukhara: U.S.S.R.	85	40N	65E
Bukittinggi: Indon.	92	0	100E
Bukoba: Tanzania	110	1S	32E
Bulagan: Mongolia	83	49N	103E
Bulawayo: Rhodesia (Zimbabwe)	111	20S	29E
BULGARIA: *cap.* Sofiya (Sofia)	69	42N	25E
Buller: *mtns.*, N.Z.	104	42S	172E
Bulloo: *r.*, Australia	100	26S	143E
Bulloo, L.: Australia	100	28S	142E
Bull Shoals Res.: U.S.A.	46	37N	93W
Bumthang: Bhutan	89	27N	91E
Bunbury: Australia	100	33S	116E
Bundaberg: Austl.	100	25S	152E
Bunguran Is.: *see* Natuna Is.			
Buraida: Saudi Arabia	87	27N	44E
Buraimi: United Arab Emirates	87	24N	56E
Burbank: U.S.A.	37	34N	118W
Burdekin: *r.*, Austl.	100	20S	147E
Burdur: Turkey	86	38N	30E
Bureya: U.S.S.R.	83	50N	130E
Burgas: Bulgaria	69	42N	27E
Burgdorf: Switzerland	75	47N	8E
Burgersdorp: S. Africa	111	31S	26E
Burgos: Spain	67	42N	4W
Burgundy: *Old Prov.*, France	72/3	47N	5E
Burley: U.S.A.	48	42N	114W
Burlington: Colo., U.S.A.	49	39N	103W
Burlington: Iowa, U.S.A.	49	41N	91W
Burlington: Mass., U.S.A.	51	42N	71W
Burlington: N.C., U.S.A.	47	36N	80W
Burlington: Vt., U.S.A.	19	44N	73W
BURMA: *cap.* Rangoon	92	—	—
Burnie: Tasmania	99	41S	146E
Burnley: England	62	54N	2W
Burns: U.S.A.	48	44N	119W
Burra: Australia	101	34S	139E
Burrinjuck Res.: Australia	101	35S	149E
Bursa: Turkey	86	40N	29E
Burton upon Trent: England	63	53N	2W
BURUNDI: *cap.* Bujumbura	110	3S	30E
Bury: England	62	53N	2W
Bury St. Edmunds: England	63	52N	1E
Būshehr: Iran	87	29N	51E
Busselton: Australia	100	34S	115E
Bute: *i.*, Scotland	62	56N	5W
Butler: U.S.A.	47	41N	80W
Butte: U.S.A.	48	46N	113W
Butterworth: Malaysia	92	5N	100E
Butterworth: S. Africa	111	32S	28E
Butt of Lewis: Scotland	61	58N	6W
Butung: *i.*, Indon.	91	5S	123E
Buxton: England	63	53N	2W
Buyaga: U.S.S.R.	83	60N	127E
Buzău: Romania	69	45N	27E
Buzuluk: U.S.S.R.	84	53N	52E
Bydgoszcz: Poland	68	53N	18E
Byelorussian S.S.R.: U.S.S.R.	68	53N	27E
Byrd Land: Antarctica	116	80S	130W
Bytom: Poland	68	50N	19E
Caballo Res.: U.S.A.	48	33N	107W
Cabimas: Venezuela	45	10N	71W
Cabinda: *prov.*, Angola	110	5S	12E
Čačak: Yugoslavia	69	44N	20E
Cáceres: Spain	67	39N	6W
Cadillac: U.S.A.	19	44N	85W
Cádiz: & Golfo de, Spain	67	37N	6W
Caen: France	72	49N	0
Caernarfon: & *Bay*, Wales	63	53N	4W
Cágliari: Sardinia	67	39N	9E
Cahors: France	73	44N	1E
Caicos Is.: Caribbean Sea	45	22N	72W
Cairngorm Mts.: Scotland	62	57N	4W
Cairns: Australia	99	17S	146E
CAIRO: Egypt	86	30N	31E
Calabozo: Venezuela	45	9N	67W
Calais: France	72	51N	2E
Calais: U.S.A.	15	45N	67W
Calamian Group: Philippines	91	12N	120E
Călăraşi: Romania	69	44N	27E
Calcutta: India	88	22N	88E
Caldera: Chile	54	27S	71W
Caldwell: U.S.A.	48	44N	117W
Calexico: U.S.A.	48	33N	115W
Calf of Man: I. of Man	62	54N	5W
Cali: Colombia	54	3N	77W
Caliente: U.S.A.	48	38N	115W
California: *State*, U.S.A.	48	—	—
California, Gulf of: Mexico	44	27N	112W
Calipatria: U.S.A.	48	33N	115W
Callao: Peru	54	12S	77W
Caltanissetta: Sicily	69	37N	14E
Calumet City: U.S.A.	34	41N	87W
Calvi: Corsica	67	43N	9E
Calvinia: S. Africa	111	32S	20E
Cam: *r.*, England	63	52N	0
Camagüy: Cuba	53	21N	78W
Camargue: *reg.*, France	73	44N	4E
Cambay: & *Gulf*, India	88	22N	73E
Camberley: England	112	51N	0
CAMBODIA: *cap.* Phnom Penh	92	13N	105E
Cambrai: France	72	50N	3E
Cambrian Mts.: Wales	63	52N	4W
Cambridge: & *Co.*, England	63	32N	0
Cambridge: Del., U.S.A.	47	39N	76W
Cambridge: Mass., U.S.A.	33	42N	71W
Camden: U.S.A.	46	34N	93W
Cameron: U.S.A.	46	31N	97W
CAMEROUN: *cap.* Yaoundé	108	5N	12E
Camocim: Brazil	54	3S	41W
Camooweal: Australia	98	20S	138E
Campbeltown: Scot.	62	55N	6W
Campeche, & Bahia de: Mexico	53	20N	93W
Campinas: Brazil	56	23S	47W
Campine: *reg.*, Belg./Neth.	72	51N	5E
Campo Grande: Brazil	54	20S	55W
Cam Ranh: Vietnam	92	11N	109E
Canadian: *r.*, U.S.A.	46	35N	97W
Çanakkale: Turkey	69	40N	26E
Canary Basin: Atl. O.	57	32N	25W
Canary Islands: Atlantic Ocean	57	28N	15W
Canaveral, Cape: U.S.A.	47	29N	81W
CANBERRA: Australia	101	35S	149E
Candia: *see* Iráklion			
Canea: *see* Khania			
Canna: *i.*, Scotland	61	57N	7W
Cannes: France	73	44N	7E
Cannock: England	63	53N	2W
Cannonball: *r.*, U.S.A.	49	46N	102W
Canon City: U.S.A.	49	38N	105W
Cantábrica, Cordillera (Cantabrian Mts.): Spain	67	43N	5W
Canterbury: England	63	51N	1E
Canterbury Bight: New Zealand	104	44S	172E
Canterbury Plains: New Zealand	104	43S	172E
Can Tho: Vietnam	92	10N	105E
Canton: China	95	23N	113E
Canton: Ill., U.S.A.	49	41N	90W
Canton: Mass., U.S.A.	51	42N	71W
Canton: Ohio, U.S.A.	47	41N	81W
Canton: S. Dakota, U.S.A.	49	43N	97W
Canudos: Brazil	54	7S	57W
Canvey Island: England	112	52N	1E
Cape Giradeaux: *city*, U.S.A.	47	37N	90W
Cape Province: South Africa	111	32S	23E
Cape Rise: Atl. O.	57	45S	12E
Cape Town: S. Africa	111	34S	18E
Cape Verde Basin: Atl. Ocean	57	25N	25W
Cape Verde Is.: Atlantic Ocean	57	18N	25W
Cape York Penin.: Australia	99	13S	143E
Cap Haitien: *town*, Haiti	45	20N	72W
Capri: *i.*, Italy	69	40N	14E
Capricorn Channel: Australia	100	23S	152E
Capricorn Group:			

The World

Coats Land — Dirk Hartog I.

	Page	Lat.	Long.
Coats Land: Antarc.	116	78S	30W
Coatzacoalcos: Mexico	53	18N	94W
Cobar: Australia	101	31S	146E
Cobh: R. of Ireland	61	52N	8W
Coburg: W. Germany	74	50N	11E
Cochabamba: Bolivia	54	17S	66W
Cochin: India	88	10N	76E
Cochrane, L.: Chile/Argentina	55	47S	72W
Cocoa: U.S.A.	47	28N	81W
Cocos Is.: Indian O.	102	11S	97E
Cocos Is.: Pacific O.	103	6N	87W
Cocos Ridge: Pacific O.	103	4N	85W
Cod, Cape: U.S.A.	51	42N	70W
Cody: U.S.A.	48	45N	109W
Coeur d'Alene: U.S.A.	48	48N	117W
Coffeyville: U.S.A.	49	37N	96W
Coff's Harbour: Australia	101	30S	153E
Cognac: France	73	46N	0
Cohasset: U.S.A.	51	42N	71W
Coimbatore: India	88	11N	77E
Coimbra: Portugal	67	40N	8W
Colac: Australia	101	38S	144E
Colatina: Brazil	54	20S	40W
Colby: U.S.A.	49	39N	101W
Colchester: England	63	52N	1E
Coleraine: N. Ireland	61	55N	7W
Colfax: U.S.A.	48	47N	117W
Colima: Mexico	52	19N	104W
Coll: *i.*, Scotland	62	57N	7W
Collie: Australia	100	33S	116E
Colmar: France	72	48N	7E
Cologne (Köln) W. Germany	64	51N	7E
COLOMBIA: *cap.* Bogotá	54	5N	72W
COLOMBO: Sri Lanka	88	7N	80E
Colón: Cuba	53	23N	81W
Colón: Panama	45	*Inset*	
Colonsay: *i.*, Scotland	62	56N	6W
Colorado: *r.*, Arg.	55	39S	65W
Colorado: *r.*, Texas, U.S.A.	46	29N	96W
Colorado: *r.*, U.S.A./Mexico	48	33N	114W
Colorado: *State*, U.S.A.	48/9	39N	106W
Colorado Plateaux: U.S.A.	48	37N	111W
Colorado Springs: U.S.A.	49	39N	105W
Columbia: Mo., U.S.A.	49	39N	92W
Columbia: S.C., U.S.A.	47	34N	81W
Columbia: *r.*, U.S.A.	48	46N	120W
Columbia: Tenn., U.S.A.	47	36N	87W
Columbus: Ga., U.S.A.	47	32N	85W
Columbus: Ind., U.S.A.	47	39N	86W
Columbus: Miss., U.S.A.	47	33N	89W
Columbus: Nebr., U.S.A.	49	41N	97W
Columbus: Ohio, U.S.A.	47	40N	83W
Colville: U.S.A.	48	49N	118W
Comilla: Bangladesh	89	23N	91E
Communism, Mt.: U.S.S.R.	85	39N	72E
Como: & *lake*, Italy	75	46N	9E
Comodoro Rivadavia: Argentina	55	46S	67W
Comorin, C.: India	88	8N	77E
Compiègne: France	72	49N	3E
CONAKRY: Guinea	108	10N	14W
Concarneau: France	72	48N	4W
Concepción: Chile	55	37S	73W
Concepción del Uruguay: Uruguay	56	32S	58W
Conchos: *r.*, Mexico	52	28N	105W
Concord: Mass., U.S.A.	33	42N	71W
Concord: N.C., U.S.A.	47	35N	80W
Concord: N.H., U.S.A.	51	43N	71W
Condamine: Australia	100	27S	150E
Condobolin: Austl.	101	33S	147E
Conecuh: *r.*, U.S.A.	47	31N	87W
Coney Island: U.S.A.	35	41N	74W
Congleton: England	63	53N	2W
CONGO: *cap.* Brazzaville	110	0	15E
Congo: *r.*, *see* Zaire			
Conn, L.: R. of Ireland	61	54N	9W
Connecticut: *r.*, U.S.A.	51	43N	73W
Connecticut: *State*, U.S.A.	51	41N	72W
Connemara: *reg.*, R. of Ireland	61	54N	10W
Connersville: U.S.A.	47	40N	85W
Conrad: U.S.A.	48	48N	112W
Consett: England	62	55N	2W
Constance, Lake (Bodensee): Switz./W. Germany	75	48N	9E
Constanța: Rom.	69	44N	29E
Constantine: Algeria	108	37N	7E
Conway: U.S.A.	47	34N	79W
Cooch Behar: India	89	26N	90E
Cook Is.: Pacific O.	102	20S	160W
Cook, Mt.: N.Z.	104	44S	170E
Cook Strait: N.Z.	104	41S	174E
Cooktown: Australia	99	15S	145E
Coolangatta: Austl.	100	28S	153E
Coolgardie: Australia	100	31S	121E
Coonamble: Australia	101	31S	148E
Cooper Creek: Austl.	100	27S	140E
Coorong, The: *lag.*, Australia	99	36S	139E
Cootamundra: Austl.	101	35S	148E
COPENHAGEN: Den.	71	56N	13E
Copiapó: Chile	54	27S	70W
Coral Gables: U.S.A.	47	26N	80W
Coral Sea: Pacific O.	99	15S	152E
Corbeil-Essonnes: France	113	49N	3E
Corbières: *mtns.*, Fr.	73	43N	2E
Corby: England	63	52N	1W
Cordele: U.S.A.	47	32N	84W
Cordillera de Mérida: Venezuela	45	9N	71W
Córdoba: Argentina	56	31S	64W
Córdoba: Mexico	53	19N	97W
Córdoba: Spain	67	38N	5W
Cordova: U.S.A.	12	61N	145W
Corinth: & *gulf*, Greece	69	38N	23E
Corinth: U.S.A.	47	35N	89W
Cork: R. of Ireland	61	52N	8W
Çorlu: Turkey	69	41N	28E
Cornwall: *Co.*, Eng.	63	50N	5W
Coromandel Ra.: New Zealand	104	37S	176E
Coromandel Coast: India	88	13N	81E
Corpus Christi: & *bay*, U.S.A.	47	28N	79W
Corrib, L.: R. of Ireland	61	53N	9W
Corrientes: Arg.	56	27S	59W
Corsica: *i.*, Medit. Sea	64	42N	9E
Corsicana: U.S.A.	46	32N	96W
Corumbá: Brazil	54	19S	57W
Corunna: *see* La Coruña			
Corvallis: U.S.A.	48	45N	123W
Coryton: England	112	52N	1E
Cosenza: Italy	69	39N	16E
Cosne: France	73	47N	3E
Costa Brava: *coast*, Spain	67	42N	3E
Costa del Sol: *coast*, Spain	67	36N	4W
COSTA RICA: *cap.* San José	45	10N	84W
Côte d'Azur: France	73	43N	7E
Côte d'Or: *mts.*, France	73	47N	5E
Cotentin: *penin.*, France	72	49N	2W
Côtes de Moselle: *hills*, France	72	49N	6E
COTONOU: Benin	108	6N	2E
Cotopaxi: *volc.*, Ec.	54	1S	78W
Cotswolds: *hills*, Eng.	63	52N	2W
Cottbus: E. Germany	74	52N	14E
Cottian Alps: Fr./It.	73	45N	7E
Coubre, Pte. de la: Fr.	73	46N	1W
Council Bluffs: U.S.A.	49	41N	96W
Coutances: France	72	49N	1W
Coventry: England	63	53N	2W
Covilhã: Portugal	67	40N	7W
Covington: U.S.A.	47	37N	80W
Cowal, Lake: Austl.	101	33S	147E
Cowan, Lake: Austl.	100	32S	122E
Cowes: England	63	51N	1W
Cowra: Australia	101	34S	149E
Cozumel, I. de: Caribbean Sea	53	20N	87W
Cracow (Kraków): Poland	68	50N	20E
Craiova: Romania	69	44N	24E
Crater L. Nat. Park: U.S.A.	48	43N	122W
Crawfordsville: U.S.A.	47	40N	88W
Crawley: England	63	51N	0
Crécy: *hist.*, France	72	50N	2E
Creil: France	72	49N	2E
Cremona: Italy	75	45N	10E
Cres: *i.*, Yugoslavia	69	45N	14E
Crescent City: U.S.A.	48	42N	124W
Crestview: U.S.A.	47	31N	87W
Crete: *i.* & *sea*, Greece	69	35N	25E
Crete: U.S.A.	49	41N	97W
Creuse: *r.*, France	71	46N	2E
Crewe: England	63	53N	2W
Crieff: Scotland	62	56N	4W
Crimea: *penin.*, U.S.S.R.	84	45N	34E
Cromer: England	63	53N	1E
Cromwell: N.Z.	104	45S	169E
Cronulla: Australia	115	34S	151E
Crosby: England	62	54N	3W
Crosby: Minn., U.S.A.	49	46N	94W
Crosby: N. Dakota, U.S.A.	49	49N	103W
Cross Sound: U.S.A.	24	58N	137W
Crotone: Italy	69	39N	17E
Croydon: England	112	51N	0
Crozet Basin: Indian Ocean	89	40S	62E
Cruzeiro do Sul: Brazil	54	8S	73W
CUBA: *cap.* La Habana (Havana)	53	*Inset*	
Cubango: *r.*, Angola	111	17S	18E
Cúcuta: Colombia	54	8N	73W
Cuernavaca: Mexico	52	19N	99W
Cuddalore: India	88	12N	80E
Cuddapah: India	88	15N	79E
Cuenca: Spain	67	40N	2W
Cuiabá: Brazil	54	16S	56W
Cuito: *r.*, Angola	111	17S	19E
Culiacán: Mexico	52	23N	106W
Cullman: U.S.A.	47	34N	87W
Culoz: France	73	46N	6E
Cumana: Venezuela	45	10N	64W
Cumberland: U.S.A.	50	40N	79W
Cumberland Is: Australia	100	21S	149E
Cumberland L.: U.S.A.	47	37N	85W
Cumbria: *Co.*, Eng.	62	55N	3W
Cumnock: Scotland	62	55N	4W
Cuneo: Italy	75	44N	8E
Cunnamulla: Austl.	101	28S	146E
Cupar: Scotland	62	56N	3W
Curaçao: *i.*, Carib. Sea	45	12N	69W
Curicó: Chile	55	35S	71W
Curitiba: Brazil	56	25S	49W
Cuttack: India	88	20N	86E
Cuxhaven: W. Germany	74	54N	9E
Cuzco: Peru	54	14S	72W
Cyclades: *is.*, Greece	69	37N	25E
CYPRUS: *cap.* Nicosia	86	35N	33E
CZECHOSLOVAKIA: *cap.* Prague	68	49N	17E
Czestochowa: Poland	68	51N	19E
Dacca: Bangladesh	89	24N	90E
Dagenham: England	112	52N	0
Dahlak Arch.: Red Sea	87	16N	40W
Dajarra: Australia	99	22S	140E
DAKAR: Senegal	108	15N	17W
Dakhla: W. Sahara	108	24N	16W
Dakhla Oasis: Egypt	109	25N	29E
Dalabandin: Pakistan	88	29N	64E
Dalby: Australia	100	27S	151E
Dalhousie: India	88	33N	76E
Dallas: U.S.A.	46	33N	97W
Dall I.: U.S.A.	24	55N	133W
Dalton: U.S.A.	47	35N	85W
Daltonganj: India	88	24N	84E
Daly: *r.*, Australia	98	14S	132E
Daly Waters: *town*, Australia	98	16S	133E
Daman: *Union Territ.*, India	88	20N	73E
DAMASCUS: Syria	86	34N	36E
Damietta: Egypt	86	31N	32E
Damodar: *r.*, India	88	24N	86E
Dampier Land: Australia	98	17S	123E
Danilovka: U.S.S.R.	85	53N	71E
Dannevirke: N.Z.	104	40S	176E
Danube: *r.*, Europe	68/9	—	—
Danushkodi: India	88	9N	80E
Danville: Ill., U.S.A.	47	40N	88W
Danville: Va., U.S.A.	47	37N	79W
Dardanelles: *str.*, Turkey	86	40N	26E
Dar es Salaam: Tanzania	110	7S	40E
Darfur: *Prov.*, Sudan	109	13N	25E
Dargaville: N.Z.	104	36S	174E
Darien, Gulf of: Colombia	54	9N	77W
Darjeeling: India	88	27N	88E
Darling: *r.*, Australia	101	31S	145E
Darling Downs: Australia	100	27S	150E
Darling Range: Australia	100	32S	116E
Darlington: England	62	55N	2W
Darmstadt: W. Ger.	74	50N	9E
Dart: *r.*, England	63	50N	4W
Dartford: England	112	51N	0
Dartmoor: England	63	51N	4W
Dartmouth: England	63	50N	4W
Darwin: Australia	98	12S	131E
Dasht-e Kavir: *desert*, Iran	87	34N	55E
Dasht-e Lūt: *desert*, Iran	87	32N	57E
Datteln: W. Germany	64	52N	7E
Daugava: *r.*, *see* West Dvina			
Daugavpils: U.S.S.R.	68	56N	26E
Dauphiné: *Old Prov.*, France	73	45N	6E
Dauphiné Alps: France	73	45N	6E
Davao: Philippines	91	7N	126E
Davenport: U.S.A.	49	41N	90W
Davis: Antarc.	116	64S	92E
Davos: Switzerland	75	47N	10E
Dawna Range: Burma/Thailand	92	13N	99E
Dawson: *r.*, Australia	100	24S	150E
Dax: France	73	44N	1W
Dayton: U.S.A.	47	40N	84W
Daytona Beach: U.S.A.	47	29N	81W
De Aar: S. Africa	111	31S	24E
Dead Sea: Israel/			
Jordan	86	32N	35E
Deadwood: U.S.A.	49	44N	104W
Dearborn: & *Heights*, U.S.A.	33	42N	83W
Death Valley: & *Nat. Monument*, U.S.A.	48	37N	117W
Deauville: France	72	49N	0
Debrecen: Hungary	68	48N	22E
Decatur: Alabama, U.S.A.	47	35N	87W
Decatur: Ill., U.S.A.	47	40N	89W
Decazeville: France	73	45N	2E
Deccan: *reg.*, India	88	17N	77E
Děčín: Czech.	74	51N	14E
Dee: *r.*, Eng./Wales	63	53N	3W
Dee: *r.*, Gramp., Scot.	62	57N	3W
Dee: *r.*, Dumfr. & Gall. Scotland	62	55N	4W
Deerfield: U.S.A.	34	42N	88W
Deer Lodge: U.S.A.	48	46N	113W
Dehra Dun: India	88	30N	78E
Deir ez Zor: Syria	87	35N	40E
De Kalb: U.S.A.	49	42N	89W
Delagoa Bay: Moz.	111	25S	33E
Delano: U.S.A.	48	36N	119W
Delano Peak: U.S.A.	48	38N	114W
Delaware: *State*, & *bay*, U.S.A.	47	39N	75W
Delft: Netherlands	74	52N	4E
Delmenhorst: W. Ger.	74	53N	9E
Delray Beach: *city*, U.S.A.	47	26N	80W
Del Rio: U.S.A.	46	29N	101W
DELHI: India	88	29N	77E
Demarcation Pt.: U.S.A.	12	70N	141W
Demavand: *mtn.*, Iran	87	36N	52E
Deming: U.S.A.	48	32N	108W
Demmin: E. Germany	74	54N	13E
Denbigh: Wales	63	53N	3W
Dendermonde: Belg.	72	51N	4E
Denham Range: Australia	100	22S	148E
Den Helder: Neth.	74	53N	5E
Deniliquin: Australia	101	36S	145E
Denison: U.S.A.	49	34N	97W
Denizli: Turkey	86	38N	29E
DENMARK: *cap.* Copenhagen	71	56N	10E
Denton: U.S.A.	49	33N	98W
D'Entrecasteaux Is.: Papua New Guinea	99	10S	151E
D'Entrecasteaux, Pt.: Australia	100	35S	116E
Denver: U.S.A.	49	40N	105W
Denville: U.S.A.	51	41N	74W
De Pere: U.S.A.	49	44N	88W
Dera'a: Syria	86	32N	36E
Dera Ghazi Khan: Pakistan	88	30N	70E
Dera Ismail Khan: Pakistan	88	32N	71E
Derbent: U.S.S.R.	84	42N	48E
Derby: Australia	98	17S	123E
Derby: & *Co.*, Eng.	63	53N	1W
Derg, L.: R. of Ireland	61	53N	8W
Derna: Libya	86	33N	22E
Derwent: *r.*, Cumbria, England	62	55N	4W
Derwent: *r.*, Derby., England	63	53N	2W
Derwent: *r.*, N. Yorks., England	63	54N	1W
Des Moines: & *r.*, U.S.A.	46	42N	94W
Des Plaines: U.S.A.	34	42N	88W
Dessau: E. Germany	74	52N	12E
Detroit: U.S.A.	33	—	—
Dettingen: *hist.*, W. Ger.	74	50N	9E
Deva: Romania	68	46N	23E
Deventer: Neth.	74	52N	6E
Dévoluy: *mtns.*, France	73	45N	6E
Devonport: England	63	50N	4W
Devonshire: *Co.*, England	63	51N	4W
Dewsbury: England	63	54N	2W
Dexter: U.S.A.	15	45N	69W
Dhahran: Saudi Arabia	87	26N	50E
Dharwar: India	88	15N	75E
Dhulia: India	88	21N	75E
Diamantina: Brazil	54	18S	44W
Dibrugarh: India	89	28N	95E
Dieciocho de Marzo: Mexico	46	26N	98W
Diego Suarez: *see* Antsirane			
Dieppe: France	72	50N	1E
Digne: France	73	44N	6E
Dijon: France	73	47N	5E
Dili: Indon.	90	8S	126E
Dimitrovgrad: Bulgaria	69	42N	26E
Dinajpur: Bangladesh	88	26N	89E
Dinan: France	72	48N	2W
Dinant: Belgium	72	50N	5E
Dinard: France	72	49N	2W
Dinaric Alps: Yugo.	69	44N	16E
Dingwall: Scotland	61	58N	4W
Dinslaken: W. Germany	64	52N	7E
Diomede Is: Bering Strait	12	66N	169E
Diredawa: Ethiopia	109	10N	42E
Dirk Hartog I.:			

The World

Fall River — Goiânia

	Page	Lat.	Long.
Fall River: *city*, U.S.A.	51	42N	71W
Falmouth: England	63	50N	5W
False Bay: S. Africa	111	34S	19E
Falun: Sweden	71	61N	16E
Famagusta: Cyprus	86	35N	34E
Fanning I.: Pacific O.	102	4N	159W
Fano: Italy	75	44N	13E
Farasan Is.: Red Sea	87	17N	42E
Fareham: England	63	51N	1W
Farewell: U.S.A.	12	63N	154W
Farewell, Cape: Greenland	13	60N	44W
Farewell, Cape: N.Z.	104	40S	173E
Fargo: U.S.A.	49	47N	97W
Faribault: U.S.A.	49	44N	93W
Farmington: U.S.A.	48	37N	108W
Farnborough: England	112	51N	1W
Farnham: England	112	51N	1W
Faro: Portugal	67	37N	8W
Fārs: *reg.*, Iran	87	29N	51E
Faxa Bay: Iceland	70	64N	23W
Fayette: U.S.A.	47	34N	88W
Fayetteville: Ark., U.S.A.	46	36N	94W
Fayetteville: N.C., U.S.A.	47	35N	79W
Fayîd: Egypt	109	*Inset*	
F'Dérik: Mauritania	108	23N	13W
Fear, C.: U.S.A.	47	34N	78W
Fécamp: France	72	50N	0
Feilding: N.Z.	104	40S	176E
Feira de Santana: Brazil	54	12S	39W
Feldkirch: Austria	75	47N	10E
Fen: *r.*, China	94	36N	112E
Fengtai: China	114	40N	116E
Fenouillèdes: *mtns.*, France	73	43N	2E
Fens, The: *reg.*, Eng.	63	53N	0
Fenyang: China	94	37N	112E
Fergana: U.S.S.R.	85	40N	72E
Fergus Falls: *city*, U.S.A.	49	46N	96W
Fernando de Noronha: *i.*, Brazil	54	4S	32W
Ferndale: U.S.A.	33	42N	83W
Ferrara: Italy	75	45N	12E
Ferret, Cap: France	73	45N	1W
Fès: Morocco	108	34N	5W
Fethiye: Turkey	86	36N	29E
Fianarantsoa: Malagasy Rep.	110	22S	47E
Fife Ness: Scotland	62	56N	3W
Figeac: France	73	4N	52E
FIJI: *cap.* Suva	102	18S	178E
Filchner Ice Shelf: Antarctica	116	78S	50W
Findlay: U.S.A.	47	41N	84W
Finistère: *Dept.*, France	72	48N	4W
Finisterre, Cape: Sp.	67	43N	9W
FINLAND: *cap.* Helsinki	70/1	—	—
Finschhafen: Papua New Guinea	99	7S	148E
Finsteraarhorn: *mtn.*, Switzerland	75	47N	8E
Fiordland: *district & Nat. Park*, N.Z.	104	46S	167E
Firenze: *see* Florence			
Fishguard: Wales	63	52N	5W
Fitchburg: U.S.A.	51	43N	72W
Fitzroy: *r.*, Queens., Australia	100	23S	150E
Fitzroy: *r.*, W. Austl.	98	18S	124E
Flagstaff: U.S.A.	48	35N	112W
Flamborough Head: England	62	54N	0
Flanders: *reg.*, Belgium	72	51N	4E
Flathead L.: U.S.A.	48	48N	114W
Flattery, C.: U.S.A.	48	48N	125W
Fleetwood: England	62	54N	3W
Flensburg: W. Germany	68	55N	9E
Flers: France	72	49N	1W
Flinders: *r.*, Australia	99	20S	141E
Flinders Range: Australia	101	31S	139E
Flinders Reefs: Coral Sea	100	18S	149E
Flint: U.S.A.	19	43N	84W
Flint: *r.*, U.S.A.	47	31N	85W
Flora: Norway	70	62N	5E
Florence (Firenze): Italy	75	44N	11E
Florence: Alabama U.S.A.	47	35N	88W
Florence: Arizona U.S.A.	48	33N	111W
Florence: S.C., U.S.A.	47	34N	80W
Florencia: Colombia	54	2N	76W
Flores: *i. & sea*, Indonesia	91	9S	121E
Floreshty: U.S.S.R.	68	48N	28E
Floriano: Brazil	54	7S	43W
Florianópolis: Brazil	56	27S	48W
Florida: Cuba	53	22N	78W
Florida: *State*, U.S.A.	47	28N	82W
Florida, Straits of: U.S.A.	47	24N	81W
Florida Keys: *is.*, U.S.A.	47	25N	81W
Flórina: Greece	69	41N	21E
Flushing (Vlissingen): Netherlands	74	51N	4E
Fly: *r.*, Papua New Guinea	99	8S	142E
Foggia: Italy	69	41N	16E
Foix: & *Old Prov.*, Fr.	73	43N	2E
Foligno: Italy	69	43N	13E
Folkestone: England	63	51N	1E
Fond du Lac: U.S.A.	49	44N	88W
Fontainebleau: France	72	48N	3E
Fontainebleau, Forêt de: France	72	48N	3E
Fontenoy: *hist.*, Belgium	72	51N	3E
Foochow: China	95	26N	118E
Forbes: Australia	101	33S	148E
Forcalquier: France	73	44N	6E
Fordlândia: Brazil	54	4S	55W
Forel, Mt.: Greenland	13	67N	37W
Forez, Monts du: France	73	45N	4E
Forfar: Scotland	62	57N	3W
Forlì: Italy	75	44N	12E
Formentera: *i.*, Balearic Is.	67	38N	1E
Formosa (Taiwan): *i. & str.*, China	90	24N	121E
Forrest: Australia	98	31S	128E
Forrest City: U.S.A.	46	35N	91W
Forsayth: Australia	99	19S	144E
Forsyth: U.S.A.	48	46N	107W
Fortaleza: Brazil	54	4S	38W
Fort Collins: U.S.A.	49	41N	105W
Fort Dauphin: Malagasy Rep.	110	25S	47E
FORT-DE-FRANCE: Martinique	45	15N	61W
Fort Dodge: U.S.A.	49	43N	94W
Fortescue: *r.*, Austl.	98	22S	118E
Forth Bridge: Scotland	62	56N	3W
Forth, Firth of: Scot.	62	56N	3W
Fort Johnston: Malawi	111	15S	35E
Fort Lauderdale: U.S.A.	47	26N	80W
Fort Madison: U.S.A.	48	41N	91W
Fort Morgan: U.S.A.	49	40N	104W
Fort Myers: U.S.A.	47	27N	82W
Fort Peck Res.: U.S.A.	48	47N	107W
Fort Pierce: U.S.A.	47	27N	80W
Fort Sandeman: Pakistan	88	31N	70E
Fort Shevchenko: U.S.S.R.	84	45N	50E
Fort Smith: U.S.A.	46	35N	94W
Fort Sumner: U.S.A.	49	34N	104W
Fort Wayne: U.S.A.	47	41N	85W
Fort William: Scotland	61	57N	5W
Fort Worth: U.S.A.	46	33N	97W
Forty Mile: *r.*, U.S.A.	30	65N	142W
Fort Yukon: U.S.A.	30	67N	145W
Foshan: China	95	23N	113E
Fougères: France	72	48N	1W
Foul Bay: Red Sea	86	23N	36E
Foulness I.: England	63	52N	1E
Foulwind, C.: N.Z.	104	42S	172E
Fourmies: France	72	50N	4E
Foveaux Strait: N.Z.	104	47S	168E
Foyle, L.: Ireland	61	55N	7W
Framingham: U.S.A.	51	42N	71W
FRANCE: *cap.* Paris	72/3	—	—
Franche Comté: *Old Prov.*, France	72/3	47N	6E
Francistown: Bots.	111	21S	27E
Franconian Heights: W. Germany	74	49N	10E
Franconian Jura: W. Germany	74	49N	11E
Frankfort: Indiana, U.S.A.	47	40N	86W
Frankfort: Kentucky, U.S.A.	47	38N	85W
Frankfurt am Main: W. Germany	74	50N	9E
Frankfurt an der Oder: E. Germany	74	52N	15E
Franklin D. Roosevelt Lake: U.S.A.	48	48N	118W
Franz Josef Land: U.S.S.R.	82/3	80N	55E
Fraserburgh: S. Africa	111	33S	22E
Fraser I.: Australia	100	25S	153E
Fray Bentos: Uruguay	56	33S	58W
Fredericia: Denmark	71	56N	10E
Frederick: U.S.A.	46	34N	99W
Fredericksburg: U.S.A.	47	38N	78W
Frederikshavn: Den.	71	57N	11E
Frederikstad: Norway	71	59N	11E
Freeport: U.S.A.	46	29N	97W
FREETOWN: Sierra Leone	108	7N	13W
Freiburg im Breisgau: W. Germany	75	48N	8E
Freising: W. Germany	75	48N	12E
Fréjus: France	73	43N	7E
Fremantle: Australia	100	32S	116E
Fremont: U.S.A.	49	41N	97W
FRENCH GUIANA: *cap.* Cayenne	54	4N	53W
Frenchman Creek: U.S.A.	49	40N	102W
Fresnillo de Gonzáles Echeverría: Mexico	52	23N	103W
Fresno: U.S.A.	48	37N	120W
Fribourg: Switzerland	75	47N	7E
Friedrichshafen: W. Germany	75	48N	9E
Friesland: *Prov.*, Netherlands	74	53N	6E
Frisian Is., East: W. Ger.	74	54N	7E
Frisian Is., North: W. Germany	71	55N	8E
Frisian Is., West: Netherlands	74	53N	5E
Frome, Lake: Austl.	101	31S	140E
Frunze: U.S.S.R.	85	43N	75E
Fuchu: Japan	114	36N	139E
Fuerteventura: *i.*, Canary Islands	108	29N	14W
Fuji San: *mtn.*, Japan	93	35N	139E
Fujisawa: Japan	114	35N	139E
Fukien: *Prov.*, China	95	26N	118E
Fukui: Japan	93	36N	136E
Fukuoka: Japan	93	34N	130E
Fukushima: Japan	93	38N	140E
Fulda: & *r.*, W. Ger.	74	50N	10E
Fulton: U.S.A.	49	39N	92W
Funabashi: Japan	114	36N	140E
Funchal: Madeira	108	33N	17W
Furka Pass: Switzerland	75	47N	8E
Furneaux Group: *is.*, Australia	99	40S	148E
Fürth: Germany	74	49N	11E
Fushun: China	90	42N	124E
Fyn: *i.*, Denmark	71	55N	10E
Fyne, L.: Scotland	62	56N	5W
Gabès: & *gulf*, Tunisia	108	34N	11E
GABON: *cap.* Libreville	110	2N	12E
GABORONE: Botswana	111	24S	26E
Gabrovo: Bulgaria	69	43N	25E
Gadames: Libya	108	30N	10E
Gadsden: U.S.A.	47	34N	86W
Gaffney: U.S.A.	47	35N	81W
Gail: *r.*, Austria	75	47N	13E
Gaillard Cut: Panama Canal	45	*Inset*	
Gainesville: Georgia, U.S.A.	47	34N	84W
Gainesville: Texas, U.S.A.	46	34N	97W
Gainsborough: Eng.	63	53N	1W
Gainsville: Florida, U.S.A.	47	30N	82W
Gairdner, L.: Austl.	98	32S	136E
Galápagos Is.: Pacific O.	103	1S	91W
Galashiels: Scotland	68	56N	3W
Galati: Romania	68	45N	28E
Galena: U.S.A.	12	65N	157W
Galesburg: U.S.A.	49	41N	90W
Galilee, Sea of: Israel	86	33N	36E
Gallarate: Italy	75	46N	9E
Galle: Sri Lanka	88	6N	80E
Gallegos: *r.*, Arg.	55	52S	71W
Gallinas, Pt.: Colombia	54	13N	72W
Gällivare: Sweden	70	67N	21E
Gallup: U.S.A.	48	36N	109W
Galveston: & *bay*, U.S.A.	46	30N	95W
Galway: & *bay*, R. of Ireland	61	53N	9W
GAMBIA, THE: *cap.* Banjul	108	13N	15W
Gambier Is.: Pac. O.	103	22S	135W
Gand: *see* Ghent			
Gandak: *r.*, India	88	27N	85E
Ganga (Ganges): *r.*, Bangl./India	88	25N	86E
Ganges: France	73	44N	4E
Ganges: *r.*, *see* Ganga			
Gap: France	73	45N	6E
Gard: *r.*, France	73	44N	4E
Garda, L. of: Italy	75	46N	11E
Garden City: Mich., U.S.A.	33	42N	83W
Garden City: N.Y., U.S.A.	35	41N	74W
Garden Grove: U.S.A.	37	34N	118W
Gardez: Afghan.	88	34N	69E
Gardner I.: Pac. O.	102	5S	175W
Garfield: U.S.A.	35	41N	74W
Gargano, C.: Italy	69	42N	16E
Garnett: U.S.A.	49	38N	95W
Garonne: *r.*, France	73	45N	0
Garoua: Cameroun	108	9N	13E
Garrigues: *mtns.*, Fr.	73	44N	4E
Garron Pt.: N. Ireland	62	55N	6W
Gartok: China	88	32N	80E
Gary: U.S.A.	34	42N	86W
Gascony: *Old Prov.*, France	73	44N	0
Gastonia: U.S.A.	47	35N	81W
Gata, C. de: Spain	67	37N	2W
Gateshead: England	62	55N	2W
Gâtine, Hauteurs de: *hills*, France	73	47N	1W
Gatooma: Rhodesia (Zimbabwe)	111	18S	30E
Gatun Lake: & *locks*, Panama Canal	45	*Inset*	
Gauhati: India	89	26N	92E
Gävle: Sweden	71	61N	17E
Gawler: Australia	101	35S	139E
Gaya: India	88	25N	85E
Gaya: Niger	108	12N	4E
Gaza: Egypt	86	31N	34E
Gaziantep: Turkey	87	37N	37E
Gdansk: & *Gulf*, Poland	68	54N	19E
Gdynia: Poland	68	55N	18E
Geelong: Australia	101	38S	144E
Geerardsbergen: Belgium	72	51N	4E
Geissen: W. Germany	75	51N	9E
Gelibolu: Turkey	69	10N	27E
Gelsenkirchen: W. Ger.	64	51N	7E
Geneva: & *l.*, Switz.	75	46N	6E
Génissiat Dam: France	73	46N	6E
Genoa: & *gulf*, Italy	75	44N	9E
Gent: *see* Ghent			
George: S. Africa	111	34S	22E
George, L.: Austl.	101	35S	149E
GEORGETOWN: Guyana	54	7N	58W
George Town: Mal.	92	5N	100E
Georgetown: U.S.A.	47	33N	79W
Georgia: *State*, U.S.A.	47	33N	84W
Georgian S.S.R.: U.S.S.R.	84	43N	45E
Gera: E. Germany	74	51N	12E
Geraldton: Australia	100	29S	115E
GERMANY, EAST *cap.* Berlin	74	—	—
GERMANY, WEST: *cap.* Bonn	74/5	—	—
Gerona: Spain	67	42N	3E
Gers: *r.*, France	73	44N	1E
Gettysburg: U.S.A.	47	40N	77W
Gevelsberg: W. Ger.	64	51N	7E
Ghaghra: *r.*, India	88	27N	82E
GHANA: *cap.* Accra	108	7N	0
Ghardaia: Algeria	108	33N	4E
Ghazipur: India	88	26N	83E
Ghent (Gand, Gent): Belgium	72	51N	4E
GIBRALTAR: & *strait*	67	36N	5W
Gibson Desert: Austl.	98	24S	124E
Gien: France	73	47N	3E
Gifu: Japan	93	35N	137E
Gijón: Spain	67	44N	6W
Gila: *r.*, U.S.A.	48	33N	113W
Gila Bend: U.S.A.	48	33N	113W
Gilbert: *r.*, Australia	99	17S	142E
Gilbert Is.: Pacific O.	102	0	175E
Gilgit: India	88	36N	74E
Gillingham: England	112	51N	0
Gineifa: Egypt	109	*Inset*	
Ginir: Ethiopia	109	7N	41E
Gippsland: *reg.*, Austl.	101	38S	148E
Girga: Egypt	86	26N	32E
Gironde: *r.*, France	73	45N	1W
Girvan: Scotland	62	55N	5W
Gisborne: N.Z.	104	39S	178E
Giurgiu: Romania	69	44N	26E
Givors: France	73	46N	5E
Giza: Egypt	86	30N	31E
Gjinokastër: Albania	69	40N	20E
Gladbeck: W. Germany	64	52N	7E
Gladstone: Australia	100	24S	151E
Glåma: *r.*, Norway	71	61N	12E
Glamorgan, Mid-: *Co.*, Wales	63	52N	4W
Glamorgan, South: *Co.*, Wales	63	52N	4W
Glamorgan, West: *Co.*, Wales	63	52N	4W
Glasgow: Ky., U.S.A.	47	37N	86W
Glasgow: Montana, U.S.A.	48	48N	107W
Glasgow: Scotland	62	56N	4W
Glastonbury: England	63	51N	3W
Glauchau: E. Germany	74	51N	13E
Glazov: U.S.S.R.	84	58N	53E
Glencoe: U.S.A.	49	45N	94W
Glen Cove: U.S.A.	35	41N	74W
Glenelg: *r.*, Australia	101	37S	141E
Glen Innes: Australia	101	30S	152E
Glenmorgan: Australia	100	27S	150E
Glenwood: U.S.A.	49	46N	95W
Gliwice: Poland	68	50N	19E
Globe: U.S.A.	48	33N	111W
Gloucester: & *Co.*, England	63	52N	2W
Gloucester: U.S.A.	51	43N	71W
Gloversville: U.S.A.	51	43N	74W
Gniezno: Poland	68	53N	18E
Goa: *Union Territ.*, India	88	15N	74E
Gobabis: S.W. Africa (Namibia)	111	23S	18E
Gobi Desert: Mong.	83	43N	105E
Godavari: *r.*, India	88	20N	81E
GODTHAAB: Grnld.	13	64N	52W
Goiânia: Brazil	54	17S	49W

Jessore — Kompong Som

The World

	Page	Lat.	Long.
Jessore: Bangladesh	88	23N	89E
Jesup: U.S.A.	47	32N	82W
Jhansi: India	88	25N	79E
Jhelum: r., Pakistan	88	31N	72E
Jibhalanta: see Uliastay			
Jidda: Saudi Arabia	87	22N	39E
Jiménez: Mexico	52	27N	105W
João Pessoa: Brazil	54	7S	35W
Jodhpur: India	88	26N	73E
Joensuu: Finland	70	63N	30E
Jofra Oasis: Libya	86	30N	15E
Jogjakarta: Indon.	91	8S	110E
Johannesburg: S. Afr.	111	26S	28E
Johnson City: U.S.A.	47	36N	82W
Johnstown: U.S.A.	50	40N	79W
Johor Bahru: Malaysia	92	1N	104E
Joliet: U.S.A.	34	42N	88W
Jolo: i., Philippines	91	6N	121E
Jonesboro: U.S.A.	46	36N	91W
Jonglei: Sudan	109	7N	31E
Jonkoping: Sweden	71	58N	14E
Joplin: U.S.A.	49	37N	94W
JORDAN: cap. Amman	86	31N	37E
Jordan: r., Jordan	86	32N	36E
Jorhat: India	89	27N	94E
Jos: & plateau, Nigeria	108	10N	9E
Joseph Bonaparte Gulf: Australia	98	14S	128E
Josselin: France	72	48N	3W
Jostedalsbreen: mtns., Norway	70	62N	7E
Jotunheimen: mtns., Norway	70	61N	9E
Juan de Fuca, Str. of: Canada/U.S.A.	28	48N	125W
Juan Fernández Is.: Pacific Ocean	103	34S	79W
Juba: Sudan	109	5N	32E
Juba: r., Somali Rep.	109	2N	42E
Júcar: r., Spain	67	39N	1W
Juist: i., W. Germany	74	54N	7E
Juiz de Fóra: Brazil	54	22S	43W
Jukao: China	94	33N	121E
Julian Alps: It./Yugo.	75	46N	13E
Julich: W. Germany	74	51N	6E
Julier Pass: Switz.	75	46N	9E
Jullundur: India	88	31N	76E
Junction City: U.S.A.	49	39N	97W
Juneau: U.S.A.	24	58N	135W
Junee: Australia	101	35S	148E
Jungfrau: mt., Switz.	75	47N	8E
Jur: r., Sudan	109	9N	28E
Jura, The: mtns., France/Switz.	73	47N	6E
Jura: i. & sound, Scotland	62	56N	6W
Juruá: r., Brazil	54	5S	67W
Jussey: France	72	48N	6E
Juticalpa: Honduras	53	15N	86W
Jyekundo: see Yushu			
Jylland: penin., Den.	71	36N	9E
Jyväskylä: Finland	70	62N	26E
K2: mtn., India	88	36N	77E
Kabaena: i., Indonesia	91	5S	122E
KABUL: Afghanistan	88	35N	69E
Kabwe: Zambia	111	15S	29E
Kadina: Australia	101	34S	138E
Kaduna: Nigeria	108	11N	7E
Kafue: & r., Zambia	111	16S	28E
Kagoshima: Japan	93	32N	131E
Kahsing: China	95	31N	121E
Kaieteur Falls: Guyana	54	5N	59W
Kaifeng: China	94	35N	115E
Kai Is.: Indonesia	91	6S	133E
Kaikohe: N.Z.	104	35S	174E
Kaikoura: & Range, N.Z.	104	42S	173E
Kailas Range: China	88	32N	81E
Kaimanawa Mts.: New Zealand	104	39S	176E
Kaipara Harbour: New Zealand	93	36S	174E
Kaiserslautern: W. Ger.	74	49N	8E
Kaitangata: N.Z.	104	46N	170E
Kajaani: Finland	70	64N	28E
Kakinada: India	88	17N	82E
Kakogawa: Japan	93	35N	135E
Kalachinsk: U.S.S.R.	85	55N	75E
Kalahari Desert: Botswana	111	24S	23E
Kalamata: Greece	69	37N	22E
Kalamazoo: U.S.A.	47	42N	86W
Kalat: Pakistan	88	29N	67E
Kalemie: Zaire	110	6S	29E
Kalgan: see Changkiakow			
Kalgoorlie: Australia	100	31S	122E
Kalinin: U.S.S.R.	84	57N	36E
Kaliningrad: U.S.S.R.	68	55N	20E
Kalispell: U.S.A.	48	48N	114W
Kalisz: Poland	68	52N	18E
Kalmar: Sweden	71	57N	16E
Kalomo: Zambia	111	17S	26E
Kaluga: U.S.S.R.	84	55N	36E
Kama: r., U.S.S.R.	84	55N	51E
Kamakura: Japan	114	35N	140E
Kamaran Is.: Yemen P.D.R.	87	15N	42E
Kamchatka: penin., U.S.S.R.	83	55N	160E
Kamchatka Bay: U.S.S.R.	83	55N	163E
Kamenskoye: U.S.S.R.	83	63N	165E
Kamensk-Uralskiy: U.S.S.R.	85	57N	62E
Kamet: mtn., India/China	88	31N	79E
Kamina: Zaire	110	9S	25E
KAMPALA: Uganda	110	0	33E
Kampen: Netherlands	74	53N	6E
Kamp-Lintfort: W. Ger.	64	52N	7W
Kamyshlov: U.S.S.R.	85	57N	63E
Kananga: Zaire	110	6S	22E
Kanazawa: Japan	93	37N	137E
Kanchanaburi: Thailand	92	14N	99E
Kanchow: China	95	26N	115E
Kandagach: U.S.S.R.	85	49N	57E
Kandahar: Afghanistan	88	32N	66E
Kandalaksha: U.S.S.R.	70	67N	32E
Kandi: Benin	108	11N	3E
Kandla: India	88	23N	70E
Kandy: Sri Lanka	88	7N	81E
Kangaroo I.: Australia	101	36S	137E
Kangchenjunga: mtn., Nepal/India	89	27N	88E
Kangean Is.: Indonesia	91	7S	116E
Kangting: China	90	30N	102E
Kanin, C.: U.S.S.R.	82	68N	45E
Kankakee: U.S.A.	47	41N	88W
Kankan: Guinea	108	10N	9W
Kannapolis: U.S.A.	47	35N	80W
Kano: Nigeria	108	12N	8E
Kanoya: Japan	93	31N	131E
Kanpur: India	88	26N	80E
Kansas: State, U.S.A.	46	39N	98W
Kansas City: Kansas, U.S.A.	46	39N	95W
Kansas City: Mo., U.S.A.	46	39N	95W
Kansk: U.S.S.R.	85	56N	95E
Kansu: Prov., China	94	35N	105E
Kaohsiung: Taiwan	95	23N	120E
Kapellen: W. Germany	64	51N	7E
Kaposvár: Hungary	68	46N	18E
Kapurthala: India	88	31N	75E
Kara: U.S.S.R.	82	69N	65E
Kara-Bogaz-Gol: l., U.S.S.R.	84	42N	54E
Karabuk: Turkey	86	41N	32E
Karachi: Pakistan	88	25N	67E
Karaganda: U.S.S.R.	85	50N	73E
Karakoram Pass: China/India	88	35N	76E
Kara-Kum: desert, U.S.S.R.	84	39N	60E
Karasberg: S.W. Africa (Namibia)	111	28S	19E
Kara Sea: U.S.S.R.	82	72N	62E
Kara-Tau: mtns., U.S.S.R.	85	44N	68E
Karaul: U.S.S.R.	83	70N	83E
Karbalā: Iraq	87	33N	44E
Kargil: India	88	35N	76E
Kariba: l., dam & gorge, Rhod. (Zim.)/Zambia	111	17S	29E
Karibib: S.W. Africa (Namibia)	111	22S	16E
Karl-Marx-Stadt: E. Germany	74	51N	13E
Karlovac: Yugoslavia	69	45N	16E
Karlovy Vary: Czech.	69	50N	13E
Karlshamn: Sweden	71	56N	15E
Karlskoga: Sweden	71	59N	15E
Karlskrona: Sweden	71	56N	16E
Karlsruhe: W. Germany	74	49N	8E
Karlstad: Sweden	71	59N	13E
Karnataka: State, India	88	14N	76E
Kárpathos: i., Greece	69	36N	27E
Kartaly: U.S.S.R.	85	53N	60E
Karwar: India	88	15N	74E
Kasai: r., Zaire	110	4S	19E
Kasempa: Zambia	111	13S	26E
Kasese: Uganda	110	0	30E
Kāshān: Iran	87	34N	51E
Kashgar: China	82	39N	76E
Kaskaskia: r., U.S.A.	49	39N	89W
Kasli: U.S.S.R.	85	56N	61E
Kásos: i. & str., Greece	69	35N	27E
Kassala: Sudan	86	15N	36E
Kassala: Prov., Sudan	86	20N	35E
Kassel: W. Germany	74	51N	9E
Katahdin, Mt.: U.S.A.	15	46N	69W
Katanning: Australia	100	34S	118E
Katase: Japan	114	35N	139E
Katherine: Australia	98	14S	133E
Kathiawar: penin., India	88	22N	71E
KATMANDU: Nepal	88	28N	85E
Katoomba: Australia	101	34S	150E
Katowice: Poland	68	50N	19E
Katrineholm: Sweden	71	59N	16E
Kattegat: str., Denmark/Sweden	71	57N	11E
Kauai: i., Pacific O.	103	22N	160W
Kaufman: U.S.A.	46	33N	96W
Kaunas: U.S.S.R.	68	55N	24E
Kaura Namoda: Nigeria	108	13N	7E
Kavacha: U.S.S.R.	83	60N	170E
Kaválla: Greece	69	41N	24E
Kavieng: Papua New Guinea	99	3S	151E
Kawagoe: Japan	93	36N	139E
Kawaguchi: Japan	114	36N	140E
Kawasaki: Japan	114	36N	140E
Kawerau: N.Z.	104	38S	177E
Kayes: Mali	108	14N	11W
Kayseri: Turkey	86	39N	36E
Kazach'ye: U.S.S.R.	83	71N	136E
Kazakh S.S.R.: U.S.S.R.	84/5	—	—
Kazakh Uplands: U.S.S.R.	85	49N	75E
Kazalinsk: U.S.S.R.	85	46N	62E
Kazan': U.S.S.R.	84	56N	49E
Kazanlák: Bulgaria	69	43N	25E
Kéa: i., Greece	69	38N	24E
Kearney: U.S.A.	49	41N	99W
Kebbi: r., Nigeria	108	13N	4E
Kecskemét: Hungary	68	47N	20E
Keene: U.S.A.	51	43N	72W
Keetmanshoop: S.W. Africa (Namibia)	111	26S	18E
Keflavik: Iceland	70	64N	22W
Keighley: England	62	54N	2W
Kelang: Malaysia	92	3N	101E
Kelso: U.S.A.	48	46N	123W
Kemerovo: U.S.S.R.	85	55N	86E
Kemi: & r., Finland	70	66N	25E
Kempsey: Australia	101	31S	153E
Kendal: England	62	54N	3W
Kenitra: Morocco	108	34N	7W
Kenmare: R. of Ireland	61	52N	10W
Kenmore: U.S.A.	49	49N	102W
Kennebec: r., U.S.A.	15	45N	70W
Kennett: U.S.A.	46	36N	90W
Kennewick: U.S.A.	48	46N	119W
Kennicott: U.S.A.	12	62N	143W
Kenosha: U.S.A.	47	43N	88W
Kensington: England	112	51N	0
Kent: Co., England	63	51N	1E
Kentucky: State, U.S.A.	47	37N	85W
Kentucky L.: U.S.A.	47	36N	88W
KENYA: cap. Nairobi	110	0	37E
Kenya, Mt.: Kenya	110	0	37E
Keokuk: U.S.A.	46	40N	92W
Keppel Bay: Australia	100	23S	151E
Kerala: State, India	88	10N	76E
Kerang: Australia	101	36S	144E
Kerch': U.S.S.R.	84	45N	36E
Kerki: U.S.S.R.	85	38N	65E
Kerkira: i. & town, Greece	69	40N	20E
Kermadec Islands: & trench, Pacific Ocean	102	30S	179W
Kermān: Iran	87	30N	57E
Kermānshāh: Iran	87	34N	47E
Kerulen: r., Mongolia	90	48N	111E
Keswick: England	62	55N	3W
Ketchikan: U.S.A.	24	55N	132W
Kettering: England	63	52N	1W
Kewanee: U.S.A.	49	41N	90W
Keweenaw Penin.: U.S.A.	49	47N	88W
Key West: U.S.A.	47	25N	82W
Khabarovsk: U.S.S.R.	83	48N	135E
Khairpur: Pakistan	88	28N	69E
Khalkís: Greece	69	38N	24E
Khandwa: India	88	22N	76E
Khaniá: (Canea) Crete	69	35N	24E
Khanka, L.: U.S.S.R.	83	45N	133E
Khan Tengri: mtn., China	85	42N	80E
Khanty-Mansiysk: U.S.S.R.	85	61N	69E
Kharagpur: India	88	22N	87E
Kharan Kalat: Pakistan	88	28N	65E
Khārg: i., Persian G.	87	29N	50E
Khar'kov: U.S.S.R.	84	50N	36E
KHARTOUM: Sudan	86	16N	33E
Khasi Hills: India	89	26N	91E
Khatanga: U.S.S.R.	83	72N	102E
Khemmarat: Thailand	92	16N	105E
Kherson: U.S.S.R.	84	47N	33E
Khimki: U.S.S.R.	114	55N	38E
Khiumaa: i., see Hiiumaa			
Khiva: U.S.S.R.	85	41N	60E
Khodzheyli: U.S.S.R.	85	42N	60E
Kholmsk: U.S.S.R.	83	47N	142E
Khorāsān: reg., Iran	87	35N	57E
Khorog: U.S.S.R.	85	37N	72E
Khorramshahr: Iran	87	30N	48E
Khrom-Tau: U.S.S.R.	85	50N	58E
Khuzestān: reg., Iran	87	31N	50E
Khyber Pass: Afghan./Pak.	88	34N	71E
Kiamusze: China	90	47N	130E
Kian: China	95	27N	115E
Kiangsi: Prov., China	95	27N	115E
Kiangsu: Prov., China	94	33N	119E
Kiangtu: China	95	32N	119E
Kidderminster: England	63	52N	2W
Kiel: W. Germany	68	54N	10E
Kiel Canal: W. Germany	74	54N	10E
Kielce: Poland	68	51N	21E
Kiev: U.S.S.R.	68	51N	30E
Kigoma: Tanzania	110	5S	30E
Kii-suidō: chan., Japan	93	34N	135E
Kildare: R. of Ireland	61	53N	7W
Kildonan: Rhodesia (Zimbabwe)	111	17S	31E
Kilimanjaro: mt., Tanzania	110	3S	37E
Kilkeel: N. Ireland	62	54N	6W
Kilkenny: R. of Ireland	61	53N	7W
Killarney: R. of Ireland	61	52N	9W
Kilmarnock: Scotland	62	56N	4W
Kilrush: R. of Ireland	61	53N	9W
Kimberley: S. Africa	111	29S	25E
Kindu: Zaire	110	3S	26E
Kingaroy: Australia	100	27S	152E
King I.: Australia	99	40S	144E
Kingman: Arizona, U.S.A.	48	35N	114W
Kingman: Kansas, U.S.A.	49	38N	98W
King's Lynn: England	63	53N	0
Kingsport: U.S.A.	47	37N	84W
Kingston: Australia	101	37S	140E
KINGSTON: Jamaica	53	18N	77W
Kingston: N.Z.	104	45S	169E
Kingston: U.S.A.	51	42N	74W
Kingston upon Hull: England	63	54N	0
Kingston-upon-Thames: England	112	51N	0
Kingsville: U.S.A.	46	28N	98W
King William's Town: S. Africa	111	33S	27E
Kinhwa: China	95	29N	120E
Kinleith: N.Z.	104	38S	176E
Kinsha: r., see Yangtze			
KINSHASA: Zaire	110	4S	15E
Kinston: U.S.A.	47	35N	78W
Kintyre: penin., Scot.	62	55N	6W
Kirchheim: W. Germany	75	49N	9E
Kirgiz S.S.R.: U.S.S.R.	85	42N	75E
Kirin: China	90	44N	126E
Kirkcaldy: Scotland	62	56N	3W
Kirkenes: Norway	70	70N	30E
Kirklareli: Turkey	69	42N	27E
Kirksville: U.S.A.	49	40N	93W
Kirkuk: Iraq	87	35N	44E
Kirkwall: Scotland	61	59N	3W
Kirov: U.S.S.R.	84	59N	50E
Kirovabad: U.S.S.R.	84	41N	46E
Kirovograd: U.S.S.R.	84	49N	32E
Kirovsk: U.S.S.R.	85	38N	60E
Kiruna: Sweden	70	68N	20E
Kisangani: Zaire	110	1N	25E
Kisarazu: Japan	93	35N	140E
Kishinev: U.S.S.R.	84	47N	29E
Kishi Wada: Japan	93	34N	135E
Kishm: Afghanistan	85	37N	70E
Kiskunfélegyháza: Hungary	68	47N	20E
Kissimmee: r., U.S.A.	47	27N	81W
Kisumu: Kenya	110	0	35E
Kithira: i., Greece	69	36N	23E
Kithnos: i., Greece	69	37N	24E
Kitwe: Zambia	111	13S	28E
Kitzbühel Alps: Austria	75	47N	12E
Kiuchuan: China	90	40N	99E
Kiukiang: China	95	30N	116E
Kivak: U.S.S.R.	83	65N	174W
Kivu, L.: Zaire	110	2S	29E
Kızılırmak: r., Turkey	86	41N	34E
Kjølen Mtns.: Nor./Sweden	75	65N	15E
Kjustendil: Bulgaria	69	42N	23E
Klagenfurt: Austria	75	47N	14E
Klaipėda: U.S.S.R.	71	56N	21E
Klamath Falls: U.S.A.	48	42N	122W
Klerksdorp: S. Africa	111	27S	26E
Klipplaat: S. Africa	111	33S	24E
Knokke: Belgium	72	51N	3E
Knoxville: U.S.A.	47	36N	84W
Kobe: Japan	93	35N	135E
København: see Copenhagen			
Koblenz: W. Germany	74	50N	8E
Kobrin: U.S.S.R.	68	52N	24E
Kōchi: Japan	93	34N	134E
Kodiak I.: U.S.A.	12	57N	154W
Kodaira: Japan	114	36N	139E
Kodok: Sudan	109	10N	32E
Kōfu: Japan	93	36N	139E
Kohat: Pakistan	88	34N	71E
Kohima: India	89	26N	94E
Koganei: Japan	114	36N	140E
Kokand: U.S.S.R.	85	40N	71E
Kokchetav: U.S.S.R.	85	54N	70E
Kokkola: Finland	70	64N	23E
Kokomo: U.S.A.	47	41N	86W
Koko Nor: see Tsing Hai			
Kola Penin.: U.S.S.R.	82	67N	38E
Kolhapur: India	88	17N	74E
Köln: see Cologne			
Kolomna: U.S.S.R.	84	55N	39E
Kolomyya: U.S.S.R.	68	48N	25E
Kolyma Plain: U.S.S.R.	83	68N	155E
Kolyma Range: see Gydan Range			
Kolyuchin, Gulf of: U.S.S.R.	83	67N	175W
Kolyvan': U.S.S.R.	85	51N	83E
Komandor Is.: U.S.S.R.	83	55N	166E
Komárno: Czech.	68	48N	18E
Komatipoort: S. Africa	111	25S	32E
Komba: Zaire	110	3N	24E
Kompong Cham: Cambodia	92	11N	105E
Kompong Som			

Limerick — Manizales

The World

	Page	Lat.	Long.
Netherlands	74	51N	6E
Limerick: R. of Ireland	61	53N	9W
Limnos: *i.*, Greece	69	40N	25E
Limoges: France	73	46N	1E
Limousin: *Old Prov.*, France	73	46N	1E
Limpopo: *r.*, Moz.	111	23S	33E
Linares: Mexico	52	25N	100W
Linares: Spain	67	38N	4W
Lincoln: & Co., Eng.	63	53N	1W
Lincoln: U.S.A.	49	41N	97W
Lincoln Park: U.S.A.	33	42N	83W
Lincolnwood: U.S.A.	34	42N	87W
Line Is.: Pacific O.	102/3	0	158W
Lingen: W. Germany	74	52N	7E
Lingga: *i.*, Indonesia	91	0	105E
Linguère: Senegal	108	15N	15W
Linköping: Sweden	71	58N	16E
Linnhe, L.: Scotland	62	57N	5W
Linton: U.S.A.	49	46N	100W
Linz: Austria	75	48N	14E
Lions, G. of (Golfe du Lion): France	73	43N	4E
Lipari Is.: Italy	69	38N	15E
Lipetsk: U.S.S.R.	84	53N	40E
Lippstadt: W. Germany	74	52N	8E
LISBON: Portugal	67	39N	9W
Lisburn: N. Ireland	62	55N	6W
Lisburne, C.: U.S.A.	12	69N	166W
Lisianski: *i.*, Pacific O.	102	27N	175W
Lisieux: France	72	49N	0
Lismore: Australia	101	29S	153E
Lithgow: Australia	101	33S	150E
Lithuanian S.S.R.: U.S.S.R.	84	55N	24E
Little Bitter Lake: Egypt	109	*Inset*	
Little Black: *r.*, U.S.A.	30	67N	144W
Littlefield: U.S.A.	46	34N	102W
Little Karroo: *plat.*, S. Africa	111	34S	22E
Little Minch: *chan.*, Scotland	61	58N	7W
Little Rock: U.S.A.	46	35N	92W
Little St. Bernard Pass: France/Italy	75	46N	7E
Liuchow: China	95	24N	109E
Livermore, Mt.: U.S.A.	46	30N	105W
Liverpool: Australia	115	34S	151E
Liverpool: England	62	53N	3W
Liverpool Range: Australia	101	32N	150E
Livingstone: *see* Maramba			
Livingstone Falls: Zaire	110	5S	14E
Livorno: *see* Leghorn			
Livradois, Massif du: *mtns.*, France	73	45N	3E
Lizard Point: England	63	50N	5W
Ljubljana: Yugoslavia	68	46N	14E
Ljungan: *r.*, Sweden	70	62N	17E
Llandrindod Wells: Wales	63	52N	3W
Llandudno: Wales	63	53N	4W
Llanelli: Wales	63	52N	4W
Llangollen: Wales	63	53N	3W
Llanidloes: Wales	63	52N	4W
Llano Estacado: *plat.*, U.S.A.	46	33N	103W
Llanos de Guarayos: *plains*, Bolivia	54	15S	63W
Lleyn: *penin.*, Wales	63	53N	5W
Lo: *r.*, China	94	36N	109E
Lobito: Angola	111	12S	14E
Lockerbie: Scotland	62	55N	3W
Lod (Lydda): Israel	86	32N	35E
Lodi: Italy	75	45N	9E
Łódź: Poland	68	52N	19E
Lofoten Is.: Norway	70	69N	15E
Logan: Utah, U.S.A.	48	42N	112W
Logan W. Va., U.S.A.	47	38N	82W
Logansport: U.S.A.	47	41N	86W
Logroño: Spain	67	42N	2W
Loir: *r.*, France	72	48N	0
Loire: *r.*, France	73	47N	1W
Lója: Ecuador	54	4S	79W
Lokchang: China	95	25N	113E
Lolland: *i.*, Denmark	71	55N	11E
Lombard: U.S.A.	34	42N	88W
Lombardy: & *Plain*, Italy	75	45N	9E
Lomblen: *i.*, Indonesia	91	8S	123E
Lombok: *i.* & *str.*, Indonesia	91	8S	116E
LOMÉ: Togo	108	6N	1E
Lommel: Belgium	72	51N	5E
Lomond, L.: Scotland	62	56N	5W
LONDON: England	112	—	—
Londonderry: N. Ireland	61	55N	7W
Londrina: Brazil	56	23S	51W
Long Bay: U.S.A.	47	34N	79W
Long Beach: *city*, Calif. U.S.A.	37	34N	118W
Long Beach: *city*, N.Y. U.S.A.	35	41N	73W
Longford: R. of Ireland	61	54N	8W
Long I.: Australia	100	22S	150E
Long I.: The Bahamas	45	23N	75W
Long I.: U.S.A.	47	41N	73W
Longmont: U.S.A.	49	40N	105W

	Page	Lat.	Long.
Longreach: Australia	99	23S	144E
Longuyon: France	72	49N	6E
Longview: Oregon, U.S.A.	48	46N	123W
Longview: Texas, U.S.A.	46	33N	95W
Longwy: France	72	49N	6E
Lons-le-Saunier: Fr.	73	47N	6E
Lookout, C.: U.S.A.	47	35N	77W
Lopei: China	90	48N	131E
Lorain: U.S.A.	47	41N	83W
Lorca: Spain	67	38N	2W
Lord Howe Rise: Pacific Ocean	102	30S	163E
Lorestān: *reg.*, Iran	87	33N	48E
Lorient: France	72	48N	3W
Lorne, Firth of: Scot.	62	56N	6W
Lorrach: W. Germany	75	48N	8E
Lorraine: *Old Prov.*, France	72	49N	6E
Los Alamos: U.S.A.	48	36N	106W
Los Andes: Chile	55	33S	71W
Los Angeles: U.S.A.	37	—	—
Lossiemouth: Scotland	61	58N	3W
Lot: *r.*, France	73	44N	1E
Lothian: *Reg.*, Scotland	62	56N	4W
Loue: *r.*, France	73	47N	6E
Loughborough: Eng.	63	53N	1W
Loughton: England	112	52N	0
Louislade Archipelago: Coral Sea	99	11S	153E
Louisiana: *State*, U.S.A.	46	33N	93W
Louis Trichardt: S. Africa	111	23S	30E
Louisville: U.S.A.	47	38N	86W
Loup City: U.S.A.	46	41N	99W
Lourdes: France	73	43N	0
Louth: England	63	53N	0
Louvain: *see* Leuven			
Lowell: U.S.A.	51	43N	71W
Lower California: *Territ.*, Mexico	44	27N	113W
Lower Tunguska: *r.*, U.S.S.R.	83	64N	95E
Lowestoft: England	63	52N	2E
Lowville: U.S.A.	19	44N	75W
Loyalty Is.: Pac. O.	102	20S	165E
Loyang: China	94	35N	112E
Lu (Salween): *r.*, China	90	30N	97E
Lualaba: *r.*, Zaire	110	6S	26E
LUANDA: Angola	110	9S	13E
Luang Prabang: Laos	92	20N	102E
Luanshya: Zambia	111	13S	28E
Lubango (Sá da Bandiera): Angola	111	15S	14E
Lubbock: U.S.A.	46	34N	102W
Lübeck: & *bay*, W. Germany	74	54N	11E
Lubéron, Montagne du: France	73	44N	5E
Lublin: Poland	68	51N	23E
Lubumbashi: Zaire	110	12S	27E
Lucca: Italy	75	44N	10E
Luce Bay: Scotland	62	55N	5W
Lucerne, L.: Switz.	75	47N	8E
Lucin: U.S.A.	48	41N	114W
Luckenwalde: E. Ger.	74	52N	13E
Lucknow: India	88	27N	81E
Lüdenscheid: W. Ger.	74	51N	8E
Lüderitz: S.W. Africa (Namibia)	111	27S	15E
Ludhiana: India	88	31N	76E
Ludlow: England	63	52N	3W
Ludlow: U.S.A.	48	35N	116W
Ludvika: Sweden	71	60N	15E
Ludwigsburg: W. Ger.	74	49N	9E
Ludwigshafen: W. Ger.	74	49N	8E
Ludwigslust: E. Ger.	74	53N	12E
Lufkin: U.S.A.	46	31N	95W
Luga: U.S.S.R.	71	59N	30E
Lugano: Switzerland	75	46N	9E
Lugo: Spain	67	43N	8W
Lugoj: Romania	68	46N	22E
Luichow Penin.: China	90	21N	110E
Luleå: Sweden	70	66N	22E
Lüleburgaz: Turkey	69	41N	27E
Lumberton: U.S.A.	47	34N	79W
Lumsden: N.Z.	104	46S	168E
Lund: Sweden	71	56N	13E
Lundy I.: England	63	51N	5W
Lune: *r.*, England	62	54N	3W
Lüneburg: & *Heath*, Germany	74	53N	10E
Lunéville: France	72	49N	6E
Lungkiang: *see* Tsitsihar			
Lure: France	72	48N	6E
Lurgan: N. Ireland	62	54N	6W
LUSAKA: Zambia	111	15S	28E
Lusambo: Zaire	110	5S	23E
Lushai Hills: India	89	23N	93E
Lushun: China	94	39N	121E
Lussac-les-Châteaux: France	73	46N	1E
Lüta: China	94	39N	121E
Luton: England	63	52N	0
Lutsk: U.S.S.R.	68	51N	25E
LUXEMBOURG: *cap.* Luxembourg	72	50N	6E
Luxor: Egypt	86	26N	33E

	Page	Lat.	Long.
Luzern (Lucerne): Switzerland	75	47N	8E
Luzon: *i.*, Phil.	91	15N	121E
Luzy: France	73	47N	4E
L'vov: U.S.S.R.	68	50N	24E
Lyakhov Is.: U.S.S.R.	83	73N	142E
Lyallpur: Pakistan	88	31N	73E
Lydda: *see* Lod			
Lydenburg: S. Africa	111	25S	30E
Lyme Bay: England	63	51N	3W
Lynchburg: U.S.A.	47	37N	79W
Lynn: U.S.A.	33	42N	71W
Lyonnais: *Old Prov.*, France	73	46N	4E
Lyons (Lyon): France	73	46N	5E
Lys: *r.*, France/Belgium	72	51N	3E
Lys'va: U.S.S.R.	85	58N	58E
Lyttleton: N.Z.	104	44S	173E
Lyubertsy: U.S.S.R.	114	55N	38E
Lyublino: U.S.S.R.	114	55N	38E
Ma'ān: Jordan	86	30N	36E
Maanshan: China	94	32N	119E
Maarianhamina: Fin.	71	60N	20E
Maas: *r.*, Netherlands	74	52N	5E
Maastricht: Neth.	74	51N	6E
McAlester: U.S.A.	46	35N	96W
McAllen: U.S.A.	46	26N	98W
Macao: China	95	22N	113E
Macclesfield: England	63	53N	2W
McComb: U.S.A.	46	31N	90W
McCook: U.S.A.	46	40N	101W
Macdonnell Ranges: Australia	98	24S	132E
Maceió: Brazil	54	10S	36W
Macequece: Moz.	111	19S	33E
Macerata: Italy	69	43N	13E
McGehee: U.S.A.	46	34N	91W
Macgillycuddy's Reeks: *mtns.*, R. of Ireland	61	52N	10W
Machida: Japan	114	36N	139E
Machrihanish: Scotland	62	55N	6W
McIntosh: U.S.A.	49	46N	101W
Mackay: Australia	100	21S	149E
Mackay, L.: Australia	98	23S	128E
Mackenzie: Guyana	54	6N	58W
Mackenzie: *r.*, Australia	100	23S	149E
Mackinac, Str. of: U.S.A./Canada	19	46N	85W
McKinley, Mt.: U.S.A.	12	63N	151W
McKinney: U.S.A.	46	33N	97W
McMurdo: Antarctica	116	78S	168E
Macias Nguema Biyogo: *i.*, Eq. Guinea	108	4N	9E
Mâcon: France	73	46N	5E
Macon: U.S.A.	47	33N	84W
Macquarie I.: Pac. O.	102	55S	159E
McRae: U.S.A.	47	32N	83W
Madagascar: *see* **MALAGASY REP.**			
Madagascar Basin: Indian Ocean	89	25S	55E
Madagascar Ridge: Indian Ocean	89	30S	45E
Madang: Papua New Guinea	99	5S	146E
Maddalena Pass: France/Italy	75	44N	7E
Madeira: *i.*, Atlantic Ocean	57	33N	17W
Madeira: *r.*, Brazil	54	5S	61W
Madera: U.S.A.	48	37N	120W
Madhya Pradesh: *State*, India	88	23N	78E
Madison: Florida, U.S.A.	47	30N	84W
Madison: Ind., U.S.A.	47	39N	85W
Madison: S. Dakota, U.S.A.	49	44N	97W
Madison: Wisc., U.S.A.	49	43N	89W
Madison Heights: U.S.A.	33	43N	83W
Madisonville: U.S.A.	47	37N	88W
Madiun: Indonesia	91	8S	112E
Madras: India	88	13N	80E
MADRID: Spain	67	40N	4W
Madura: *i.*, Indon.	91	7S	113E
Madurai: India	88	10N	78E
Maebashi: Japan	93	36N	139E
Mafeking: S. Africa	111	26S	25E
Magadan: U.S.S.R.	83	60N	150E
Magallenes: *see* Punta Arenas			
Magdalena: *r.*, Colombia	54	7N	74W
Magdeburg: E. Ger.	74	52N	12E
Magellan, Str. of: Chile/Argentina	55	53S	70W
Maggiore, Lake: Italy/Switzerland	75	46N	9E
Magnitogorsk: U.S.S.R.	85	53N	59E
Magnolia: U.S.A.	46	33N	93W
Magude: Moz.	111	25S	33E
Magwe: Burma	92	20N	95E
Mahanadi: *r.*, India	88	22N	83E
Maharashtra: *State*, India	88	24N	76E
Mahia Penin.: N.Z.	104	39S	178E
Mahón: Minorca	67	40N	4E
Maidenhead: England	112	52N	1W

	Page	Lat.	Long.
Maidstone: England	112	51N	1E
Maiduguri: Nigeria	108	12N	13E
Maimana: Afghan.	85	36N	65E
Main: *r.*, W. Germany	74	50N	10E
Main: *Old Prov.*, France	72	48N	1W
Main Barrier Range: Australia	101	32S	141E
Mai Ndombe, L.: Zaire	110	2S	17E
Maine: *State*, U.S.A.	19	45N	70W
Mainland: *i.*, Orkney Is.	61	59N	3W
Mainz: W. Germany	74	50N	8E
Maiskhal: Bangladesh	89	21N	92E
Maitland: Australia	101	33S	152E
Majorca (Mallorca): *i.*, Balearic Is.	67	39N	3E
Majunga: Malagasy Republic	110	16S	46E
Makeni: Sierra Leone	108	9N	12W
Makarikari Salt Pan: Botswana	111	21S	26E
Makassar: *str.*, Indonesia	91	5S	120E
Makeyevka: U.S.S.R.	84	48N	38E
Makhachkala: U.S.S.R.	84	43N	48E
Makran: *reg.*, Iran/Pakistan	87	26N	62E
Makushino: U.S.S.R.	85	55N	67E
Malabar Coast: India	88	12N	75E
Malacca: *str.*, Malaysia	92	2N	102E
Maladetta Massif: France/Spain	73	43N	1E
Málaga: Spain	67	37N	4W
MALAGASY REP.: *cap.* Tananarive	110	*Inset*	
Malahide: R. of Ireland	62	53N	6W
Malaita: *i.*, Solomon Is.	99	9S	161E
Malakal: Sudan	109	10N	32E
Malang: Indonesia	91	8S	112E
Malanje: Angola	110	9S	16E
Mälar, L.: Sweden	71	59N	17E
Malatya: Turkey	87	38N	38E
MALAWI: *cap.* Lilongwe	110	13S	34E
Malawi (Nyasa), Lake: Africa	110	13S	34E
Malaya: *State*, Malaysia	91	4N	102E
MALAYSIA: *Fed. cap.* Kuala Lumpur	91	5N	110E
Malbork: Poland	68	54N	19E
Malden: U.S.A.	33	42N	71W
Malden I.: Pacific O.	103	5S	155W
MALDIVES: *cap.* Mahé	89	7N	73E
Malebo, Pool: *l.*, Zaire	110	4S	15E
Malesherbes: France	72	48N	2E
Malheur L.: U.S.A.	48	43N	119W
MALI: *cap.* Bamako	108	15N	5W
Malines: *see* Mechelen			
Malin Head: R. of Ireland	61	55N	7W
Malinmore Head: R. of Ireland	61	55N	9W
Mallaig: Scotland	62	57N	6W
Mallorca (Majorca): *i.*, Spain	67	39N	3E
Mallow: R. of Ireland	61	52N	9W
Malmberget: Sweden	70	67N	21E
Malmédy: Belgium	72	50N	6E
Malmesbury: S. Africa	111	33S	19E
Malmö: Sweden	71	56N	13E
Maloja Pass: Switz.	75	46N	10E
Malonga: Zaire	110	10S	23E
Malpelo I.: Pacific O.	54	4N	82W
Malplaquet: *hist.*, France	72	50N	4E
MALTA: *cap.* Valletta	69	36N	14E
Malta: U.S.A.	48	48N	108W
Malvan: India	88	16N	73E
Malvern: England	63	52N	2W
Man, I. of: *cap.* Douglas	62	54N	5W
Manaar: & *gulf*, Sri Lanka	88	9N	80E
Manado: Indonesia	91	2N	125E
MANAGUA: Nic.	45	12N	86W
MANAMA: Bahrain	87	26N	51E
Mana Pass: China	88	31N	79E
Manaus: Brazil	54	3S	60W
Manchester: England	62	54N	2W
Manchester: U.S.A.	51	43N	71W
Mandalay: Burma	92	22N	96E
Mandan: U.S.A.	49	47N	101W
Mandasor: India	88	24N	75E
Mangalore: India	88	13N	75E
Mangyshlak Penin.: U.S.S.R.	84	44N	51E
Manhattan: Kansas, U.S.A.	49	39N	97W
Manhattan: N.Y., U.S.A.	35	41N	74W
Manifold, C.: Australia	100	23S	151E
Manila: Philippine Is.	91	15N	121E
Manipur: *State*, India	89	25N	94E
Manistee: *r.*, U.S.A.	19	44N	85W
Manitou Is.: U.S.A.	49	47N	87W
Manitowoc: U.S.A.	19	44N	88W
Manizales: Colombia	54	5N	76W

Monroeville — Newton
The World

	Page	Lat.	Long.
U.S.A.	47	42N	83W
Monroeville: U.S.A.	47	31N	87W
MONROVIA: Liberia	108	6N	11W
Mons: Belgium	72	50N	4E
Montague I.: U.S.A.	12	60N	147W
Montana: *State*, U.S.A.	48	47N	110W
Montargis: France	72	48N	3E
Montauban: France	73	44N	1E
Montauk Pt.: U.S.A.	51	41N	72W
Montbéliard: France	73	47N	7E
Montceau-les-Mines: France	73	47N	4E
Mont Cenis Pass: France/Italy	75	45N	7E
Montclair: U.S.A.	35	41N	74W
Mont de Marsan: Fr.	73	44N	1W
Montdidier: France	72	50N	3E
Monte Bello Is.: Australia	98	20S	115E
MONTE CARLO: Monaco	73	44N	7E
Montego Bay: *town*, Jamaica	53	18N	78W
Montélimar: France	73	45N	5E
Monterey: & *Bay*, U.S.A.	48	37N	122W
Monterrey: Mexico	52	26N	100W
MONTEVIDEO: Uruguay	56	35S	56W
Montgomery: U.S.A.	47	32N	86W
Montluçon: France	73	46N	3E
Montmédy: France	72	50N	5E
Montmirail: France	72	49N	4E
Montpelier: U.S.A.	19	44N	73W
Montpellier: France	73	44N	4E
Montreuil: France	72	50N	2E
Montreuil Bellay: Fr.	73	47N	0
Montreux: Switz.	75	46N	7E
Montrose: Scotland	62	57N	2W
Montrose: U.S.A.	48	38N	108W
Mont St. Michel: Fr.	72	49N	2W
Montserrat: *i.*, West Indies	45	17N	62W
Montvalier, Pic de: Spain/France	73	43N	1E
Monza: Italy	75	46N	9E
Moorhead: U.S.A.	49	47N	97W
Moorreesburg: South Africa	111	33S	18E
Moosehead, L.: U.S.A.	15	46N	69W
Moradabad: India	88	29N	79E
Morava: *r.*, Czech.	68	49N	17E
Moray Firth: Scot.	61	58N	4W
Morbihan: *Dept.*, Fr.	72	48N	3W
Moreau: *r.*, U.S.A.	49	45N	102W
Morecambe: England	62	54N	3W
Moree: Australia	101	29S	150E
Morelia: Mexico	52	20N	101W
Moreton in Marsh: England	63	52N	2W
Morgan City: U.S.A.	46	30N	91W
Morgantown: U.S.A.	47	40N	80W
Morkalla: Australia	101	34S	141E
Morlaix: France	72	49N	4W
MOROCCO: *cap.* Rabat	108	32N	5W
Morón: Cuba	53	22N	78W
Morotai: *i.*, Indon.	91	3N	128E
Morpeth: England	62	55N	2W
Morristown: U.S.A.	35	41N	75W
Morton Grove: U.S.A.	34	42N	87W
Morvan: *reg.*, France	73	47N	4E
Moscow: U.S.A.	48	47N	117W
MOSCOW: U.S.S.R.	84	56N	37E
Mosel (Moselle): *r.*, Fr./W. Ger.	74	50N	7E
Moses Lake: *city*, U.S.A.	48	47N	119W
Moshi: Tanzania	110	3S	37E
Moss: Norway	70	59N	11E
Mosselbaai: *town*, South Africa	111	34S	22E
Most: Czech.	74	50N	14E
Mostaganem: Algeria	67	36N	0
Mostar: Yugoslavia	69	43N	18E
Mosul: Iraq	87	36N	43E
Motala: Sweden	71	59N	15E
Motherwell: Scot.	62	56N	3W
Motueka: N.Z.	104	41S	173E
Moulins: France	73	47N	3E
Moulmein: Burma	92	17N	97E
Moultrie: U.S.A.	47	31N	84W
Moundsville: U.S.A.	47	40N	81W
Mountain Home: U.S.A.	48	43N	116W
Mount Eba: *town*, Australia	98	30S	136E
Mount Gambier: *town*, Australia	101	38S	141E
Mount Isa: *town*, Australia	98	21S	140E
Mount Lofty Range: Australia	101	35S	138E
Mount Lyell: *town*, Australia	99	42S	146E
Mount Magnet: *town*, Australia	100	28S	118E
Mount Morgan: *town*, Australia	100	24S	150E
Mount Pleasant: *city*, U.S.A.	19	44N	85W
Mount Prospect: *city*, U.S.A.	34	42N	88W
Mount Vernon: *city*, Ill., U.S.A.	47	38N	89W
Mount Vernon: *city*, N.Y., U.S.A.	35	41N	74W
Mount Vernon: *city*, Wash., U.S.A.	48	48N	122W
Mourne Mts.: N. Irel.	61	54N	6W
Moyale: Kenya	110	4N	39E
MOZAMBIQUE: *cap.* Maputo	110	—	—
Mozambique: Moz.	111	15S	40E
Mozambique Chan.	110	15S	41E
Mpanda: Tanzania	110	6S	31E
Mtwara: Tanzania	110	10S	40E
Muang Khon Kaen: Thailand	92	16N	103E
Muang Lamsang: Thailand	92	18N	99E
Muang Nan: Thailand	92	19N	101E
Muang Phrae: Thailand	92	18N	100E
Muang Phitsanulok: Thailand	92	17N	100E
Muchinga Mts.: Zambia	111	13S	32E
Mudgee: Australia	101	32S	150E
Muğla: Turkey	86	37N	28E
Muhammad Qol: Sudan	86	21N	37E
Mühlhausen: E. Ger.	74	51N	10E
Mukachevo: U.S.S.R.	68	48N	23E
Mukallā: Yemen P.D.R.	87	15N	49E
Mukden (Shenyang): China	94	42N	124E
Mülheim: W. Ger.	74	51N	7E
Mülheim an der Ruhr: W. Germany	64	51N	7E
Mulhouse: France	72	48N	7E
Mull: *i.*, Scotland	62	56N	6W
Müller Mts.: Indon.	91	1N	114E
Mullewa: Australia	100	28S	116E
Mull Hd.: Scotland	61	59N	3W
Mullingar: R. of Irel.	61	54N	7W
Mull of Oa.: Scotland	62	56N	6W
Mulobezi: Zambia	111	17S	25E
Multan: Pak.	88	30N	71E
Muna: *i.*, Indonesia	91	5S	122E
Muncie: U.S.A.	47	40N	85W
Mungbere: Zaire	110	3N	28E
Munich (München): W. Germany	75	48N	12E
Münster: W. Ger.	74	52N	8E
Muonio: *r.*, Finland	70	68N	24E
Mur: France	72	48N	3W
Mur: *r.*, Austria	75	47N	14E
Murat: France	73	45N	3E
Murchison: *r.*, Austl.	98	27S	116E
Murcia: Spain	67	38N	1W
Muret: France	73	43N	1E
Murfreesboro: U.S.A.	47	36N	86W
Murmansk: U.S.S.R.	70	69N	33E
Murom: U.S.S.R.	84	56N	42E
Muroran: Japan	93	42N	141E
Murray: *r.*, Austl.	101	35S	139E
Murray Bridge: Australia	101	35S	139E
Murrumbidgee: *r.*, Australia	101	35S	146E
Murupara: N.Z.	104	38S	177E
Murwillumbah: Australia	100	28S	153E
Musashino: Japan	114	36N	140E
MUSCAT: Oman	85	24N	59E
Muscatine: U.S.A.	49	41N	91W
Muskegon: *r.*, U.S.A.	19	43N	86W
Muskogee: U.S.A.	46	36N	95W
Mussoorie: India	88	30N	78E
Mustafakemalpaşa: Turkey	69	40N	28E
Mustang I.: U.S.A.	46	27N	97W
Muswellbrook: Austl.	101	32S	151E
Mutankiang: China	90	45N	130E
Mutano: Angola	111	17S	15E
Muyun-Kum: *desert*, U.S.S.R.	85	44N	71E
Muzaffarpur: India	88	26N	85E
Mwanza: Tanzania	110	3S	33E
Mweru, L.: Zambia/Zaire	110	9S	29E
Myingyan: Burma	92	21N	95E
Myitkyina: Burma	92	26N	97E
Mymensingh: Bangl.	88	25N	90E
Mysore: India	88	12N	77E
My Tho: Vietnam	92	10N	106E
Naas: R. of Ireland	61	53N	7W
Nacala: Mozambique	111	15S	40E
Nacogdoches: U.S.A.	46	32N	95W
Naestved: Denmark	71	55N	12E
Nafud: *desert*, Saudi Arabia	87	28N	41E
Naga Hills: India/Burma	89	26N	95E
Nagaland: *State*, India	89	26N	95E
Nagaoka: Japan	93	37N	139E
Nagapattinam: India	88	11N	80E
Nagasaki: Japan	93	33N	130E
Nagoya: Japan	93	35N	137E
Nagpur: India	88	21N	79E
Nagykanizsa: Hung.	68	46N	16E
Naha: Okinawa I.	92	26N	127E
Naini Tal: India	88	29N	80E
Nairn: Scotland	61	58N	4W
NAIROBI: Kenya	110	2S	37E
Najaf: Iraq	87	32N	44E
Najd: *reg.*, Saudi Arabia	87	26N	42E
Najran: Saudi Arabia	87	17N	44E
Nakhon Phanom: Thailand	92	17N	105E
Nakhon Ratchasima: Thailand	92	15N	102E
Nakhon Sawan: Thailand	92	16N	100E
Nakhon Si Thammarat: Thailand	92	8N	100E
Namangan: U.S.S.R.	85	41N	72E
Nam Dinh: Vietnam	92	20N	106E
Namib Desert: S.W. Afr. (Namibia)	111	23S	15E
NAMIBIA: *see* South West Africa			
Nampa: U.S.A.	48	44N	117W
Nampula: Moz.	111	15S	40E
Namsos: Norway	70	64N	11E
Namur: Belgium	72	50N	5E
Nanchang: China	95	28N	116E
Nancy: France	72	49N	6E
Nanda Devi: *mtn.*, India	88	30N	80E
Nangchen Japo: *mtn.*, China	90	33N	94E
Nanking: China	94	32N	119E
Nanling: *mts.*, China	95	25N	112E
Nanning: China	95	23N	108E
Nanping: China	95	27N	118E
Nansei Is.: *see* Ryukyu Is.			
Nan Shan: *mts.*, China	90	38N	100E
Nantes: France	72	47N	2W
Nantung: China	94	32N	121E
Nanumea: *i.*, Pac. O.	102	5S	176E
Nanyang: China	94	33N	112E
Nanyuan: China	114	40N	116E
Nanyuki: Kenya	110	0	37E
Nao, C. de la: Spain	67	39N	0
Napa: U.S.A.	46	38N	122W
Napier: N.Z.	104	39S	177E
Naples: Italy	69	41N	14E
Naracoorte: Austl.	101	37S	141E
Narbada: *r.*, India	88	22N	75E
Narbonne: France	73	43N	3E
Narrabri: Australia	101	30S	150E
Narrandera: Austl.	101	35S	147E
Narrogin: Australia	100	33S	117E
Narva: U.S.S.R.	84	59N	28E
Narvik: Norway	70	68N	17E
Nar'yan-Mar: U.S.S.R.	82	67N	53E
Nashua: U.S.A.	51	43N	72W
Nashville: U.S.A.	47	36N	87W
Nasik: India	88	20N	74E
Nasiriya: Iraq	87	31N	46E
NASSAU: The Bahamas	45	25N	77W
Nassau Mts.: Indonesia	98	4S	136E
Nasser, L.: Egypt	86	23N	33E
Nassjö: Sweden	71	58N	15E
Natal: Brazil	54	6S	35W
Natal: *Prov.*, S. Afr.	111	28S	31E
Natchez: U.S.A.	46	32N	91W
Natchitoches: U.S.A.	46	33N	93W
Natick: U.S.A.	33	41N	71W
Natuna Is. (Bunguran Is.): Indon.	91	4N	108E
Naturaliste, Cape: Australia	100	34S	115E
Nauru: *i.*, Pac. O.	102	1S	167E
Navan: R. of Irel.	61	54N	7W
Navarin, C.: U.S.S.R.	83	62N	179E
Navasota: *r.*, U.S.A.	46	31N	96W
Návpaktos: Greece	69	38N	21E
Návplion: Greece	69	38N	23E
Náxos: *i.*, Greece	69	37N	26E
Nazareth: Israel	86	33N	35E
Naze, The: *marshes*, England	63	52N	1E
N'DJAMENA: Chad	108	12N	15E
Ndola: Zambia	111	13S	29E
Neagh, L.: N. Irel.	61	55N	6W
Nebit-Dag: U.S.S.R.	84	40N	55E
Nebraska: *State*, U.S.A.	49	42N	100W
Nebraska City: U.S.A.	49	41N	96W
Neches: *r.*, U.S.A.	46	31N	95W
Neckar: *r.*, W. Germany	74	49N	9E
Needham: U.S.A.	33	42N	71W
Needles, The: *cliffs*, England	63	51N	2W
Negeb: *desert*, Israel	86	30N	35E
Negro: *r.*, Argentina	55	40S	64W
Negro: *r.*, Brazil	54	1S	64W
Negros: *i.*, Phil.	91	10N	123E
Nehbandān: Iran	87	32N	60E
Neisse (Nysa): *r.*, Pol./E. Ger.	74	52N	15E
Neiva: Colombia	54	3N	75W
Nellore: India	88	14N	80E
Nelson: N.Z.	104	41S	173E
Neman: *r.*, U.S.S.R.	71	53N	25E
Nemours: France	72	48N	3E
Nemuro: Japan	90	43N	145E
Nenagh: R. of Irel.	61	53N	8W
Nenana: U.S.A.	12	64N	149W
Nene: *r.*, England	63	53N	0
Neosho: *r.*, U.S.A.	46	38N	96W
NEPAL: *cap.* Katmandu	88	28N	85E
Nerchinsk: U.S.S.R.	83	52N	116E
Neskaupstadhur: Ice.	70	65N	14W
Ness, L.: Scotland	61	57N	4W
NETHERLANDS: *cap.* The Hague	74	52N	5E
Neubrandenburg: E. Germany	74	53N	13E
Neuchâtel: & *lake*, Switzerland	75	47N	7E
Neufchâteau: Belg.	72	50N	5E
Neufchâteau: France	72	48N	6E
Neukirchen-Vluyn: W. Germany	64	51N	7E
Neumünster: W. Ger.	72	54N	10E
Neunkirchen: W. Ger.	74	49N	7E
Neuquén: Argentina	55	39S	68W
Neuse: *r.*, U.S.A.	47	35N	78W
Neuss: W. Germany	64	51N	7E
Neustrelitz: E. Ger.	74	53N	13E
Nevada: *State*, U.S.A.	48	39N	117W
Nevada City: U.S.A.	48	39N	121W
Never: U.S.S.R.	83	54N	124E
Nevers: France	73	47N	3E
Nevis: *i.*, W. Indies	45	17N	63W
New Amsterdam: *i.*, Indian Ocean	89	38S	78E
Newark: N.J., U.S.A.	35	41N	74W
Newark: Ohio, U.S.A.	47	40N	82W
Newark upon Trent: England	63	53N	1W
New Bedford: U.S.A.	51	42N	71W
New Bern: U.S.A.	47	35N	77W
Newberry: U.S.A.	19	46N	85W
New Braunfels: U.S.A.	46	30N	98W
New Britain: *i.*, Papua, New Guinea	99	6S	150E
New Brunswick: U.S.A.	35	40N	74W
Newbury: England	63	51N	1W
New Caledonia: *i.*, Pacific Ocean	102	21S	165E
Newcastle: Australia	101	33S	152E
Newcastle: N. Ireland	62	54N	6W
New Castle: Pa., U.S.A.	47	41N	80W
Newcastle: S. Africa	111	28S	30E
Newcastle: Wyo., U.S.A.	49	44N	104W
Newcastle under Lyme: England	63	53N	2W
Newcastle upon Tyne: England	62	55N	2W
Newdegate: Austl.	100	33S	119E
New Delhi: India	115	28N	77E
Newenham, Cape: U.S.A.	12	59N	162W
New Forest: *reg.*, England	63	51N	2W
New Guinea: *i.*, East Indies	98/9	5S	140E
New Hampshire: *State*, U.S.A.	19	44N	72W
Newhaven: England	63	51N	0
New Haven: U.S.A.	51	41N	73W
New Hebrides: *is.*, Pacific Ocean	102	15S	168E
New Hyde Park: U.S.A.	35	41N	74W
New Iberia: U.S.A.	46	30N	92W
New Ireland: *i.*, Papua New Guinea	99	3S	152E
New Jersey: *State*, U.S.A.	50/1	40N	75W
Newmarket: Eng.	63	52N	0
New Mexico: *State*, U.S.A.	48/9	34N	107W
Newnan: U.S.A.	47	33N	85W
New Orleans: U.S.A.	46	30N	90W
New Plymouth: N.Z.	104	39S	174E
Newport: Wales	63	52N	3W
Newport: England	63	51N	1W
Newport: Rhode Island, U.S.A.	51	41N	71W
Newport: Vt., U.S.A.	19	45N	72W
Newport News: U.S.A.	47	37N	76W
New Providence: *i.*, The Bahamas	47	25N	77W
Newquay: England	63	50N	5W
New Rochelle: U.S.A.	35	41N	74W
Newry: N. Ireland	62	54N	6W
New South Wales: *State*, Australia	101	32S	146E
Newton: Iowa, U.S.A.	49	42N	93W

Ottawa — Port Jackson

The World

	Page	Lat.	Long.
Ottawa: Ill., U.S.A.	49	41N	89W
Ottawa: Kansas, U.S.A.	49	39N	95W
Otway Cape: Austl.	101	39S	144E
Otztal Alps: Austria	75	47N	11E
Ouachita: r., U.S.A.	46	33N	92W
OUAGADOUGOU: Upper Volta	108	12N	2W
Ouargla: Algeria	108	32N	5E
Oubangui: r., Africa	109	4N	21E
Oudenaarde: Belg.	72	51N	4E
Oudtshoorn: S. Afr.	111	34S	22E
Ouessant, Î. d': Fr.	72	48N	5W
Oulu: & lake, Fin.	70	65N	25E
Ou-sammyaku: mtns., Japan	93	39N	141E
Ourthe: r., Belgium	72	50N	6E
Ouse: r., East Anglia, England	63	53N	0
Ouse: r., Sussex, England	63	51N	0
Oust: r., France	72	48N	2W
Outer Hebrides: is., Scotland	61	58N	7W
Outjo: S.W. Africa (Namibia)	111	20S	17E
Ouyen: Australia	101	35S	142E
Oviedo: Spain	67	43N	6W
Owen, Mt.: N.Z.	104	42S	172E
Owen Falls: Uganda	110	0	33E
Owens: l., U.S.A.	48	36N	118W
Owensboro: U.S.A.	47	38N	87W
Owen Stanley Range: Papua New Guinea	99	9S	147E
Owyhee Res.: & r., U.S.A.	48	43N	118W
Oxford: & Co., Eng.	63	52N	1W
Oxnard: U.S.A.	48	34N	119W
Oxus: r. see Amu Dar'ya			
Oyonnax: France	73	46N	6E
Ozark Plat.: U.S.A.	46	37N	93W
Ozarks, L. of the: U.S.A.	46	38N	93W
Ózd: Hungary	68	48N	20E
Paarl: S. Africa	111	34S	19E
Pachuca de Soto: Mexico	52	27N	99W
Pacific Grove: U.S.A.	48	37N	122W
Pacific Ocean	102/3	—	—
Padang: Indonesia	91	1S	100E
Padangsidempuan: Indonesia	92	1N	99E
Paderborn: W. Ger.	74	52N	9E
Padre I.: U.S.A.	46	27N	97W
Padua (Padova): It.	75	45N	12E
Paducah: U.S.A.	47	37N	89W
Pafuri: Moz.	111	22S	33E
Paignton: England	63	50N	4W
Paimboeuf: France	73	47N	2W
Paimpol: France	72	49N	3W
Paisley: Scotland	62	56N	4W
Pakanbaru: Indonesia	92	1N	102E
PAKISTAN: cap. Islamabad	88	—	—
Pak Lay: Laos	92	18N	101E
Pakokku: Burma	92	21N	95E
Pakse: Laos	92	15N	105E
Palapye Road: Botswana	111	22S	26E
Palatka: U.S.A.	47	30N	82W
Palau Is.: Caroline Is.	91	7N	135E
Palawan: i., Phil.	91	10N	119E
Palembang: Indonesia	91	3S	105E
Palencia: Spain	67	42N	5W
Palermo: Sicily	69	38N	13E
Palestine: U.S.A.	46	32N	96W
Palghat: India	88	11N	76E
Palisade: U.S.A.	48	41N	116W
Palk Strait: India/Sri Lanka	88	10N	80E
Palliser, C.: N.Z.	104	42S	175E
Palma de Mallorca: Spain	67	40N	3E
Palma Sorlano: Cuba	53	20N	76W
Palmas, C.: Liberia	108	4N	8W
Palm Beach: U.S.A.	45	27N	80W
Palmer Land: Antarctica	116	64S	63W
Palmerston North: New Zealand	104	40S	176E
Palmyra I.: Pac. O.	102	6N	162W
Palo Alto: U.S.A.	36	36N	122W
Palos, C. de: Spain	67	38N	1W
Pamiers: France	73	43N	2E
Pamirs: mts., U.S.S.R./Afghanistan	85	37N	73E
Pamlico Sd.: U.S.A.	47	35N	76W
Pampa: reg., Argentina	49	33S	64W
Pampa: U.S.A.	46	35N	101W
Pamplona: Spain	67	43N	2W
PANAMA: cap. Panama	45	8N	80W
Panama Canal	45	Inset	
Panama City: U.S.A.	47	30N	86W
Panay: i., Phil.	91	11N	122E
Pangong Ra.: China	88	34N	80E
Panjim: India	88	15N	74E
Pantar: i., Indonesia	91	8S	124E
Pantellaria: i., Italy	69	37N	12E
Paoki: China	94	34N	107E
Paoshan: China	92	25N	99E
Paoting: China	94	39N	115E
Paotow: China	94	41N	110E
Papua: & gulf, Papua New Guinea	99	7S	145E
PAPUA NEW GUINEA: cap. Port Moresby	99	5S	145E
Pará: r., Brazil	54	1S	48W
Paracel Is.: S. China S.	91	16N	112E
PARAGUAY: cap. Asuncion	56	23S	58W
Paraguay: r., S. Am.	49	26S	58W
Parakou: Benin	108	9N	3E
PARAMARIBO: Surinam	54	6N	55W
Paramus: U.S.A.	35	41N	74W
Paramushir: i., U.S.S.R.	83	51N	155E
Paraná: Argentina	56	32S	60W
Paraná: r., S. Am.	56	25S	53W
Parbati: r., India	88	23N	77E
Parbhani: India	88	19N	77E
Parchim: E. Germany	74	53N	12E
Pardubice: Czech.	68	50N	16E
PARIS: France	113	—	—
Paris: U.S.A.	46	34N	96W
Parkersburg: U.S.A.	47	39N	82W
Parkes: Australia	101	33S	148E
Park Range: U.S.A.	48	40N	107W
Park Rapids: town, U.S.A.	49	47N	95W
Parma: Italy	75	45N	10E
Parma: U.S.A.	47	41N	82W
Parnaiba: Brazil	54	3S	42W
Parnassós: mtn., Greece	69	38N	22E
Páros: i., Greece	69	37N	25E
Parramatta: Austl.	115	34S	151E
Parsons: U.S.A.	49	37N	95W
Parthenay: France	73	47N	0
Partizansk: U.S.S.R.	83	43N	133E
Pasadena: U.S.A.	37	34N	118W
Pascagoula: & r., U.S.A.	47	30N	89W
Pasco: U.S.A.	48	46N	119W
Passaic: U.S.A.	35	41N	74W
Passau: W. Germany	75	49N	13E
Passchendaele: Belg.	72	51N	3E
Passero, C.: Sicily	69	37N	15E
Pasto: Colombia	54	1N	77W
Patagonia: reg., Arg.	55	45S	70W
Patay: France	72	48N	2E
Paterson: U.S.A.	35	41N	74W
Pathankot: India	88	32N	76E
Pathfinder Res.: U.S.A.	48	42N	107W
Patiala: India	88	30N	76E
Patna: India	88	26N	85E
Patos, Lagoa dos: Brazil	56	31S	51W
Pátrai (Patras): Greece	69	38N	22E
Pattani: Thailand	92	6N	101E
Pau: France	73	43N	0
Paulistana: Brazil	54	8S	41W
Paulo Afonso Falls: Brazil	54	9S	38W
Pavia: Italy	75	45N	9E
Pavlodar: U.S.S.R.	85	52N	77E
Payette: & r., U.S.A.	48	44N	117W
Paysandu: Uruguay	56	32S	58W
Pearl: r., U.S.A.	46	32N	90W
Pease: r., U.S.A.	46	34N	100W
Pechenga: U.S.S.R.	70	70N	31E
Pechora: r., U.S.S.R.	84	63N	56E
Pecos: & r., U.S.A.	46	31N	104W
Pécs: Hungary	68	46N	18E
Pedro, Pt.: Sri Lanka	88	10N	80E
Pedro Miguel Locks: Panama Canal	45	Inset	
Peebinga: Australia	101	35S	141E
Peebles: Scotland	62	56N	3W
Pee Dee: r., U.S.A.	47	34N	79W
Peel: I. of Man	62	54N	5W
Pegasus Bay: N.Z.	104	43S	173E
Pegu: Burma	92	17N	96E
Peh: r., China	95	24N	113E
Peian: China	90	48N	127E
Peine: W. Germany	74	52N	10E
Peipus, L.: U.S.S.R.	71	58N	27E
PEKING (Peiping): China	114	—	—
Pelee: i., U.S.A.	47	42N	83W
Pelican Point: S.W. Afr. (Namibia)	111	23S	14E
Peloponnese: penin., Greece	69	38N	22E
Pelotas: Brazil	56	32S	52W
Pelusium, Bay of: Egypt	109	Inset	
Pelvoux, Mont: Fr.	73	45N	6E
Pematangsiantar: Indonesia	92	2N	99E
Pemba: Zambia	111	17S	27E
Pemba: i., Tanzan.	110	5S	40E
Pembroke: Wales	63	52N	5W
Pendembu: Sierra Leone	108	8N	11W
Pendleton: U.S.A.	48	46N	119W
Pend Oreille L.: U.S.A.	48	48N	116W
Penganga: r., India	88	20N	77E
Pengpu: China	94	33N	117E
Penmarch, Pte. de: France	72	48N	4W
Pennar: r., India	88	14N	77E
Pennine Alps: Switzerland/Italy	75	46N	7E
Pennines: mtns., Eng.	62	54N	2W
Pennsylvania: State, U.S.A.	47	41N	77W
Penobscot: r., U.S.A.	15	45N	68W
Penrith: Australia	101	34S	151E
Penrith: England	62	55N	3W
Pensacola: U.S.A.	47	30N	87W
Pentland Firth: Scot.	61	59N	3W
Penza: U.S.S.R.	84	53N	45E
Penzance: England	63	50N	6W
Peoria: U.S.A.	49	41N	90W
Perche, Collines du: hills, France	72	49N	1E
Percy Is.: Australia	100	22S	150E
Perdu, Mont: Fr./Sp.	73	43N	0
Pergamino: Arg.	56	34S	61W
Périgord: reg., France	73	45N	1E
Périgueux: France	73	45N	1E
Perim I.: Yemen P.D.R.	87	13N	43E
Perm: U.S.S.R.	84	57N	55E
Pernik: Bulgaria	69	43N	23E
Péronne: France	72	50N	3E
Perpignan: France	73	43N	3E
PERSIA: see IRAN			
Persian Gulf	87	27N	52E
Perth: Australia	100	32S	116E
Perth: Scotland	62	56N	3W
Perth Amboy: U.S.A.	35	41N	74W
PERU: cap. Lima	54	10S	75W
Peru Basin: Pacific O.	103	15S	85W
Peru-Chile Trench: Pacific Ocean	103	20S	75W
Perugia: Italy	69	43N	12E
Pesaro: Italy	75	44N	13E
Pescadores: is., Taiwan	95	24N	120E
Pescara: Italy	69	42N	14E
Peshawar: Pakistan	88	34N	71E
Pessac: France	73	45N	1W
Petange: Lux.	72	50N	6E
Peterborough: Austl.	101	33S	139E
Peterborough: Eng.	63	53N	0
Peterhead: Scotland	61	57N	2W
Petersburg: Alaska, U.S.A.	24	57N	133W
Petersburg: Va., U.S.A.	47	37N	78W
Petone: N.Z.	104	41S	175E
Petoskey: U.S.A.	19	45N	85W
Petropavlovsk: U.S.S.R.	85	55N	69E
Petropavlovsk-Kamchatskiy: U.S.S.R.	83	53N	159E
Petrópolis: Brazil	56	23S	43W
Petroşeni: Romania	69	45N	23E
Petrozavodsk: U.S.S.R.	84	62N	35E
Petukhovo: U.S.S.R.	85	55N	68E
Pfälzer Bergland: plat., W. Germany	74	49N	8E
Pforzheim: W. Ger.	74	49N	9E
Phanom Dongrak: mtns., Thailand	92	14N	103E
Phan Rang: Vietnam	92	12N	109E
Phan Thiet: Vietnam	92	10N	108E
Phenix City: U.S.A.	47	32N	85W
Phet Buri: Thailand	92	13N	99E
Philadelphia: U.S.A.	50	40N	75W
PHILIPPINES, THE: cap. Manila	91	10N	123E
Philippine Sea	91	18N	130E
Philip Smith Mts.: U.S.A.	30	68N	147W
PHNOM PENH: Cambodia	93	11N	105E
Phoenix: U.S.A.	48	34N	112W
Phoenix Is.: Pac. O.	102	3S	175W
Phong Saly: Laos	92	21N	102E
Phu Cuong: Vietnam	92	10N	106E
Phuket: Thailand	93	8N	98E
Piacenza: Italy	75	45N	10E
Piatra-Neamţ: Rom.	68	47N	26E
Piave: r., Italy	75	46N	12E
Picardy: Old Prov., France	72	50N	2E
Picton: N.Z.	104	41S	174E
Piedmont: Reg., It.	75	45N	8E
Piedras Negras: Mex.	52	29N	101W
Pierre: U.S.A.	49	44N	100W
Pietarsaari: Finland	70	64N	23E
Pietermaritzburg: South Africa	111	30S	30E
Piet Retief: S. Africa	111	27S	31E
Pigeon: r., U.S.A./Canada	49	48N	90W
Pikeville: U.S.A.	47	37N	83W
Pilcomayo: r., S. Am.	54	23S	62W
Pilsen: see Plzen			
Pinang: i., Malaysia	92	5N	100E
Pinar del Rio: Cuba	53	22N	84W
Pindus Mts.: Greece	69	40N	21E
Pine Bluff: U.S.A.	46	34N	92W
Pine Island Sound: U.S.A.	47	27N	82W
Pinerolo: Italy	75	45N	7E
Pinkiang: see Harbin			
Pinnaroo: Australia	101	35S	141E
Pinos, I. de: Cuba	53	22N	83W
Pinsk: U.S.S.R.	71	52N	26E
Piraieus: Greece	69	38N	24E
Pirgos: Greece	69	38N	22E
Pirmasens: W. Ger.	74	49N	8E
Pisa: Italy	75	44N	10E
Pistoia: Italy	75	44N	11E
Pit: r., U.S.A.	48	41N	121W
Pitcairn I.: Pac. O.	103	25S	130W
Piteşti: Romania	69	45N	25E
Pittsburg: Kansas, U.S.A.	49	37N	95W
Pittsburg: Texas, U.S.A.	46	33N	95W
Pittsburgh: U.S.A.	47	40N	80W
Piura: Peru	54	5S	81W
Placetas: Cuba	53	22N	80W
Plainfield: U.S.A.	35	41N	74W
Plantaurel, Mts. du: France	73	43N	1E
Plata, Rio de la: r., S. America	56	35S	57W
Platte: r., U.S.A.	49	41N	100W
Plattsburg: U.S.A.	19	45N	74W
Plauen: E. Germany	74	50N	12E
Plenty, Bay of: N.Z.	104	38S	177E
Plentywood: U.S.A.	49	49N	105W
Pleven: Bulgaria	69	43N	25E
Ploeşti: Romania	69	45N	26E
Plomb du Cantal: mtn., France	73	45N	3E
Plombières: France	72	48N	6E
Plovdiv: Bulgaria	69	42N	25E
Plumtree: Rhodesia (Zimbabwe)	111	20S	28E
Plymouth: England	63	50N	4W
Plzen (Pilsen): Czech.	68	50N	13E
Po: r., Italy	75	45N	10E
Pocatello: U.S.A.	48	43N	112W
Poçoes: Brazil	54	15S	40W
Pointe Noire: Congo	110	5S	12E
Poissy: France	72	49N	2E
Poitiers: France	73	47N	0
Poitou: Old Prov., Fr.	73	47N	1W
Poix: France	72	50N	2E
POLAND: cap. Warsaw	68	52N	20E
Polotsk: U.S.S.R.	68	55N	29E
Poltava: U.S.S.R.	84	50N	35E
Polunochnoye: U.S.S.R.	85	62N	60E
Pomeranian Bay: E. Ger./Pol.	71	54N	14E
Pomona: S.W. Africa (Namibia)	111	27S	15E
Ponape: i., Pacific O.	102	8N	159E
Ponca City: U.S.A.	49	37N	97W
Ponce: Puerto Rico	45	18N	67W
Pondicherry: India	88	12N	80E
Ponta Grossa: Brazil	56	24S	47W
Pont-à-Mousson: Fr.	72	49N	6E
Ponta Porã: Brazil	54	22S	56W
Pontarlier: France	73	47N	6E
Pontchartrain, L.: U.S.A.	47	30N	90W
Pontevedra: Spain	67	42N	9W
Pontiac: U.S.A.	47	43N	83W
Pontianak: Indonesia	91	0	109E
Pontic Mts.: Turkey	86/7	42N	35E
Pontivy: France	72	48N	3W
Pontoise: France	113	49N	2E
Pontresina: Switz.	75	46N	10E
Pontypool: Wales	63	52N	3W
Pontypridd: Wales	63	52N	3W
Poole: England	63	51N	2W
Poona: India	88	18N	74E
Poopo, L.: Bolivia	54	18S	67W
Poperinghe: Belg.	72	51N	3E
Poplar Bluff: U.S.A.	46	37N	90W
Popocatepetl: volc., Mexico	52	19N	99W
Porbandar: India	88	22N	70E
Porcupine: r., Canada/U.S.A.	30	67N	142W
Pori: Finland	70	61N	22E
Port Adelaide: Austl.	101	35S	139E
Portadown: N. Irel.	62	54N	6W
Portaferry: N. Irel.	62	54N	6W
Portalegre: Portugal	67	39N	7W
Port Alfred: S. Afr.	111	34S	27E
Port Angeles: U.S.A.	48	48N	123W
Port Antonio: Jam.	53	18N	76W
Port Arthur: U.S.A.	46	30N	94W
Port Augusta: Austl.	101	32S	138E
PORT-AU-PRINCE: Haiti	45	19N	72W
Port Chalmers: N.Z.	104	46S	171E
Port Elizabeth: South Africa	111	34S	26E
Port Ellen: Scotland	62	56N	6W
Port Fuad: Egypt	109	Inset	
Port Harcourt: Nig.	108	5N	7E
Port Hedland: Austl.	98	20S	119E
Port Huron: U.S.A.	19	43N	82W
Port Jackson: sd., Austl.	115	34S	151E

Rosario — Saranac Lake

The World

Place	Page	Lat.	Long.
Rosario: Argentina	56	33S	61W
Roscoff: France	72	49N	4W
Roseburg: U.S.A.	48	43N	123W
Roseires: Sudan	109	12N	34E
Rosendaël: France	72	51N	2E
Rosenheim: W. Ger.	75	48N	12E
Rosetta: Egypt	86	32N	30E
Ross Ice Shelf: Antarctica	116	80S	180
Rosslare Harbour: R. of Ireland	62	52N	6W
Ross-on-Wye: Eng.	62	52N	3W
Ross Sea: Antarctica	116	76S	175W
Rostock: E. Germany	74	54N	12E
Rostov: U.S.S.R.	84	47N	40E
Roswell: U.S.A.	49	33N	105W
Rothbury: England	62	55N	2W
Rothenburg: W. Ger.	74	49N	10E
Rotherham: England	63	53N	1W
Rothesay: Scotland	62	56N	5W
Roti: i., Indonesia	91	10S	124E
Roto: Australia	101	33S	146E
Rotorua: N.Z.	104	38S	176E
Rotterdam: Neth.	74	52N	4E
Rottweil: W. Ger.	74	48N	9E
Roubaix: France	72	51N	3E
Rouen: France	72	49N	1E
Roundup: U.S.A.	48	46N	109W
Roussillon: Old Prov., France	73	43N	3E
Rovaniemi: Finland	70	66N	26E
Rovereto: Italy	75	46N	11E
Rovigo: Italy	75	45N	12E
Rovno: U.S.S.R.	84	51N	26E
Roxburgh: N.Z.	104	46S	169E
Royale, Isle: U.S.A.	49	48N	89W
Royal Tunbridge Wells: England	63	51N	0
Royan: France	72	46N	1W
Royston: England	63	52N	0
Ruahine Range: N.Z.	104	40S	176E
Ruapehu: mtn., N.Z.	104	39S	176E
Rub' al Khali: desert, Saudi Arabia	87	20N	50E
Rubtsovsk: U.S.S.R.	85	52N	81E
Rudok: China	88	34N	80E
Ruffec: France	73	46N	0
Rugby: England	63	52N	1W
Rügen: i., E. Germany	68	54N	13E
Ruhr: district, W. Ger.	64	Inset	
Rukwa, L.: Tanzania	110	8S	32E
Rum Jungle: Austl.	98	13S	131E
Ruse: Bulgaria	69	44N	26E
Rush: R. of Ireland	62	54N	6W
Russian Soviet Fed. Socialist Rep.: U.S.S.R.	82/3	—	—
Rutland: U.S.A.	19	44N	73W
Ruvuma: r., Africa	110	11S	37E
Ruwenzori, Mt.: Uganda	110	1N	30E
RWANDA: cap. Kigali	110	2S	30E
Ryazn': U.S.S.R.	84	55N	40E
Rybach'ye: U.S.S.R.	85	43N	76E
Rybinsk: & res., U.S.S.R.	84	58N	38E
Ryukyu Is. (Nansei Is.): Japan	90	27N	127E
Ryukyu Trench: Pacific Ocean	102	27N	130E
Rzeszów: Poland	68	50N	22E
Rzhev: U.S.S.R.	84	56N	35E
Saale: r., E. Germany	74	50N	12E
Saalfeld: E. Germany	74	51N	11E
Saar: Land, W. Ger.	74	49N	7E
Saar: r., W. Germany	74	50N	7E
Saarbrucken: W. Ger.	74	49N	7E
Saaremaa: i., U.S.S.R.	71	58N	23E
Sabadell: Spain	67	42N	2E
Sabah: State, Malaysia	91	5N	118E
Sabinas: Mexico	52	28N	101W
Sabine: r., U.S.A.	46	31N	94W
Sabkhat Minjora: salt flat, Saudi Arabia	87	20N	53E
Sable, Cape: U.S.A.	47	25N	81W
Saco: U.S.A.	19	43N	70W
Sacramento: & r., U.S.A.	48	39N	121W
Sacramento Mts.: U.S.A.	46	34N	105W
Sá da Bandeira (Lubango): Angola	111	15S	14E
Sado: i., Japan	93	38N	138E
Safford: U.S.A.	48	32N	110W
Safi: Morocco	108	32N	9W
Sagaing: Burma	92	21N	95E
Saginaw: U.S.A.	19	44N	84W
Sagua la Grande: Cuba	53	23N	80W
Sahara Desert: North Africa	108/9	—	—
Saharan Atlas: mts., Algeria	108	33N	3E
Saharanpur: India	88	30N	78E
Sai: r., India	88	26N	82E
Saigon: see Ho Chi Minh City			
St. Affrique: France	73	44N	3E
St. Albans: England	62	52N	0
St. Amand: France	72	50N	3E
St. Amand-Mont-Rond: France	73	47N	2E
St. André, Plaine de: France	72	49N	1E
St. Andrews: Scot.	62	56N	3W
St. Anne's: England	62	54N	3W
St. Augustine: U.S.A.	47	30N	81W
St. Bride's Bay: Wales	63	52N	5W
St. Brieuc: France	72	49N	3W
St. Catherine's Pt.: England	63	51N	1W
St. Chamond: France	73	45N	5E
St. Christopher (St. Kitts): i., W. Indies	45	17N	63W
St. Clair, L.: U.S.A.	19	43N	83W
Saint Clair Shores: U.S.A.	33	42N	83W
St. Claude: France	73	46N	6E
St. Cloud: U.S.A.	49	46N	94W
St. Croix: i., W. Ind.	45	18N	65E
St. David's Head: Wales	63	52N	5W
St. Denis: France	113	49N	2E
St. Dié: France	72	48N	7E
St. Dizier: France	72	49N	5E
St. Elias, Mt.: & mtns., U.S.A./Canada	12	60N	140W
Saintes: France	73	46N	1W
Saintes, Les: is., West Indies	45	16N	62W
St. Étienne: France	73	45N	4E
St. Flour: France	73	45N	3E
St. Francis: r., U.S.A.	46	35N	90W
St. Francis, C.: South Africa	111	34S	25E
St. Gallen: Switz.	75	47N	9E
St. George: U.S.A.	48	37N	114W
St. George, C.: U.S.A.	47	30N	85W
St. George's Chan.: Wales/R. of Irel.	63	52N	6W
St. Germain-en-Laye: France	113	49N	2E
St. Gothard Pass: Switzerland	75	47N	9E
St. Govan's Head: Wales	63	52N	5W
St. Helena: i., Atl. O.	57	16S	8W
St. Helena Bay: South Africa	111	32S	18E
St. Helens: England	62	53N	3W
Saint Helens: U.S.A.	48	46N	123W
St. Helier: Chan. Is.	63	Inset	
St. Ingbert: Germany	74	49N	7E
St. Ives: England	63	50N	5W
St. Jean-de-Luz: Fr.	73	43N	2W
St. Jean de Maurienne: Fr.	73	45N	6E
St. Jean Pied-de-Port: France	73	43N	1W
St. John: r., U.S.A.	15	47N	69W
St. Johns: r., U.S.A.	47	30N	82W
St. Joseph: Mo., U.S.A.	46	40N	95W
St. Joseph: & r., Mich., U.S.A.	47	42N	87W
St. Julien: France	73	46N	6E
St. Junien: France	73	46N	1E
St. Kitts: see St. Christopher			
St. Lawrence: i., Bering Sea	12	63N	170W
St. Lô: France	72	49N	1W
St. Louis: U.S.A.	46	39N	90W
St. Louis: Senegal	108	16N	16W
St. Lucia: i., W. Ind.	45	14N	61W
St. Malo: & gulf, Fr.	72	49N	2W
St. Martin: i., West Indies	45	18N	63W
St. Mary's: England	63	50N	6W
St. Mary's: Australia	99	42S	148E
St. Marys: U.S.A.	50	41N	79W
St. Matthew: i., Bering Sea	12	60N	172W
St. Maurice: Switz.	75	46N	7E
Ste. Menehould: Fr.	72	49N	5E
St. Moritz: Switz.	75	46N	10E
St. Nazaire: France	72	47N	2W
St. Omer: France	72	51N	2E
Saintonge: Old Prov., France	75	45N	1W
St. Paul: i., Indian O.	89	39S	78E
St. Paul: U.S.A.	49	45N	93W
St. Paul, C.: Ghana	108	6N	1E
St. Paul Rocks: Atlantic Ocean	57	0	30W
St. Peter Port: Channel Islands	63	Inset	
St. Petersburg: U.S.A.	47	28N	83W
St. Pierre-Quilbignon: France	72	48N	5W
St. Pol: France	72	50N	2E
St. Pons: France	73	43N	3E
St. Quentin: France	72	50N	3E
St. Raphaël: France	73	43N	7E
Ste. Savine: France	72	48N	4E
St. Servan: France	72	49N	2W
St. Thomas: i., West Indies	45	18N	65W
St. Tropez: France	73	43N	7E
St. Valéry en Caux: France	72	50N	1E
St. Vincent, C. (Cabo de São Vincent): Portugal	67	37N	9W
St. Vincent: i., West Indies	45	13N	61W
Saipan: i., Pac. O.	102	15N	145E
Saiwūn: Yemen P.D.R.	87	16N	49E
Sakai: Japan	93	35N	135E
Sakaka: Sau. Arab.	87	30N	40E
Sakakawea, L.: U.S.A.	49	48N	102W
Sakata: Japan	93	39N	140E
Sakhalin: i., U.S.S.R.	83	50N	143E
Sakhalin Bay: U.S.S.R.	83	54N	141E
Sakishima Group: Japan	90	24N	124E
Salado: r., Argentina	56	30S	61W
Salala: Oman	87	17N	54E
Salamanca: Mexico	52	21N	101W
Salamanca: Spain	67	41N	6W
Sala-y-Gomez: i., Pacific Ocean	103	26S	105W
Salekhard: U.S.S.R.	82	66N	66E
Salem: India	88	12N	78E
Salem: Mass., U.S.A.	51	42N	71W
Salem: Oregon, U.S.A.	48	45N	123W
Salem: Va., U.S.A.	47	37N	80W
Salerno: Italy	69	41N	15E
Salida: U.S.A.	49	38N	106W
Salima: Malawi	110	14S	35E
Salina: U.S.A.	49	39N	98W
Salinas: U.S.A.	48	37N	122W
Saline: r., U.S.A.	46	34N	92W
Salisbury: Australia	101	35S	139E
Salisbury: & Plain, England	63	51N	2W
SALISBURY: Rhodesia (Zimbabwe)	111	18S	31E
Salmon: r., U.S.A.	48	45N	116W
Salmon River Mts.: U.S.A.	48	45N	115W
Salon de Provence: France	73	44N	5E
Salonica: see Thessalonica			
Salop: Co., England	63	53N	3W
Salpausselka: moraine, Finland	71	61N	25E
Salt: r., U.S.A.	46	40N	92W
Salta: Argentina	56	25S	65W
Saltillo: Mexico	52	25N	101W
Salt Lake City: U.S.A.	48	41N	112W
Salt Range: Pakistan	88	33N	73E
Salto: Uruguay	56	31S	58W
Saluzzo: Italy	75	45N	7E
Salvador (Bahia): Brazil	54	13S	38W
Salween: r., Burma	90	20N	98E
Salzach: r., Austria	75	47N	12E
Salzburg: & Prov., Austria	75	48N	13E
Salzgitter: W. Ger.	74	52N	10E
Samah de Langreo: Spain	67	43N	7W
Samah: China	93	18N	110E
Samar: i., Phil.	91	12N	125E
Samarinda: Indon.	91	0	117E
Samarkand: U.S.S.R.	85	40N	67E
Samarra: Iraq	87	34N	44E
Sambalpur: India	88	22N	84E
Sambor: U.S.S.R.	68	50N	23E
Sambre: r., France/Belgium	72	50N	4E
Samoa Is.: Pac. O.	102	12S	172W
Sámos: i., Greece	69	38N	27E
Samothrace: i., Greece	69	40N	26E
Samsun: Turkey	86	41N	36E
SAN'A: Yemen	87	15N	44E
Sanandaj: Iran	87	35N	47E
San Angelo: U.S.A.	46	31N	100W
San Antonio: U.S.A.	46	29N	99W
San Antonio: r., U.S.A.	46	29N	97W
San Benito Is.: Mex.	44	28N	115W
San Bernardino: U.S.A.	48	34N	117W
San Blas, C.: U.S.A.	47	30N	85W
Sancerre: France	73	47N	3E
San Clemente: i., U.S.A.	48	33N	118W
San Cristóbal: Venez.	54	8N	72W
Sancti Spiritus: Cuba	53	22N	79W
Sandakan: Malaysia	91	6N	118E
Sandgate: Australia	100	27S	153E
San Diego: U.S.A.	48	33N	117W
Sandpoint: U.S.A.	48	48N	117W
Sandringham: Eng.	63	53N	1E
Sandusky: U.S.A.	47	41N	83W
San Félix I.: Pac. O.	103	26S	80W
San Fernando: Chile	54	34S	71W
San Fernando: r., Mexico	52	25N	98W
San Fernando: Phil.	91	17N	120E
Sanford: Fla., U.S.A.	47	29N	80W
Sanford: Maine, U.S.A.	19	43N	71W
Sanford: N.C., U.S.A.	47	35N	79W
San Francisco: r., U.S.A.	48	33N	109W
San Francisco: U.S.A.	36	—	—
Sangar: U.S.S.R.	83	64N	127E
Sangre de Cristo Range: U.S.A.	49	37N	105W
San Joaquin: r., U.S.A.	48	37N	120W
SAN JOSÉ: Costa Rica	45	10N	84W
San Jose: U.S.A.	48	37N	122W
San Jose: r., U.S.A.	48	35N	108W
San Juan: Argentina	55	32S	69W
SAN JUAN: Puerto Rico	45	18N	66W
San Juan Mts.: U.S.A.	48	37N	107W
San Justo: Argentina	56	31S	61W
San Luis: Argentina	55	33S	66W
San Luis Obispo: U.S.A.	48	35N	121W
San Luis Potosi: Mex.	52	22N	101W
San Marcos: U.S.A.	46	30N	98W
SAN MARINO: cap. San Marino	75	44N	12E
San Mateo: U.S.A.	36	38N	122W
San Pedro: r., U.S.A.	48	33N	111W
Sanquhar: Scotland	62	55N	4W
San Rafael: Arg.	54	35S	68W
San Rafael: U.S.A.	36	38N	123W
San Remo: Italy	75	44N	8E
SAN SALVADOR: El Salvador	44	14N	89W
San Sebastián: Spain	67	43N	2W
San Severo: Italy	69	42N	15E
Santa Ana: U.S.A.	37	34N	118W
Santa Barbara: & chan., U.S.A.	48	34N	120W
Santa Barbara Is.: U.S.A.	48	34N	120W
Santa Catalina: i. & gulf, U.S.A.	48	33N	118W
Santa Clara: Cuba	53	22N	80W
Santa Clara: U.S.A.	48	37N	122W
Santa Cruz: Bolivia	54	18S	63W
Santa Cruz: U.S.A.	48	37N	122W
Santa Cruz: i., U.S.A.	48	34N	120W
Santa Cruz de Tenerife: Canary Islands	108	28N	16W
Santa Fé: Argentina	56	32S	61W
Santa Fe: U.S.A.	49	36N	106W
Santa Maria: Brazil	56	30S	54W
Santa Maria: U.S.A.	48	35N	120W
Santa Marta: Col.	45	11N	74W
Santa Monica: U.S.A.	37	34N	118W
Santana do Livramento: Brazil	56	31S	55W
Santander: Spain	67	43N	4W
Santa Paula: U.S.A.	48	34N	119W
Santarém: Portugal	67	39N	9W
Santa Rosa: Arg.	55	37S	64W
Santa Rosa: Calif., U.S.A.	48	38N	123W
Santa Rosa: N. Mex., U.S.A.	49	35N	105W
Santa Rosa: i., U.S.A.	48	34N	120W
SANTIAGO: Chile	55	33S	71W
Santiago: Dom. Rep.	45	20N	71W
Santiago, Rio Grande de: r., Mexico	52	21N	104W
Santiago de Compostelo: Spain	67	43N	9W
Santiago de Cuba: Cuba	53	20N	76W
Santiago del Estero: Argentina	54	28S	64W
Santo André: Brazil	56	24S	47W
Santo Antônio: Brazil	54	9S	64W
SANTO DOMINGO: Dom. Repub.	45	19N	70W
Santos: Brazil	56	24S	46W
Sanvic: France	72	49N	0
Sanyate: r., Rhodesia (Zimbabwe)	111	17S	29E
São Bernardo do Campo: Brazil	56	24S	47W
São Francisco: r., Brazil	54	12S	43W
São Leopoldo: Brazil	56	30S	51W
São Luis: Brazil	54	3S	44W
Saône: r., France	73	46N	5E
São Paulo: Brazil	56	24S	46W
São Roque, C. de: Brazil	54	5S	35W
São Vicente: Brazil	56	24S	46W
São Vicente, Cabo de (C. St. Vincent): Portugal	67	37N	9W
Sapporo: Japan	93	43N	141E
Saragossa: see Zaragoza			
Sarajevo: Yugo.	69	44N	18E
Saranac Lake: city, U.S.A.	19	44N	74W

The World

Saransk — South Australia

	Page	Lat.	Long.
Saransk: U.S.S.R.	84	54N	45E
Sarasota: U.S.A.	47	27N	83W
Saratov: U.S.S.R.	84	52N	46E
Saravane: Laos	92	15N	106E
Sarawak: *State,* Malaysia	91	3N	113E
Sardina: *i.,* Medit. Sea	64	40N	9E
Sargasso Sea	57	30N	60W
Sark: *i.,* Chan. Is.	63	*Inset*	
Sarny: U.S.S.R.	84	51N	27E
Sarpsborg: Norway	71	59N	11E
Sarrebourg: France	72	49N	7E
Sarreguemines: Fr.	72	49N	7E
Sarthe: *r.,* France	72	48N	0
Sasebo: Japan	93	33N	130E
Sassari: Sardinia	67	41N	9E
Satara: India	88	17N	74E
Satpura Range: India	88	22N	77E
Satu-Mare: Romania	68	48N	23E
SAUDI ARABIA: *cap.* Riyadh	87	—	—
Sauerland: *upland,* W. Germany	74	51N	8E
Saugor: India	88	24N	79E
Sauk Center: U.S.A.	49	46N	95W
Sault Ste. Marie: U.S.A.	19	46N	84W
Saumur: France	73	47N	0
Sauternes: France	73	45N	0
Sava: *r.,* Yugoslavia	69	45N	17E
Savannah: & *r.,* Ga., U.S.A.	47	32N	81W
Savannah: Tenn., U.S.A.	47	35N	88W
Savannakhet: Laos	93	17N	105E
Saverne: France	72	49N	7E
Savigliano: Italy	75	45N	8E
Savona: Italy	75	44N	8E
Savonlinna: Finland	70	62N	29E
Savoy: *Old Prov.,* Fr.	73	46N	6E
Savoy Alps: France	73	46N	7E
Sawu: *i.* & *sea,* Indon.	91	10S	122E
Saxmundham: Eng.	63	52N	1E
Sayn Shanda: Mong.	83	45N	110E
Sca Fell: *mtn.,* Eng.	62	54N	3W
Scapa Flow: *inlet,* Scotland	61	59N	3W
Scarborough: Eng.	62	54N	0
Schaerbeek: Belgium	72	51N	4E
Schaffhausen: Switz.	75	48N	8E
Scheldt: *r.,* Belgium/Netherlands	72	51N	4E
Schenectady: U.S.A.	51	43N	74W
Schiedam: Neth.	74	52N	4E
Schio: Italy	75	46N	11E
Schleswig: W. Ger.	68	54N	10E
Schmalkalden: E. Ger.	74	51N	10E
Schoonebeek: Neth.	74	53N	7E
Schouwen-Duiveland: *i.,* Netherlands	72	52N	4E
Schwäbisch-Gmünd: W. Germany	75	49N	10E
Schwandorf: W. Ger.	74	49N	12E
Schweinfurt: W. Ger.	74	50N	10E
Schwelm: W. Ger.	64	51N	7E
Schwerin: E. Ger.	74	54N	11E
Schwerte: W. Ger.	64	51N	8E
Schwyz: Switz.	75	47N	9E
Scilly, Is. of: Eng.	63	50N	6W
Scoresby Sound: Greenland	13	71N	23W
Scotia Sea: S. Atlantic Ocean	55	57S	50W
SCOTLAND: *cap.* Edinburgh	61	—	—
Scottsbluff: U.S.A.	49	42N	104W
Scranton: U.S.A.	50	41N	76W
Scunthorpe: England	62	54N	1W
Seal, C.: S. Africa	111	34S	24E
Seattle: U.S.A.	36	—	—
Sebakwe: *r.,* Rhodesia (Zimbabwe)	111	18S	30E
Sebcha di Tauorga: *bay,* Libya	86	32N	15E
Sebha Oasis: Libya	108	27N	15E
Sechura Desert: Peru	54	6S	80W
Sedalia: U.S.A.	46	39N	93W
Sedan: France	72	50N	5E
Sedbergh: England	62	54N	3W
Seeheim: S.W. Afr. (Namibia)	111	27S	18E
Segovia: Spain	67	42N	4W
Segovia: *r.,* Hond./Nicaragua	45	15N	84W
Ségre: *r.,* Spain	67	42N	1E
Segura: *r.,* Spain	67	38N	2W
Seine: *r.,* France	72	49N	1E
Seine, Baie de la: Fr.	72	49N	1W
Sekondi-Takoradi: Ghana	108	5N	2W
Selby: England	62	54N	1W
Selenga: *r.,* Mongolia	83	49N	101E
Sélestat: France	72	48N	7E
Selety-Tengiz, L.: U.S.S.R.	85	53N	73E
Selkirk: Scotland	62	56N	3W
Selma: U.S.A.	47	32N	87W
Selsey Bill: *hd.,* Eng.	63	51N	1W
Selukwe: Rhodesia (Zimbabwe)	111	20S	30E
Selvas: *geog. reg.,* Brazil	54	6S	65W
Semarang: Indonesia	91	7S	110E
Seminoe Res.: U.S.A.	48	42N	107W
Semiozernoye: U.S.S.R.	85	52N	64E
Semipalatinsk: U.S.S.R.	85	50N	80E
Semnān: Iran	87	35N	53E
Senanga: Zambia	111	16S	23E
Sendai: Japan	93	38N	141E
Seneca L.: U.S.A.	50	43N	77W
SENEGAL: & *r., cap.* Dakar	108	15N	15W
Senja: *i.,* Norway	70	69N	18E
Senlis: France	72	49N	3E
Sennar: & *dam,* Sudan	86	13N	34E
Sens: France	72	48N	3E
SEOUL (KYONGSONG): S. Korea	90	38N	127E
Septentrional, Meseta: *plat.,* Spain	67	42N	5W
Seremban: Malaysia	92	3N	102E
Seria: Brunei	91	4N	114E
Serian: Malaysia	92	1N	111E
Serio: *r.,* Italy	75	45N	10E
Serov: U.S.S.R.	85	60N	60E
Serowe: Botswana	111	23S	27E
Serra dos Parecis: Brazil	54	12S	60W
Serra Geral: *mtns.,* Brazil	56	25S	51W
Sérrai: Greece	69	41N	23E
Sète: France	73	43N	4E
Sétif: Algeria	67	36N	5E
Setúbal: Portugal	67	38N	9W
Sevan, L.: U.S.S.R.	84	41N	46E
Sevastopol': U.S.S.R.	84	45N	34E
Sevenoaks: England	112	51N	0
Severn: *r.,* England	63	52N	2W
Severnaya Zemlya: *is.:* U.S.S.R.	83	79N	95E
Severn Tunnel: Eng.	63	52N	3W
Severoural'sk: U.S.S.R.	85	60N	60E
Seville: Spain	67	37N	6W
Sèvre Nantaise: *r.,* France	73	47N	1W
Sèvre Niortaise: *r.,* France	73	46N	1W
Sèvres: France	113	49N	2E
Seward: U.S.A.	12	60N	150W
Seward Peninsula: U.S.A.	12	66N	165W
Seychelles-Mauritius Plateau: Indian O.	89	10S	57E
Seydhisfjördhur: Ice.	70	65N	14W
Seymour: U.S.A.	46	33N	99W
Sézanne: France	72	49N	4E
Sfax: Tunisia	108	35N	11E
'S-GRAVENHAGE: *see* HAGUE, THE			
Shabwah: Yemen P.D.R.	87	16N	47E
Shackleton Range: Antarctica	116	82S	160E
Shaftesbury: England	63	51N	2W
Shahjahanpur: India	88	28N	80E
Shahrezā: Iran	87	32N	52E
Shahrūd: Iran	87	36N	55E
Shakhty: U.S.S.R.	84	48N	40E
Shalym: U.S.S.R.	85	53N	88E
Shamrock: U.S.A.	46	35N	100W
Shamva: Rhodesia (Zimbabwe)	111	17S	32E
Shangani: *r.,* Rhod. (Zimbabwe)	111	19S	28E
Shanghai: China	95	31N	121E
Shangkiu: China	94	34N	116E
Shanklin: England	63	51N	1W
Shannon: *r.,* R. of Ireland	61	53N	9W
Shansi: *Prov.,* China	94	37N	112E
Shan States: Burma	93	22N	98E
Shantung: *Prov.,* China	94	36N	117E
Shantung Peninsula: China	94	37N	120E
Shaohing: China	95	30N	121E
Shaokuan (Kükong): China	95	25N	113E
Shaoyang: China	95	27N	111E
Sharjah: U.A.E.	87	25N	55E
Sharon: U.S.A.	47	41N	81W
Shasta, Lake: U.S.A.	48	41N	122W
Shasta, Mt.: U.S.A.	48	41N	122W
Shawnee: U.S.A.	46	35N	97W
Sheboygan: U.S.A.	49	44N	88W
Sheenjek: *r.,* U.S.A.	30	68N	144W
Sheffield: England	63	53N	1W
Sheffield: U.S.A.	47	35N	88W
Shelby: U.S.A.	48	48N	112W
Shelbyville: U.S.A.	47	35N	86W
Shelekhov Bay: U.S.S.R.	83	60N	157E
Shenandoah: *r.,* U.S.A.	47	38N	79W
Shensi: *Prov.,* China	94	35N	109E
Shenyang (Mukden): China	94	42N	123E
Shepparton: Austl.	101	36S	145E
Sheppey, I. of: Eng.	63	51N	1E
Sherborne: England	63	51N	3W
Sheridan: U.S.A.	48	45N	107W
Sherlovaya Gora: U.S.S.R.	83	51N	116E
Sherman: U.S.A.	46	34N	97W
's-Hertogenbosch: Netherlands	74	52N	5E
Shetland Is.: Scot.	61	60N	2W
Sheyenne: *r.,* U.S.A.	49	48N	99W
Shibeli: *r.,* Ethiopia/Somali Republic	109	6N	43E
Shigatse: China	89	29N	89E
Shihchan: China	83	51N	126E
Shihkiachwang: China	94	38N	115E
Shikoku: *i.,* Japan	93	34N	134E
Shillong: India	89	26N	92E
Shimoga: India	88	14N	76E
Shimonoseki: Japan	93	34N	131E
Shipki Pass: India/China	88	32N	79E
Shiraz: Iran	87	30N	53E
Shire: *r.,* Malawi	111	16S	35E
Shizuoka: Japan	93	35N	139E
Shkodër: Albania	69	42N	19E
Shoalwater Bay: Australia	100	22S	150E
Sholapur: India	88	18N	76E
Shortland Is.: Solomon Is.	99	7S	156E
Shreveport: U.S.A.	46	32N	94W
Shrewsbury: England	63	53N	3W
Shrewsbury: U.S.A.	51	42N	72W
Shuntak: China	95	23N	113E
Shwangliao: China	90	44N	123E
Shwebo: Burma	92	23N	96E
Si: *r.,* China	95	23N	112E
Sialkot: Pakistan	88	32N	75E
SIAM: *see* **THAILAND**			
Siam, Gulf of	92	10N	102E
Sian: China	94	34N	109E
Siang: *r.,* China	95	27N	112E
Siangfan: China	94	32N	112E
Siangtan: China	95	28N	112E
Siauliai: U.S.S.R.	68	56N	23E
Sibenik: Yugoslavia	69	44N	16E
Sibi: Pakistan	88	30N	68E
Sibiu: Romania	68	46N	25E
Sibu: Malaysia	92	2N	112E
Sicilian Channel: Medit. Sea	69	37N	12E
Sicily: *i.* & *Reg.,* Italy	69	—	—
Sidi-bel-Abbès: Alg.	67	35N	1W
Sidmouth: England	63	51N	3W
Sidney: U.S.A.	49	48N	104W
Sidra, Gulf of: Libya	109	32N	17E
Sieg: *r.,* W. Germany	74	51N	8E
Siegburg: W. Germany	74	51N	7E
Siegen: W. Germany	74	51N	8E
Siem Reap: Cambodia	92	13N	103E
Siena: Italy	69	43N	11E
Sierra de Juárez: *mtns.,* Mexico	48	32N	116W
SIERRA LEONE: *cap.* Freetown	108	8N	12W
Sierra Madre Occidental (W. Sierra Madre): *mtns.,* Mexico	52	25N	105W
Sierra Madre Oriental (E. Sierra Madre): *mtns.,* Mexico	52	25N	100W
Sierra Madre del Sur (S. Sierra Madre): *mtns.,* Mexico	52	17N	100W
Sierra Morena: *mtns.,* Spain	67	38N	5W
Sierra Nevada: *mtns.,* Spain	67	37N	3W
Sierra Nevada: *mtns.,* U.S.A.	48	38N	120W
Siglufjördhur: Ice.	70	66N	19W
Sihanoukville: *see* Kompong Som			
Siirt: Turkey	87	38N	42E
Sikeston: U.S.A.	47	37N	89W
Sikhote Alin' Range: U.S.S.R.	83	47N	137E
Sikkim: *State,* India	88	27N	88E
Silchar: India	89	25N	93E
Silistra: Bulgaria	69	44N	27E
Silverton: Colorado, U.S.A.	48	38N	108W
Silverton: Oregon, U.S.A.	48	45N	123W
Simanggang: Malaysia	92	1N	111E
Simferopol': U.S.S.R.	84	45N	34E
Simla: India	88	31N	77E
Simonstown: S. Afr.	111	34S	18E
Simplon Pass: Switz.	75	46N	8E
Simpson Desert: Australia	98	25S	137E
Sinai: *penin.* & *mtn.,* Egypt	86	28N	34E
Sind: *Prov.,* Pakistan	88	26N	69E
SINGAPORE: *cap.* Singapore	92	1N	104E
Singaradja: Indon.	91	8S	115E
Singkep: *i.,* Indon.	91	1S	104E
Singleton: Australia	101	33S	151E
Singtai: China	94	37N	114E
Sining: China	90	36N	102E
Sinkiang Uighur A.R.: China	82/3	40N	85E
Sinuiju: N. Korea	90	40N	124E
Sinyang: China	94	32N	113E
Sion: Switzerland	75	46N	7E
Sioux City: U.S.A.	49	42N	96W
Sioux Falls: *city,* U.S.A.	49	44N	97W
Siretul: *r.,* Romania	68	47N	26E
Sirte: Libya	84	31N	17E
Sisak: Yugoslavia	69	45N	16E
Sisseton: U.S.A.	49	46N	97W
Sīstān: *geog. reg.,* Iran/Afghan.	87	31N	61E
Sisteron: France	73	44N	6E
Sitapur: India	88	27N	81E
Sittang: *r.,* Burma	92	18N	97E
Sivas: Turkey	86	40N	37E
Siwa: Egypt	86	29N	25E
Skagerrak: *str.,* Denmark/Nor.	71	57N	8E
Skagway: U.S.A.	24	60N	135W
Skåne: *reg.,* Sweden	71	56N	14E
Skegness: England	63	53N	0
Skellefte: *r.,* Sweden	70	65N	20E
Skellefteå: Sweden	70	65N	21E
Skerries: R. of Irel.	62	54N	6W
Skien: Norway	71	59N	10E
Skikda: Algeria	67	37N	7E
Skipton: England	62	54N	2W
Skiros: *i.,* Greece	69	39N	25E
Skive: Denmark	71	57N	9E
Skokie: U.S.A.	34	42N	88W
Skomer I.: Wales	63	52N	5W
Skopje: Yugoslavia	69	42N	21E
Skövde: Sweden	71	58N	14E
Skye: *i.,* Scotland	61	57N	6W
Slavonski Brod: Yugoslavia	69	49N	18E
Slieve Donard: *mtn.,* N. Ireland	62	54N	6W
Sligo: R. of Ireland	61	54N	8W
Sliven: Bulgaria	69	43N	26E
Slonim: U.S.S.R.	68	53N	25E
Slough: England	112	52N	1W
Smoky Hill: *r.,* U.S.A.	49	39N	100W
Smolensk: U.S.S.R.	84	55N	32E
Snaefell: *mtn.,* I. of Man	62	54N	4W
Snake: *r.,* U.S.A.	48	46N	118W
Snowdon: *mtn.,* Wales	63	53N	4W
Snowy: *mtns.* & *r.,* Australia	101	37S	148E
Snyder: U.S.A.	46	33N	101W
Sochi: U.S.S.R.	84	44N	40E
Society Is.: Pac. O.	103	17S	150W
Socotra: *i.,* Arab. Sea	87	13N	54E
Soda Mts.: Libya	84	29N	15E
Söderhamn: Sweden	71	61N	17E
Soest: W. Germany	74	52N	8E
Soest: Netherlands	74	52N	5E
Sofala: Moz.	111	20S	35E
SOFIYA: Bulgaria	69	43N	23E
Sognafjorden: *fd.,* Norway	71	61N	6E
Soissons: France	72	49N	3E
Sokoto: Nigeria	108	13N	5E
Solent, The: *chan.,* England	63	51N	1W
Solihull: England	63	52N	2W
Solikamsk: U.S.S.R.	84	60N	57E
Solimões: *r., see* Amazon			
Solingen: W. Germany	64	51N	7E
Sologne: *reg.,* France	72	48N	2E
Solomon Is.: Pacific O.	99	10S	155E
Solothurn: Switz.	75	47N	8E
Solway Firth: Eng./Scotland	62	55N	4W
SOMALI REPUBLIC: *cap.* Mogadiscio	109	—	—
Sombor: Yugoslavia	68	46N	19E
Sombrero: *i.,* West Indies	45	18N	63W
Somerset: *Co.,* Eng.	63	51N	3W
Somerset: U.S.A.	47	37N	85W
Somerville: Mass., U.S.A.	33	42N	71W
Somerville: N.J., U.S.A.	50	41N	75W
Somme: *r.,* France	72	50N	2E
Sommières: France	73	44N	4E
Son: *r.,* India	88	24N	81E
Sondre Stromfjörd: Greenland	13	67N	52W
Songea: Tanzania	110	11S	36E
Songkhla: Thailand	92	7N	101E
Sonoyta: Mexico	48	32N	113W
Soonwald: *mtns.,* W. Germany	74	50N	8E
Sopron: Hungary	68	48N	16E
Soria: Spain	67	42N	2W
Sorocaba: Brazil	56	23S	48W
Souk Ahras: Algeria	67	36N	8E
Souris: *r.,* U.S.A./Canada	49	49N	101W
Sousse: Tunisia	108	36N	11E
Southampton: Eng.	63	51N	1W
South Australia:			

South Bend — Tay

The World

Place	Page	Lat.	Long.
State, Australia	98	30S	135E
South Bend: U.S.A.	47	42N	86W
South Carolina: *State*, U.S.A.	47	34N	81W
South China Sea	91	15N	115E
South Dakota: *State*, U.S.A.	49	45N	100W
South Downs: Eng.	63	51N	0
Southeast Indian Ridge: Indian Ocean	89	45S	95E
Southeast Pacific Basin: Pacific Ocean	103	45S	100W
Southend-on-Sea: England	63	52N	1E
Southern Alps: N.Z.	104	43S	170E
Southern Cross: Australia	100	31S	119E
Southern Ocean	102/3	—	—
Southern Sierra: *see* Sierra Madre del Sur			
Southern Uplands: Scotland	62	55N	4W
Southfield: U.S.A.	33	42N	83W
South Foreland: Eng.	63	51N	1E
Southgate: U.S.A.	33	42N	83W
South Georgia: *i.*, Atlantic Ocean	55	54S	37W
South Island: N.Z.	104	—	—
SOUTH KOREA: *cap.* Seoul	90	37N	127E
Southland: *district*, N.Z.	104	46S	168E
South Orkney Is.: Southern Ocean	57	61S	45W
Southport: England	62	54N	3W
South Sandwich Is.: Southern Ocean	55	57S	27W
South Sandwich Trench: Southern O.	57	57S	25W
South Shetland Is.: Antarctica	55	62S	60W
South Shields: Eng.	62	55N	1W
South Sioux City: U.S.A.	49	42N	96W
South Uist: *i.*, Scot.	53	57N	7W
South West Africa (Namibia): S. Africa	111	24S	17E
Southwest Indian Ridge: Indian Ocean	89	35S	55E
Southwest Pacific Basin: Pacific Ocean	103	35S	150W
Southwark: England	112	52N	0
Southwest Cape: New Zealand	104	47S	168E
Sovetsk: U.S.S.R.	68	55N	22E
Soviet Harbour: U.S.S.R.	83	49N	140E
SPAIN: *cap.* Madrid	67	—	—
Spalding: England	63	53N	0
Spandau: W. Germany	113	53N	13E
Spanish Town: Jam.	53	18N	77W
Sparks: U.S.A.	48	40N	120W
Spartanburg: U.S.A.	47	35N	82W
Spárti: Greece	69	37N	22E
Spartivento, C.: Italy	69	38N	16E
Spasskoye: U.S.S.R.	85	52N	69E
Speedwell, C.: U.S.S.R.	82	75N	55E
Spencer Gulf: Austl.	101	34S	137E
Spennymoor: Eng.	62	55N	2W
Spenser Mts.: N.Z.	104	42S	173E
Spessart: *mts.*, W. Ger.	74	50N	9E
Spey: *r.*, Scotland	61	57N	3W
Speyer: W. Germany	74	49N	8E
Spiekeroog: *i.*, W. Ger.	74	54N	8E
Spitsbergen (Svalbard): *i.*, Arctic Ocean	82	78N	20E
Split: Yugoslavia	69	44N	16E
Spokane: U.S.A.	48	48N	117W
Spree: *r.*, E. & W. Ger.	113	52N	14E
Springbok: S. Africa	111	30S	18E
Springdale: U.S.A.	46	36N	94W
Springfield: Colo., U.S.A.	49	37N	103W
Springfield: Illinois, U.S.A.	49	40N	90W
Springfield: Mass., U.S.A.	51	42N	73W
Springfield: Mo., U.S.A.	49	37N	93W
Springfield: Ohio, U.S.A.	47	40N	84W
Springfield: Oregon, U.S.A.	48	44N	123W
Springsure: Austl.	100	24S	148E
Spungabera: Moz.	111	20S	33E
Spurn Hd.: England	62	54N	0
Sretensk: U.S.S.R.	83	52N	118E
SRI LANKA: *cap.* Colombo	88	7N	81E
Srinagar: India	88	34N	75E
Stafford: & *Co.*, Eng.	62	53N	2W
Staines: England	112	51N	1W
Stamford: England	63	53N	0
Stamford: U.S.A.	51	41N	74W
STANLEY: Falkland Is.	55	52S	58W
Stanthorpe: Austl.	101	29S	152E
Stara Zagora: Bulg.	69	42N	26E
Start Pt.: England	63	50N	4W
Stassfurt: E. Germany	74	52N	12E
State College: *city*, U.S.A.	50	41N	78W
Staten I.: U.S.A.	35	41N	74W
Statesville: U.S.A.	47	36N	81W
Staunton: U.S.A.	47	38N	79W
Stavanger: Norway	71	59N	6E
Stavelot: Belgium	72	50N	6E
Stavropol': U.S.S.R.	84	45N	42E
Steigerwald: *mts.*, W. Germany	74	50N	10E
Steinkjer: Norway	70	64N	11E
Stellenbosch: S. Afr.	111	34S	19E
Stelvio Pass: Switz./Italy	75	47N	10E
Stendal: E. Germany	74	53N	12E
Steppes: *geog. reg.*, U.S.S.R.	82	50N	70E
Sterling: Colorado, U.S.A.	49	41N	103W
Sterling: Ill., U.S.A.	49	42N	90W
Sterlitamak: U.S.S.R.	84	54N	56E
Steubenville: U.S.A.	47	40N	81W
Stevens Point: *City*, U.S.A.	49	45N	89W
Stewart I.: N.Z.	104	47S	168E
Steyr: Austria	75	48N	14E
Stillwater: U.S.A.	46	36N	97W
Štip: Yugoslavia	69	42N	22E
Stirling: Scotland	62	56N	4W
Stirling Range: Austl.	100	34S	118E
STOCKHOLM: Sweden	71	59N	18E
Stockport: England	63	53N	2W
Stockton: U.S.A.	48	38N	121W
Stockton on Tees: England	62	55N	1W
Stockton Plateau: U.S.A.	46	30N	102W
Stoke on Trent: Eng.	63	53N	2W
Stonehaven: Scot.	62	57N	2W
Stonehenge: *hist.*, England	63	51N	2W
Stonington I.: Antarctica	116	67S	67W
Stony Tunguska: *r.*, U.S.S.R.	83	61N	95E
Store Bælt: *str.*, Den.	71	55N	11E
Stor L.: Sweden	61	63N	14E
Stornoway: Scot.	70	58N	6W
Storuman: Sweden	70	65N	17E
Stour: *r.*, Dorset, England	63	51N	2W
Stour: *r.*, Kent, Eng.	63	51N	1E
Stour: *r.*, Suff., Eng.	63	52N	1E
Stowmarket: Eng.	63	52N	1E
Stralsund: E. Germany	68	54N	13E
Strangford L.: N. Ireland	62	54N	6W
Stranraer: Scotland	62	55N	5W
Strasbourg: France	72	49N	8E
Stratford on Avon: England	63	52N	2W
Stratford: N.Z.	104	39S	174E
Strathclyde: *Reg.*, Scot.	62	56N	4W
Strathmore: *valley*, Scotland	62	57N	3W
Straubing: W. Ger.	74	49N	12E
Strawberry Mt.: U.S.A.	48	44N	119W
Stromboli: *volc.*, Italy	69	39N	15E
Stroud: England	63	52N	2W
Strumble Head: Wales	63	52N	5W
Stuart Highway: Australia	98	20S	134E
Sturt Desert: Austl.	101	28S	141E
Stuttgart: W. Germany	75	49N	9E
Stuttgart: U.S.A.	46	35N	91W
Suakin: Sudan	109	19N	37E
Suanhwa: China	94	41N	115E
Subotica: Yugoslavia	68	46N	20E
Suceava: Romania	68	48N	26E
Suchiate: Mexico	44	15N	92W
Suchow (Tungshan): China	94	34N	117E
Suchow: China	95	32N	121E
Sucre: Bolivia	54	19S	65W
SUDAN: *cap.* Khartoum	109	—	—
Sudbury: England	63	52N	1E
Sudeten Mts.: Czech./Poland	68	51N	16E
Sue Peaks: *mtn.*, U.S.A.	46	30N	103W
Suez: & *gulf*, Egypt	86	30N	32E
Suez Canal: Egypt	109	*Inset*	
Suffolk: *Co.*, Eng.	63	52N	1E
Suffolk: U.S.A.	47	37N	77W
Sugarloaf Pt.: Austl.	101	32S	153E
Suir: *r.*, R. of Ireland	61	52N	7W
Suita: Japan	93	35N	135E
Sukhona: *r.*, U.S.S.R.	84	60N	42E
Sukhumi: U.S.S.R.	84	43N	41E
Sukkur: Pakistan	88	28N	69E
Sula: *is.*, Indonesia	91	2S	125E
Sulaiman Range: Pakistan	88	30N	70E
Sulawesi: *see* Celebes			
Sulphur Springs: U.S.A.	46	33N	96W
Sulu Sea: Phil.	91	8N	120E
Sumatra: *i.*, Indon.	91	0	100E
Sumba: *i.*, Indonesia	91	10S	120E
Sumbawa: *i.*, Indon.	91	8S	117E
Sumen: Bulgaria	69	43N	27E
Sumgait: U.S.S.R.	84	40N	50E
Summan Dahna: *desert*, Saudi Arabia	87	26N	47E
Summit: Alaska, U.S.A.	12	63N	149W
Summit: N.J., U.S.A.	35	41N	74W
Sumter: U.S.A.	47	34N	80W
Sumy: U.S.S.R.	84	51N	35E
Sunbury: U.S.A.	50	41N	77W
Sundarbans: *district*, India/Bangladesh	88	22N	90E
Sunda Str.: Indon.	91	6S	106E
Sunderland: England	62	55N	1W
Sundsvall: *I.*, Sweden	70	62N	17E
Sungari Res.: China	90	43N	127E
Sungkiang: China	95	31N	121E
Suo-nada: *gulf*, Japan	93	34N	132E
Superior: U.S.A.	49	47N	92W
Superior, L.: U.S.A./Canada	19	47N	90W
Suphan Buri: Thailand	92	14N	100E
Sur (Tyre): Lebanon	86	33N	35E
Surabaja: Indonesia	91	7S	113E
Surakarta: Indonesia	91	7S	111E
Surat: India	88	21N	73E
SURINAM: *cap.* Paramaribo	54	4N	56W
Surrey: *Co.*, Eng.	63	51N	0
Susa: Italy	75	45N	7E
Susquehanna: *r.*, U.S.A.	50	40N	76W
Sussex, E.: *Co.*, England	63	51N	0
Sussex, W.: *Co.*, England	63	51N	1W
Susuman: U.S.S.R.	83	63N	148E
Sutlej: *r.*, Pakistan/India	88	30N	73E
Sutherland: Australia	115	34S	151E
Sutton: England	112	51N	0
Suttor: *r.*, Australia	100	21S	147E
SUVA: Fiji	99	18S	178E
Suwannee: *r.*, U.S.A.	47	30N	83W
Suzuka: Japan	93	35N	137E
Svalbard *see* Spitsbergen			
Svendborg: Den.	71	55N	11E
Sverdlovsk: U.S.S.R.	85	57N	61E
Svir': *r.*, U.S.S.R.	84	61N	34E
Swabian Jura: *mts.*, W. Germany	75	48N	9E
Swaffham: England	63	53N	1E
Swain Reefs: Austl.	100	22S	152E
Swakopmund: S.W. Africa (Namibia)	111	23S	14E
Swale: *r.*, England	62	54N	2W
Swan: *r.*, Australia	100	32S	116E
Swanage: England	63	51N	2W
Swan Hill: *town*, Australia	101	35S	144E
Swansea: Wales	63	52N	4W
Swatow: China	95	23N	117E
SWAZILAND: *cap.* Mbabane	111	27S	32E
SWEDEN: *cap.* Stockholm	70/1	—	—
Sweetwater: U.S.A.	46	32N	100W
Sweetwater Canal: Egypt	109	*Inset*	
Swellendam: S. Afr.	111	34S	20E
Swilly, L.: R. of Irel.	61	55N	8W
Swindon: England	63	52N	2W
Swinoujście: Poland	68	54N	14E
SWITZERLAND: *cap.* Bern	75	47N	8E
Sydney: Australia	115	34S	151E
Syktyvkar: U.S.S.R.	84	62N	51E
Sylacauga: U.S.A.	47	33N	86W
Sylhet: Bangladesh	89	25N	92E
Syracuse: Sicily	69	37N	15E
Syracuse: U.S.A.	50	43N	76W
Syr Darya (Jaxartes): *r.*, U.S.S.R.	85	43N	67E
SYRIA: *cap.* Damascus	86/7	—	—
Syrian Desert: Arabia	87	32N	40E
Syzran': U.S.S.R.	84	53N	48E
Szczecin: Poland	68	53N	15E
Szczecinek: Poland	68	54N	17E
Szechwan: *Prov.*, China	95	30N	105E
Szeged: Hungary	68	46N	20E
Szolnok: Hungary	68	47N	20E
Szombathely: Hung.	68	47N	17E
Tabora: Tanzania	110	5S	33E
Tabriz: Iran	87	38N	46E
Tacna: Peru	54	18S	70W
Tacoma: U.S.A.	48	47N	122W
Tacuarembó: Uruguay	56	32S	56W
Tadzhik S.S.R.: U.S.S.R.	85	38N	72E
Taegu: S. Korea	90	36N	128E
Taejon: S. Korea	90	37N	127E
Taff: *r.*, Wales	63	52N	3W
Tafilalet Oasis: Mor.	108	31N	4W
Taganrog: U.S.S.R.	84	47N	39E
Tagliamento: *r.*, Italy	75	46N	13E
Tagus: *r.*, Sp./Port.	67	40N	8W
Tahiti: *i.*, Pacific O.	103	18S	150W
Tahoe, Lake: U.S.A.	48	39N	120W
Tai, Lake: China	95	31N	121E
Taichow: China	94	32N	120E
Taichung: Taiwan	95	24N	121E
Taif: Saudi Arabia	87	21N	40E
Taihape: N.Z.	104	40S	176E
Tainan: Taiwan	95	23N	120E
TAIPEI: Taiwan	95	25N	122E
Taipeh Shan: *ra.*, China	95	31N	116E
Taiping: Malaysia	92	5N	101E
Taitao Penin.: Chile	55	47S	75W
T'aitung: Taiwan	93	23N	121E
TAIWAN *cap.* Taipei	95	24N	121E
Taiyuan: China	94	38N	112E
Ta'iz: Yemen	87	14N	44E
Tak: Thailand	92	17N	99E
Takamatsu: Japan	93	34N	134E
Takaoka: Japan	93	37N	137E
Takla Makan: *desert*, China	82/3	39N	83E
Talara: Peru	54	5S	81W
Talaud Is.: Indon.	91	4N	127E
Talavera de la Reina: Spain	67	40N	5W
Talbot, C.: Austl.	98	14S	127E
Tali: China	92	35N	110E
Talladega: U.S.A.	47	33N	86W
Tallahassee: U.S.A.	47	30N	84W
Tallinn: U.S.S.R.	71	59N	25E
Tamale: Ghana	108	9N	1W
Tamana: *r.*, U.S.A.	30	63N	143W
Tamar: *r.*, England	63	51N	4W
Tamatave: Malagasy Republic	110	18S	49E
Tambov: U.S.S.R.	84	53N	41E
Tamil Nadu: *State*, India	88	10N	78E
Tampa: & *bay*, U.S.A.	47	28N	82W
Tampere: Finland	70	61N	24E
Tampico: Mexico	52	23N	98W
Tamsag Bulag: Mongolia	83	47N	117E
Tamworth: Australia	101	31S	151E
Tana: *fd.*, Norway	70	70N	28E
Tana, L.: Ethiopia	109	12N	37E
Tanana: U.S.A.	12	65N	152W
TANANARIVE: Malagasy Rep.	110	18S	47E
Tandil: Argentina	55	37S	59W
Tandou, L.: Austl.	101	33S	142E
Tanezrouft: *geog. reg.*, Algeria	108	23N	0
Tanga: Tanzania	110	5S	39E
Tanganyika, L.: Afr.	110	8S	30E
Tangier: Morocco	67	36N	6W
Tangshan: China	94	39N	118E
Tanimbar Is.: Indon.	91	7S	131E
Tanta: Egypt	86	31N	31E
TANZANIA: *cap.* Dodoma	110	—	—
Tapajos: *r.*, Brazil	54	6S	57W
Tapa Shan: *mts.*, China	94	32N	108E
Tapti: *r.*, India	88	21N	75E
TARABULUS: Tripoli	86	33N	13E
Tarakan: Indonesia	91	3N	118E
Taranaki: *dist.*, N.Z.	104	39S	174E
Taranto: & *gulf*, Italy	69	40N	17E
Tarare: France	73	46N	4E
Tararua Ra.: N.Z.	104	41S	175E
Tarascon: France	73	44N	5E
Tarawa: *i.*, Pac. O.	102	1N	173E
Tarbes: France	73	43N	0
Tardenois: *hills*, Fr.	72	49N	4E
Taree: Australia	101	32S	152E
Tarim: *r.*, China	85	41N	83E
Tarko-Sale: U.S.S.R.	83	65N	78E
Tarn: *r.*, France	73	44N	2E
Târnovo: Bulgaria	69	43N	26E
Tarragona: Spain	67	41N	1E
Tarsus: Turkey	86	37N	35E
Tartary, Gulf of: U.S.S.R.	83	50N	140E
Tartu: U.S.S.R.	71	58N	27E
Tashkent: U.S.S.R.	85	41N	69E
Tasman, Mt.: N.Z.	104	44S	170E
Tasman Bay: & *mts.*, New Zealand	104	41S	173E
Tasmania: *i.* & *State*, Australia	99	42S	146E
Tasman Sea: Pac. O.	99	35S	165E
Tassili-n-Ajjer: *plat.*, Algeria	108	26N	8E
Tatarsk: U.S.S.R.	85	55N	76E
Tateyama: Japan	93	35N	140E
Tatry: *mtns.*, Czech.	68	49N	20E
Tatung: China	94	40N	113E
Taumarunui: N.Z.	104	39S	175E
Taunton: England	63	51N	3W
Taunton: U.S.A.	51	42N	71W
Taunus: *mts.*, W. Ger.	74	50N	8E
Taupo: & *lake*, N.Z.	104	39S	176E
Tauranga: N.Z.	104	38S	176E
Taurus Mts.: Turkey	86	37N	35E
Tavda: & *r.*, U.S.S.R.	85	58N	65E
Tavistock: England	63	51N	4W
Tavoy: Burma	92	14N	98E
Taw: *r.*, England	63	51N	4W
Tawas Pt.: U.S.A.	19	44N	83W
Tawitawi: *i.*, Phil.	91	5N	120E
Tay: *r.*, Scotland	62	56N	3W

The World

Tay, L — Udon Thani

	Page	Lat.	Long.
Tay, L.: Scotland	62	56N	4W
Tayside: *Reg.*, Scotland	62	57N	3W
Taymyr, L.: U.S.S.R.	83	75N	102E
Taymyr Peninsula: U.S.S.R.	83	75N	105E
Tayshet: U.S.S.R.	85	56N	97E
Tbilisi: U.S.S.R.	84	42N	45E
Teague: U.S.A.	46	32N	96W
Te Anau, L.: N.Z.	104	45S	168E
Te Awamatu: N.Z.	104	38S	175E
Tecuci: Romania	68	46N	27E
Tees: *r.*, England	62	55N	1W
Teesside: England	62	55N	1W
TEGUCIGALPA: Honduras	45	14N	87W
TEHRĀN: Iran	87	35N	51E
Tehuacán: Mexico	52	18N	97W
Tehuantepec: *gulf & isthmus*, Mexico	53	17N	94W
Teifi: *r.*, Wales	63	52N	4W
Tekely: U.S.S.R.	85	45N	79E
Tekirdağ: Turkey	69	41N	27E
Tell Atlas: *mtns.*, Algeria	67	37N	7E
Tell el Kebir: Egypt	109	*Inset*	
Telok Anson: Malaysia	92	4N	101E
Telukbetung: Indon.	91	5S	105E
Temir-Tau: U.S.S.R.	85	50N	73E
Temora: Australia	101	34S	148E
Temple: U.S.A.	46	31N	97W
Temuco: Chile	55	39S	73W
Tenda Pass: Fr./Italy	75	44N	7E
Tende: France	73	44N	8E
Tenerife: *i.*, Canary Is.	108	28N	16W
Tengchung: China	92	25N	98E
Tengiz, L.: U.S.S.R.	85	50N	69E
Tenkiller Ferry Res.: U.S.A.	46	36N	95W
Tennant Creek: *town*, Australia	98	20S	134E
Tennessee: *r.*, & *State*, U.S.A.	47	36N	88W
Tenterfield: Austl.	101	29S	152E
Ten Thousand Is.: U.S.A.	47	26N	82W
Tepic: Mexico	52	21N	105W
Teramo: Italy	69	43N	14E
Teresina: Brazil	54	5S	43W
Terme di Valdieri: Italy	75	44N	7E
Termez: U.S.S.R.	85	37N	67E
Ternate: *i.*, Indon.	91	1N	127E
Terneuzen: Neth.	74	51N	4E
Terni: Italy	69	43N	13E
Ternopol': U.S.S.R.	68	50N	26E
Terre Haute: U.S.A.	47	39N	87W
Terschelling: *i.*, Netherlands	74	53N	5E
Teruel: Spain	67	40N	1W
Tessenei: Ethiopia	109	15N	37E
Test: *r.*, England	63	51N	1W
Tete: Mozambique	111	16S	34E
Tetlin Junction: U.S.A.	30	63N	142W
Tetuan: Morocco	67	36N	5W
Teutoburger Wald: W. Germany	74	52N	8E
Tewkesbury: Eng.	63	52N	2W
Texarkana: U.S.A.	46	33N	94W
Texas: *State*, U.S.A.	46	32N	100W
Texas City: U.S.A.	46	29N	95W
Texel: *i.*, Neth.	74	53N	5E
Texoma, L.: U.S.A.	46	34N	97W
Tezpur: India	89	27N	93E
Thabazimbi: S. Afr.	111	25S	27E
THAILAND: *cap.* Bangkok	92	15N	102E
Thal: *desert*, Pakistan	88	32N	72E
Thames: N.Z.	104	37S	176E
Thames: *r.*, England	63	52N	0
Thanet, Isle of: *dist.*, England	63	51N	1E
Thanh Hoa: Vietnam	92	19N	105E
Thanjavur: India	88	11N	79E
Thar Desert: India/Pakistan	88	27N	72E
Thásos: *i.*, Greece	69	41N	25E
Thaton: Burma	92	16N	97E
Thayetmyo: Burma	92	19N	95E
Thebes: *hist.*, Egypt	86	26N	33E
The Dalles: U.S.A.	48	46N	121W
The Hague: *see* Hague			
Thermopolis: U.S.A.	48	44N	108W
Thessalonica (Salonica): Greece	69	41N	23E
Thetford: England	63	52N	1E
Thief River Falls: *city*, U.S.A.	49	48N	96W
Thiérache: *hills*, France	72	50N	4E
Thiers: France	73	46N	4E
Thionville: France	72	49N	6E
Thira: *i.*, Greece	69	36N	25E
Thirsk: England	62	54N	1W
Thomasville: Ala., U.S.A.	47	32N	88W
Thomasville: Ga., U.S.A.	47	31N	84W
Thonon: France	73	46N	7E
Thore: *r.*, France	73	44N	2E
Thouars: France	73	47N	0
Three Kings Is.: N.Z.	104	34S	172E
Three Points, C.: Ghana	108	5N	2W
Three Springs: Austl.	100	30S	116E
Thule: Greenland	13	76N	68W
Thun: & *l.*, Switz.	75	47N	8E
Thur: *r.*, Switz.	75	48N	9E
Thüringer Wald: *mts.*, E. Germany	74	50N	11E
Thursday I.: Austl.	99	11S	142E
Thurso: Scotland	61	59N	3W
Tiaret: Algeria	67	35N	1E
Tiber: *r.*, Italy	69	43N	12E
Tibesti: *highlands*, Chad	108/9	—	—
Tibet: *Aut. Reg.*, China	88/9	33N	85E
Ticino: *r.*, Italy	75	45N	9E
Tien Shan: *range*, China/U.S.S.R.	85	42N	80E
Tientsin: China	94	39N	117E
Tierra del Fuego: *i.*, Argentina	55	54S	67W
Tiffin: U.S.A.	47	41N	83W
Tignes Res.: France	72	45N	7E
Tigris: *r.*, Turkey/Iraq	87	35N	44E
Tihama: *plain*, Sau. Arab.	87	20N	41E
Tijuana: Mexico	48	32N	117W
Tiksi: U.S.S.R.	83	72N	129E
Tilburg: Neth.	74	52N	5E
Tilbury: England	112	51N	0
Tillabéry: Niger	108	14N	1E
Timaru: N.Z.	104	44S	171E
Timbuktu: *see* Tombouctou			
Timişoara: Romania	68	46N	21E
Timor: *i. & sea*, Indonesia	91	10S	125E
Timsah, L.: Egypt	109	*Inset*	
Tipperary: R. of Ireland	61	52N	8W
TIRANE: Albania	69	41N	20E
Tiraspol': U.S.S.R.	68	47N	30E
Tire: Turkey	69	38N	28E
Tiree: *i.*, Scotland	61	56N	7W
Tirgu-Jiu: Romania	69	45N	23E
Tirgu Mureş: Romania	68	46N	25E
Tiruchirappalli: India	88	11N	79E
Tirunelveli: India	88	9N	78E
Tista: *r.*, Bangl./India	88	27N	89E
Titicaca, Lake: Peru/Bolivia	54	16S	69W
Titograd: Yugoslavia	69	42N	19E
Titovo Užice: Yugo.	69	44N	20E
Titov Veles: Yugo.	69	42N	22E
Tiverton: England	63	51N	4W
Tivoli: Italy	69	42N	13E
Tlálpan: Mexico	52	19N	99W
Tlemcen: Algeria	67	35N	1W
Tobago: *i.*, Trinidad & Tobago	45	11N	61W
Tobermory: Scot.	62	57N	6W
Tobol': *r.*, U.S.S.R.	85	56N	66E
Tobol'sk: U.S.S.R.	85	58N	68E
Tobruk: Libya	86	32N	24E
Tocantins: *r.*, Brazil	54	4S	50W
Toccoa: U.S.A.	47	35N	84W
Tocumwal: Austl.	101	36S	146E
TOGO: *cap.* Lomé	108	8N	1E
Tokelau: *is.*, Pac. O.	102	9S	171W
Tokorozawa: Japan	114	36N	139E
Tokushima: Japan	93	34N	134E
TOKYO: Japan	93	36N	140E
Tolbuhin: Bulgaria	69	44N	28E
Toledo: & *mtns.*, Spain	67	40N	4W
Toledo: Ohio, U.S.A.	47	42N	84W
Toledo: Oregon, U.S.A.	48	45N	124W
Tolo, G. of: Indon.	91	2S	122E
Tolstoy, C.: U.S.S.R.	83	59N	155E
Toluca de Lerdo: Mexico	52	19N	100W
Tomatlan: Mexico	44	20N	105W
Tombigbee: *r.*, U.S.A.	47	32N	88W
Tombouctou (Timbuktu): Mali	108	17N	3W
Tomini, Gulf of: Indonesia	91	0	121E
Tomsk: U.S.S.R.	85	56N	85E
Tonbridge: England	112	51N	0
TONGA: & *Trench*, Pacific Ocean	102	20S	175W
Tonkin, Gulf of: S.E. Asia	92	21N	108E
Tonle, Sap: *L.*, Cambodia	92	13N	104E
Tønsberg: Norway	71	59N	11E
Tooele: U.S.A.	48	41N	112W
Toowoomba: Austl.	100	28S	152E
Topeka: U.S.A.	49	39N	96W
Topozero: *L.*, U.S.S.R.	70	66N	32E
Torbay: England	63	60N	4W
Torgau: E. Germany	74	52N	13E
Torne: *r.*, Sweden/Finland	70	68N	19E
Tornio: Finland	70	66N	24E
Tororo: Uganda	110	1N	34E
Torquay: England	63	50N	4W
Torrance: U.S.A.	37	34N	118W
Torrens, L.: Austl.	101	31S	137E
Torreón: Mexico	52	26N	103W
Torres Strait: Austl.	99	10S	142E
Torridge: *r.*, England	61	51N	4W
Tortona: Italy	75	45N	9E
Tortosa: Spain	67	41N	1E
Toruń: Poland	68	53N	19E
Tosa-wan: *bay*, Japan	93	33N	134E
Touba: Senegal	108	15N	16W
Touggourt: Algeria	108	33N	6E
Toul: France	72	49N	6E
Toulon: France	73	43N	6E
Toulouse: France	73	44N	1E
Toungoo: Burma	92	19N	96E
Touraine: *Old Prov.*, France	73	47N	1E
Tourcoing: France	72	51N	3E
Tournai: Belgium	72	51N	3E
Tours: France	73	47N	1E
Towcester: England	63	52N	1W
Townshend I.: Austl.	100	22S	151E
Townsville: Austl.	100	19S	147E
Toyama: Japan	93	37N	137E
Toyohashi: Japan	93	35N	137E
Toyonaka: Japan	93	35N	135E
Toyota: Japan	93	35N	137E
Trabzon: Turkey	87	41N	40E
Trafalgar, C.: Spain	64	36N	6W
Tralee: R. of Ireland	61	52N	10W
Tranås: Sweden	70	58N	15E
Transkei: *self-governing State*, South Africa	111	31S	29E
Transvaal: *Prov.*, Rep. of South Africa	111	25S	29E
Transylvanian Alps: Romania	69	45N	24E
Trapani: Sicily	69	38N	12E
Traunstein: W. Ger.	75	48N	13E
Traveller's L.: Austl.	101	33S	142E
Traverse City: U.S.A.	19	45N	85W
Trelleborg: Sweden	71	55N	13E
Tremadoc Bay: Wales	63	53N	4W
Trent: *r.*, England	63	53N	1W
Trentino: *Reg.*, Italy	75	46N	11E
Trento: Italy	75	46N	11E
Trenton: Missouri, U.S.A.	49	40N	94W
Trenton: N.J., U.S.A.	51	40N	75W
Treviso: Italy	75	46N	12E
Trier: W. Germany	74	50N	7E
Trieste: Italy	75	46N	14E
Trikkala: Greece	69	40N	22E
Trincomalee: Sri Lanka	88	8N	81E
Trinidad: U.S.A.	49	37N	105W
TRINIDAD & TOBAGO: *cap.* Port of Spain	45	10N	61W
Trinity: *r.*, U.S.A.	46	31N	96W
Tripoli: Lebanon	86	34N	36E
Tripolis: Greece	69	38N	22E
Tripura: *State*, India	89	24N	92E
Tristan da Cunha: *i.*, Atlantic Ocean	57	38S	12W
Trivandrum: India	88	8N	77E
Troitsk: U.S.S.R.	85	54N	62E
Trollhättan: Sweden	71	58N	12E
Tromsø: Norway	70	70N	19E
Trona: U.S.A.	48	36N	117W
Trondheim: Norway	70	63N	11E
Trondheimsfjorden: *fd.*, Norway	70	64N	11E
Trowbridge: England	63	51N	2W
Troy: Ala., U.S.A.	47	32N	86W
Troy: N.Y., U.S.A.	51	42N	74W
Troy: *hist.*, Turkey	86	40N	26E
Troyes: France	72	48N	4E
Trujillo: Honduras	45	16N	86W
Trujillo: Peru	54	8S	79W
Truro: England	63	50N	5W
Truth or Consequences: U.S.A.	48	33N	107W
Tsaidam Swamps: China	90	37N	95E
Tsangpo: *r.*, China	89	29N	86E
Tselinograd: U.S.S.R.	85	51N	71E
Tsetserlig: Mong.	90	47N	102E
Tsimlyansk Res.: U.S.S.R.	84	48N	43E
Tsinan: China	94	37N	117E
Tsing Hai (Koko Nor): *l.*, China	90	37N	100E
Tsingtao: China	94	36N	120E
Tsining: Inner Mongolia; China	94	41N	113E
Tsining: Shantung, China	94	35N	117E
Tsinkiang (Chuanchow): China	95	25N	119E
Tsinling Shan: China	94	34N	108E
Tsitsihar: China	90	47N	124E
Tsu: Japan	93	35N	137E
Tsushima: *is.*, Japan	93	34N	129E
Tsumeb: S.W. Africa (Namibia)	111	19S	18E
Tsuni: China	92	27N	106E
Tsuyung: China	92	25N	101E
Tuam: R. of Ireland	61	54N	9W
Tuamotu Arch.: Pacific Ocean	103	15S	140W
Tuapse: U.S.S.R.	84	44N	39E
Tuatapere: N.Z.	104	46S	168E
Tubai Is.: Pac. O.	103	25S	150W
Tubarão: Brazil	56	28S	49W
Tübingen: W. Ger.	75	49N	9E
Tucson: U.S.A.	48	32N	111W
Tucumcari: U.S.A.	49	35N	104W
Tucupita: Venez.	54	9N	62W
Tudela: Spain	67	42N	2W
Tufts Abyssal Plain: Pacific Ocean	103	45N	140W
Tugssâq: Greenland	13	73N	55W
Tula: U.S.S.R.	84	54N	37E
Tulare: U.S.A.	48	36N	119W
Tulear: Malagasy Rep.	110	23S	44E
Tulia: U.S.A.	46	35N	102W
Tullahoma: U.S.A.	47	35N	86W
Tullamore: R. of Ireland	61	53N	7W
Tulle: France	73	45N	2E
Tulsa: U.S.A.	46	36N	96W
Tulufan: China	90	43N	89E
Tumaco: Colombia	54	2N	79W
Tumkur: India	88	13N	77E
Tungabhadra: *r.*, India	88	16N	76E
Tungchuan: China	94	35N	119E
Tunghsien (Tungchow): China	114	40N	117E
Tunghwa: China	90	42N	126E
Tungkwan: China	94	34N	110E
Tungshan: *see* Suchow			
Tungting, L.: China	95	29N	112E
TUNIS: Tunisia	108	37N	10E
TUNISIA: *cap.* Tunis	108	35N	10E
Tunja: Colombia	54	6N	73W
Tupelo: U.S.A.	46	34N	89W
Turanian Plain: U.S.S.R.	85	43N	60E
Turbat: Pakistan	88	26N	63E
Turbo: Colombia	54	8N	77W
Turda: Romania	68	47N	24E
Turfan Depression: China	83	43N	89E
Turgay: & *r.*, U.S.S.R.	85	50N	64E
Turgutlu: Turkey	69	39N	28E
Turin: Italy	75	45N	8E
Turkana (Rudolf), L.: Kenya	110	4N	36E
Turkestan: U.S.S.R.	85	43N	68E
TURKEY: *cap.* Ankara	86/7	—	—
Turkmen S.S.R.: U.S.S.R.	82/3	39N	57E
Turks Is.: W. Indies	45	22N	71W
Turku (Åbo): Finland	71	60N	22E
Turlock: U.S.A.	48	37N	121W
Turnagain, C.: N.Z.	104	40S	177E
Turnhout: Belgium	72	51N	5E
Turnu Măgurele: Romania	69	44N	25E
Turnu Severin: Romania	69	45N	23E
Tuscaloosa: U.S.A.	47	33N	88W
Tuscany: *Reg.*, Italy	75	44N	11E
Tushino: U.S.S.R.	114	55N	38E
Tuttlingen: W. Ger.	75	48N	9E
Tuvalu: *is.*, Pacific O.	102	8S	180
Tuxpan: Mexico	52	21N	97W
Tuxtla Gutiérrez: Mexico	53	17N	93W
Tuy Hoa: Vietnam	92	13N	109E
Tuyun: China	95	26N	107E
Tuz, L.: Turkey	86	38N	33E
Tweed: *r.*, England/Scotland	62	56N	2W
Twenty Mile House: U.S.A.	30	66N	144W
Twin Bridges: U.S.A.	48	45N	112W
Twin Falls: *city*, U.S.A.	48	43N	115W
Tygda: U.S.S.R.	83	53N	126E
Tyler: U.S.A.	46	32N	95W
Tyne, N. & S.: *rivs.*, England	62	32N	2W
Tyne and Wear: *Co.*, England	62	55N	1W
Tynemouth: England	62	55N	1W
Tyre: *see* Sur			
Tyrol: *Prov.*, Austria	75	47N	11E
Tyrrhenian Sea	69	40N	12E
Tywi: *r.*, Wales	63	52N	4W
Tyumen': U.S.S.R.	85	57N	65E
Tzepo: China	94	37N	118E
Ube: Japan	93	34N	131E
Uberaba: Brazil	54	20S	48W
Ubon Ratchathani: Thailand	92	15N	105E
Ubsa Nor: *L.*, Mong.	90	50N	93E
Ubundi: Zaire	110	0	25E
Ucayali: *r.*, Peru	54	7S	74W
Udaipur: India	88	25N	74E
Uddevalla: Sweden	71	58N	12E
Udd L.: Sweden	70	66N	18E
Udine: Italy	75	46N	13E
Udon Thani: Thailand	92	17N	103E

The World

Weifang – Zwolle

Place	Page	Lat.	Long.
Weifang: China	**94**	37N	118E
Weihai: China	**94**	38N	122E
Weimar: E. Germany	**74**	51N	11E
Weirton: U.S.A.	**47**	41N	81W
Weiser: U.S.A.	**48**	44N	117W
Weisshorn: mtn., Switzerland	**75**	46N	8E
Welkon: S. Africa	**111**	27S	27E
Welland: r., Eng.	**63**	52N	0
Wellesley Is.: Austl.	**98**	17S	139E
Wellesley: U.S.A.	**33**	42N	71W
Wellingborough: England	**63**	52N	1W
Wellington: Austl.	**101**	32S	149E
Wellington: England	**63**	53N	3W
WELLINGTON: N.Z.	**104**	41S	175E
Wells: U.S.A.	**48**	41N	115W
Welper: W. Germany	**64**	51N	7E
Welshpool: Wales	**63**	53N	3W
Welwyn Garden City: England	**112**	52N	0
Wem: England	**63**	53N	3W
Wembley: England	**112**	52N	0
Wenatchee: U.S.A.	**48**	47N	121W
Wenchow: China	**95**	28N	121E
Wendover: U.S.A.	**48**	41N	114W
Wenshan: China	**92**	23N	104E
Wensum: r., Eng.	**63**	53N	1E
Wentworth: Austl.	**101**	34S	141E
Wernigerode: E. Ger.	**74**	52N	11E
Wesel: W. Germany	**64**	52N	6E
Weser: r., W. Germany	**74**	53N	9E
Wesergebirge: mts., W. Germany	**74**	52N	9E
West Australian Basin: Indian Ocean	**89**	20S	100E
West Bengal: State, India	**88**	23N	87E
West Dvina (Daugava): r., U.S.S.R.	**84**	56N	28E
Westerholt: W. Ger.	**64**	52N	7E
Western Australia: State, Australia	**98**	25S	120E
Western Ghats: range, India	**88**	15N	75E
Western Sahara: disputed territory W. Africa	**108**	25N	14W
Western Sayan Mts.: U.S.S.R.	**85**	52N	91E
Western Sierra Madre: see Sierra Madre Occidental			
Westerwald: mts., W. Germany	**74**	51N	8E
West Indies	**45**	—	—
West Irian: State, Indonesia	**98**	5S	137E
Westland: district, N.Z.	**104**	43S	171E
Westland: U.S.A.	**33**	42N	83W
West Midland: Co., England	**63**	52N	2W
Westminster: Eng.	**112**	51N	0
Weston: Malaysia	**91**	5S	116E
Weston-super-Mare: England	**63**	51N	3W
West Palm Beach: U.S.A.	**47**	27N	80W
Westphalia: Länd, W. Germany	**74**	52N	7E
Westport: N.Z.	**104**	42S	172E
Westport: R. of Ireland	**61**	54N	10W
Westport: U.S.A.	**51**	41N	73W
West Siberian Plain: U.S.S.R.	**82/3**	60N	73E
West Virginia: State, U.S.A.	**47**	38N	80W
Westwood: U.S.A.	**48**	40N	121W
Wetar: i., Indonesia	**91**	7S	126E
Wetzlar: W. Germany	**74**	51N	9E
Wexford: R. of Irel.	**61**	52N	6W
Wexford: Co., R. of Ireland	**63**	52N	6W
Wey: r., England	**63**	51N	1W
Weymouth: England	**63**	51N	2W
Weymouth: U.S.A.	**51**	42N	71W
Whakatane: N.Z.	**104**	38S	177E
Whangarei: N.Z.	**104**	36S	174E
Wharfe: r., England	**62**	54N	1W
Wharton Basin: Indian Ocean	**89**	16S	107E
Wheaton: U.S.A.	**34**	42N	88W
Wheeler L.: U.S.A.	**47**	35N	87W
Wheeling: U.S.A.	**47**	40N	81W
Whitby: England	**62**	54N	1W
Whitchurch: Eng.	**63**	53N	3W
White: r., Arkansas, U.S.A.	**46**	35N	91W
White: r., Indiana, U.S.A.	**47**	39N	87W
White: r., S. Dak., U.S.A.	**49**	44N	100W
Whitefish: U.S.A.	**48**	48N	115W
Whitehead: N. Irel.	**62**	55N	6W
White Nile (Bahr el Jebel): r., Sudan	**109**	7N	31E
White Plains: U.S.A.	**51**	41N	74W
White Sea: U.S.S.R.	**82**	65N	37E
White Volta: r., West Africa	**108**	12N	2W
Whitney, Mt.: U.S.A.	**48**	37N	118W
Whitsunday I.: Australia	**100**	20S	149E
Whyalla: Australia	**101**	33S	138E
Wichita: U.S.A.	**46**	38N	97W
Wichita: r., U.S.A.	**46**	34N	100W
Wichita Falls: city, U.S.A.	**46**	34N	98W
Wick: Scotland	**61**	58N	3W
Wicklow: R. of Irel.	**61**	53N	6W
Wicklow Mts.: R. of Ireland	**61**	53N	6W
Widnes: England	**63**	53N	3W
Wiener-Neustadt: Austria	**68**	48N	16E
Wiesbaden: W. Ger.	**74**	50N	8E
Wigan: England	**62**	53N	3W
Wight, I. of: Eng.	**63**	51N	1W
Wigtown: Scotland	**62**	55N	4W
Wigtown Bay: Scot.	**62**	54N	4W
Wilcannia: Australia	**101**	32S	143E
Wilhelmshaven: W. Germany	**74**	54N	8E
Wilkes-Barre: U.S.A.	**50**	41N	76W
Wilkes Land: Antarctica	**116**	71S	120E
Willamette: r., U.S.A.	**48**	45N	123W
Williamson: U.S.A.	**47**	37N	82W
Williamsport: U.S.A.	**50**	41N	77W
Willich: W. Germany	**64**	51N	7E
Williston: U.S.A.	**49**	48N	104W
Willmar: U.S.A.	**43**	45N	95W
Willoughby, Cape: Australia	**101**	36S	138E
Willow South: U.S.A.	**12**	62N	150W
Wilmette: U.S.A.	**34**	42N	88W
Wilmington: Del., U.S.A.	**50**	40N	75W
Wilmington: N.C., U.S.A.	**47**	34N	78W
Wilson: U.S.A.	**47**	36N	78W
Wiltshire: Co., Eng.	**63**	51N	2W
Wiluna: Australia	**98**	27S	120E
Winchester: England	**63**	51N	1W
Winchester: Ky., U.S.A.	**47**	38N	84W
Winchester: Va., U.S.A.	**50**	39N	78W
Windermere: l., England	**62**	54N	3W
Windhoek: S.W. Africa (Namibia)	**111**	22S	17E
Wind River Range: U.S.A.	**48**	43N	110W
Windsor: England	**112**	51N	1W
Windward Is.: W. Indies	**45**	13N	62W
Windward Passage: Cuba/Haiti	**45**	20N	73W
Winfield: U.S.A.	**46**	37N	97W
Winnemucca: & l., U.S.A.	**48**	41N	118W
Winner: U.S.A.	**49**	43N	100W
Winnibago, L.: U.S.A.	**49**	44N	88W
Winona: U.S.A.	**47**	33N	90W
Winslow: U.S.A.	**48**	35N	111W
Winston-Salem: U.S.A.	**47**	36N	80W
Winter Haven: U.S.A.	**47**	28N	82W
Winterthur: Switz.	**75**	48N	9E
Winton: Australia	**99**	22S	143E
Wisbech: England	**63**	53N	0
Wisconsin: State, U.S.A.	**49**	45N	90W
Wisconsin Rapids: city, U.S.A.	**49**	44N	90W
Wismar: E. Germany	**74**	54N	11E
Witbank: S. Africa	**111**	26S	29E
Witdraai: S. Africa	**111**	27S	21E
Witney: England	**63**	52N	2W
Witten: W. Germany	**64**	51N	7E
Wittenberge: E. Ger.	**74**	53N	12E
Wittlaer: W. Germany	**64**	51N	7E
Włocławek: Poland	**68**	52N	19E
Woburn: U.S.A.	**33**	42N	71W
Woking: England	**112**	51N	1W
Wolf: r., U.S.A.	**49**	45N	89W
Wolfenbüttel: W. Ger.	**74**	52N	10E
Wolf Rock: England	**63**	50N	6W
Wolfsburg: W. Ger.	**74**	52N	11E
Wollongong: Austl.	**101**	34S	151E
Wolverhampton: England	**63**	53N	2W
Wolverton: England	**63**	52N	1W
Wonsan: N. Korea	**90**	39N	127E
Wonthaggi: Austl.	**101**	38S	146E
Woodland: U.S.A.	**48**	39N	122W
Woodville: N.Z.	**104**	40S	176E
Woodville: U.S.A.	**46**	31N	94W
Woodward: U.S.A.	**46**	36N	99W
Woomera: Australia	**98**	31S	137E
Woonsocket: U.S.A.	**51**	42N	72W
Woosung: China	**95**	31N	121E
Worcester: & Co., England	**63**	52N	2W
Worcester: S. Africa	**111**	34S	20E
Worcester: U.S.A.	**51**	42N	73W
Workington: Eng.	**62**	55N	3W
Worksop: England	**63**	53N	1W
Worms: W. Germany	**74**	50N	8E
Worms Hd.: Wales	**63**	52N	4W
Worth: U.S.A.	**34**	42N	88W
Worthing: England	**63**	51N	0
Wrangell: U.S.A.	**24**	56N	132W
Wrath, C.: Scotland	**61**	59N	5W
Wrexham: Wales	**63**	53N	3W
Wrocław: Poland	**68**	51N	17E
Wuchang: China	**95**	30N	114E
Wuchow: China	**95**	23N	111E
Wuhan: China	**95**	30N	115E
Wuhsi: China	**95**	32N	120E
Wuhu: China	**95**	31N	118E
Wulanhaote: China	**90**	46N	112E
Wulfrath: W. Germany	**64**	51N	7E
Wulumuchi (Urumchi): China	**83**	44N	87E
Wuppertal: W. Ger.	**64**	51N	7E
Würzburg: W. Ger.	**74**	50N	10E
Wuyi Shan: mtns., China	**95**	27N	117E
Wyandotte: U.S.A.	**33**	42N	83W
Wyangala Res.: Australia	**101**	34S	149E
Wye: r., England	**63**	52N	3W
Wyndham: Austl.	**98**	15S	128E
Wyoming: State, U.S.A.	**42/3**	43N	107W
Xánthi: Greece	**69**	41N	25E
Xingu: r., Brazil	**54**	7S	53W
Xochimilco: Mexico	**52**	19N	99W
Yaan: China	**90**	30N	103E
Yakima: & r., U.S.A.	**48**	47N	120W
Yakuta: & bay, U.S.A.	**30**	60N	140W
Yakutsk: U.S.S.R.	**83**	62N	130E
Yallourn: Australia	**101**	38S	146E
Yalta: U.S.S.R.	**84**	45N	34E
Yamagata: Japan	**93**	38N	140E
Yamal Peninsula: U.S.S.R.	**82/3**	70N	70E
Yamatu: China	**85**	46N	84E
Yamma Yamma, L.: Australia	**100**	26S	141E
Yampa: r., U.S.A.	**48**	40N	108W
Yampi Sound: Austl.	**98**	16S	123E
Yamuna: r., India	**88**	25N	81E
Yanbu: Saudi Arabia	**87**	24N	38E
Yangchow: China	**94**	38N	113E
Yangtze: r., China	**95**	31N	118E
Yao: Japan	**93**	35N	136E
YAOUNDÉ: Cameroun	**108**	4N	11E
Yaraka: Australia	**99**	25S	144E
Yarkand: China	**82**	38N	77E
Yaroslavl': U.S.S.R.	**84**	58N	40E
Yazd: Iran	**87**	32N	54E
Yazoo City: & r., U.S.A.	**46**	33N	90W
Yellow Sea: China	**90**	35N	122E
Yellowstone: L.& Nat. Park, U.S.A.	**48**	45N	111W
Yellowstone: r., U.S.A.	**48**	46N	108W
YEMEN: cap. San'a	**87**	15N	44E
YEMEN P.D.R.: cap. Aden	**87**	15N	50E
Yenakiyevo: U.S.S.R.	**84**	48N	38E
Yenangyaung: Burma	**90**	20N	95E
Yencheng: China	**94**	34N	120E
Yenisey: r., U.S.S.R.	**83**	58N	88E
Yenisey, Gulf of: U.S.S.R.	**83**	72N	83E
Yeniseysk: U.S.S.R.	**85**	58N	92E
Yentai (Chefoo): China	**94**	38N	121E
Yeovil: England	**63**	51N	3W
Yerevan: U.S.S.R.	**84**	40N	44E
Yeungkong: China	**95**	22N	112E
Yeysk: U.S.S.R.	**84**	46N	38E
Yinchwan (Yin-chuan, Ninghsia): China	**94**	38N	106E
Yingkow: China	**94**	40N	122E
Yin Shan: desert, China	**90**	42N	108E
Yokkaichi: Japan	**93**	35N	137E
Yokohama: Japan	**114**	35N	140E
Yokosuka: Japan	**114**	35N	140E
Yonkers: U.S.A.	**35**	41N	74W
Yonne: r., France	**72**	48N	3E
York: England	**62**	54N	1W
York, Cape: Austl.	**98**	11S	143E
York: Nebr., U.S.A.	**49**	41N	98W
York: Pa., U.S.A.	**50**	40N	77W
Yorke Penin.: Austl.	**99**	35S	138E
Yorkshire, N.: Co., England	**62**	54N	1W
Yorkshire, S.: Co., England	**62**	54N	1W
Yorkshire, W.: Co., England	**62**	54N	2W
Yoshkar-Ola: U.S.S.R.	**84**	57N	48E
Youghal: R. of Irel.	**61**	52N	8W
Young: Australia	**101**	34S	148E
Youngstown: U.S.A.	**47**	41N	81W
Ypres: Belgium	**72**	51N	3E
Yreka: U.S.A.	**48**	42N	123W
Yuan: r., China	**95**	29N	110E
Yuba City: U.S.A.	**48**	39N	122W
Yucatan Channel: Mexico/Cuba	**45**	22N	86W
Yucatán Penin.: Mexico	**53**	20N	88W
YUGOSLAVIA: cap. Belgrade	**69**	44N	20E
Yukagir Plateau: U.S.S.R.	**83**	66N	157E
Yukon: r., Canada/U.S.A.	**12**	63N	159W
Yulin: China	**94**	38N	109E
Yuma: U.S.A.	**48**	33N	115W
Yunkwei Plat.: China	**90**	27N	106E
Yunnan: Prov., China	**92**	25N	103E
Yushu (Jyekundo): China	**90**	33N	97E
Yuzhno Sakhalinsk: U.S.S.R.	**83**	47N	143E
Yverdon: Switz.	**75**	47N	7E
Zabul: Iran	**87**	31N	62E
Zacatecas: Mexico	**52**	23N	103W
Zadar: Yugoslavia	**69**	44N	15E
Zagreb: Yugoslavia	**68**	46N	16E
Zagros Mts.: Iran	**87**	32N	50E
Zāhedan: Iran	**87**	29N	61E
ZAÏRE: cap. Kinshasa	**110**	—	—
Zaire (Congo): r., Zaire	**110**	2N	21E
Zambezi: r., S. Afr.	**111**	16S	31E
ZAMBIA: cap. Lusaka	**110**	—	—
Zamboanga: Phil.	**91**	7N	122E
Zamora: Spain	**67**	41N	6W
Zamora de Hidalgo: Mexico	**52**	20N	102W
Zamość: Poland	**68**	51N	23E
Zanesville: U.S.A.	**47**	40N	82W
Zante: i., Greece	**69**	38N	21E
Zanthus: Australia	**98**	31S	123E
Zanzibar: State & town, Tanzania	**110**	6S	39E
Zaporozh'ye: U.S.S.R.	**84**	48N	35E
Zaragoza (Saragossa): Spain	**67**	42N	1W
Zárate: Argentina	**56**	34S	59W
Zaria: Nigeria	**108**	11N	8E
Zaysan, L.: U.S.S.R.	**85**	48N	84E
Zeebrugge: Belgium	**72**	51N	3E
Zeerust: S. Africa	**111**	26S	26E
Zeila: Somali Rep.	**109**	11N	43E
Zeitz: E. Germany	**74**	51N	12E
Zella Mehlis: E. Ger.	**74**	51N	11E
Zemz: r., Libya	**84**	31N	14E
Zermatt: Switz.	**75**	46N	8E
Zeya: U.S.S.R.	**83**	54N	127E
Zhdanov: U.S.S.R.	**84**	47N	37E
Zhigalovo: U.S.S.R.	**83**	55N	105E
Zhitomir: U.S.S.R.	**84**	50N	29E
Zielona Góra: Pol.	**68**	52N	16E
ZIMBABWE: see **RHODESIA**			
Zittau: E. Germany	**74**	51N	15E
Ziatoust: U.S.S.R.	**85**	55N	60E
Zliten: Libya	**86**	32N	14E
Znojmo: Czech.	**68**	49N	16E
Zomba: Malawi	**111**	15S	35E
Zongo: Zaire	**109**	4N	18E
Zonguldak: Turkey	**86**	41N	32E
Zrenjanin: Yugo.	**69**	45N	20E
Zuara: Libya	**86**	33N	13E
Zug: Switzerland	**75**	47N	8E
Zuider Zee: see Ijsselmeer			
Zuni: r., U.S.A.	**48**	35N	109W
Zurich: & L., Switz.	**75**	47N	8E
Zushi: Japan	**114**	35N	140E
Zwickau: E. Germany	**74**	51N	12E
Zwolle: Neth.	**74**	53N	6E

Chester Hubbard
was
here!

Maybye

Maybe

Maybye